Handbook of Production Management Methods

Gideon Halevi

OXFORD   AUCKLAND   BOSTON   JOHANNESBURG   MELBOURNE   NEW DELHI

Butterworth-Heinemann
Linacre House, Jordan Hill, Oxford OX2 8DP
225 Wildwood Avenue, Woburn, MA 01801-2041
A division of Reed Educational and Professional Publishing Ltd

 A member of the Reed Elsevier plc group

First published 2001

British Library Cataloguing in Publication Data
A catalogue record for this book is available from the British Library

Library of Congress Cataloguing in Publication Data
A catalogue record for this book is available from the Library of Congress

ISBN 0 7506 5088 5

Typeset in India at Integra Software Services Pvt Ltd, Pondicherry 605 005
For information on all Butterworth-Heinemann publications visit our website at
www.bh.com
Printed and bound in Great Britain by Biddles Ltd. *www.biddles.co.uk*

Contents

Preface _____

Manufacturing processes require a knowledge of many disciplines, including design, process planning, costing, marketing, sales, customer relations, costing, purchasing, bookkeeping, inventory control, material handling, shipping and so on. It is unanimously agreed that each discipline in the manufacturing process must consider the interests of other disciplines. These interests of the different disciplines may conflict with one another, and a compromise must be made. Managers and the problems they wish to solve in their organization set particular requirements, and compromises are made by 'weighting' each of these requirements. Different organizations will have different needs and thus differently weighted requirements.

More than 110 different methods have been proposed to improve the manufacturing cycle. Each of the proposed methods improves a certain aspect or several aspects of the manufacturing cycle. The list of methods shows that some are of a technological nature, while others are organizational and architectural, and yet others focus on information technology. Some are aimed at lead-time reduction, while others aim at inventory reduction, and yet others focus on customer satisfaction or organizational and architectural features. In some methods environmental issues are becoming dominating, while others focus on respect for people (workers); many of these proposed methods are based on human task groups.

Such a variety of methods and objectives makes it difficult for a manager to decide which method best suits his/her business.

The aim of this book is to present to the reader a brief description of published manufacturing methods, their objectives, the means to achieve the objectives, and to assist managers in making a method selection decision. To meet the objective, over 1000 published papers in journals, conferences, books, and commercial brochures were reviewed and summarized to the best of our ability. Other authors might consider some methods differently. We hope that we have been objective in our summations. The reader may refer to the bibliography to find further details of each method.

Although some specific decision-making methods are described, they are not obligatory. They are used merely to demonstrate that a methodic decision can be made. Each manager should examine and decide how best to make this decision.

The first chapter is an overview of the evolution of manufacturing methods and techniques. It main purpose is to show trends and how new technologies, such as computers, have been adapted and improved. Some of the adapted technologies failed while others were successful.

Chapter 2 lists the 110 manufacturing methods that are described in this book. Survey shows that many of the early-period methods are still in use in industry. Therefore this book presents known methods, regardless of their 'age'. This chapter can be used as an index to the methods listed in Chapter 5.

In addition the methods are mapped according to their type (Technological, Software, Management, Philosophical, Auxiliary) and according to the topics that they focus on. These rough mappings may assist in the selection of a group of methods to be considered.

Chapter 3 considers method mapping by objectives and by Functions. Sixteen objectives are considered, including: rapid response to market demands, lead-time reduction, and progress towards zero defects (quality control). Twenty-four functions are considered, such as focus on cost, focus on enterprise flexibility and focus on lead-time duration. Each of the 110 methods is graded for each of the 40 mapping categories. This grading has been done to the best of our ability, however, the user should not regard the gradings as absolutes – other 'experts' could arrive at alternative gradings.

Chapter 4 proposes a general technique for decision-making. One manufacturing method may support several objectives and functions, while the user might wish to improve several objectives. A decision-making table is described with several examples.

Chapter 5 is the main part of the book, in which the 110 manufacturing methods are briefly described and for which a comprehensive bibliography is provided.

Installing a manufacturing method might be a very expensive and time-consuming project. There is no one system that is best for everyone. We hope that this book will be of assistance in making the right decision, in selecting an appropriate manufacturing method/methods for specific company needs.

Gideon Halevi

1
Trends in manufacturing methods

The role of management in an enterprise is to:

- implement the policy adopted by the owners or the board of directors
- optimize the return on investment
- efficiently utilize men, machines and money;

and most of all – to make profit.

The manufacturing environment may differ with respect to:

- size of plant;
- type of industry;
- type of production (mass production, job shop, etc.).

The activities may involve

- developing and producing products;
- producing parts or products designed by the customer;
- reproducing items that have been manufactured in the past.

However, the fundamental principles of the manufacturing process are the same for all manufacturing concerns, and thus a general cycle can be formulated. Because each mode of manufacturing is subject to different specific problems, the emphasis on any particular phase of the cycle will vary accordingly.

In order to ensure good performance the manufacturing process must consider the requirements of many disciplines, such as:

- marketing and sales
- customer relations
- product definition and specifications
- product design
- process planning and routing
- production management: MRP, capacity planning, scheduling, dispatching, etc.

- shop floor control
- economics
- purchasing
- inventory management and control
- costing and bookkeeping
- storage, packing and shipping
- material handling
- human resource planning.

Management's task is to make sure that the requirements of all disciplines are considered and to coordinate and direct their activities.

As enterprises grew in size and complexity, the problem of coordinating and managing the various activities increased. As a result, an organizational structure developed wherein independent departments were established, each having responsibility for performing and managing a given general type of activity. This organizational structure established a chain of activities. Each discipline (department) accepts the decisions made by the previous department, regards them as constraints, optimizes its own task, makes decisions and transfers them to the next department. While this organizational approach helped to create order out of chaos, it nevertheless tended to reduce the operation of a manufacturing enterprise to an ungainly yet comfortable amalgam of independent bits and pieces of activity, each performed by a given department or individual. As a result, interaction and communication between the various departments and individuals carrying out these activities suffered greatly. Therefore, the attainment of such attributes as overall efficiency and excellence of performance in manufacturing, although improved by the organizational approach, was still handicapped by its shortcomings.

The initial attempt by management to coordinate and control enterprise operations involved building an organizational structure that encompassed mainly the technological departments and tasks. The philosophy and assumption was that if the technology disciplines could accomplish the objectives of:

- meeting delivery dates;
- keeping to a minimum the capital tied up in production;
- reducing manufacturing lead time;
- minimizing idle times on the available resources;
- providing management with up-to-date information;

management objective could be accomplished.

The above assumption did not prove to be correct, since the stated objectives conflict with each other. To minimize the capital tied up in production, work should start as closely as possible to the delivery date; this also reduces manufacturing lead time. However, this approach increases idle time in an environment in which resources are not continuously overloaded.

Keeping to a minimum the capital tied up in production calls for minimum work-in-process. It can be done, but might affect the objective of meeting delivery dates, as items or raw material might be missing and delay in assembly might occur.

Minimizing idle time on the available resources could be accomplished by maintaining buffers before each resource. This can guarantee that a resource will have the next task ready for processing. However, by accomplishing this objective, inventory will be increased, and thus capital tied up in production.

The initial steps in developing manufacturing methods in the 1960s and 1970s were directed towards production solutions. The proposed technology methods may be divided into three groups each with its main philosophies:

1. *Production is very complex.* Therefore we need more and more complex computer programs and systems to regulate and control it.
2. *Production is very complex.* Therefore THE only way to make such systems more effective is to simplify them.
3. *Production is very complex.* Therefore there is no chance of building a system to solve the problems. Hence the role of computers should be limited to supplying data and humans should be left to make decisions.

The first group believes that more and more complex computer programs and systems need to be developed to regulate and control production management. Such methods include:

- PICS – production information and control system
- COPICS – communication-oriented production information and control system
- IMS – integrated manufacturing system.

These methods (and others) use logic and production theories as with previous manual methods, but by computer rather than manually. The disciplines considered include:

- Engineering design
- Process planning
- Master production planning
- Material requirement/Resource planning
- Capacity planning
- Shop floor control
- Inventory management and control.

Engineering design and process planning tasks are the major contributors to product cost, processing lead time, resources requirements and inventory size. These two tasks depend heavily on human experts to make their decisions.

They are regarded as stand-alone tasks, presumably done by CAD – computer-aided design, and supply production management with product structure (termed the bill of materials – BOM), and CAPP – computer-aided process planning which supply production management with routings – which specify how each item and assembly are to be processed, indicating resources and processing time. The bill of materials and routing are regarded as constraints to the production planning stages.

PICS, which was very popular in the 1960s, is a systematic method of performing the technological disciplines and consists of the following stages:

Master production planning   Master production planning transforms the manufacturing objectives of quantity and delivery dates for the final product, which are assigned by marketing or sales, into an engineering production plan. The decisions at this stage depend on either the forecast or the confirmed orders, and the optimization criteria are meeting delivery dates, minimum level of work-in-process, and plant load balance. These criteria are subject to plant capacity constraints and to the constraints set by the routing stage.

The master production schedule is a long-range plan. Decisions concerning lot size, make or buy, additional resources, overtime work and shifts, and confirmation or change of promised delivery dates are made until the objectives can be met.

Material requirements planning (MRP)   The purpose of this stage is to plan the manufacturing and purchasing activities necessary in order to meet the targets set forth by the master production schedule. The number of production batches, their quantity and delivery date are set for each part of the final product.

The decisions in this stage are confined to the demands of the master production schedule, and the optimization criteria are meeting due dates, minimum level of inventory and work-in-process, and department load balance. The parameters are on-hand inventory, in-process orders and on-order quantities.

Capacity planning   The goal here is to transform the manufacturing requirements, as set forth in the MRP stage, into a detailed machine loading plan for each machine or group of machines in the plant. It is a scheduling and sequencing task. The decisions in this stage are confined to the demands of the MRP stage, and the optimization criteria are capacity balancing, meeting due dates, minimum level of work-in-process and manufacturing lead time. The parameters are plant available capacity, tooling, on-hand material and employees.

Shop floor   The actual manufacturing takes place on the shop floor. In all previous stages, personnel dealt with documents, information, and paper. In this stage workers deal with material and produce products. The shop floor foremen are responsible for the quantity and quality of items produced and for keeping the workers busy. Their decisions are based on these criteria.

Inventory control   The purpose of this stage is to keep track of the quantity of material and number of items that should be and that are present in inventory at any given moment; it also supplies data required by the other stages of the manufacturing cycle and links manufacturing to costing, bookkeeping, and general management.

PICS was regarded at one time as the ultimate manufacturing method. However, problems at the implementation start prevented its success. The logic seemed to be valid but problems occurred with the reliability of the data. The PICS method requires data from several sources, such as customer orders, available inventory, status of purchasing orders, status of items on the shop floor, status of items produced by subcontractors, and status of items in the quality assurance department. The data from all sources must be synchronized at the instant that the PICS programs are updated. For example, as a result of new jobs and shop floor interruptions, capacity planning must be updated at short intervals. PICS can do this, however, feedback data must be introduced into the system. At that time data collection terminals were not available and manual data collection, using lists and punched cards, was used. Manual data collection takes time, and shop floor status varies during this time, hence updated capacity plans were made with incorrect data. Similar problems occurred when updating inventory and purchasing information to run MRP.

As computer technology advanced and data collection terminals were introduced as stand-alone or on-line media, they were able to overcome the main practical problems of PICS, and COPICS – Computer-oriented PICS – was introduced.

COPICS solved the data problem but revealed logical problems. A material requirements planning (MRP) system performs its planning and scheduling function based on the assumption that resources have infinite capacities. This simple assumption leads to unrealistic and infeasible plans and schedules. The infinite capacity assumption forces procurement of materials earlier than is actually needed and sets unrealistic due dates. To reduce the impact of these problems, a more recent generation of MRP systems introduces rough-cut capacity planning within the MRP, and is termed MRPII – manufacturing resource planning. It improves planning but does not eliminate the problems altogether.

MRP starts with the product but the planning logic breaks this down into individual items. When one item falls behind the scheduled plan, there is no easy way to re-plan all other items of the affected product, thus increasing work-in-process and jeopardizing delivery dates. A modification in the form of 'pegging' is added as a patch, but it is informative data rather than working data.

Capacity planning logic to solve an overload or underload situation involves pulling jobs forward or pushing jobs backward. This logic contradicts the objectives of production management. Pulling jobs forward increases work-in-progress (WIP) and therefore increases the capital tied up in production. Pushing jobs backwards is almost certain to delay delivery dates.

To solve these problems, systems developers turned to the third philosophy; developing 'user friendly' systems. Here, the user is responsible for storing and retrieving data in the appropriate files and making decisions accordingly. It is the user's responsibility to decide what data to store, the quality of the data, its validity and completeness and its correctness. Therefore, the 'production systems' are always in the clear. If unreasonable decisions are made, it is the user's fault.

While solving the logistics of the production planning problem, another problem arose, the interdisciplinary information system, information such as customer orders, purchasing, inventory, etc. Each of these disciplines developed its own data processing system to serve its own needs. IMS – integrated manufacturing system (sometimes called MIS – management integrated system) – was developed in order to integrate production planning systems and the relevant interdisciplinary systems. Such integration is needed to manage information flow from one discipline to another. For example items ordered and supplied should update (close) open purchasing orders, but at the same time should update the inventory file. However, the data needed to update the purchasing open order file are not the same data needed to update the inventory file. They may even work with different keys; purchasing with order numbers and inventory with item numbers. In the 1960s and 1970s this was a real problem, and although the logic and intention was clear and justified, systems failed to deliver the expected results.

The second philosophy '*Production is very complex.* Therefore THE only way to make such systems more effective is to simplify them' resulted in production methods such as Group Technology (GT), Kanban and Just-in-Time (JIT).

Group Technology (started in the 1940s) preached organization of the processing departments of the enterprise into work cells, where each work cell can produce a family of products/items. A cell consists of all resources required to produce a family of parts. Item processing starts and finishes in one work cell. The workers in the cell are responsible for finishing the job on time, for the quality of the items and the transfer of items from one workstation to another. The cell is an autonomous functional unit. Production planning is very simple and consists of only one decision – which work cell to direct the order to. The GT scope of applications was broadened to include product design and process planning. The main message of GT in these areas is 'do not invent the wheel all over again', i.e. one solution may serve many problems – a family of problems.

Although the GT philosophy is an excellent one, it had its ups and downs and generally was not recognized as being in vogue because of implementation problems. One of the main deficiencies of GT was the method of forming the families. Although promoted quite hard in the 1970s, only a few factories implemented GT as a processing method, but it had some success in CAPP – computer-aided process planning.

Kanban is a Japanese word that means 'visual record' and refers to a manufacturing control system developed and used in Japan. The kanban, or card as it is generally referred to, is a mechanism by which a workstation signals the need for more parts from the preceding station. The type of signal used for a kanban is not important. Cards, coloured balls, lights and electronic systems have all been used as kanban signals. A unique feature that separates a true kanban system from other card systems (such as a 'travel card' used by most companies), is the incorporation of a 'pull' production system. Pull production refers to a demand system whereby products are produced only on demand from the using function. Thus production planning is simple and actually runs itself without the need to schedule and plan.

The system raised some interest in the west, but only a few plants used this method, probably because kanban is most suited to plants with a repeated production cycle. For one-time orders the cards are used only once, and the benefit of pulling jobs cannot be obtained.

Kanban systems are most likely to be associated with just-in-time (JIT) systems.

The philosophy of JIT manufacturing is to operate a simple and efficient manufacturing system capable of optimizing the use of manufacturing resources such as capital, equipment and labour. This results in the development of a production system capable of meeting a customer's quality and delivery demands at the lowest manufacturing price. The production system motto is to obtain or produce something only when it is needed (just in time). Simply put, JIT is having just WHAT is needed, just WHEN it is needed.

The biggest misconception about JIT is that it is an inventory control system: although structuring a system for JIT will control inventory, that is not its major function.

JIT created vast interest in the west, but only a few plants used this method, probably because it requires very tight control and a special mentality that is not usually found in the west.

During the 1970s and early 1980s there was a breakthrough in the computer world; computers became less expensive, smaller in size, and faster in performance. These features introduced new engineering capabilities and new computer engineering applications. Engineers have abandoned their slide rules and drawing boards, and replaced them by computers. Even handbooks are stored in a computer database. All this makes the work of engineers much faster and more accurate. Engineers can consider many alternatives, compute, and display each alternative on a monitor. The ease of changing parameters and shapes, contributes to improved design.

Thus many computerized basic engineering applications were developed. Computer-aided design (CAD) became one of the most useful and beneficial applications of computers in industry. The trend kept on spreading, and today there are many different computer-aided systems, such as computer graphics, computer-aided engineering, computer-aided testing and troubleshooting.

Furthermore, industry recognized the potential of using computers as 'machine members'. A new era emerged: computer-aided manufacturing (CAM). CAM brought the message that a computer is a working tool, not merely a tool for information storage and number crunching. A computer can control machine motion, and thus computer numerical control (CNC) machines were developed. A computer can read sensors and replace switching circuits software and hardware, and thus industrial robots were developed. A computer can read signals from any binary device and employ a selected algorithm to make decisions and execute them by means of computer output signals, and thus automated guided vehicles were developed. Because there are virtually no limits to the possible applications that may benefit from the use of computer-aided manufacturing systems, the trend is to use more and more computer-controlled manufacturing resources.

The potential for using computers as machine members was far too great to stop at individual machines, and soon spread to combined applications such as automatic warehousing, flexible manufacturing cells (FMC), flexible manufacturing systems (FMS), and the ideas of the automatic or unmanned factory.

The three fields of computer applications in industry – computers as data processing, computers as machine members, and computers as engineering aids – were rapidly accepted. However, they were developed as islands of automation. The transfer of data and information between one and the other was by manual means. Therefore, it was logical that the next step in the development of computer applications in industry would be to combine the three separate application fields in one integrated system. This system was called Computer Integrated Manufacturing (CIM). CIM is a technology that combines all advanced manufacturing technologies into one manufacturing system that is capable of:

- rapid response to manufacturing and market demands;
- batch processing with mass-production efficiency;
- mass production with the flexibility of batch production;
- reducing manufacturing cost.

The change from the IMS era (the leading technology from the 1960s to the early 1970s) to the CIM era is primarily in the structure of the system. The main objective of the intelligent manufactuary system (IMS) was to create a central database to serve all applications, thus eliminating redundancy of data, and ensuring synchronization of data.

CIM retains the central database, and in addition incorporates design tools such as group technology, simulation models, and a design application. Computer integrated manufacturing encompasses the total manufacturing enterprise and therefore includes marketing, finance, strategic planning and human resource management.

The plurality of goal conflicts which came up in the production field shows that the competitiveness of an enterprise cannot be fully guaranteed if solutions are used which cover only part of the whole production system. All disciplines of an enterprise that are directly or indirectly involved in the production process have to be optimized all the time.

The potential benefits of implementing CIM began to be demonstrated as a few companies throughout the world began to achieve major improvements in performance. However, most companies, worldwide, were failing to attain the level of benefits being experienced by these few companies. In fact, many comparies actually experienced serious failures where these new concepts and technologies were introduced. Why?

One reason is that implementation of CIM requires knowledge and technology in the following disciplines:

1. communication between computers, terminals and machines;
2. computer science to solve data storage and processing problems;
3. computer-operated resources, such as CNC, robots, automatic guided vehicles, etc.;
4. algorithms and methodology in the fields of basic engineering and production management.

Such technologies were not available in the early 1980s.

Another reason might be that CIM systems technology is especially sensitive to the neglect of human factors.

The fact that CIM could not deliver the required control and benefits created a need for a new paradigm for manufacturing methods. In addition, the competitive markets of the late 1980s and early 1990s imposed new demands and objectives on the manufacturing process that also called for a new paradigm for manufacturing methods. The new demands were: short time to market; product diversity and options; quality products; customer satisfaction and customer seductiveness and competitive prices. The addition of the above market demands resulted in substantial rethinking of the initial CIM system concept. This led to the realization that the initial CIM system concept needed to be broadened from one which encompassed primarily the technological operation of an enterprise to one that encompasses both technological and managerial operations of an enterprise as an integrated manufacturing operation.

From the late 1980s to the late 1990s there were tremendous advances in the field of computer science. The technological problems that inhibited the success of CIM were solved. Communication between computers, terminals and machines became common practice. Database capacity grew tremendously while now storage and retrieval time shortened. Using computers as machine members is taken for granted, and most processing resources are computerized.

However, there was no breakthrough in developing algorithms and methodology in the field of basic engineering and production management. Developing algorithms for management methods and for processing in different fields takes a lot of time and large-scale effort. Research and development in this area, although necessary, can be irksome. Industry needs solutions and methods without having to wait a long time for algorithms to be developed. Serious research was neglected with the excuse that manufacturing and processing is not totally deterministic. Effective operation of such systems therefore requires use of logic but also inference, intuition and experience. Hence, developing management and processing methods became a topic for the disciplines of artificial intelligence, expert systems and computer science.

There was a need for new management methods, but solutions were not readily available. Thus a competition arose to create new manufacturing methods and to obtain recognition. This competition brought over 110 proposals for manufacturing methods. Some of the most famous are enterprise resource planning (ERP), concurrent engineering, total quality management (TQM), business process modelling, world class manufacturing, agile manufacturing, lean manufacturing, bionic manufacturing, virtual manufacturing, mission statements, etc.

Some of the proposed methods are of a technological nature, while others are organizational and architectural, and yet others focus on information technology. Some are aimed at lead-time reduction, while others aim at inventory reduction, and yet others focus on customer satisfaction, or organizational and architectural aspects. In some methods environmental issues dominate (environment-conscious manufacturing), while others focus on respect for people (workers) and promote continual improvements, many of the proposed methods are based on human task groups

Some of the proposed management methods are computerized versions of previous manual methods, for example, flexible manufacturing systems (FMS) are computerized versions of the work cells of the group technology method. Enterprise resource planning reminds one very much of CIM. The difference between the new computerized methods and the previous methods is that technology and engineering which were the basis of the previous methods disappear and are replaced by expert system know-how. The new methods are based on teamwork and computer programs that provide storage retrieval, computation and simulation services. Humans were made the centrepiece of the architecture of the system because they must be the overall driving force and controllers of the functions to be performed in the plant. The basic technology and engineering data is supplied by the human user who also makes logical decisions. Most of the proposed methods emphasize the need for each discipline of the manufacturing process to consider the objectives and problems of other disciplines. However, each proposed method is mainly directed to respond to the needs of a specific discipline.

The flood of proposals, with each one directed towards the needs of a different discipline, makes it difficult to decide which method is the best manufacturing method for any specific enterprise. In the 1960s and 1970s there were only a few methods to select from and the manufacturing methods life cycle was several years. The life cycle in the 1990s was much shorter. For example total quality management (TQM) was a 'hit' in 1994; and billions of dollars were spent on its installation. In 1997 a new paradigm took its place; enterprise resource planning (ERP) became the new fashion. And again billions of dollars were spent on installing it. Towards 1998 enterprise resource management (ERM) replaced or enhanced ERP. In 1999 competition between customer relation management (CRM) and supply chain management occurred.

In this book the proposed methods are introduced, and mapped according to the activities they aimed to improve, such as reduced inventory; reduced lead time and time to market, improved communication, etc. In this way a manager will be able to select a method that is most suited to his/her organization.

2
List of manufacturing methods

The trends in manufacturing methods in industry were presented in Chapter 1. Methods are described which have been used since the early 1960s up to the present time.

Survey shows that many of the early-period methods are still in use in industry, while many of the new methods are really only of academic interest. Therefore this book will present known methods, regardless of their 'age'.

2.1 List of manufacturing methods

This book lists 110 manufacturing methods. A detailed description of these methods is given in Chapter 5, including an extended bibliography.

Number	Method name and abbreviation
1	Activity-based costing – ABC
2	Agent-driven approach
3	Agile manufacturing
4	Artificial intelligence
5	Autonomous enterprise
6	Autonomous production cells
7	Benchmarking
8	Bionic manufacturing system
9	Borderless corporation
10	Business intelligence and data warehousing
11	Business process re-engineering – BPR
12	CAD/CAM, CNC, ROBOTS – computer-aided design and manufacturing
13	Cellular manufacturing
14	Client/server architecture
15	Collaborative manufacturing in virtual enterprises
16	Common-sense manufacturing – CSM
17	Competitive edge

18	Competitive intelligence – CI
19	Computer-aided process planning – CAPP
20	Computer integrated manufacturing – CIM
21	Concurrent engineering – CE
22	Constant work-in-process – CONWIP
23	Cooperative manufacturing
24	Computer-oriented PICS – COPICS
25	Core competence
26	Cost estimation
27	Cross-functional leadership
28	Customer relationship management – CRM
29	Customer retention
30	Cycle time management – CTM
31	Demand chain management
32	Digital factory
33	Drum buffer rope – DBR
34	E-business
35	E-manufacturing – F2B2C
36	Electronic commerce
37	Electronic data interchange – EDI
38	Electronic document management – EDM
39	Enterprise resource planning – ERP
40	Environment conscious manufacturing – ECM
41	Executive excellence
42	Expert systems
43	Extended enterprise
44	Flat organization
45	Flexible manufacturing system – FMS
46	Fractal manufacturing system
47	Fuzzy logic
48	Genetic manufacturing system
49	Global manufacturing network – GMN
50	Global manufacturing system
51	Group technology
52	Holonic manufacturing systems – HMS
53	Horizontal organization
54	House of quality – HOQ
55	Human resource management – HRM
56	Integrated manufacturing system – IMS
57	Intelligent manufacturing system – IMS
58	Just-in-time manufacturing – JIT
59	Kaizen Blitz
60	Kanban system
61	Knowledge management

62	Lean manufacturing
63	Life-cycle assessment – LCA
64	Life-cycle management
65	Life-cycle product design
66	Manufacturing enterprise wheel
67	Manufacturing excellence
68	Manufacturing execution system – MES
69	Master product design
70	Master production scheduling
71	Material requirements planning – MRP
72	Material resource planning – MRPII
73	Matrix shop floor control
74	Mission statement
75	Mobile agent system
76	Multi-agent manufacturing system
77	One-of-a-kind manufacturing – OKM
78	Optimized production technology – OPT
79	Outsourcing
80	Partnerships
81	Performance measurement system
82	Product data management – PDM and PDMII
83	Product life-cycle management
84	Production information and control system – PICS
85	Quality function deployment – QFD
86	Random manufacturing system
87	Reactive scheduling
88	Self-organizing manufacturing methods
89	Seven paths to growth
90	Simultaneous engineering – SE
91	Single minute exchange of dies – SMED
92	Statistical process control – SPC
93	Strategic sourcing
94	Supply chain management
95	Taguchi method
96	Team performance measuring and managing
97	Theory of constraint – TOC
98	Time base competition – TBC
99	Total quality management – TQM
100	Value chain analysis
101	Value engineering
102	Virtual company
103	Virtual enterprises
104	Virtual manufacturing
105	Virtual product development management – VPDM

106	Virtual reality for design and manufacturing
107	Virtual reality
108	Waste management and recycling
109	Workflow management
110	World class manufacturing

Some of the methods are referred to by their abbreviations. Although the abbreviations are given on the above method list, the following lists the abbreviations sorted by alphabet order. The method full name and its number are also displayed.

Abbreviation	Method	Method number
ABC	Activity-based costing	1
BPR	Business process re-engineering	11
CAD	Computer-aided design	12
CAM	Computer-aided manufacturing	12
CE	Concurrent engineering	21
CI	Competitive intelligence	18
CIM	Computer integrated manufacturing	20
CNC	Computerized numerical control	12
CONWIP	Constant work-in-process	22
COPICS	Computer-oriented PICS	24
CRM	Customer relationship management	28
CSM	Common-sense manufacturing	16
CTM	Cycle time management	30
DBR	Drum buffer rope	33
E-business	Electronic business	34
E-commerce	Electronic commerce	36
ECM	Environment-conscious manufacturing	40
EDI	Electronic data interchange	37
EDM	Electronic document management	38
ERP	Enterprise resource planning	39
F2B2C	E-manufacturing	35
FMS	Flexible manufacturing system	45
GMN	Global manufacturing network	49
HMS	Holonic manufacturing systems	52
HOQ	House of quality	54
HRM	Human resource management	55
IMS	Integrated manufacturing system	56

IMS	Intelligent manufacturing system	57
JIT	Just-in-time manufacturing	58
LCA	Life-cycle assessment	63
MES	Manufacturing execution system	68
MRP	Material requirements planning	71
MRPII	Material resource planning	72
OKM	One-of-a-kind manufacturing	77
OPT	Optimized production technology	78
PDM and PDMII	Product data management	82
PICS	Production information and control system	84
QFD	Quality function deployment	85
SE	Simultaneous engineering	90
SMED	Single minute exchange of dies	91
SPC	Statistical process control	92
TBC	Time base competition	98
TOC	Theory of constraint	97
TQM	Total quality management	99
VE	Value engineering	101
VPDM	Virtual product development management	105
VR	Virtual reality	107
WCM	World class manufacturing	110

2.2 Classification of methods by type

The list of manufacturing methods includes methods of many different types. Some of the methods are of a technological nature, while others are organizational and architectural, and yet others focus on information technology. Some are of a practical nature while others are of a philosophical nature.

In this section are classified types by a one-letter code as follows:

T – Technological solution, requires hardware resources
S – Software solution, requires computer
M – Management – methodic directions for organization and managing
P – Philosophical – modern management methods
X – Auxiliary programs to the methods that support the objective

Each manufacturing method is coded using the above classification to the best of the authors' judgement. (Each user is entitled to adjust the coding according to his/her preference.)

The manufacturing methods, sorted by codes are listed below.

Manufacturing method	Method number	Method type
2	Agent-driven approach	M
3	Agile manufacturing	M
6	Autonomous production cells	M
9	Borderless corporation	M
11	Business process re-engineering – BPR	M
13	Cellular manufacturing	M
18	Competitive intelligence – CI	M
26	Cost estimation	M
43	Extended enterprise	M
51	Group technology	M
54	House of quality – HOQ	M
55	Human resource management – HRM	M
56	Integrated manufacturing system – IMS	M
58	Just-in-time manufacturing – JIT	M
59	Kaizen blitz	M
60	Kanban system	M
62	Lean manufacturing	M
69	Master product design	M
70	Master production scheduling	M
77	One-of-a-kind manufacturing – OKM	M
79	Outsourcing	M
81	Performance measurement system	M
83	Product life-cycle management	M
89	Seven paths to growth	M
93	Strategic sourcing	M
94	Supply chain management	M
96	Team performance measuring and managing	M
98	Time base competition – TBC	M
99	Total quality management – TQM	M
101	Value engineering	M
103	Virtual enterprises	M
108	Waste management and recycling	M
109	Workflow management	M
5	Autonomous enterprise	P
8	Bionic manufacturing system	P
16	Common-sense manufacturing – CSM	P
17	Competitive edge	P
22	Constant work-in-process – CONWIP	P

23	Cooperative manufacturing	P
25	Core competence	P
27	Cross-functional leadership	P
29	Customer retention	P
30	Cycle time management – CTM	P
35	E-manufacturing – F2B2C	P
40	Environment-conscious manufacturing – ECM	P
41	Executive excellence	P
44	Flat organization	P
46	Fractal manufacturing system	P
48	Genetic manufacturing system	P
50	Global manufacturing system	P
52	Holonic manufacturing systems – HMS	P
53	Horizontal organization	P
57	Intelligent manufacturing system – IMS	P
63	Life-cycle assessment – LCA	P
64	Life-cycle management	P
65	Life-cycle product design	P
66	Manufacturing enterprise wheel	P
67	Manufacturing excellence	P
73	Matrix shop floor control	P
74	Mission statement	P
76	Multi-agent manufacturing system	P
80	Partnerships	P
85	Quality function deployment – QFD	P
86	Random manufacturing system	P
87	Reactive scheduling	P
88	Self-organizing manufacturing methods	P
97	Theory of constraint – TOC	P
100	Value chain analysis	P
105	Virtual product development management – VPDM	P
107	Virtual reality	P
110	World class manufacturing	P
1	Activity-based costing – ABC	S
7	Benchmarking	S
10	Business intelligence and data warehousing	S
19	Computer-aided process planning – CAPP	S
20	Computer integrated manufacturing – CIM	S
21	Concurrent engineering – CE	S
24	Computer-oriented PICS – COPICS	S

28	Customer relationship management – CRM	S
31	Demand chain management	S
32	Digital factory	S
33	Drum buffer rope – DBR	S
34	E-business	S
36	Electronic commerce	S
39	Enterprise resource planning – ERP	S
71	Material resource planning – MRP	S
72	Material resource planning – MRPII	S
78	Optimized production technology – OPT	S
82	Product data management – PDM and PDMII	S
84	Production information and control system – PICS	S
90	Simultaneous engineering – SE	S
92	Statistical process control – SPC	S
95	Taguchi method	S
102	Virtual company	S
104	Virtual manufacturing	S
12	CAD/CAM, CNC, ROBOTS	T
15	Collaborative manufacturing in virtual enterprises	T
45	Flexible manufacturing system – FMS	T
68	Manufacturing execution system – MES	T
106	Virtual reality for design and manufacturing	T
4	Artificial intelligence	X
14	Client/server architecture	X
37	Electronic data interchange – EDI	X
38	Electronic document management – EDM	X
42	Expert systems	X
47	Fuzzy logic	X
49	Global manufacturing network – GMN	X
61	Knowledge management	X
75	Mobile agent system	X
91	Single minute exchange of dies – SMED	X

2.3 Mapping the methods by main class

In this section the methods are grouped according to the main focus of the method. The grouping is done to the best of the authors' judgement. (Each user is entitled to adjust the groups according to his/her preference.)

Method number	Manufacturing method	Method type
	Focus on manufacturing hardware	
12	CAD/CAM, CNC, ROBOTS	T
15	Collaborative manufacturing in virtual enterprises	T
45	Flexible manufacturing system – FMS	T
68	Manufacturing execution system – MES	T
	Focus on auxiliary software support	
4	Artificial intelligence	X
14	Client/server architecture	X
37	Electronic data interchange – EDI	X
38	Electronic document management – EDM	X
42	Expert systems	X
47	Fuzzy logic	X
49	Global manufacturing network – GMN	X
61	Knowledge management	X
75	Mobile agent system	X
91	Single minute exchange of dies – SMED	X
	Focus on production planning and control	
62	Lean manufacturing	M
97	Theory of constraint – TOC	P
10	Business intelligence and data warehousing	S
32	Digital factory	S
33	Drum buffer rope – DBR	S
71	Material requirements planning – MRP	S
72	Material resource planning – MRPII	S
78	Optimized production technology – OPT	S
84	Production information and control system – PICS	S
	Focus on next generation production management	
8	Bionic manufacturing system	P
23	Cooperative manufacturing	P
35	E-manufacturing – F2B2C	P
46	Fractal manufacturing system	P
48	Genetic manufacturing system	P
52	Holonic manufacturing systems – HMS	P
73	Matrix shop floor control	P

86	Random manufacturing system	P
87	Reactive scheduling	P
88	Self-organizing manufacturing methods	P

Focus on processing manufacturing methods

6	Autonomous production cells	M
13	Cellular manufacturing	M
51	Group technology	M
58	Just-in-time manufacturing – JIT	M
59	Kaizen blitz	M
60	Kanban system	M
77	One-of-a-kind manufacturing – OKM	M
16	Common-sense manufacturing – CSM	P
22	Constant work in process – CONWIP	P

Focus on commercial aspects

9	Borderless corporation	M
18	Competitive intelligence – CI	M
79	Outsourcing	M
94	Supply chain management	M
17	Competitive edge	P
25	Core competence	P
29	Customer retention	P
30	Cycle time management – CTM	P
80	Partnerships	P
100	Value chain analysis	P
28	Customer relationship management – CRM	S
31	Demand chain management	S
34	E-business	S
36	Electronic commerce	S

Focus on organization

11	Business process re-engineering – BPR	M
56	Integrated manufacturing system – IMS	M
99	Total quality management – TQM	M
57	Intelligent manufacturing system – IMS	P
20	Computer integrated manufacturing – CIM	S
24	Computer-oriented PICS – COPICS	S
39	Enterprise resource planning – ERP	S
82	Product data management – PDM and PDMII	S

Focus on advanced organizational manufacturing methods

2	Agent-driven approach	M
3	Agile manufacturing	M
70	Master production scheduling	M
81	Performance measurement system	M
89	Seven paths to growth	M
103	Virtual enterprises	M
109	Workflow management	M
5	Autonomous enterprise	P
44	Flat organization	P
50	Global manufacturing system	P
53	Horizontal organization	P
66	Manufacturing enterprise wheel	P
110	World class manufacturing	P

Focus on product design methods

43	Extended enterprise	M
54	House of quality – HOQ	M
69	Master product design	M
93	Strategic Sourcing	M
101	Value engineering	M
85	Quality function deployment – QFD	P
105	Virtual product development management – VPDM	P
107	Virtual reality	P
7	Benchmarking	S
21	Concurrent engineering – CE	S
90	Simultaneous engineering (SE)	S
102	Virtual company	S
104	Virtual manufacturing	S
106	Virtual reality for design and manufacturing	T

Focus on human factors in manufacturing

55	Human resource management – HRM	M
96	Team performance measuring and managing	M
98	Time base competition – TBC	M
27	Cross functional leadership	P
41	Executive excellence	P
67	Manufacturing excellence	P
74	Mission statement	P
76	Multi-agent manufacturing system	P

Focus on environmental manufacturing methods

83	Product life-cycle management	M
108	Waste management and recycling	M
40	Environment-conscious manufacturing – ECM	P
63	Life-cycle assessment – LCA	P
64	Life-cycle management	P
65	Life-cycle product design	P

Focus on cost and quality manufacturing methods

26	Cost estimation	M
1	Activity-based costing – ABC	S
19	Computer-aided process planning – CAPP	S
92	Statistical process control – SPC	S
95	Taguchi method	S

3
Mapping systems

To assist managers in selecting the best method to achieve certain criteria two mapping methods are presented: one based on the objectives of the method, and the other based on the functions that the methods may serve.

3.1 Mapping by method objective

The objectives considered are:

1. Meeting delivery dates – production planning and control
2. Reduce production costs
3. Rapid response to market demands – product design
4. Reduce lead time – production
5. Progress towards zero defects – quality control
6. Progress towards zero inventory – increase inventory turnround
7. Improve management knowledge and information – enterprise communication
8. Improve and increase teamwork collaboration
9. Improve customer and supplier relationships
10. Improve procurement management and control
11. Management strategic planning – competitiveness – globalization
12. Improve human resources management
13. Improve enterprise integration – improving supply chain globally
14. Continuous improvement
15. Environmental production
16. Marketing – market share.

A particular method may be an answer for more than one objective. In some cases a method is specifically intended for one objective, but other objectives are by-products. The suitability of each method to a specific objective is graded according to the following:

a – Excellent for specific dedicated objective
b – Very good

c – Good
d – Fair

Blank means that the method has nothing to do with the objective at hand.

Interpreting the objective terms

1. Meeting delivery dates – production planning and control

   This objective refers to a method that plans enterprise production activities. The planning objective is to meet the promised delivery dates, on the one hand, and on the other hand might be used to assist sales in promising practical delivery dates. It considers only the planning but not the actual performance.

2. Reduce production costs

   This objective refers to methods that actually control expenditures, calling for efficient methods of processing, and general management techniques. Note: production costs are a parameter at all stages of production planning methods. General methods are not included in this objective.

3. Rapid response to market demands – product design

   This objective refers to methods that are aimed at decreasing the time from an idea for a product to the time that actual production starts. This includes all production preparatory tasks such as product specifications, product realization, product design, process planning, preparing product documentation.

4. Reduce lead time – production

   This objective refers to methods that are aimed at decreasing the processing time. It may refer to hardware solutions, technological or organizational methods on the shop floor or external.

5. Progress towards zero defects – quality control

   This objective refers to methods that improve processing quality, by any means, including technology, machining, process planning, administrative and control techniques.

6. Progress toward zero inventories – increase inventory turnround

   This objective refers to any methods or programs that deal with the subject of inventory management and control

7. Improve management knowledge and information – enterprise communication

   This objective refers to data collection methods and interpretation from all aspects of the enterprise, such as methods of converting information into useful knowledge and methods that capture ideas, technologies, business ventures. Internal and external communications networks systems.

8. Improve and increase teamwork collaboration

   This objective refers to methods that deal with enterprise functions that are performed by groups, such as in design, production, and partnering with external and virtual companies. Furthermore it includes such topics as communication skills, problem solving skills, negotiation skills, etc.

9. Improve customer and supplier relationships

This objective refers to methods that deal with topics such as customer expectations, customer retention, responsiveness to customers, and strategic methods of satisfying the market. Suppliers are referred to as those that produce items that are part of the processing activity externally. Purchased commercial items will be referred to in the next objective of procurement. Other topics include organization structure, how to apply supply chain and choose partners, how to manage the use of temporary and contract workers, how to outsource production etc.

10. Improve procurement management and control

Procurement is the purchasing of commercial items and raw materials. This objective refers to methods that involve selecting vendors and suppliers, terms negotiations, communications, methods of lead-time reduction, and commitment to delivery schedule.

11. Management strategic planning – competitiveness – globalization

This objective refers to methods that deal with general management operational decision-making in the following fields: setting enterprise goals, when and how to integrate the enterprise, extended enterprise, innovative management, and similar strategic planning topics.

12. Improve human resources management

This objective refers to methods that are concerned with the human element. Topics include human resource intelligence, responsiveness of human resources, workforce flexibility, career planning, employee motivation, employee autonomy, and leadership.

13. Improve enterprise integration – improving supply chain globally

This objective refers to methods that connect and combine people, processes, systems and technology to ensure that the right information is available at the right location with the right resources at the right time.

14. Continuous improvement

This objective refers to methods that continually measure and analyse organization processes with the aim of improving procedures and technologies, to identify time and material waste in production.

15. Environmental production

This objective refers to methods that deal with life-cycle manufacturing: design for disassembly, and technology assessment that understands social, ecological and political environments.

16. Marketing – market share

This objective refers to methods that deal with marketing techniques, market competition, global markets, sales promotion, distribution, and aspects of product design.

3.2 Mapping by functions that the method focuses on

In this mapping system manufacturing methods are grouped into four categories according to the following main focus topics:

1. Focus on organization
2. Focus on product life-cycle
3. Focus on performance measurement
4. Focus on management functions

Each one of the above main topics is divided further into detailed functions. A particular method may be an answer for more than one objective. In some cases a method is specifically intended for one objective, but other objectives are byproducts. The suitability of each method to a specific objective is graded according to the following tables given for each topic.

1. Focus on organization
    1.1 Focus on top management
        The grades are:
        b – Top management involvement is a must
        c – Top management involvement is required
        d – Top management involvement is optional
    1.2 Focus on management staff (purchasing, finance, marketing, computing, etc.)
        The grades are:
        b – Controlled by management staff
        c – Involvement of staff management must be high
        d – Involvement of staff management is optional
    1.3 Focus on line management (processing, shop floor, production planning, etc.)
        The grades are:
        b – Controlled by line management
        c – Involvement of line management must be high
        d – Involvement of line management is optional
    1.4 Focus on employees
        The grades are:
        b – Employees must lead the process
        c – Involvement of employees must be high
        d – Low involvement of employees is required
    1.5 Focus on customers
        The grades are:
        b – Customers affect organization performance in meeting objectives

    c – Customer involvement must be high

    d – Low involvement of customer is required

  1.6 Focus on suppliers

    The grades are:

    b – The organization must rely on supplier's relations

    c – Suppliers involvement must be high

    d – Low involvement of suppliers is required

Blank means that the method has nothing to do with the objective at hand.

2. Focus on product life-cycle

  2.1 Focus on product conceptualization and specification

  2.2 Focus on product design

  2.3 Focus on production planning

  2.4 Focus on processing

  2.5 Focus on auxiliary functions (maintenance, quality, etc.)

  2.6 Focus on end of product life (disassembly, etc.)

  The grade for all is as follows:

    b – Dominant factor in product life-cycle

    c – Involves and affects product life-cycle

    d – Minor effect on product life-cycle

Blank means that the method has nothing to do with the objective at hand.

3. Focus on performance achievement (measurement – maximize or minimize)

  3.1 Focus on quality and functionality

  3.2 Focus on cost

  3.3 Focus on enterprise flexibility

  3.4 Focus on customer satisfaction

  3.5 Focus on meeting delivery dates

  3.6 Focus on lead-time duration

  The grade for all is as follows:

    b – Dominant factor in performance achievement

    c – Involves and affects performance achievement

    d – Minor effect on performance achievement

Blank means that the method has nothing to do with the objective at hand.

4. Focus on management functions

  4.1 Focus on strategic planning

  4.2 Focus on operational organization

  4.3 Focus on management control

  4.4 Focus on decision-making methods

  4.5 Focus on human resource utilization

  4.6 Focus on guidance

  The grade for all is as follows:

    b – The method depends on the relevant topic

    c – The method is involved with the relevant topic

    d – The method is independent of the relevant topic

Blank means that the method has nothing to do with the objective at hand.

3.3 Mapping the manufacturing methods

In this section the grades of the methods are presented in alphabetical order. The manufacturing methods are graded according to the grading method described in Section 3.1 and 3.2. The grades are in the following format:

The type of objective followed by a dash (–); the objective number (from Section 3.1) followed by its grade. Several objectives may follow. A semi-colon separates them (;). A star (*) denotes the end of the objectives. Then follow the functions with their grade. Two digits separated by a full-stop give the function (.), separation between functions is by a semi-colon (;).

1. **Activity-based costing – ABC**
   S – 2c; 7c; 11d; 14c; * 1.2b; 3.2b; 4.3b
2. **Agent-driven approach**
   M – 3d; 4b; 7c; 13d; * 2.3c; 3.3c; 4.3d
3. **Agile manufacturing**
   M – 2c; 3c; 4b; 7b; 8c; 13c; 14c; * 1.2b; 1.3b; 3.3c; 3.6c; 4.3c; 4.5c; 4.6c
4. **Artificial intelligence**
   X – 1c; 3c; 5c; 6c; 7b; 11c; 13c; * 1.3c; 2.2b; 2.3b; 2.4b; 4.1c; 4.2c; 4.4b
5. **Autonomous enterprise**
   P – 7c; 11c; 13b; * 1.1b; 1.2c; 4.2c; 4.3c
6. **Autonomous production cells**
   M – 1.b; 2c; 4b; 6c; 7c; * 1.3b; 2.4b; 3.3b; 4.2c
7. **Benchmarking**
   S – 3b; 7c; 9c; 11b; 14c; 16b; * 1.2c; 2.1b; 2.2b; 3.1b; 3.4b; 4.1c
8. **Bionic manufacturing system**
   P – 1c; 2c; 3d; 4c; 8d; 9d; 13c; 14c; 16c; * 1.3b; 1.4c; 2.4c; 3.3b; 3.5c; 3.6c; 4.4c; 4.6c
9. **Borderless corporation**
   M – 1c; 2c; 3b; 4b; 6b; 7b; 8b; 9b; 10b; 11b; 13c; * 2.4b; 3.2c; 3.3b; 3.4b; 3.5c; 3.6b; 4.1b; 4.2c; 4.3c; 4.4c
10. **Business intelligence and data warehousing**
    S – 6b; 7b; 9c; 10b; 11b; 13c; 16b; * 1.1b; 1.2c; 1.3b; 3.3c; 4.1a; 4.2b; 4.3b; 4.4a
11. **Business process re-engineering – BPR**
    M – 7b; 8c; 9b; 13c; 14c; * 1.2b; 2.5c; 3.2c; 3.3c; 4.1c; 4.2b; 4.3d; 4.6c
12. **CAD/CAM, CNC, Robots, computer-aided design and manufacturing**
    T ; S – 3b; 4b; 5c; 7c; * 1.2d; 1.3d; 2.2b; 2.4c

13. **Cellular manufacturing**

   M – 2c; 4c; 5d; 6b; 8c; 12c; * 1.1d; 1.3b; 1.4c; 2.4c; 2.5c; 3.2c; 3.5c; 3.6b ; 4.5d

14. **Client/server architecture**

   X – 1b; 2b; 3c; 4c; 5d; 6b; 7b; 13c; * 1.3b; 2.3c; 2.4b; 2.5c; 3.2c; 3.5c; 4.3c

15. **Collaborative manufacturing**

   T – 3d; 7b; 11c; 13b; * 1.1c; 1.2b; 3.3c; 4.3b

16. **Common-sense manufacturing – CSM**

   P – 1c; 2c; 4b; 6b; 8c; * 1.3b; 2.3d; 2.4b; 3.5c; 3.6b; 4.2c

17. **Competitive edge**

   P – 9c; 11b; 16c; * 1.1b; 1.2c; 1.5c; 3.4b; 4.1b; 4.6c

18. **Competitive intelligence – CI**

   M – 7b; 9d; 11b; 13c; 16c; * 1.1b; 1.2b; 4.1b; 4.3d; 4.4d

19. **Computer-aided process planning – CAPP**

   S – 1b; 2c; 4c; * 2.3c; 2.4b; 2.5c; 3.1c; 3.2b

20. **Computer integrated manufacturing – CIM**

   S – 1d; 2c; 3d; 6d; 7b; 10c; 13b; * 1.2b; 1.3c; 2.3c; 3.2c; 3.3b; 3.5c; 3.6c; 4.2b; 4.3c; 4.4c

21. **Concurrent engineering – CE**

   S – 3b; 4c; 5d; 8c; 13c; * 1.2c; 1.3c; 2.1c; 2.2b; 2.5c; 3.2d; 3.6d

22. **Constant work in process – CONWIP**

   P – 1c; 2d; 4b; 6b; 14d; * 1.3b; 2.3d; 2.4b; 3.2d; 3.5c; 3.6c; 4.2c

23. **Cooperative manufacturing**

   P – 1b; 3c; 4b; 8c; 12d; 14d; 16d; * 1.3b; 1.4d; 2.4b; 3.3c; 3.5d; 3.6c; 4.2c; 4.5c

24. **Computer-oriented PICS – COPICS**

   S – 1b; 2c; 4d; 6d; 7c; 10c; 13c; * 1.2c; 1.3b; 2.3b; 2.4b; 2.5d; 4.2c; 4.3b; 4.4c; 4.5c

25. **Core competence**

   P – 3d; 4d; 7c; 9c; 10c; 11c; 13b; 16d; * 1.1c; 1.2c; 1.5c; 1.6b; 3.3c; 4.1b; 4.2c; 4.3c

26. **Cost estimation**

   M – 2b; 4d; 11d; * 1.2b; 3.2b; 4.2d; 4.4c

27. **Cross-functional leadership**

   P – 2c; 3c; 8b; 9c; 12b; 13c; 14c; * 1.1b; 1.2b; 1.3c; 3.1c; 3.2c; 4.2c; 4.5b; 4.6c

28. **Customer relationship management – CRM**

   S – 7c; 9b; 10b; 11c; 13c; 16b; * 1.1b; 1.2c; 1.3b; 1.5b; 1.6b; 3.3c; 3.4c; 4.1c; 4.2c; 4.3c; 4.4c

29. **Customer retention**

   P – 3d; 7c; 9b; 11c; 12c; * 1.1d; 1.2c; 1.4c; 1.5b; 2.5c; 3.4b; 4.1c; 4.2c; 4.6b

30. **Cycle time management – CTM**
    P – 2c; 5c; 6b; 11c; 8b; 12b; 15b; * 1.1b; 1.2c; 1.3b; 1.4b; 1.5d; 2.4c; 2.6c; 3.1d; 4.1b; 4.2c; 4.5b
31. **Demand chain management**
    S – 3b; 4c; 6c; 7b; 9b; 10c; 11c; 13b; * 1.1d; 1.2b; 1.5c; 1.6c; 3.3c; 3.4c; 4.1d; 4.2b; 4.3c; 4.4d
32. **Digital factory**
    S – 1a; 3a; 4a; 6a; 7b; 13c * 1.1a; 1.5b; 2.x b; 4.xb
33. **Drum buffer rope (DBR)**
    S – 1d; 2d; 4b; 6c; * 1.3c; 1.4c; 2.4c; 3.5c; 4.2c
34. **E-business**
    S – 2c; 3c; 4b; 6c; 7c; 9b; 10c; 1.2b; 1.5b; 1.6b; 3.2d; 3.3d; 3.4c; 4.2c; 4.4.c
35. **E-manufacturing – F2B2C**
    P – 3a; 4a; 7c; 9b; 10c; 11a; 1.1b; 1.5b; 1.6c; 3.3b3.4b; 3.5b; 4.1b
36. **Electronic commerce**
    S – 7b; 9b; 11b; * 1.1b; 1.2c; 1.5b; 3.4c; 4.2c
37. **Electronic data interchange – EDI**
    X – 2c; 3c; 4b; 6b; 7b; 8b; 9b; 10b; 13b; 16c; 1.2d; 1.3b; 1.5b; 1.6b; 3.3c; 4.1c; 4.3c
38. **Electronic document management – EDM**
    X – 2d; 3c; 4c; 6c; 7b; 8c; 13c; * 1.2b; 1.3b; 2.5c; 3.3c; 4.2c; 4.4d
39. **Enterprise resource planning (ERP)**
    S – 1c; 2b; 3b; 4c; 6b; 7b; 9b; 10c; 13b; * 1.2b; 1.3c; 1.4c; 1.5c; 1.6c; 2.3b; 2.4b; 3.3c; 3.4d; 3.5c; 4.2c; 4.3b
40. **Environment conscious manufacturing – ECM**
    P – 11c; 15b; * 1.1b; 1.2c; 2.1b; 2.2b; 2.6b; 3.4c
41. **Executive excellence**
    P – 7b; 8d; 9b; 13c; 16c; * 1.1b; 3.3c; 4.3c; 4.5b
42. **Expert systems**
    X – 1c; 3c; 5c; 6c; 7b; 11c; 13c; * 1.3c; 2.2b; 2.3b; 2.4b; 4.1c; 4.2c; 4.4b
43. **Extended enterprise**
    M – 1c; 2c; 3b; 4b; 6b; 7b; 8b; 9b; 10b; 11b; 13c; * 2.4b; 3.2c; 3.3b; 3.4b; 3.5c; 3.6b; 4.1b; 4.2c; 4.3c; 4.4c
44. **Flat organization**
    P – 2b; 3b; 4d; 7c; 8c; 9c; 13c; 14c; * 1.1b; 1.2c; 1.3c; 1.5c; 3.2c; 3.3b; 4.2b; 4.3d; 4.4c
45. **Flexible manufacturing system – FMS**
    T – 1a; 3a; 4a; 6a; 7b; 13c * 1.1b; 2.4b; 2.5c; 3.3b
46. **Fractal manufacturing system**
    P – 1c; 2c; 3d; 4c; 8d; 9d; 13c; 14c; 16c; * 1.3b; 1.4c; 2.4c; 3.3b; 3.5c; 3.6c; 4.4c; 4.6c

47. **Fuzzy logic**
    X – 1c; 2c; 3c; 4c; 5d; 11c; 13d; 16c; * 2.2c; 2.3c; 2.4c; 2.5c; 3.1c; 3.2c; 3.5c; 3.6c; 4.3d; 4.4b; 4.6c

48. **Genetic manufacturing system**
    P – 1c; 2c; 3d; 4c; 8d; 9d; 13c; 14c; 16c; * 1.3b; 1.4c; 2.4c; 3.3b; 3.5c; 3.6c; 4.4c; 4.6c

49. **Global manufacturing network (GMN)**
    X – 3b; 5b; 7c; 9c; 10c; * 1.6b; 2.2b

50. **Global manufacturing system**
    P – 1b; 2b; 3c; 4b; 5d; 6c; 7c; 11b; 12c; 13b; 14d; * 1.1d; 1.2c; 1.3b; 2.3b; 2.4b; 2.5c; 3.1d; 3.2c; 3.3b; 3.5b; 3.6b; 4.1b

51. **Group technology**
    M – 1b; 2b; 3b; 4b; 5d; 6c; 7b; 8c; * 1.3b; 1.4d; 2.2c; 2.3c; 2.4b; 2.5c; 3.2c; 3.3c; 3.5d; 3.6b

52. **Holonic manufacturing systems (HMS)**
    P – 1c; 2c; 3d; 4c; 8d; 9d; 13c; 14c; 16c; * 1.3b; 1.4c; 2.4c; 3.3b; 3.5c; 3.6c; 4.4c; 4.6c

53. **Horizontal organization**
    P – 2b; 3b; 4d; 7c; 8c; 9c; 13c; 14c; * 1.1b; 1.2c; 1.3c; 1.5c; 3.2c; 3.3b; 4.2b; 4.3d; 4.4c

54. **House of quality (HOQ)**
    M – 3b; 5c; 8c; 9b; * 1.3c; 1.5d; 2.2b; 2.5d; 2.6c; 3.1b; 3.2d; 3.4c

55. **Human resource management – HRM**
    M – 8d; 12b; * 1.1b; 1.2c; 1.4b; 4.2d; 4.5b

56. **Integrated manufacturing system – IMS**
    M – 1b; 2b; 4c; 6c; 7b; 10d; 13c; * 1.2c; 1.3b; 1.4d; 1.6d; 2.3b; 3.3d; 3.5b; 4.2c; 4.3d

57. **Intelligent manufacturing system (IMS)**
    P – 2c; 3b; 4c; 7b; 8b; 9b; 11c; 13b; * 1.1b; 1.5c; 1.6b; 2.x c; 3.x c; 4.xc (x means all functions)

58. **Just in time manufacturing – JIT**
    M – 2c; 3d; 4b; 5c; 6b; 8c; 9c; 10c; 13d; 14b; * 1.1b; 1.2c; 1.3b; 1.4c; 1.5c; 1.6c; 2.3c; 2.4b; 2.5c; 3.6c; 4.2c

59. **Kaizen blitz**
    M – 4c; 5c; 6c; 8b; 12c; 14b; * 1.3b; 1.4b; 2.4b; 2.5c; 3.1b; 3.3c

60. **Kanban system**
    M – 1c; 2d; 4c; 6b; 8c; 14b; * 1.3b; 1.4b; 2.4b; 3.3c; 3.5c; 3.6c

61. **Knowledge management**
    X – 1c; 3c; 5c; 6c; 7b; 11c; 13c; * 1.3c; 2.2b; 2.3b; 2.4b; 4.1c; 4.2c; 4.4b

62. **Lean manufacturing**
    M – 1c; 2c; 3b; 4b; 5b; 6c; 8c; 9b; 14b; * 1.1b; 1.2b; 1.3b; 1.4b; 1.5c; 1.6c; 2.2b; 2.3b; 2.4b; 2.5b; 3.1b; 3.2c; 3.3b; 3.4b; 3.6c; 4.2b; 4.3c; 4.5b

63. **Life-cycle assessment –LCA**
    P – 11c; 15b; * 1.1b; 1.2c; 2.1b; 2.2b; 2.6b; 3.4c
64. **Life-cycle management**
    P – 11c; 15b; * 1.1b; 1.2c; 2.1b; 2.2b; 2.6b; 3.4c
65. **Life-cycle product design**
    P – 3c; 11c; 15b; * 1.1b; 1.2c; 2.1b; 2.2b; 2.6b; 3.4c
66. **Manufacturing enterprise wheel**
    P – 5c; 6c; 7c; 8b; 9b; 13b; 14b; 16b; * 1.5b; 2.2c; 2.3c; 2.4c; 2.5c;
    2.6c; 3.1c; 3.3b; 3.4b; 4.2b
67. **Manufacturing excellence**
    P – 2c; 3c; 4c; 8b; 9c; 12b; 14c; * 1.1b; 1.3c; 1.4b; 1.5c; 2.4c;
    3.3c; 3.4c; 4.2c; 4.5b
68. **Manufacturing execution system (MES)**
    T – 1b; 2b; 3c; 4c; 5d; 6b; 7b; 13c; 1.3b; 2.3c; 2.4b; 2.5c; 3.2c;
    3.5c; 4.3c
69. **Master product design**
    M – 2c; 3b; 4d; 7c; * 1.2b; 1.5d; 2.1b; 2.2b; 3.2c; 3.4d; 3.6b
70. **Master production scheduling**
    M – 1b; 2c; 3b; 4c; 7b; 10d; 11c; 13c; 16d; * 1.1b; 1.2c; 1.3d;
    2.1d; 2.3c; 3.2c; 3.3b; 3.5b; 3.6c; 4.3b; 4.4b
71. **Material requirements planning – MRP**
    S – 1b; 4c; 6c; 7b; 10c; 13c; * 1.2c; 1.3b; 1.6c; 2.3b; 2.4c; 2.5c;
    3.5c; 3.6d
72. **Material resource planning – MRP II**
    S – 1b; 4c; 6c; 7b; 10c; 13c; * 1.2c; 1.3b; 1.6c; 2.3b; 2.4c; 2.5c;
    3.5c; 3.6d
73. **Matrix shop floor control**
    P – 1b; 2c; 3d; 4b; 8d; 9d; 13b; 14c; 16c; * 1.2b; 1.3b; 1.4c; 2.3b;
    2.4c; 3.3b; 3.5b; 3.6b; 4.4c; 4.6c
74. **Mission statement**
    P – 8b; 9c; 12b; 14d; * 1.1b; 1.4b; 3.3c; 4.3c; 4.5b
75. **Mobile agent system**
    X – 3b; 7b; 11c; 13c; * 1.1b; 3.3b; 4.1c; 4.2c; 4.3c
76. **Multi-agent manufacturing system**
    P – 1c; 2d; 4c; 6d; 8c; 12b; 13c; 14c; * 1.3c; 1.4b; 2.3d; 2.4b; 3.6c;
    4.2c; 4.5b
77. **One-of-a-kind manufacturing (OKM)**
    M – 2c; 3b; 4c; 7c; 14d; * 1.1d; 1.2d; 1.3b; 2.3b; 2.4b; 2.5c; 3.1c;
    3.2b; 4.1b; 4.2b
78. **Optimized production technology – OPT**
    S – 1c; 4c; 6c; * 1.3c; 2.4b; 3.5c
79. **Outsourcing**
    M – 2c; 3c; 4b; 6c; 9d; 10b; 14c; * 1.1d; 1.2c; 1.3d; 1.6b; 2.4c;
    3.2c; 3.3b; 4.1b; 4.2c; 4.5d

80. **Partnerships**
    P – 3d; 4d; 5c; 6c; 9b; 10b; 11c; * 1.1c; 1.2c; 1.6b; 3.2c; 3.5c
81. **Performance measurement system**
    M – 7a; 8b; 9c; 11b; 13b; * 1.3b; 3.3b; 4.1a; 4.3a; 4.4b
82. **Product data management – PDM and PDMII**
    S – 2d; 3b; 4c; 6d; 7b; 8d; 14c; 15d; * 1.2c; 1.3d; 2.1c; 2.2b; 2.3c;
    2.5c; 2.6c; 3.1d; 3.2c; 4.3c
83. **Product life-cycle management**
    M – 3c; 4c; 5d; 7b; 9b; 11d; 14c; 15c; 16c; * 1.1d; 1.2b; 1.5b;
    2.2c; 2.6b; 3.1d; 3.4c; 4.6c
84. **Production information and control system – PICS**
    S – 1b; 2c; 4d; 6d; 7c; 10c; 13c; * 1.2c; 1.3b; 1.6c; 2.3b; 2.4b;
    2.5d; 3.5b
85. **Quality function deployment – QFD**
    P – 3b; 5c; 8c; 9b; * 1.3c; 1.5d; 2.2b; 2.5d; 2.6c; 3.1b; 3.2d;
    3.4c
86. **Random manufacturing system**
    P – 1c; 2c; 3d; 4c; 8d; 9d; 13c; 14c; 16c; * 1.3b; 1.4c; 2.4c; 3.3b;
    3.5c; 3.6c; 4.4c; 4.6c
87. **Reactive scheduling**
    P – 1b; 2d; 4c; 13d; * 1.3b; 1.4d; 2.4b; 3.3c; 3.5d
88. **Self-organizing manufacturing methods**
    P – 1c; 2c; 3d; 4c; 8d; 9d; 13c; 14c; 16c; * 1.3b; 1.4c; 2.4c; 3.3b;
    3.5c; 3.6c; 4.4c; 4.6c
89. **Seven paths to growth**
    M – 11b; 16b; * 1.1b; 1.5b; 2.6c; 4.1b; 4.2c; 4.3c; 4.6c
90. **Simultaneous engineering (SE)**
    S – 3b; 4c; 5d; 8c; 13c; * 1.2c; 1.3c; 2.1c; 2.2b; 2.5c; 3.2d; 3.6d
91. **Single minute exchange of dies (SMED)**
    X – 2b; 3c; 4c; 14c; * 1.3b; 2.4b; 3.3c
92. **Statistical process control (SPC)**
    S – 2c; 3d; 5b; 14b; * 1.3d; 1.4b; 2.5b; 3.2d; 4.2c
93. **Strategic sourcing**
    M – 2c; 3d; 4c; 9b; 10b; 11c; 14d; * 1.1c; 1.2b; 1.6b; 3.3c; 4.2c
94. **Supply chain management**
    M – 1c; 2c; 3b; 4b; 6b; 7b; 8b; 9b; 10b; 11b; 13c; * 2.4b; 3.2c;
    3.3b; 3.4b; 3.5c; 3.6b; 4.1b; 4.2c; 4.3c; 4.4c
95. **Taguchi method**
    S – 2c; 3b; 5b; 14b; * 1.3d; 1.4b; 2.5b; 3.2d; 4.2c
96. **Team performance measuring and managing**
    M – 8b; 12c; * 1.1c; 1.2b; 1.4d; 4.3b; 4.5b
97. **Theory of constraint (TOC)**
    P – 1b; 2d; 4c; 6b; 13d; * 1.2d; 1.3b; 2.3b; 2.5d; 3.5d; 4.3c

98. Time base competition – TBC

M – 2d; 3b; 4b; 6b; 7c; 8b; 9d; 13c; 14c; * 1.1d; 1.2d; 1.3b; 1.4b; 2.2c; 2.4b; 3.3c; 4.5b; 4.6c

99. Total quality management (TQM)

M – 2d; 5b; 6d; 8c; 9b; 12c; 14b; * 1.1b; 1.3b; 1.4b; 1.5c; 1.6c; 2.5b; 3.1b; 3.2d; 3.4b

100. Value chain analysis

P – 7c; 9c; 11b; 16c; * 1.1b; 3.2b; 4.1b

101. Value engineering

M – 2b; 3b; 5c; 8b; 14b; 16d; * 1.3c; 1.5c; 2.2b; 3.2c

102. Virtual company

S – 3b; 4c; 8c; 11b; 13d; 14c; * 1.1b; 1.2c; 2.2b; 3.3c; 3.6c; 4.2c

103. Virtual enterprises

M – 2c; 3b; 4c; 7c; 8b; 9c; 10c; 11b; 13b; 16c; * 1.1b; 1.2c; 1.6c; 3.2c; 3.6c; 4.1b; 4.2c; 4.3c

104. Virtual manufacturing

S – 3b; 4c; 8c; 11b; 13d; 14c; * 1.1b; 1.2c; 2.2b; 3.3c; 3.6c; 4.2c

105. Virtual product development management (VPDM)

P – 2d; 3b; 4c; 6d; 7b; 8d; 14c; 15d; * 1.2c; 1.3d; 2.1c; 2.2b; 2.3c; 2.5c; 2.6c; 3.1d; 3.2c; 4.3c

106. Virtual reality for design and manufacturing

T – 3b; 7c; 8c; * 1.2b; 2.1c; 2.2b; 3.3c; 3.6c; 4.2c

107. Virtual reality

P – 2c; 3c; 4d; 8d; 9b; 10c; 13c; * 1.1b; 1.2b; 1.3c; 1.6d; 2.2b; 3.2c; 3.3c; 4.1b; 4.2c

108. Waste management and recycling

M – 13d; 15b; * 1.2b; 2.2b; 2.4b; 2.5c; 4.1c; 4.6c

109. Workflow management

M – 3c; 6b; 7a; 13a; * 1.1b; 1.6d; 3.2d; 3.3b; 3.5b; 4.1b; 4.2b; 4.3b; 4.4c

110. World class manufacturing

P – 5c; 6c; 7c; 8c; 9c; 11d; 14b; 15c; 16d; * 1.1b; 1.2c; 1.3d; 1.4d; 1.5c; 3.1c; 3.2c; 3.3c; 3.4c; 4.1c; 4.3b; 4.4c; 4.5c; 4.6c

4
Decision-making – method selection

The objective of this book is to assist managers to evaluate and select the most appropriate manufacturing method or methods for their needs.

The book does not pretend to supply a single technique for selection, but rather proposes several techniques, allowing the user to decide which one is most suitable. Alternatively, the user may devise his/her own technique.

Section 4.2 enables the user to select a method according to its type. The list of methods is sorted by type, classified into five categories, coded as follows:

M – Management – a methodic scheme for organization and managing
P – Philosophical – modern management methods
S – Software solution, requires a computer
T – Technological solution, requires hardware resources
X – Auxiliary programs to methods that support the objective

Section 4.3 enables the user to select a method according to the main focus of the method, which is selected from 12 focus areas as follows:

1. Focus on manufacturing hardware
2. Focus on auxiliary support software
3. Focus on production planning and control
4. Focus on next generation production management
5. Focus on processing manufacturing methods
6. Focus on commercial aspects
7. Focus on organization
8. Focus on advanced organizational manufacturing methods
9. Focus on product design methods
10. Focus on human factors in manufacturing
11. Focus on environmental manufacturing methods
12. Focus on cost and quality manufacturing methods

In Section 4.1 a systematic technique is proposed that results in selection of a single method to meet user-specified needs. The proposed decision-making procedure is based on a decision-making table. This method ensures that the decision is not improperly influenced by the decision maker. The decision depends on the objectives and functions considered, and on the grading given to each method. In this book we use gradings given to the best of our ability. One may not agree with our grading, we might be wrong. Readers may adjust the given gradings, and even add or delete objectives. As long as this is done before solving the decision table, the decision-making procedure remains valid, and an honest impartial decision will result.

The user is recommended to consult with the bibliography, and/or with marketing representatives of the appropriate methods to verify the soundness of the final decision. Implementing a manufacturing method is a costly venture, and it is wise to consider it very carefully before adapting a method.

4.1   Objective grading tables

Table 4.1 is a table of objectives. The first column contains the method number; the second column contains the method initial for verification purposes; the third column contains the method classification as defined in Chapter 2. The following 16 columns are the 16 objectives (see Chapter 3).

The content of the method rows in these 16 columns contains the grading assigned to each method, as given in Chapter 5, and in condensed form in Section 3.3.

Table 4.1 Objective table, sorted alphabetically

Method number	Method initial	Classification	1	2	3	4	5	6	7	8	9	10	11	12	13	14	15	16
1	A	S		c					c				d		c			
2	A	M			d	b			c						d			
3	A	M		c	c	b			b	c					c	c		
4	A	X	c		c		c	c	b				c		c			
5	A	P	b						c				c		b			
6	A	M	b	c		b		c	c									
7	B	S			b				c		c		b			c		b
8	B	P	c	c	d	c				d	d				c	c		c
9	B	M	c	c	b	b		b	b	b	b	b	b		c			
10	B	S						b	b		c	b	b		c			b
11	B	M							b	c	b				c	c		
12	C	T			b	b	c		c									
13	C	M		c			c	d	b		c			c				
14	C	X	b	b	c	c	d	b	b						c			
15	C	T			d				b				c		b			
16	C	P	c	c		b		b		c								
17	C	P									c		b					c
18	C	M							b		d		b		c			c

Table 4.1 (*Continued*)

Method number	Method initial	Classification	Objective															
			1	2	3	4	5	6	7	8	9	10	11	12	13	14	15	16
19	C	S	b	c		c												
20	C	S	d	c	d			d	b			c			b			
21	C	S			b	c	d			c					c			
22	C	P	c	d		b		b								d		
23	C	P	b		c	b			b		c			d		d		d
24	C	S	b	c		d		d	c			c			c			
25	C	P			d	d			c		c	c	c		b			d
26	C	M		b		d							d					
27	C	P		c	c					b	c			b	c	c		
28	C	S							c		b	b	c		c			b
29	C	P				d			c		b		c	c				
30	C	P		c			c	b		b			c	b			b	
31	D	S			b	c		c	b		b	c	c		b			
32	D	S	a		a	a		a	b						c			
33	D	S	d	d		b		c										
34	E	S		c	c	b		c	c		b	c						
35	E	P			a	a			c		b	c	a					
36	E	S							b		b		b					
37	E	X		c	c	b		b	b	b	b	b			b			c
38	E	X		d	c	c		c	b	c					c			
39	E	S	c	b	b	c		b	b		b	c			b			
40	E	P											c				b	
41	E	P							b	d	b				c			c
42	E	X	c		c		c	c	b				c		c			
43	E	M	c	c	b	b		b	b	b	b	b	b		c			
44	F	P			b	b	d		c	c	c				c	c		
45	F	T	a		a	a		a	b						c			
46	F	P	c	c	d	c				d	d				c	c		c
47	F	X	c	c	c	c	d						c		d			c
48	G	P	c	c	d	c				d	d				c	c		c
49	G	X			b		b		c			c	c					
50	G	P	b	b	c	b	d	c	c				b	c	b	d		
51	G	M	b	b	b	b	d	c	b	c								
52	H	P	c	c	d	c				d	d				c	c		c
53	H	P			b	b	d		c	c	c				c	c		
54	H	M			b		c			c	b							
55	H	M								d				b				
56	I	M	b	b			c		c	b			d		c			
57	I	P		c	b	c			b	b	b		c		b			
58	J	M			c	d	b	c	b		c	c	c		d	b		
59	K	M					c	c	c		b			c		b		
60	K	M	c	d		c			b		c					d		
61	K	X	c		c		c	c	b				c		c			
62	L	M	c	c	b	b	b	c			c	b			b			
63	L	P											c				b	
64	L	P											c				b	

No.																		
65	L	P				c									c		b	b
66	M	P						c	c	c	b	b			b	b		b
67	M	P		c	c	c				b	c			b		c		
68	M	T	b	b	c	c	d	b	b							c		
69	M	M		c	b	d			c									
70	M	M	b	c	b	c		b				d	c		c			d
71	M	S	b			c		c	b			c		c				
72	M	S	b			c		c	b			c		c				
73	M	P	b	c	d	b				d	d			b	c		c	
74	M	P								b	c		b		d			
75	M	X		b				b				c	c					
76	M	P	c	d		c		d		c			b	c	c			
77	O	M		c	b	c			c						d			
78	O	S	c			c		c							d			
79	O	M		c	c	b		c			d	b			c			
80	P	P			d	d	c	c			b	b	c					
81	P	M							a	b	c		b		b			
82	P	S		d	b	c		d	b	d				c	d			
83	P	M			c	c	d		b		b		d		c	c	c	
84	P	S	b	c		d		d	c			c		c				
85	Q	M			b		c			c	b							
86	R	P	c	c	d	c				d	d			c	c		c	
87	R	P	b	d		c								d				
88	S	P	c	c	d	c				d	d			c	c		c	
89	S	M									b						b	
90	S	S			b	c	d		c				c					
91	S	X		b	c	c							c					
92	S	S		c	d		b						b					
93	S	M		c	d	c			b	b	c		d					
94	S	M	c	c	b	b		b	b	b	b	b	b	b	c		b	
95	T	S		c	b		b						b					
96	T	M							b					c				
97	T	P	b	d		c		b						d				
98	T	M		d	b	b		b	c	b	d			c	c			
99	T	M		d			b	d		c	b		c		b			
100	V	P						c		c		b						c
101	V	M		b	b	c		b			b			b			d	
102	V	S		b	c			c		b			d	c				
103	V	M	c	b	c		c	b	c	c	b		b				c	
104	V	S		b	c			c		b			d	c				
105	V	P		d	b	c		d	b	d				c	d			
106	V	T			b			c	c									
107	V	P	c	c	d			d	b	c			c					
108	W	M												d		b		
109	W	M		c			b	a						a				
110	W	P		c	c	c	c	c		d			b	c	d			

4.1.1   Selecting a method using a single objective

The procedure for selecting a manufacturing method using a single objective is as follows:

1. Select the column that represents the objective in Table 4.1.
2. Scan the rows in this column for grades a or b.
3. Make an objective table that contains only the methods filtered in step 2.
4. Decide which class of method to use.
5. Narrow down the table made in step 3 to those that correspond to the desired class.
6. Decide which of the proposed methods is preferred.
   6.1 The decision may be based on methods that are supported by commercial software (class S).
   6.2 The decision may be based on selected class.
   6.3 The decision may be based on the maximum number of objectives that the method supports.
   6.4 The decision is up to the user.

4.1.2 Decision-making example

Step 1: A method to meet delivery dates – production planning and control is needed – objective 1.

Steps 2 and 3: Scan Table 4.1 and build a new table (Table 4.1.1) that contains only methods with grades a or b in the column objective 1.

Table 4.1.1 Table of methods that meet the desired objective 1

Method	Initial	Class	Objective															
			1	2	3	4	5	6	7	8	9	10	11	12	13	14	15	16
6	A	M	b	c		b		c	c						c			
14	C	X	b	b	c	c	d	b	b						c			
19	C	S	b	c		c												
23	C	P	b		c	b				c			d		d			d
24	C	S	b	c		d		d	c			c			c			
32	D	S	a		a	a		a	b						c			
45	F	T	a		a	a		a	b						c			
50	G	P	b	b	c	b	d	c	c				b	c	b	d		
51	G	M	b	b	b	b	d	c	b	c					c			
56	I	M	b	b		c		c	b			d			c			
68	M	T	b	b	c	c	d	b	b						c			
70	M	M	b	c	b	c			b			d	c		c			d
71	M	S	b			c		c	b			c			c			
72	M	S	b			c		c	b			c			c			
73	M	P	b	c	d	b				d	d				b	c		c
84	P	S	b	c		d		d	c			c			c			
87	R	P	b	d		c									d			
97	T	P	b	d		c		b							d			

Table 4.1.2 Table of methods that meet the desired objective and are of class S

Method	Initial	Class	Objective															
			1	2	3	4	5	6	7	8	9	10	11	12	13	14	15	16
19	C	S	b	c		c												
24	C	S	b	c		d		d	c			c			c			
32	D	S	a		a	a		a	b						c			
71	M	S	b			c		c	b			c			c			
72	M	S	b			c		c	b			c			c			
84	P	S	b	c		d		d	c			c			c			

Step 4: In the case that a method that is supported by computer software is preferred, i.e. class S, proceed to step 5.

Step 5: Build a new table that includes only methods of class S (see Table 4.1.2, which now includes only five methods).

The proposed methods, as given in Table 4.1.2 are:

19 Computer integrated manufacturing – CIM
24 Computer-oriented PICS – COPICS
32 Digital factory
71 Material requirements planning – MRP
72 Material resource planning – MRPII
84 Production information and control system – PICS

Note: Method 32 (Digital factory) is the newest and the most expensive.

4.1.3   Second example

Step 1: A method to progress towards zero inventory – increase inventory turn-round (objective 6) is needed.

Steps 2 and 3: Scanning Table 4.1 a new table (4.1.3) that contains only methods with grade a or b for objective 6 is built.

Step 4: If a method that is supported by computer software, i.e. class S, is preferred, then the table indicates one of the methods:

10 – Business intelligence and data warehousing
32 – Digital factory, or
39 – Enterprise resource planning – ERP

should be selected.

Note: Method 32 (Digital factory) is the newest and most expensive.

Table 4.1.3 Table of methods that meet objective 6

Method	Initial	Class	1	2	3	4	5	6	7	8	9	10	11	12	13	14	15	16
9	B	M	c	c	b	b		b	b	b	b	b	b		c			
10	B	S						b	b		c	b	b		c			b
13	C	M		c		c	d	b		c				c				
14	C	X	b	b	c	c	d	b	b						c			
16	C	P	c	c		b		b		c								
22	C	P	c	d		b		b								d		
30	C	P			c		c	b		b			c	b			b	
32	D	S	a		a	a		a	b						c			
37	E	X			c	c	b	b	b	b	b	b			b			c
39	E	S	c	b	b	c		b	b		b	c			b			
43	E	M	c	c	b	b		b	b	b	b	b	b		c			
45	F	T	a		a	a		a	b						c			
58	J	M		c	d	b	c	b		c	c	c			d	b		
60	K	M	c	d		c		b		c						d		
68	M	T	b	b	c	c	d	b	b						c			
94	S	M	c	c	b	b		b	b	b	b	b	b		c			
97	T	P	b	d		c		b							d			
98	T	M		d	b	b		b	c	b	d				c	c		
109	W	M			c			b	a						a			

Table 4.1.4 Table of methods that meet objective 6 and are of class M

Method	Initial	Class	1	2	3	4	5	6	7	8	9	10	11	12	13	14	15	16
9	B	M	c	c	b	b		b	b	b	b	b	b		c			
13	C	M		c		c	d	b		c				c				
43	E	M	c	c	b	b		b	b	b	b	b	b		c			
58	J	M		c	d	b	c	b		c	c	c			d	b		
60	K	M	c	d		c		b		c						d		
94	S	M	c	c	b	b		b	b	b	b	b	b		c			
98	T	M		d	b	b		b	c	b	d				c	c		
109	W	M			c			b	a						a			

In the case that management would like to select less-expensive methods, the table recommends class M methods as shown in Table 4.1.4.

Alternative methods are listed with an indication of how many objectives may benefit:

9. Borderless corporation	8
13. Cellular manufacturing	1

43.	Extended enterprise	8
58.	Just-in-time manufacturing – JIT	3
60.	Kanban system	1
94.	Supply chain management	8
98.	Time base competition – TBS	4
109.	Workflow management	3

If the method is selected on the basis of the number of objectives that the method supports with 'b' grade, the proposed methods are reduced to three (with eight objectives). The most popular within these is supply chain management, and probably this method would be selected.

Examining Table 4.1.4 reveals that if the objectives inventory control (6) and continuous improvement (14) are priorities then method 58 – just-in-time – is recommended.

The method selections described in this section select the best method for a single objective. For satisfaction of several objectives a more advanced selection method is required and this is detailed in Section 4.3.

4.2   Function grading tables

Table 4.2 is a Functions table. The first column contains the method number; the second column contains the method initial for verification purposes; the third column contains the method classification.

The following 24 columns are the 24 functions (see Chapter 3) grouped into four main functions. The number includes the main function, followed by a (.) and six subfunctions as below.

1. Focus on organization
   1.1 Focus on top management
   1.2 Focus on management staff (purchasing, finance, marketing, computing, etc.)
   1.3 Focus on line management (processing, shop floor, production planning, etc.)
   1.4 Focus on employees
   1.5 Focus on customers
   1.6 Focus on suppliers
2. Focus on product life-cycle
   2.1 Focus on product conceptualization and specification
   2.2 Focus on product design
   2.3 Focus on production planning
   2.4 Focus on processing
   2.5 Focus on auxiliary functions (maintenance, quality, etc.)
   2.6 Focus on end of product life (disassembly, etc.)

3. Focus on performance achievement (measurement – maximize or minimize)
   3.1 Focus on quality and functionality
   3.2 Focus on cost
   3.3 Focus on enterprise flexibility
   3.4 Focus on customer satisfaction
   3.5 Focus on meeting delivery dates
   3.6 Focus on lead-time duration
4. Focus on management functions
   4.1 Focus on strategic planning
   4.2 Focus on operational organization
   4.3 Focus on management control
   4.4 Focus on decision-making methods
   4.5 Focus on human resource utilization
   4.6 Focus on guidance

The content of the method rows in these 24 columns are the gradings assigned to each method, as given in Chapter 5 and in condensed format in Section 3.3.

Table 4.3.7 is constructed to include objective grading table and function grading table (Table 4.1 and Table 4.2) in one table. It is sorted alphabetically.

Table 4.2 Function table sorted alphabetically

Method number	Method initial	Classifi-cation	Function																							
			1						2						3						4					
			1	2	3	4	5	6	1	2	3	4	5	6	1	2	3	4	5	6	1	2	3	4	5	6
1	A	S		b												b							b			
2	A	M								c						c							d			
3	A	M		b	b											c		c					c		c	c
4	A	X			c				b	b	b										c	c		b		
5	A	P	b	c																		c	c			
6	A	M			b						b					b							c			
7	B	S		c					b	b					b		b				c					
8	B	P			b	c					c					b		c	c				c		c	
9	B	M									b				c	b	b	c	b	b	b	c	c	c		
10	B	S	b	c	b											c					a	b	b	a		
11	B	M		b									c		c	c					c	b	d			c
12	C	T			d	d			b		c															
13	C	M	d			b	c				c	c			c				c	b					d	
14	C	X				b			c	b	c				c			c				c				
15	C	T	c	b												c					b					
16	C	P				b			d	b							c	b			c					
17	C	P	b	c			c									b					b					c
18	C	M	b	b																	b		d	d		
19	C	S							c	b	c				c	b										
20	C	S		b	c						c				c	b		c	c		b	c	c			
21	C	S		c	c				c	b			c		d				d							

22	C	P			b					d	b				d			c	c		c				
23	C	P			b	d				b					d	c	c		c		c				
24	C	S				c	b			b	b	d		c				c	b	c	c				
25	C	P	c	c			c	b						c				b	c	c					
26	C	M			b					b								d			c				
27	C	P	b	b	c					c	c						c			b		c			
28	C	S	b	c	b		b	b					c	c				c	c	c	c				
29	C	P	d	c		c	b				c				b			c	c					b	
30	C	P	b	c	b	b	d				c		c	d			b	c			b				
31	D	S	d	b			c	c					c	c				d	b	c	d				
32	D	S	a					b		b	b	b	b	b	b			b	b	b	b	b	b		
33	D	S				c	c				c				c				c						
34	E	S			b			c	b			d	d	c				c		c					
35	E	P	b				b	c			b	b	b		b			c							
36	E	S	b	c			b				c				c										
37	E	X		d	b		b	b			c				c			c							
38	E	X		b	b					c				c				c		d					
39	E	S		b	c	c	c	c		b	b		c	d	c			c	b						
40	E	P	b	c			b	b			b			c											
41	E	P	b								c							c		b					
42	E	X			c		b	b	b				c				c	c		b					
43	E	M		b						b	c	b	b	c	b	b	c	c	c						
44	F	P	b	c	c		c				c	b			b			d	c						
45	F	T	b				b	c			b														
46	F	P			b	c				c		b		c	c			c				c			
47	F	X					c	c	c	c	c	c		c	c			d	b			c		c	
48	G	P			b	c				c		b		c	c			c				c			
49	G	X				b		b			b	b	c		d	c	b	b	b	b					
50	G	P	d	c	b		b	b	c		d	c	b		b	b	b								
51	G	M			b	d		c	c	b	c		c	c			d	b							
52	H	P			b	c				c		b		c	c			c				c			
53	H	P	b	c	c		c				c	b			b			d	c						
54	H	M			c		d			b		d	c	b	d		c		d				b		
55	H	M	b	c		b				b				b				d				b			
56	I	M		c	b	d		d		b				d			b	c	d						
57	I	P	b				c	b	c	c	c	c	c	c	c	c	c	c	c	c	c	c	c	c	c	c
58	J	M	b	c	b	c	c	c		c	b	c					c		c						
59	K	M			b	b				b	c		b		c										
60	K	M			b	b				b				c		c	c								
61	K	X			c		b	b	b				c	c			b								
62	L	M	b	b	b	b	c	c	b	b	b	b	b	c	b	b	c		b	c		b			
63	L	P	b	c		b	b				b			c											
64	L	P	b	c		b	b				b			c											
65	L	P	b	c		b	b				b			c											
66	M	P			b	c	c	c	c	c	c	b	b		b										
67	M	P	b		c	b	c			c	c	c		c			b								
68	M	T			b		c	b	c		c		c		b			c							
69	M	M		b		d	b	b		c		d			c										
70	M	M	b	c	d	d	c			c	b		b	c			b	b							
71	M	S	c	b		c	b	c	c		c	c	d												
72	M	S	c	b		c	b	b	c		c	c													
73	M	P	b	b	c	b	c			b		b	b				c		c						
74	M	P	b		b					c		b					c	b							
75	M	X	b							b			c	c	c										
76	M	P	c	b		d	b	c		c		c					b								
77	O	M	d	d	b	b	b	c	c	b	c	b		b	b										
78	O	S		c		b				c															
79	O	M	d	c	d		b			c			c	b			b	c		d					

Table 4.2 (*Continued*)

Method number	Method initial	Classification	Function																							
			1						2						3						4					
			1	2	3	4	5	6	1	2	3	4	5	6	1	2	3	4	5	6	1	2	3	4	5	6
80	P	P	c	c				b							c		c									
81	P	M			b											b					a		a	b		
82	P	S		c	d				c	b	c	c	c	d	c								c			
83	P	M	d	b			b				c				b	d		c								c
84	P	S			c	b		c		b	b	d				b										
85	Q	M				c		d	b				d	c	b	d		c								
86	R	P			b	c						c				b			c	c				c		c
87	R	P			b	d					b					c		d								
88	S	P			b	c						c				b			c	c				c		c
89	S	M	b				b							c							b	c	c			c
90	S	S		c	c				c	b			c		d				d							
91	S	X			b							b				c										
92	S	S			d	b							b		d								c			
93	S	M	c	b				b								c							c			
94	S	M										b			c	b	b	c	b	b	b	c	c	c		
95	T	S				d	b						b		d								c			
96	T	M	c	b		d																	b		b	
97	T	P			d	b					b		d					d					c			
98	T	M	d	d	b	b					c		b												b	c
99	T	M	b		b	b	c	c					b		b	d		b			b					
100	V	P	b												b						b					
101	V	M			c		c		b						c											
102	V	S	b	c					b								c				c		c			
103	V	M	b	c			c		b								c				c	b	c	c		
104	V	S	b	c					b								c				c		c			
105	V	P			c	d			c	b	c	c	c	d	c								c			
106	V	T			b				c	b							c				c		c			
107	V	P	b	b	c			d	b						c	c					b	c				
108	W	M			b				b		b	c									c					c
109	W	M	b					d							d	b		b			b	b	b	c		
110	W	P	b	c	d	d	c								c	c	c	c			c		b	c	c	c

4.2.1 Selecting a method using a single function – example

The procedure for selecting a manufacturing method using a single function is the same as the selection method used for a single objective, except that the function table is used instead of the objective table.

Suppose that management wishes to select manufacturing methods that focus on management control – 4.3. To find such methods, Table 4.2 is filtered at column 4.3 by searching for grades a or b. Eleven methods were obtained as shown in Table 4.2.1

The proposed methods, as given in Table 4.2.1 are:

1 Activity-based costing – ABC
10 Business intelligence and data warehousing

Table 4.2.1   Table of methods that meet the desired function

Method	Class	Function																							
		1						2						3						4					
		1	2	3	4	5	6	1	2	3	4	5	6	1	2	3	4	5	6	1	2	3	4	5	6
1	S		b											b								b			
10	S	b	c	b											c					a	b	b	a		
15	T	c	b												c							b			
24	S		c	b						b	b	d									c	b	c	c	
32	S	a			b			b	b	b	b	b	b							b	b	b	b	b	b
39	S		b	c	c	c	c			b	b				c	d	c				c	b			
70	M	b	c	d				d		c				c	b		b	c				b	b		
81	M			b											b					a		a	b		
96	M	c	b		d										b							b		b	
109	M	b					d							d	b		b			b	b	b	c		
110	P	b	c	d	d	c							c	c	c	c				c		b	c	c	c

15   Collaborative manufacturing in virtual enterprises
24   Computer-oriented PICS – COPICS
32   Digital factory
39   Enterprise resource planning – ERP
70   Master production scheduling
81   Performance measurement system
96   Team performance measuring and managing
109   Workflow management
110   World class manufacturing

In the case that management wishes to have commercial software to support this function then only those five methods classified as 'S' should be considered. These five methods are of different types. Activity-based costing concentrates on control through cost, while COPICS controls through production and the other methods control through information.

Using the tables, management can make an intelligent decision. If, in addition to management control systems, management wishes to prioritize product life-cycle (function 2.6) and product design (function 2.2), only the digital factory method can comply with such a request.

4.3   General selection method – based on the decision table technique

This technique is used to make a decision when several objectives and/or functions are required. The technique attempts to find the best compromise between all the alternatives available, by assigning weights to each requirement, and then evaluating the grade of each method. Once the weights and grades are set, the decision is made by mathematical computations. Setting the grades and weights independently of the decision process ensures that an impartial and objective decision is reached.

The steps in the technique are (see examples in Section 4.3.1):

Step 1. List the priority objectives/functions.
Step 2. Assign weight to each requirement. Use any convenient scale, say 1 to 10. Several objectives or functions might have the same weight.
Step 3. Assign weights to each method class. (Any numerical value may be used. If there is no preference, assign the same value to all classes.)
Step 4. Filter the general table to include only columns of required objectives/functions.
Step 5. Remove from the filtered table all methods that have one or more of the columns blank (i.e. the method does not support the objective or function).
Step 6. Convert the method grades from alphabetical to numerical; use any convenient conversion factor.
Step 7. Multiply the weight (column) grades by the method grade (row) and replace the result in the grade location.
Step 8. For each method (row), sum the replaced grade values and list them in an additional column for each row.
Step 9. Multiply the values in the additional column by the class weight and place the product in that column.

The method with the maximum value in the additional column is the recommended method.

4.3.1 Example of selection of methods to meet several objectives

Step 1. The company requires a manufacturing method to:
Reduce production costs – objective 2
Rapid response to market demands – product design – objective 3
Progress towards zero inventory – increase inventory turnround – objective 6
Improve management knowledge and information – objective 7
Improve enterprise integration – improving supply chain globally – objective 13

Step 2. Assign weights to the objectives (user defined)
Objective 2   weight 10
Objective 3   weight 8
Objective 6   weight 8
Objective 7   weight 6
Objective 13   weight 6

Table 4.3.1   Selection of required objectives

Method number	Class	2	3	6	7	13	Method number	Class	2	3	6	7	13
		Objective							*Objective*				
1	S	c			c		42	X		c	c	b	c
2	M		d		c	d	43	M	c	b	b	b	c
3	M	c	c		b	c	44	P	b	b		c	c
4	X		c	c	b	c	45	T		a	a	b	c
5	P				c	b	46	P	c	d			c
6	M	c		c	c		47	X	c	c			d
7	S		b		c		48	P	c	d			c
8	P	c	d			c	49	X		b		c	
9	M	c	b	b	b	c	50	P	b	c	c	c	b
10	S			b	b	c	51	M	b	b	c	b	
11	M				b	c	52	P	c	d			c
12	T		b		c		53	P	b	b		c	c
13	M	c		b			54	M		b			
14	X	b	c	b	b	c	55	M					
15	T		d		b	b	56	M	b		c	b	c
16	P	c		b			57	P	c	b		b	b
17	P						58	M	c	d	b		d
18	M				b	c	59	M			c		
19	S	c					60	M	d		b		
20	S	c	d	d	b	b	61	X		c	c	b	c
21	S		b			c	62	M	c	b	c		
22	P	d		b			63	P					
23	P		c				64	P					
24	S	c		d	c	c	65	P		c			
25	P		d		c	b	66	P			c	c	b
26	M	b					67	P	c	c			
27	P	c	c			c	68	T	b	c	b	b	c
28	S				c	c	69	M	c	b		c	
29	P		d		c		70	M	c	b		b	c
30	P	c		b			71	S			c	b	c
31	S		b	c	b	b	72	S			c	b	c
32	S		a	a	b	c	73	P	c	d			b
33	S	d		c			74	P					
34	S	c	c	c	c		75	X		b		b	c
35	P		a		c		76	P	d		d		c
36	S				b		77	M	c	b		c	
37	X	c	c	b	b	b	78	S				c	
38	X	d	c	c	b	c	79	M	c	c	c		
39	S	b	b	b	b	b	80	P			d	c	
40	P						81	M				a	b
41	P				b	c	82	S	d	b	d	b	

Table 4.3.1 (*Continued*)

Method number	Class	2	3	6	7	13	Method number	Class	2	3	6	7	13
83	M		c		b		97	P	d		b		d
84	S	c		d	c	c	98	M	d	b	b	c	c
85	M		b				99	M	d		d		
86	P	c	d			c	100	P				c	
87	P	d				d	101	M	b	b			
88	P	c	d			c	102	S		b			d
89	M						103	M	c	b		c	b
90	S		b			c	104	S		b			d
91	X	b	c				105	P	d	b	d	b	
92	S	c	d				106	T		b		c	
93	M	c	d				107	P	c	c			c
94	M	c	b	b	b	c	108	M					d
95	S	c	b				109	M		c	b	a	a
96	M						110	P			c	c	

Step 3. Assign weights to classes (user defined)
M = 4; P = 3; S = 5; T = 5; X = 1
Step 4. Filter Table 4.1 to obtain only columns of required objectives. This step results in Table 4.3.1.
Step 5. Remove from the filtered table all methods that have one or more column blank (i.e. the method does not meet that objective). See table 4.3.2.
Step 6. Convert the methods grades from alphabetical to numerical using conversion factors as follows: a = 6; b = 4; c = 3; d = 1

Table 4.3.2

Method number	Class	2	3	6	7	13
9	M	c	b	b	b	c
14	X	b	c	b	b	c
20	S	c	d	d	b	b
37	X	c	c	b	b	b
38	X	d	c	c	b	c
39	S	b	b	b	b	b
43	M	c	b	b	b	c
50	P	b	c	c	c	b
68	T	b	c	b	b	c
94	M	c	b	b	b	c
98	M	d	b	b	c	c

Table 4.3.3

Method number	Class	2	3	6	7	13
9	M	3	4	4	4	3
14	X	4	3	4	4	3
20	S	3	1	1	4	4
37	X	3	3	4	4	4
38	X	1	3	3	4	3
39	S	4	4	4	4	4
43	M	3	4	4	4	3
50	P	4	3	3	3	4
68	T	4	3	4	4	3
94	M	3	4	4	4	3
98	M	1	4	4	3	3

The conversion is shown in Table 4.3.3.

Step 7. Multiply the weight (column) grades by the method grade (row) and replace the result in the grade location as shown in Table 4.3.4.

Step 8. For each method (row) sum the replaced grade values and list them in an additional column (method weight) for each row, as shown in Table 4.3.5.

Step 9. Multiply the values in the additional column by the class weights and place the results in the final column (Total value) of Table 4.3.5.

The highest total value is **760** and it recommended that **method 39** (**ERP**) be used.

4.3.2   Example of selection of methods to meet several functions

Step 1. The company requires a manufacturing method to:

Focus on line management (processing, shop floor, production planning, etc.) – 1.3
Focus on production planning – 2.3
Focus on processing – 2.4
Focus on meeting delivery dates – 3.5

Step 2. Assign weights to the functions (user defined)

Function   1.3   weight 1
Function   2.3   weight 1
Function   2.4   weight 1
Function   3.5   weight 1

Step 3. Assign weights to the classes (user defined)

M = 1; P = 1; S = 1; T = 1; X = 1 (See chapter 2 for definition of classes.)

Step 4. Filter from Table 4.2 the columns of required functions.

Table 4.3.4

Method number	Class	Objective					Objective				
		2	3	6	7	13	2	3	6	7	13
		Weight					Weight				
		10	8	8	6	6	10	8	8	6	6
9	M	3	4	4	4	3	30	32	32	24	18
14	X	4	3	4	4	3	40	24	32	24	18
20	S	3	1	1	4	4	30	8	8	24	24
37	X	3	3	4	4	4	30	24	32	24	24
38	X	1	3	3	4	3	10	24	24	24	18
39	S	4	4	4	4	4	40	32	32	24	24
43	M	3	4	4	4	3	30	32	32	24	18
50	P	4	3	3	3	4	40	24	24	18	24
68	T	4	3	4	4	3	40	24	32	24	18
94	M	3	4	4	4	3	30	32	32	24	18
98	M	1	4	4	3	3	10	32	32	18	18

Table 4.3.5

Method number	Class	Objective							
		2	3	6	7	13	Method weight	Class weight	Total value
		Weight							
		10	8	8	6	6			
9	M	30	32	32	24	18	136	4	544
14	X	40	24	32	24	18	138	5	138
20	S	30	8	8	24	24	94	5	470
37	X	30	24	32	24	24	134	1	134
38	X	10	24	24	24	18	100	1	100
39	S	40	32	32	24	24	152	5	**760**
43	M	30	32	32	24	18	136	4	544
50	P	40	24	24	18	24	130	3	390
68	T	40	24	32	24	18	138	5	690
94	M	30	32	32	24	18	136	4	544
98	M	10	32	32	18	18	110	4	440

Step 5. Remove from the filtered table all methods that have one of the columns blank (i.e. the method does not support that function).

Step 6. Convert the method grades from alphabetical to numerical using conversion factors as follows: a = 6; b = 4; c = 3; d = 1

Table 4.3.6

Method	Class	Function								
		1.3	2.3	2.4	3.5	1.3	2.3	2.4	3.5	Total
14	X	b	c	b	c	4	3	4	3	14
16	P	b	d	b	c	4	1	4	3	12
22	P	b	d	b	c	4	1	4	3	12
39	S	c	b	b	c	3	4	4	3	14
50	P	b	b	b	b	4	4	4	4	16
51	M	b	c	b	d	4	3	4	1	12
68	T	b	c	b	c	4	3	4	3	14
71	S	b	b	c	c	4	4	3	3	14
72	S	b	b	b	b	4	4	4	4	16
73	P	b	b	c	b	4	4	3	4	15
84	S	b	b	b	b	4	4	4	4	16

The results are shown in Table 4.3.6.

Steps 7 to 9 will not change the total value sequence, as all weights are 1.

Examining the table for the highest total value reveals that there are three methods (50, 72, 84) with total value 16 and one method (73) with total value 15. The difference is very small and method 73 should also be considered. Thus the user has to exercise judgement in making the decision. In a real situation, one might also consider methods with total value 14. One has to remember that the mathematical maximum score cannot guarantee an ideal, optimum manufacturing method. The four recommended methods are:

1. Global manufacturing system – method 50
2. Material resource planning II – method 72
3. Matrix shop floor control – method 73
4. Production information and control system (PICS) – method 84

4.3.3   Example of selection of method to meet several functions and objectives

The decision table method has thus far been demonstrated for cases of objective needs and function needs separately. However, the same method may be used for any combination of requirements. In this section the company needs are of a mixed nature as below:

1.3   Focus on line management (processing, shop floor, production planning, etc.)

2.3   Focus on production planning

2.4   Focus on processing

3.5   Focus on meeting delivery dates

2   Reduce production costs

3   Rapid response to market demands – product design
6   Progress toward zero inventory – increase inventory turnround
7   Improve management knowledge and information – enterprise communication
13   Improve enterprise integration – improving supply chain globally

The solution may be carried out manually or using a spreadsheet.
    The weight of the needs are:

Function   1.3   weight   8
Function   2.3   weight 10
Function   2.4   weight 10
Function   3.5   weight   9
Objective   2   weight   8
Objective   3   weight   6
Objective   6   weight   7
Objective   7   weight   7
Objective   13   weight   8

Step 3. Assign weights to classes (user defined)
M = 5; P = 5; S = 4; T = 3; X = 1
Step 4. In order to filter the required needs Table 4.3.7 is constructed to include objectives and functions (Table 4.1 and Table 4.2) as one table.

Table 4.3.7

Method number	Class	Function 1						Function 2						Function 3						Function 4						Objective 1	2	3	4	5	6	7	8	9	10	11	12	13	14	15	16
		1	2	3	4	5	6	1	2	3	4	5	6	1	2	3	4	5	6	1	2	3	4	5	6																
1	S	b								b							b									c				c							d			c	
2	M							c						c						d									d	b		c							d		
3	M	b	b							c				c			c			c		c c				c	c	b			b	c							c	c	
4	X		c					b	b	b								c	c	b						c		c		c c	b						c		c		
5	P	b	c													b				c	c													c				c		b	
6	M		b							b				b			b					c				b	c		b		c c							c			
7	S	c						b	b					b		b		c	c			c					b			c		c	c		b				c	c	b
8	P		b	c						c				b		c c					c				c c c d c					d	d					c	c	c
9	M		b							c			b	c	b b c b	b c c c				c c b b		b b b b	b	b		c				
10	S	b	c	b						c						a	b	b	a					b b		c	b	b					c		b
11	M	b								c			c c		c	b	d		c							b	c	b							c	c	
12	T	d	d					b		c														b	b	c		c									
13	M	d		b	c					c	c		c		c	b				d		c		c d	b		c				c				
14	X		b					c	b	c		c		c						c		b b c c d b b									c		
15	T	c	b							c									b				d			b					c		b	
16	P		b					d	b					c	b		c					c c		b		b	c							
17	P	b	c		c								b			b				c										c		b				c
18	M	b	b											b		d d								b		d		b		c		c
19	S							c	b	c		c	b								b	c		c										

20	S	b c				c			c b		c c		b c c		d c d		d b		c			b	
21	S	c c			c b		c		d		d				b c d		c					c	
22	P	b				d b		d		c c	c		c d	b	b					d		
23	P	b d			b		c	d c	c		c	b	c b		c			d		d	d
24	S	c b			b b d			c b c c		b c	d	d c		c		c				
25	P	c c		c b			c		b c c			d d		c	c c	c		b			d
26	M	b					b		d	c		b	d			d					
27	P	b b c				c c				b c	c c			b c		b	c	c		
28	S	b c b	b b			c c		c c c c		c	b b	c	c				b
29	P	d c	c b			c		b	c c c		b		d	c	b		c	c		
30	P	b c b b d		c	c d		b c		b	c		c b	b		c	b		b
31	S	d b		c c			c c		d b c d			b c	c b	b c	c		b	
32	S	a		b	b b b b b		b b b b b a	a a	a b		c			c	
33	S	c c			c		c		c		d d	b	c				
34	S	b	c b			d d c		c	c		c c b	c c	b c		b	
35	P	b		b c		b b b	b		a a		c	b c	a			
36	S	b c	b			c		c			b	b		b		
37	X	d b	b b			c		c	c		c c b	b b b b	b		b		c
38	X	b b			c		c		c	d		d c c	c b c		c		
39	S	b c c c c		b b		c d c		c b		c b b c	b b	b c		b	
40	P	b c		b b		b		c				b d b		c		b		c
41	P	b				c		c	b		b d b		c			c
42	X	c		b b b			c c	b	c	c	c c b		c		c	
43	M	b		c b b c b b c c c		c c b b	b b b b	b	b		c	
44	P	b c c	c		c b		b d c		b b d	c c c		c c	
45	T	b		b c		b		a	a a	a b		c	
46	P	b c		c		b	c c		c	c c c d c		d d		c c	c
47	X	c c c c	c c		c c		d b	c c c c c d			c	d		c
48	P	b c		c		b	c c		c	c c c d c		d d		c c	c
49	X	b	b					b	b	c	c c		
50	P	d c b		b b c	d c b	b b b		b b c b d c c		b	c	b	d
51	M	b d		c c b c		c c	d b		b b b b d c b c			
52	P	b c		c		b	c c		c	c c c d c		d d		c c	c
53	P	b c c	c		c b		b d c		b b d	c c c		c c	
54	M	c	d	b		d c b d	c		b	c	c b		
55	M	b c	b			d	b		d		d		b	c	
56	M	c b d	d	b		d	b	c d		b b	c	c b		d		c
57	P	b		c b c c c c c c c c c c c c	c c c c c c		c b c		b b b		c		b
58	M	b c b c c c		c b c			c	c		c d b c b	c c c		d	b
59	M	b b		b c	b	c			c c c	b		c		b
60	M	b b		b		c	c c		c d	c	b	c		d
61	X	c		b b b			c c	b	c	c	c c b		c		c	
62	M	b b b b c c		b b b b	b c b b	c	b c	b	c c b b b c	c b			b
63	P	b c		b b		b		c					c			b
64	P	b c		b b		b		c					c			b
65	P	b c		b b		b		c			c			c			b
66	P	b		c c c c c c	b B		b			c c c b b		b	b	b
67	P	b	c b c		c		c c		c	b	c c c		b c		b		c
68	T	b		c b c		c	c		c	b b c c d b b		c		
69	M	b	d	b b		c	d	b		c b d	c			
70	M	b c d		d	c		c b		b c		b b	b c b c		b	d c		c		d
71	S	c b		c		b c c			c d		b		c	c b		c		c	
72	S	c b		c		b b c		b c		b		c	c b		c		c	
73	P	b b c		b c			b	b b		c	c b c d b		d d		b	c		c
74	P	b	b			c		c	b		b c		b		d
75	X	b			b		c c c		b		c		c		c	
76	P	c b		d b	c		c		b	c d	c	d	c		b	c c	
77	M	d d b		b b c	c b		b b		c b c	c			d
78	S	c			b		c		c		c	c	

Table 4.3.7   (*Continued*)

Method number	Class	Function 1						Function 2						Function 3						Function 4						Obj 1	2	3	4	5	6	7	8	9	10	11	12	13	14	15	16
		1	2	3	4	5	6	1	2	3	4	5	6	1	2	3	4	5	6	1	2	3	4	5	6																
79	M	d	c	d			b			c						c	b			b	c				d	c	c	b		c			d	b			c				c	
80	P	c	c				b									c		c															d	d	c	c		b	b	c		
81	M			b															b	a			a	b							a	b	c			b		b			
82	S		c	d				c	b	c				c	c	d	c					c				d	b	c		d	b	d								c	d
83	M	d	b			b			c						b	d		c							c		c	c	d		b		b		d				c	c	c
84	S		c	b			c		b	b	d						b									b	c		d		d	c			c				c		
85	M			c		d			b		d	c	b	d			c										b		c			c	b								
86	P		b	c						c					b		c	c			c					c	c	c	d	c				d	d				c	c	c
87	P		b	d					b						c		d									b	d		c									d			
88	P		b	c					c						b		c	c			c					c	c	c	d	c				d	d				c	c	c
89	M	b			b					c				b	c	c				c																b					b
90	S		c	c				c	b		c			d			d										b	c	d		c								c		
91	X		b						b			c														b	c	c											c		
92	S		d	b						b		d			c											c	d		b									b			
93	M	c	b			b									c			c								c	d	c					b	b	c			d			
94	M				b			c	b	b	c	b	b	c	c	c										c	c	b	b		b	b	b	b		b		c			
95	S		d	b						b		d			c											c	b		b									b			
96	M	c	b		d											b		b													b						c				
97	P		d	b				b		d					d			c								b	d		c		b							d			
98	M	d	d	b	b			c		b					c					b	c					d	b	b		b	c	b	d						c	c	
99	M	b		b	b	c	c		b					b	d		b								d			b	d		c	b				c			b		
100	P	b							b						b						b									c		c		b							c
101	M		c		c			b							c											b	b		c		b							b			d
102	S	b	c					b							c		c			c						b	c			c			b			d	c				
103	M	b	c			c									c		c	b	c	c						c	b	c		c	b	c	c	c	b		b				c
104	S	b	c					b							c		c	c		c						b	c			c			b			d	c				
105	P		c	d				c	b	c				c	c	d	c					c				d	b	c		d	b	d								c	d
106	T		b					c	b						c		c	c								b			c	c											
107	P	b	b	c		d		b						c	c			b	c							c	c	d			d	b	c				c				
108	M		b					b		b	c			c											c												d		b		
109	M	b			d									d	b		b			b	b	b	c			c		b	a								a				
110	P	b	c	d	d	c								c	c	c		c		b	c	c	c			c	c	c	c		d						b	c	d		

Filtering the required objectives and function reduces table 4.3.7 to four rows (methods) as shown in Table 4.3.8.

Table 4.3.8

Method number	Class	Function 1						Function 2						Function 3						Function 4						Obj 1	2	3	4	5	6	7	8	9	10	11	12	13	14	15	16
		1	2	3	4	5	6	1	2	3	4	5	6	1	2	3	4	5	6	1	2	3	4	5	6																
14	T		b					c	b	c				c			c								c	b	b	c	c	d	b	b						c			
39	S	b	c	c	c	c		b	b						c	d	c			c	b					c	b	b	c		b	b		b	c			b			
50	P	d	c	b				b	b	c				d	c	b		b	b	b						b	b	c	b	d	c	c				b		c	b	d	
68	T		b					c	b	c				c			c								c	b	b	c	c	d	b	b						c			

Table 4.3.9

Method number	Class	Function				Objective				
		1.3	2.3	2.4	3.5	2	3	6	7	13
14	T	b	c	b	c	b	c	b	b	c
39	S	c	b	b	c	b	b	b	b	b
50	P	b	b	b	b	b	c	c	c	b
68	T	b	c	b	c	b	c	b	b	c

Filtering out the unwanted columns results in Table 4.3.9.

Step 6. Convert the method grades from alphabetical to numerical using conversion factors as follows: $a = 6$; $b = 4$; $c = 3$; $d = 1$.

Step 7. Multiply the weight (column) grades by the method grades (row) and replace the result in the grade location.

Table 4.3.10 shows the results of steps 6 and 7.

Step 8. Compute subtotals for each method.

The class weights are $M = 5$; $P = 5$; $S = 4$; $T = 3$; $X = 1$.

Step 9. Multiply the subtotals by the class weights.

The results are shown in Table 4.3.11.

The highest total is for method 50 – global manufacturing system and this is the recommended method.

This recommendation is in line with the desire to implement a philosophical and modern management method.

For a practical method supported by software, method 39 – enterprise resource planning – ERP, is recommended.

Table 4.3.10

Method number	Class	Function				Objective					Function				Objective				
		1.2	2.3	2.4	3.5	2	3	6	7	13	1.2	2.3	2.4	3.5	2	3	6	7	13
											Weight								
											8	10	10	9	8	6	7	7	8
14	T	4	3	4	3	4	3	4	4	3	32	30	40	27	32	18	28	28	24
39	S	3	4	4	3	4	4	4	4	4	24	40	40	27	32	24	28	28	32
50	P	4	4	4	4	4	3	3	3	4	32	40	40	36	32	18	21	21	32
68	T	4	3	4	3	4	3	4	4	3	32	30	40	27	32	18	28	28	24

Table 4.3.11

Method number	Class	Function				Objective							
		1.2	2.3	2.4	3.5	2	3	6	7	13	Methods subtotal	Class weight	Total
						Weight							
		8	10	10	9	8	6	7	7	8			
14	T	32	30	40	27	32	18	28	28	24	259	3	777
39	S	24	40	40	27	32	24	28	28	32	275	4	1100
50	P	32	40	40	36	32	18	21	21	32	272	5	1360
68	T	32	30	40	27	32	18	28	28	24	259	3	777

4.4 Summary

This chapter presents a methodic technique for selecting the best manufacturing method to meet specified needs.

The user must be aware that although the method incorporates mathematical procedures, it should be treated with caution and human judgement should be applied to the conclusions.

It is recommended that before making any commitment to install the recommended method, the user should read carefully the method description, some of the bibliography, and if possible consult with other plants that are using the recommended method.

5

110 manufacturing methods

5.1 Introduction to manufacturing methods

This chapter is the main part of the book, in which 110 manufacturing methods are briefly described, and a large number of bibliographical references are given.

The heading of each manufacturing method includes its number and full name, and the grading each method was assigned in Chapter 3 follows the name before the text.

Bibliographical references follow the text for each manufacturing method.

5.2 Brief descriptions of the 110 manufacturing methods

Activity-based costing – ABC

S- 2c; 7c; 11d; 14c; * 1.2b; 3.2b; 4.3b

Activity-based costing is an information system that maintains and processes data on a firm's activities and products/ services. It identifies the activities performed, traces costs to these activities, and then uses various cost drivers to trace the cost of activities to the final products/services. Cost drivers are factors that create or influence cost and reflect the consumption of activities by the products/services. An ABC system can be used by management for a variety of purposes relating to both activities and products/services.

In conventional cost accounting systems, direct costs such as the costs of specific services are billed directly to the product. However, indirect costs or overhead for the entire plant operation (including individual departments) are typically accumulated and divided by the total number of employees to determine the additional hourly rate. In this system, overhead cost per hour is the same irrespective of the job type.

However, not all overhead costs vary on a job basis. For instance, overhead costs relating to order processing do not vary with the amount of processing time that it takes to produce the order. Also, the cost per hour is not the same across all departments and job types.

ABC in the manufacturing sector has remained a focal point of interest for practitioners and academics for a number of years.

The steps in developing and implementing an ABC model are outlined below.

Step 1: Form a cross-functional steering committee. In order to establish a process for implementing ABC, first form a committee that will ultimately be responsible for the implementation and evaluation of the ABC system.

The committee and its members should meet regularly with management to identify issues that could affect implementation of the ABC system, such as utilization of resources, quality control, communication, information systems, and process improvements. It is very important to gain staff support for the ABC system. Personnel will more readily accept the new system if they are educated about the nature of the system and are concurrently involved in the development and implementation phases.

Step 2: Identify case types for analysis. Case types for analysis are typically selected based on case volume (high volume), financial impact (high cost, low profitability), variance measure, quality assurance issues, or special interest.

Step 3: Profile the manufacturing system. Using case management and critical path analysis, perform activity analysis across all operations and processes that are required to move the jobs from order to shipment.

Critical path analysis is an abbreviated report that shows the critical or key incidents that must occur in a predictable and timely sequence to achieve the order.

Case management and critical path analysis are developed and implemented typically by a multidisciplinary group. Case management along with critical path analysis has proved to be a useful framework to analyse activities and to collect data on the type and amount of resources needed and actually used for the delivery of orders. The data can be used to determine where process improvements can be made and where non-value-added activities could be eliminated.

Step 4: Aggregate activities. The number of different actions performed on a typical order is so large that it is economically infeasible to create an activity pool for each separate action. Therefore, many individual actions have to be aggregated to form a few separate distinct activity pools. A single cost driver is then used to trace the cost of these activities to different procedures.

Step 5: Analyse cost flow using cost drivers. The plant cost management system is used to develop cost information on different activities along the critical path from order to shipment. The procedure involves a detailed analysis of the company's general ledger accounts. In collecting cost information it is necessary to combine certain ledger accounts that are associated with use of similar resources. For instance, salaries and fringe benefit costs that are recorded in two separate accounts are combined for the purposes of allocation.

Step 6: Educate staff about the ABC system. On-site training seminars are held throughout the design and implementation. Staff meetings are used to report progress and to discuss any problems that the steering committee has encountered. These seminars and periodic meetings have two main objectives: to ensure that the design and implementation are appropriate and to build commitment to the ABC.

Step 7: Evaluate and analyse data and results. ABC systems in combination with case management and critical path analysis provide crucial financial details and measures to conduct variance analysis and evaluate the efficiency of the system.

Accurate costs reported by the ABC systems reduce the risk that poor case-mix decisions, faulty pricing decisions, and suboptimal capital budgeting decisions will be made because of inaccurate costs. This risk can be particularly high when competitors can take advantage of poor decisions that can occur as a result of inaccurate costs.

There are numerous challenges in implementing an ABC system. First, collecting the data needed to establish an ABC system is time-consuming and expensive. An ABC system is much more complex and detailed than a traditional cost system because costs are allocated to different activity pools and each of these pools is further broken down into several separate activities. This requires detailed analysis of financial accounting records as well as inquiries and interviews to identify and gather costs and other information on specific activities. Successful implementation of an ABC system requires a comprehensive paradigm shift in management – a move from a functional departmental view of management to a more cross-functional view of plant activities and processes.

Bibliography

1. Billinton, R. and Wang, P., 1998: Distribution system reliability cost/worth analysis using analytical and sequential simulation techniques, *IEEE Transactions on Power Systems*, **13**(4), 1245–50.
2. Checkland, P. and Holwell, S., 1998: *Information. Systems and Information Systems: Making Sense of the Field*. Chichester: Wiley.
3. Davalos, K.J. and Noble, J.S., 1998: Integrated approach for environmental cost analysis of manufacturing systems, *Engineering Design & Automation*, **4**(4), 309–23.
4. Drucker, F.P., 1994: The theory of the business, *Harvard Business Review*, pp. 95–102.
5. Rigby, K.D., 1994: How to manage the management tools, *Planning Review*, **21**(6), 8–15.

6. Riggs, L.J. and Felix, H.G., 1983: *Productivity by Objectives*. Prentice-Hall.
7. Sik-Wah-Fong-P and Dodo-Ka-Yan-Ip, 1999: Cost engineering: a separate academic discipline? *European Journal of Engineering Education*, **24**(1), 73–82.
8. Turney, P.B.B., 1990: What is the scope of activity-based costing? *Journal of Cost Management*, **3**(4), 40–42.

Agent-driven approach

M – 3d; 4b; 7c; 13d; * 2.3c; 3.3c; 4.3d

Agent-driven manufacturing systems are designed to solve shop floor control problems in manufacturing systems.

The objective of the agent-driven approach is to design a factory information system with the capabilities of computer integrated manufacturing. The agent-based architecture interprets the components of a manufacturing system as humans associated with software agents. These agents are connected to message-conveying blackboards, each of which is associated with a manufacturing planning and control domain.

The first manufacturing control architectures were usually centralized or hierarchical. The poor performance of these structures in very dynamic environments and their difficulties with unforeseen disruptions and modifications led to new control architectures based on self-organized systems that change their internal organization on their own account. An agent manufacturing system is composed of self-organizing agents that may be completely informational or may represent subsystems of the physical world.

At the workshop level, the heterogeneity of the system leads to agent identification problems. This heterogeneity of the system makes the identification of the agent rather unclear. One agent identification method is based on the idea that an agent should be autonomous and intelligent. Thus the agent basic capabilities should be:

1. To transform its environment in at least one of the dimensions shape, space and time.
2. To verify search results before presenting them.
3. To roam the network and seek information autonomously.

The control behaviour of each agent is briefly outlined as follows.

The part agent and the resource agent negotiate with each other to manage the operation of part entities and the functioning of resources. The intelligence agent provides different bidding algorithms and strategies; the monitor agent is used to supplement the system status. The database agent and management agents manipulate inter-agent information. The communication agents carry out all communications between entities.

The seven objectives are:

1. Capture shop floor data.
2. Provide a highly structured data management system to build a unified vision of the manufacturing data.
3. Supporting diagnosis, data analysis and forecasting activities.
4. Support the implementation of real-time decisions as well as decisions scenario analysis.
5. Support intelligent control and information interfaces.
6. Provide the data basis for decision support and planning system.
7. Provide the necessary interfaces to implement manufacturing planning and control.

Bibliography

1. Agent Builder Environment. http://www.networking.ibm.com/iag/iagsoft.htm.
2. Davies, C.T., 1978: Data processing spheres of control. *IBM Systems Journal*, **17**(2), 179–198.
3. Elmagarmid, A.K. (ed.), 1992: *Database Transaction Models for Advanced Applications*. Morgan Kaufmann, San Mateo,
4. Finin, T., Fritzson, R., McKay, D. and McEntire, R., 1994: Using KQML as an agent communication language. In *Proceedings of the Third International Conference on Information and Knowledge Management (CIKM'94)*, ACM Press.
5. Georgakopoulos, D., Hornick, M. and Sheth, A., 1995: An overview of workflow management: from process modeling to workflow automation infrastructure. *Distributed and Parallel Databases*, **3**(2), 119–152.
6. Gilman, C.R., Aparicio, M., Barry, J., Durniak, T., Lam, H. and Ramnath, R., 1997: Integration of design and manufacturing in a virtual enterprise using enterprise rules, intelligent agents, STEP, and work flow. In *SPIE Proceedings on Architectures, Networks, and Intelligent Systems for Manufacturing Integration*, pp. 160–171.
7. Gray, J. and Reuter, A., 1993: *Transaction Processing: Concepts and Techniques*. Morgan Kaufmann, San Mateo.
8. Huhns, M.N. and Singh, M.P. (eds), 1998: *Readings in Agents*. Morgan Kaufmann, San Francisco.
9. Labrou, Y. and Finin, T., 1998: Semantics and conversations for an agent communication language. In M.N. Huhns and M.P. Singh (eds), *Readings in Agents*, Morgan Kaufmann, San Francisco, pp. 235–242.
10. Lefranqois, P., Cloutier, L. and Montreuil, B., 1996: An agent-driven approach to design factory information systems, *Computers in Industry*, **32**, 197–217.
11. Nakamura, J., Takahara, T. and Kamigaki, 1995: Human-computer cooperative work in multi-agent manufacturing system. In E.M. Dar-el (ed.) *Proceedings of the 13th International Conference on Production Research*, Jerusalem, August 6–10, pp. 370–372.
12. Rabelo, R.J. and Spinosa, L.M., 1997: Mobile-agent-based supervision in supply-chain management in the food industry. In *Proceedings of Workshop on Supply-Chain Management in Agribusiness*, Vitoria (ES) Brazil, pp. 451–460.

13. Rabelo, R.J. and Camarinha-Matos, L.M., 1994: Negotiation in multi-agent based dynamic scheduling, *Journal on Robotics and Computer Integrated Manufacturing*, **11**(4), 303–310.
14. Sethi, A.K. and Sethi, S.P., 1990: Flexibility in manufacturing: a survey, *The International Journal of Flexible Manufacturing Systems*, **2**, pp. 289–328.
15. Singh, M.P., 1998: Agent communication languages: Rethinking the principles, *IEEE Computer*, **31**(12), 40–47.
16. SMART. http:l/smart.npo.org/

Agile Manufacturing

M – 2c; 3c; 4b; 7b; 8c; 13c; 14c; * 1.2b; 1.3b; 3.3c; 3.6c; 4.3c; 4.5c; 4.6c
Agile manufacturing can be defined as the capability of reacting quickly to changing markets, to produce high quality products, to reduce lead times, and to provide superior service. These are achieved by improving enterprise communications among all disciplines engaged in the manufacturing process.

Agile manufacturing can also be defined as the capability of surviving and prospering in a competitive environment of continuous and unpredictable change by reacting quickly and effectively to changing markets, driven by customer-designed products and services. Critical to successfully accomplishing agile manufacturing are a few enabling technologies such as the standard for the exchange of products (STEP), concurrent engineering, virtual manufacturing, component-based hierarchical shop floor control system, information and communication infrastructure, etc.

The agile manufacturing enterprise is able to bring out totally new products quickly. It assimilates field experience and technological innovation easily, continually modifying its product offerings to incorporate them. Its products evolve. As the needs of users change and improvements are introduced, users can readily reconfigure or upgrade what they have bought instead of replacing it. A reprogrammable, reconfigurable, continuously changeable production system, integrated into a new information-intensive manufacturing system make the lot size of an order irrelevant. The cost of producing is the same regardless of the quantity. Agile manufacturing thus produces to order, whereas mass production produces to stock and sell, basing its production schedule on marketing projections. Similarly, quality in agile manufacturing advances from being measured in defects per part when sold, to customer gratification over the full life of the product.

The workforce is valued as the enterprise's central long-term asset. The workforce is responsible for innovative product evolution and for manufacturing process improvements that allow cost increases to be recovered internally, rather than through price increases.

Because of the limited flexibility of mass production enterprises and their production technology, they extend the technology as long as possible in order to amortize costs. Agile enterprises see opportunities for growth and profit in constant change, of which their production technologies and managerial organization, both highly flexible, are able to take full advantage. Instead of a static organization structure based on fixed specialized disciplines, 'agile' organizations have a dynamic structure, keyed to the evolving needs of cross-functional project teams.

Agility is accomplished by integrating three resources: technology, management and workforce, into a coordinated interdisciplinary system. Highly flexible production resources are necessary, and they already exist. Design is not the province of engineering, not even of engineering and manufacturing jointly. Instead, representatives of every stage in the product life-cycle, from raw materials to ultimate disposal, participate in setting its design specifications.

Information thus flows seamlessly between agile manufacturers and their suppliers, and between manufacturers and their customers, who play an active role in product design and development. Distributed enterprise integration and distributed concurrent operations are made possible by strict, universal, data exchange standards using robust 'groupware' – software allowing many people to work on the same files at the same time. Enterprise integration is also made possible by an atmosphere of mutual responsibility for success within enterprises and between cooperating enterprises. The ethics of agile manufacturing are mutual trust. Trust and mutual responsibility require a capacity for localized decision-making that allows implementation at the point of information. The workforce does not have to wait for requests to move up and then back down the organizational hierarchy before acting. Issues locally decidable include production scheduling changes, error detection and response, cooperation with other departments in setting and pursuing shared goals, and changing pathways to those goals when problems arise.

Often the quickest route to the introduction of a new product is selecting organizational resources from different companies and then synthesizing them into a single business entity: a virtual company. If the various distributed resources, human and physical, are compatible with one another, that is, if they can perform their respective functions jointly, then the virtual company can behave as if it were a single company dedicated to one particular project. For as long as the market opportunity lasts, the virtual company continues to exist; when the opportunity passes, the virtual company dissolves and its personnel turns to other projects.

An agile enterprise has the organizational flexibility to adopt for each project the managerial vehicle that will yield the greatest competitive advantage. Sometimes this will take the form of an internal cross-functional project team with participation by suppliers and customers. At other times it might take the form of collaborative ventures with other companies, and sometimes it will take the form of a virtual company. The guiding principle of agile enterprise management is not automatic recourse to self-directed work teams, but for full utilization of corporate assets. The key to utilizing assets fully is the workforce.

Flexible production technologies and flexible management enable the workforce of agile manufacturing enterprises to implement the innovations they generate. There can be no algorithm for the conduct of such an enterprise. The only possible long-term agenda is providing physical and organizational resources to support the creativity and initiative of the workforce.

With agile manufacturing, competitive advantage will be determined by new criteria of quality and customer satisfaction. Highly competitive firms will develop:

- Products that are custom-designed and configured at the time of order.
- Products that can be reconfigured and upgraded to meet evolving requirements, extending product life and reducing the value of distinct product generations.
- Long-term relationship with customers who are committed to the development of products they use and to the companies that maintain the currency of those products.

Rapid product creation, development and modification in an agile manufacturing enterprise is made possible by:

- The routine formation of inter-disciplinary project teams, able to develop product designs and manufacturing process specifications concurrently.
- Extending the concept of design to the entire projected life-cycle of a product, from initial specifications to its eventual disposal.
- The availability of scientific knowledge of the manufacturing process, and of computers capable of accurately simulating product performance characteristics, and of modelling the entire manufacturing process.
- Modular, flexible, reconfigurable, affordable production processes and equipment.
- The ability to obtain relevant information quickly, to share it with project members distributed throughout a firm and in different firms, and to link that information directly to production machinery.
- Modular product design incorporating reconfigurability and upgradability leading to extremely long product lifetimes.

The steps needed to implement agile manufacturing are as follows.

- Identify cycle-time reduction opportunities for all enterprise activities and actively pursue their development.
- Develop intimate, responsive, supplier – vendor – customer networks, incorporating interactive information exchange systems as appropriate.
- Empower the workforce at all levels of the enterprise; and involve the workforce in setting company agendas and in exercising initiatives to accomplish them.

- Setting bold goals that create enterprise-wide challenges.
- Leverage existing resources to meet goals in proportion to current capabilities.
- Evoke personal commitment to long-term goals from everyone in the enterprise.
- Create a climate of reciprocal responsibility for the success of the enterprise.
- Encourage creativity and initiative by identifying goals clearly, but remaining vague about the means.
- Provide the workforce with the skills and the tools they need to achieve the goals.
- Monitor progress towards goals anticipating evolutionary changes in direction.
- Develop metrics that will measure the value of the workforce as corporate asset. Use these metrics to define the need for, and invest in, continuous workforce training and education.
- Assimilate into the managerial decision-making process, as an expression of corporate responsibility, workforce constitution.
- Identify the generic technological and organizational requirements to make the transition from flexible to agile manufacturing.
- Identify regulatory and legal barriers to the formation of cooperative ventures and pursue their removal.
- Identify infrastructure requirements that will enhance distributed concurrent product control, development and manufacture.

The advantages of becoming an agile enterprise are:

- enhanced flexibility and responsiveness to changing consumer and customer demand;
- lower costs;
- reduced lead times;
- greater efficiency;
- higher standards of quality;
- increased market share;
- improved turnover and profit growth.

Bibliography

1. Gilles, J. and Puttick, J., 1995: Factory of the future, CEC Eureka Project, Factory EI 1003 – Final Report Synopsis.
2. Hamlet, and Prahalad, 1991: Agile manufacturing, *Harvard Business Review*.
3. Hertz, J., Krogh, A. and Palme, R.G., 1989: *Introduction to the Theory of Neural Computation*, Lecture Notes Volume 1, Santa Fe Institute – Studies in the Sciences of Complexity, Addison-Wesley, Reading, MA.

4. HUTOP, 1999–2002: Human Sensory Factors for Total Product Life Cycle, IMS project proposal.
5. Kohli, R. and Park, H., 1994: Coordinating buyer–seller transactions across multiple products, *Management Science*, **40**(9), 1145–1150.
6. Johnson-Laird, P.N., 1983: *Mental Models*. Cambridge University Press, Cambridge
7. Neiman, D., Hildum, D., Lesser, V.R. and Sandholm, T.W., 1994: Exploiting meta-level information in a distributed scheduling system. *Proceedings of Twelfth National Conference on Artificial Intelligence (A A A I 94)*, August.
8. Nonaka, I. and Takeuchi, H., 1995: *The Knowledge Creating Company*. Oxford University Press, Oxford.
9. Polanyi, M., 1966: *The Tacit Dimension*. Routledge and Kegan Paul, London.
10. Rabelo, R.J. and Camarinha-Matos, L.M., 1996: Towards agile scheduling in extended enterprise. In L.M. Camarinha-Matos and H. Afsarmanesh (eds) *Balanced Automation Systems II – Implementation Challenges for Anthropocentric Manufacturing*, Chapman & Hall, pp. 413–424.
11. Sethi, A.K. and Sethi, S.P., 1990: Flexibility in manufacturing: a survey. *International Journal of flexible Manufacturing Systems*, **2**.
12. Westkamper, E. and Schmidt, T., 1997: Concept of a learning simulation system. In *MCPL'97 IFAC/IFIP Conference on Management and Control of Production and Logistics – Conference Proceedings*, Campinas, SP, Brazil.
13. X-CITTIC, 1996–1998: *A Planning and Control System for Semiconductor Virtual Enterprises*, Esprit project no. EP20544.

Artificial intelligence

X – 1c; 3c; 5c; 6c; 7b; 11c; 13c; * 1.3c; 2.2b; 2.3b; 2.4b; 4.1c; 4.2c; 4.4b
See Knowledge management

Autonomous enterprise

P – 7c; 11c; 13b; * 1.1b; 1.2c; 4.2c; 4.3c
The autonomous enterprise objective is to manage autonomy, that is, to maximize freedom without letting the system fall into chaos.

Open environments, such as the Internet and corporate intranets, enable a large number of interested parties to use and enhance vast quantities of information. These environments support modern applications, such as virtual enterprises, and information access at all places and all times, involving a number of information sources and component activities.

At first glance autonomy is a blessing. It enables a large number of interested parties to use and enhance vast amounts of information. However, without principled techniques to coordinate the various activities, any implementation would yield disjointed and error-prone behaviour, while requiring excessive effort to build and maintain.

The autonomous enterprise proposes that the main basis for managing autonomy lies in the notion of commitments. A flexible formulation of commitments can provide a natural means through which autonomous agents may voluntarily constrain their behaviour. By flexible, we mean that it should be possible to cancel or otherwise modify the commitments. Consider a situation in which a purchaser is trying to obtain some parts from a vendor. We would like the vendor to commit to delivering correct parts of the right quality to the purchaser. However, it is important that the supply chain be able to survive exceptions such as when the manufacturing plant fails, or when the purchaser decides that the parts need to be of a lower error tolerance than initially ordered.

Information cannot be understood independently of the processes that create or consume it. Flexibility of behaviour and the ability to recover from failures require an approach that is sensitive to how those processes interact. When agents are associated with each independent process, a flexible notion of commitments can capture the desired interactions among those processes. A multi-agent system can be viewed as a global commitment, which encapsulates the promises and obligations the agents may have towards each other. Global commitments generalize the traditional ideas of information management so as to overcome their historical weaknesses. Information management involves three main concerns, which must be addressed by any approach for constructing information-based solutions:

1. Data integrity and flow: correctness of data and how it is conveyed from one party to another.
2. Organizational structure: how the various parties relate to each other.
3. Autonomy: how the autonomy of the different parties is preserved.

A commitment is a relationship between a debtor, a creditor, a context, and a proposition. The debtor owes it to the creditor to make the proposition true; the context serves as a witness and as the adjudicator of disputes.

Bibliography

1. Agent Builder Environment. http://www.networking.ibm.com/iag/iagsoft.htm.
2. Davies, C.T., 1978: Data processing spheres of control. *IBM Systems Journal*, **17**(2), 179–198.
3. Elmagarmid, A.K. (ed.), 1992: *Database Transaction Models for Advanced Applications*. Morgan Kaufmann, San Mateo.
4. Georgakopoulos, D., Hornick, M. and Sheth, A., 1995: An overview of workflow management: From process modeling to workflow automation infrastructure, *Distributed and Parallel Databases*, **3**(2), 119–152.
5. Gilman, C.R., Aparicio, M., Barry, J., Durniak, T., Lam, H. and Ramnath, R., 1997: Integration of design and manufacturing in a virtual enterprise using enterprise rules, intelligent agents, STEP, and work flow. In *SPIE Proceedings on Architectures, Networks, and Intelligent Systems for Manufacturing Integration*, pp. 160–171.

6. Gray, J. and Reuter, A., 1993: *Transaction Processing: Concepts and Techniques.* Morgan Kaufmann, San Mateo.
7. Huhns, M.N. and Singh, M.P. (eds), 1998: *Readings in Agents.* Morgan Kaufmann, San Francisco.
8. Labrou, Y. and Finin, T., 1998: Semantics and conversations for an agent communication language. In M.N. Huhns and M.P. Singh (eds), *Readings in Agents*, Morgan Kaufmann, San Francisco, pp. 235–242.
9. Singh, M.P., An ontology for commitments in multiagent systems: Toward a unification of normative concepts, *Artificial Intelligence and Law.* To appear.
10. Singh, M.P., 1998: Agent communication languages: Rethinking the principles, *IEEE Computer*, **31**(12), 40–47.
11. SMART. http:l/smart.npo.org/

Autonomous production cells

M – 1b; 2c; 4b; 6c; 7c; * 1.3b; 2.4b; 3.3b; 4.2c

The objective of autonomous production cells is to perform machining operations autonomously with a high degree of reliability. This goal is achieved through the integration of planning, machining and monitoring functions directly on the machine. Under ideal conditions the user of such a production unit then has all the functions necessary to carry out and control the machining task directly at his disposal. Among other things in the field of process control, the architecture and conceptual design of an autonomous production cell offer enhanced possibilities for process monitoring and fault management within a production system that go beyond the capabilities of currently available monitoring systems. This is especially possible through utilization of the extensive information available from different sources connected with each other in the modular system structure, e.g. system control, sensors or measurement systems.

The concept of an autonomous production cell is characterized by the high availability of planning, control, handling and machining functions directly on the machine. Compared to currently available monitoring systems this allows for enhanced methods of process monitoring and disturbance management within a production system. A module for the analysis of the process state uses a model-based comparison of cutting forces, a multi-sensor configuration and a NC-control integrated monitoring approach.

For the detection of disturbances the described methods are interconnected and closely linked to the system control. The system for disturbance management will be improved towards an integrated system, which, dependent on the monitoring tasks and machining operations, allows for the coordinated operation of the described monitoring strategies either in parallel or in sequential modes. In order to achieve maximum reliability of the process, the state identification module is implemented as a module for cause determination and response release to be able to initiate adequate responses to the identified process disturbances.

A system for disturbance management is concerned with analysis of the ongoing machining processes and disturbances that occur during machining operations. This system is subdivided into three modules that perform

- process state identification,
- determination of the reasons for disturbances, and
- response initiation

After preprocessing the data from certain machine tool sensors, and the integration of information from the control and planning level the *module for process state analysis* has to identify the current state of the machining process. The task of the *cause determination module* is to analyse the nature of the disturbance that has been detected and to determine the reason for the occurrence of this disturbance. Using this information the *response release module* has to decide which response is appropriate. The reaction is released by the system for disturbance management and is executed in coordination with the planning and control level of the autonomous production cell.

The basic strategy of the module for process state analysis is based on the utilization of information inherent to the NC-controller and is designed to monitor machining processes.

The deployment of automatic systems like the autonomous production cell requires integrated systems architecture with a high degree of functionality in all parts of the machine. Thus a central element is the NC-controller.

Bibliography

1. Chan, H.M. and Milnrer, D.A., 1982: Direct clustering algorithm for group formation in cellular manufacturing, *Journal of Manufacturing Systems*, **1**: 65–75.
2. Chandrasekharan, M.P. and Rajagopalan, R., 1986: An ideal seed non-hierarchical clustering algorithm for cellular manufacturing, *International Journal of Production Research*, **24**: 451–464.
3. Choobineh, F., 1988: Framework for design of cellular manufacturing systems, *International Journal of Production Research*, **26**: 1511–1522.
4. Co, H.C. and Arrar, A., 1988: Configuration cellular manufacturing systems, *International Journal of Production Research*, **26**: 1511–1522.
5. Deitz, D. and Drucker, F.P., 1991: The new productivity challenge, *Harvard Business Review*, Nov.–Dec.: 69–79.
6. Drucker, F.P., 1990: The emerging theory of manufacturing, *Harvard Business Review*, May–June: 94–102.
7. Merchant, M.E., 1984: *Computer Integration of Engineering Design and Production*, Manufacturing Studies Board, National Research Council, Washington DC: National Academy Press.
8. Pritschow, G. *et al.*, 1993: Open system controllers – a challenge for the future of the machine tool industry, *Annals of the CIRP*, **41**(1), pp. 449–453.

9. Rajamani, D., Singh, N. and Aneja, Y.P., 1990: Integrated design of cellular manufacturing system in the presence of alternative process plans, *International Journal of Production Research*, **28**: 1541–1554.
10. Vakharia, A.J. and Wemmerlov, U., 1990: Designing a cellular manufacturing systems: a material flow approach based on operation sequences, *IIE Transactions*, **22**: 84–97.
11. Weck, M., Kaever, M., Brouer, N. and Rehse, M., 1997: NC Integrated process monitoring and control for intelligent, autonomous manufacturing systems, *Proceedings of the 29th CIRP International Seminar on Manufacturing Systems, New Manufacturing Era – Adaption to Environment, Culture, Intelligence and Complexity*, Osaca University, Japan, May 11–13, pp. S. 69–74.
12. Yoshida, Ham and Hitomi, 1985: *Group Technology – Applications to Production Management*, Kluwer-Nijhoff, Boston.

Benchmarking

S – 3b; 7c; 9c; 11b; 14c; 16b; * 1.2c; 2.1b; 2.2b; 3.1b; 3.4b; 4.1c

The goal of benchmarking is to keep or regain a company's competitive edge. Benchmarking is a business management tool for defining feasible change goals. It is the process of continuously comparing and measuring an organization against business leaders anywhere in the world to gain information that will help the organization to take action to improve performance.

The ability to gain superiority is dependent upon a detailed understanding of the company's own operations and those of others, and the ability to incorporate these to develop performance improvements. Even if you know that one system is better than another, a detailed analysis of the other system is necessary to understand and to explain the difference in performances.

The theoretical basis of benchmarking is the notion that consumers do not buy goods or services but rather buy the attributes of those goods or services; hence, success in the marketplace rests on creating products whose attributes match what the market wants and needs. An operational system for evaluating the 'appropriateness' of a product's attributes – its ability to satisfy consumer needs – is constructed and illustrated with reference to several types of industrial sensors. The method encourages managers to ask continually: 'what business am I in'. Or ask the question:

- How do I create value for my customers?

That question, in turn, leads to several others:

- Who are my customers?
- What particular aspects or characteristics of my product are especially important in creating value?
- How can I best enhance those value-creating properties?

Knowledge of the market value that is attached to each of the most important attributes of a technology-based product is important information for managers. Many businesses are built on products that have a single outstanding characteristic that none of the competing products can match, while satisfying minimal standards in other characteristics.

There are several types of benchmarking:

1. Internal benchmarking: a comparison of internal operations.
2. Competitive benchmarking: specific competitor – to – competitor comparison for the product of interest.
3. Functional benchmarking: comparisons of similar functions within the same broad industry or industry leaders.
4. Generic benchmarking: comparison of business functions or processes regardless of industry.

One of the proposed benchmarking procedures includes the following steps:

1. Systematize benchmarking goals.
2. Identify relevant objects to be benchmarked.
3. Assess the applicability of the current benchmarking procedure.
4. Find typical illustrative examples for benchmarking.
5. Identify potential problems and further research opportunities.

Some examples include:

Business process benchmarking – The goal is principally concerned with the company's effort to achieve long-term competitive and customer advantages.

One way that benchmarking is very useful, is in the identification of non-value-added activities within the enterprise.

Benchmarking in application systems management – Both standard and applications software are benchmarked with the following objectives.

- To compare different software packages of a certain type in order to select the one most capable of meeting particular requirements.
- To compare different releases of one product in order to control quality enhancement.

Benchmarking in infrastructure management – The main purpose of software process benchmarking for a company is to learn about its own technological opportunities by learning about other similar operations.

Hardware benchmarking – Hardware systems benchmarking is conducted with two goals in mind:

- to compare different systems on different platforms running the same application.
- to compare different machines.

Organizational benchmarking – The goals of such benchmarking studies focus on the following.

- To find the best way of using information in the organization so as to optimize information system benefits.
- To establish the best workable solution to combine information from different sources.
- To establish the best programme for promoting cooperation and communication within the organization.

Bibliography

1. Camp, R., 1989: *Benchmarking: The Search for Industry Best . . . ., 1989*. ASQC Quality Press.
2. Crawford, J., 1994: TPC auditing: How to do it better, Quarterly Report, pp. 9–11.
3. Daneva, M., 1995: Software benchmarking design and use. In J. Brown (ed.), *Reengineering the Enterprise*. Chapman & Hall, London.
4. Davenport, T.H., 1993: *Process Innovation*. Harvard Business School Press, Boston.
5. Doumengts, G. and Browne, J. (ed.), 1997: *Modelling Techniques for Business Process Reengineering and Benchmarking*. Chapman & Hall, London.
6. ESPRIT Project 2151:, SCOPE – Technology for Evaluation and Certification of software product quality. Project brochure, November 1992.
7. Hars, A., Kruse, C. and Scheer, A.W., 1992: Ways to utilizing reference modules for data engineering. *Conference Proceedings, CIM, FAIM '92*.
8. Heib, R. and Daneva, M., 1995: Benchmarking: eine Defintionklarung. Gabler, Wiesbaden.
9. Hiech, B., Thoben, D., Kromker, M. and Wickner, A., 1994: Benchmarking of bid preparation for capital goods. In A. Rolstadas (ed.), *Benchmarking – Theory and Practice*. Chapman & Hall.
10. Jones, C.V., 1996: *Pattern of Software Systems Failure and Success*. International Thompson Computer Press, Boston.
11. Mair, R., 1995: Quality of data model. In *Conference Proceedings, Third International Conference on Software Quality Management*, Seville.
12. Mettins, K., Kempf, S. and Siebert, G., 1995: How benchmarking supports reengineering. In J. Brown (ed.), *Reengineering the Enterprise*. Chapman & Hall.
13. Rostadas, A. (ed.), 1994: *Benchmarking – Theory and Practice*. Chapman & Hall. London.

14. Scheer, A.W., 1992: *Architecture of Integrated Information Systems*. Springer-Verlag, Berlin.
15. Watson, H.G., 1993: *Strategic Benchmarking*, John Wiley and Sons, pp. 3–39.

Bionic manufacturing system

P – 1c; 2c; 3d; 4c; 8d; 9d; 13c; 14c; 16c; * 1.3b; 1.4c; 2.4c; 3.3b; 3.5c; 3.6c; 4.4c; 4.6c
(See also Self-organizing manufacturing method; and Holonic manufacturing system.)

Bionic manufacturing systems are designed to solve shop floor control problems. Bionic manufacturing systems have an architecture made up of totally distributed independent autonomous modules that cooperate intelligently to create a manufacturing system that responds to future manufacturing needs. The needs are specified as:

- produced by autonomous modules;
- reduction of workforce;
- modular design that assures integration;
- inexpensive construction of production lines (reduction of 70–80% in investment);
- meeting customers needs;
- fast adjustment to market fluctuations.

The traditional approach to the design of manufacturing systems is the hierarchical approach. The design is based on a top-down approach and strictly defines the system modules and their functionality. Communication between modules is strictly defined and limited in such a way that modules communicate with their parent and child modules only. In a hierarchical architecture, modules cannot take initiatives; therefore, the system is sensitive to perturbations, and its autonomy and reaction to disturbances are weak. The resulting architecture is very rigid and therefore expensive to develop and difficult to maintain.

Heterarchical control was an approach devised to lessen the problems of hierarchical systems. The heterarchical approach bans all hierarchy in order to give full power to the basic modules, often called 'agents', in the system. A heterarchical manufacturing system consists of, for instance, workstations and orders only. Each order negotiates with the workstations to get the work done, using all possible alternatives available to face unforeseen situations. In this way, it is possible to react adequately to changes in the environment (such as new products that enter the market, new or evolving technologies, unpredictable demands for products) as well as to disturbances in the manufacturing system itself (defects, delays, variable yield of chemical reactors).

The bionic manufacturing system is inspired by biological metaphors, the main focus being on the self-organizing nature of the elements in the manufacturing system. Each organ of a life-form acts on its own while coordinating actions and maintaining harmony with other organs. An organ, in turn consists of cells. Biologically, a cell is separated from outside by a membrane, through which materials enter and exit. A cell changes its own conditions by its operation and it can perform multiple and different operations. The function of coordination in biological system is executed by enzymes. In manufacturing it is executed by the operator.

The biological viewpoint has close parallels in manufacturing. Production units on the shop floor can be compared to cells in biology. The concept of biology and the similarities to manufacturing are used to propose manufacturing concepts and supporting modelling elements.

Bibliography

1. Hardwick, M., Spooner, D.L., Rando, T. and Morris, K.C., 1996: Sharing manufacturing information in virtual enterprises, *Communications of the ACM*, **39**(2).
2. Luis, M., Camarinha-Matos, H.A., Rabelo, R.J. and Camarinha Matos, L.M. (eds) Towards agile scheduling in extended enterprise. In *Balanced Automation Systems II – Implementation Challenges for Anthropocentric Manufacturing*. Chapman & Hall, pp. 413–424.
3. Okino, N., 1992: A prototyping of bionic manufacturing system. In *Proceedings of ICOOMS'92*, pp. 297–302.
4. Okino, N., 1993: Bionic manufacturing systems. In J. Peklerik (ed.), *Flexible Manufacturing Systems, Past, Present, Future*, Ljubljana, Slovenia, pp. 73–95.
5. Bradshaw, J. (ed.), (1997) Software Agents, AAAI Press / The MIT Press.
6. Tonshoff, H.K., Winkler, M. and Aurich, J.C., 1994: Product modeling for holonic manufacturing systems. In *Proceeding of the 4th International Conference on CIM and Automation Technology*, Oct. 10–12, Troy, NY, pp. 121–127.
7. Ueda, K., 1992: An approach to bionic manufacturing systems based on DNA-type information. In *Proceedings of ICOOMS '92*, pp. 303–308.
8. Tharumarajah, A., Wells, A.J. and Nemes, L., 1996: Comparison of bionic, fractal and holonic manufacturing system concepts, *International Journal of Computer Integrated Manufacturing*, **9**(3), pp. 217–226.

Borderless corporation

M – 1c; 2c; 3b; 4b; 6b; 7b; 8b; 9b; 10b; 11b; 13c; * 2.4b; 3.2c; 3.3b; 3.4b; 3.5c; 3.6b; 4.1b; 4.2c; 4.3c; 4.4c

See Supply chain management.

Business intelligence and data warehousing

S – 6b; 7b; 9c; 10b; 11b; 13c; 16b; * 1.1b; 1.2c; 1.3b; 3.3c; 4.1a; 4.2b; 4.3b; 4.4a

The objectives of business intelligence and data warehousing are to assist managers in setting company strategy, maintaining corporate competitiveness and increasing revenue.

Managers make decisions based on data and information. Several methods from which manager may draw their data are available, such as customer relationship management, customer knowledge management, e-commerce, and e-business. These methods are viewed as key technology solutions for not only understanding customers, but also for maintaining corporate competitiveness and increasing revenue.

The business intelligence and data warehousing method proposes to have a single data source, while deriving the data from many individual sources, which include:

- E-commerce
- business-to-business
- business-to-consumer
- business-to-employee
- business-to-supplier
- financial information
- ERP information
- customer knowledge management
- customer relationship marketing
- data warehousing human resource
- other organizational information.

Business intelligence and data warehousing technologies also play an important role in the evolution of knowledge management and enterprise information portals. Although there is currently little data and/or primary research to support the existence of an enterprise information portals market, the concept of an enterprise portal with access to multiple data sources and information is sound.

Business intelligence and data warehousing play a vital role in facilitating corporate strategy and organizational initiatives, for not only understanding customers, but also for maintaining corporate competitiveness and increasing revenue. From a computing architecture viewpoint business intelligence and data warehousing may assist with the transition from client/server to distributed concurrent use and Internet access.

Many organizations are moving towards Internet/Intranet access. As organizations provide access to increasing numbers of employees nearly all members of the organization will become consumers of business intelligence information.

Bibliography

1. Auditore, P.J., 2000: The future of BI, *Enterprise Systems Journal*, **15**(2), 53–55.
2. Blackburn, J.D., 1991: *Time-Based Competition: The Next Battleground in American Manufacturing*. Business One-Irwin, Homewood ILL.
3. Chrisman, J.J., Hofer, C.W. and Boulton, W.R., 1988: Toward a system for classifying business strategies, *Academy of Management Review*, **13**, 413–28.
4. Fitzgerald, A., 1992: Enterprise resource planning (ERP)-breakthrough or buzzword? In *Third International Conference on Factory 2000. Competitive Performance Through Advanced Technology (Conference Publishing No.359)*. IEE, London, pp. 291–7.
5. Gabel, H.L., 1991: *Competitive Strategies for Product Standards*, McGraw Hill, London.
6. Hicks, D.A. and Stecke, K.E., 1995: The ERP maze: enterprise resource planning and other production and inventory control software. *IIE-Solutions*, **27**(8), 12–16.
7. Huber, G.P., 1990: A theory of the effects of advanced information technologies on organizational design, intelligence, and decision making, *Academy of Management Review*, **15**, 47–71.
8. Jenson, R.L. and Johnson, I.R., 1999: The enterprise resource planning system as a strategic solution, *Information Strategy: The Executive's Journal*, **15**(4), 28–33.
9. Jetly, N., 1999: ERP's last mile – [enterprise resource planning], *Intelligent Enterprise*, **2**(17), 38–40, 42, 44–5.
10. Kempfer, L., 1998: Linking PDM to ERP, *Computer-Aided Engineering*, **17**(2), 58–64.
11. Lacity, M. and Hirschheim, R., 1993: *Information Systems Outsourcing*, Wiley.
12. Miller, J.G. and Roth, A.V., 1994: A taxonomy of manufacturing strategies, *Management Science*, **40**, 285–304.
13. McKie, S., 1998: Packaged solution or Pandora's box? *Intelligent-Enterprise*, **1**(2), 38–9, 41, 44, 46.
14. Stein, T., 1998: ERP's future linked to E-supply chain. *Information Week*, **705**, 1.20, 1.22.
15. Teece, D.J., Pisano, G. and Shuen, A., 1997: Dynamic capabilities and strategic management, *Strategic Management Journal*, **18**, 509–533.

Business process re-engineering (BPR)

M – 7b; 8c; 9b; 13c; 14c; * 1.2b; 2.5c; 3.2c; 3.3c; 4.1c; 4.2b; 4.3d; 4.6c

The goal of business process re-engineering (BPR) is to improve customer service; increase market share; reduce the cycle time inherent in business operations; reduce the cost of operations; and achieve dramatic improvements in a company's performance in a relatively short period of time.

Many approaches exist for improving manufacturing performance (JIT, OPT, etc.) but few approaches offer the opportunity to make dramatic improvements in the non-manufacturing or "White collar" areas of a company business. Business process re-engineering focuses on examining the work-flow and processes within and between organizations. BPR can be viewed as a set of logically related tasks performed to achieve a definite business outcome.

Most business process re-engineering methodologies follow the same pattern in terms of approach to projects and deliverables. The business drivers for any integrated process improvement/information systems initiative are the company business strategy and the critical success factors of the business. This should dictate the priority for pursuing process improvement projects. The general phases of any process improvement project include the following.

1. *Define business processes and their internal/external clients.* The primary objective of this phase is to define the project goals and scope of the project. Critical business and process issues are identified and the organization's relationships and the high-level process interrelationships within the scope of the project are defined. Information technology support issues are defined and information technology goals established. In addition, the relationship of applications and databases to the current process is defined. Project plans are also developed for management of the subsequent phases of the project.

2. *Model and analyse the process that supports these products and services.* The primary purpose of this phase is to define the current process and identify the process disconnects. The current level of information techno-logy support to the process is documented in additional detail and informa-tion technology related disconnects are also identified and segregated. The information technology will be used as a basis for developing the process design phase of the project.

3. *Design of the new process.* Highlight opportunities for incremental and or radical change by identifying and eliminating waste and inefficiency. Develop new process design criteria and information technology business design criteria. Information technology business design criteria establish a framework for developing the application strategy. The new process is designed with recommendations to support the implementation phase. Cultural, organization and training issues that represent obstacles to imple-mentation are identified. In addition, measurements are established for the newly designed process. Data models and application prototypes are addi-tional deliverables that can also be developed during this phase.

4. *Implementation.* Attainment of the project goals and the benefits derived from installation of the new process, information technology support infra-structure and related recommendations are contingent upon a successful implementation phase. The foundation for success is the quality of the deliv-erables and the implementation strategy developed in the prior phase. How-ever, it is even more critical that management commitment and leadership

be provided for the duration of the implementation phase. Effective project management is a key critical success factor during the implementation phase.

5. *Build a mechanism to ensure constant improvements.* The deliverables from the process design phase represent the foundation for the implementation phase, and are the basis for developing detailed implementation plans for all the process-related recommendations. This would include process changes, organization changes, policies/ guidelines, measurements, training, and job function changes.

The following seven principles should guide any business process re-engineering effort.

1. Organize about outcomes, not tasks.
2. Have those who use the output of the process perform the process.
3. Subsume information processing work into the real work that produce the information.
4. Treat geographically dispersed resources as though they were centralized.
5. Link parallel activities instead of integrating their results.
6. Put the decision point where the work is performed, and build control into the process.
7. Capture information once and at source.

The approaches to BPR differ in degree of change – radical or incremental. Radical programmes often require heavy financial commitment and have long pay-back periods, so that financial backing is often a problem. It is often easier to secure financial backing for an incremental programme because the overall risk is smaller and project control and management are easier. The assumption is that incremental changes will lead to greater overall change.

When people try to simplify a process with existing methods, they try to remove obstacles and bottlenecks, without a vision. The real problem is that these attempts to simplify specific tasks and/or processes may lead to a less efficient overall process or target function (local optimization does not necessarily guarantee global optimization). To succeed with BPR a clear broad organization vision must be considered.

Two process-identifying approaches are considered. The exhaustive approach identifies all the organizational activities, and then sorts them by priority to be re-engineered. This is very time-consuming, and often there are insufficient resources to analyse all of the activities after process mapping. The high-impact approach identifies only major processes or those that do not support or even oppose the organizational vision and objectives.

BPR cannot be done in isolation or in separate steps. It has to be aligned with the business strategy and information technology strategy. Moreover, there has to be an innovative environment that constantly searches for opportunities to improve organizational functioning.

Bibliography

1. Bernus, P., Nemes, L. and Williams, T.J. (eds), 1996: *Architectures for Enterprise Integration*. Chapman & Hall, London.
2. Bowersox, D. and Closs, D., 1996: *Logistical Management: The Integrated Supply Chain Process*, McGraw-Hill.
3. Bradely, P., Browne. J., Jackson. S. and Jagdev, H., 1995: Business process re-engineering (BPR) – a study of the software tools currently available, *Computers in Industry*, **25**, 309–330.
4. Davenport, H.T. and Short, E.J., 1990: The new industrial engineering: information technology and business process redesign, *Sloan Management Review*, **31**(4), 11–27.
5. Davenport, T.H., 1993: *Process Innovation: Re-engineering Work Through Information Technology*. Harvard Business School Press, Boston.
6. Douglas, D.P., 1993: The role of IT in business reengineering, *I/S Analyzer*, **31**, 115–122.
7. Drucker, F.P., 1994: The theory of the business, *Harvard Business Review*, **Sep– Oct**, 95–102.
8. Hales, H.L. and Savoie, J.B., 1994: Building a foundation for successful business process reengineering, *Industrial Engineering*, **Sept.**, 17–19.
9. Hammer, M., 1990: Re-engineering work; don't automate, obliterate, *Harvard Business Revue*, **July–August**, 104–112.
10. Hammer, M. and Champy, J., 1993: *Re-engineering the Corporation: A Manifesto for Business Revolution*. Nicholas Brealey Publishing, London.
11. Kubiak, B.F. and Korowicki, A., 1999: The processes reconstruction followed by business process re-engineering. In W. Abramowicz (ed.), *Business Information Systems '99*. AE, Poznań.
12. Peppard, J. and Rowland, Ph., 1995: *The Essence of Business Process Re-engineering*, Prentice Hall International, London.
13. Teng, J.T.C., Grover, V. and Fiedler, K.D., 1994: Re-design business processes using information technology, *Long Range Planning*, **27**, 95–106.
14. Williams, C., 1993: Business process re-engineering at Rank Xerox, *Business Change & Re-engineering*, **1**, 8–15.
15. Wright, R., 1992: *Systems Thinking – A Guide to Managing in a Changing Environment*, SME Publishing.

CAD/CAM, CNC, Robots Computer-aided design and manufacturing

T; S – 3b; 4b; 5c; 7c; * 1.2d; 1.3d; 2.2b; 2.4c

Computer-aided design (CAD) is a computer software and hardware combination used in conjunction with computer graphics to allow engineers and designers to create, draft, manipulate and change designs on a computer without the use of conventional drafting. CAD systems permit greater speed, precision and flexibility than traditional drafting systems.

Computer-aided manufacturing (CAM) incorporates the use of computers to control and monitor several manufacturing elements such as robots, computerized numerical control (CNC) machines, storage and retrieval systems, and automated guided vehicles (AGV). CAM implementations are often classified into several levels. At the lowest level, it includes programmable machines that are controlled by a centralized computer. At the highest level, large-scale systems integration includes control and supervisory systems.

Working with CAD the designer is able to converse with the computer and receive a direct response from it. For example the designer may generate a sketch on the monitor, as a result of previous programming, the computer understand the sketch, makes calculations based on it, and present answers or a revised sketch to the designer within a few seconds.

The computer can carry out vast amounts of detail work, tirelessly and without error. It can evaluate the consequences of an endless series of design alternatives, performing both engineering calculations and graphical manipulation, and can file away each alternative for future reference. Optimum solutions for problems cannot be obtained in closed form, thus requiring the designer to resort to a tiresome trial-and-error process. For such problems, the computer can be instructed to increment a set of parameters and generate a family of solutions, from which the optimum one can be selected.

A typical CAD system will include software and capabilities for:

computer solution of nonlinear equations;
finite elements analysis;
motional analysis and simulation;
dynamic analysis and simulation;
design optimization.

The synergistic effort of achieving this close coupling between the designer and computer has important benefits:

1. The designer can immediately see and correct any gross error in drawings or input statements.
2. The designer can monitor the progress of a problem solution and terminate the run or modify the input data as required.
3. The designer can make subjective decisions at critical branch points which guide the computer in continuation of the problem solution.
4. The graphic display may present data that cannot be readily understood or interpreted in a computer output list or even as plotted output. Through clever programming, a computer-driven display can present multiple views, moving pictures, blinking lines, dashed lines, lines of varying intensity, solid modelling, etc.

Different CAD system vendors use different system methods for display and command. These include: wire mesh, primitives, constructive solid geometry (CSG), boundary representation (B-Rep), sweeping, spatial occupancy enumeration, cell decomposition. In the future we may find intelligent CAD systems based on artificial intelligence (IT) that might even lead to automated design systems.

The variation of products competing in the CAD market (usually offering system options and features) made it difficult to transfer data from a CAD unit from one vendor to a CAD unit purchased from another vendor. To solve this problem attempts were made to form CAD/CAM standards. CAD/CAM standards are considered no different from company standards for any other application in practice. Operational as well as exchange applications standards allows the user to be more flexible as opposed to being locked into one vendor. The common standards are IGES – Initial Graphics Exchange Specifications, PDES – Product Data Exchange Specifications, STandard for the Exchange of Product model data, STEP or ISO 10303.

Computer-aided manufacturing (CAM) has many meanings and interpretations. At one extreme, it refers to the use of a computer to run an automatic programmed tool (APT) for programming numerical control machines (CNC), while at the other extreme, it refers to what technology forecasting predicts for the future – the automatic factory. The automatic factory is a computer integrated manufacturing system that controls all phases of the industrial enterprise: product design, process planning, flow of materials, production planning, positioning of materials, automatic production, assembly and testing, automatic warehousing, and shipping.

The common interpretation of CAM is not as ambitious as the automatic factory. Most commonly it involves the utilization of CNC machines and robots. Computer numerical control (CNC) machines are locally programmable machines with dedicated microcomputers. CNC provides great flexibility by allowing the machine to be controlled and programmed in the office instead of on the shop floor. Machine setup is transferred to the office, which thus increases machine operating and processing time. CNC allows machines to be integrated with other complementary technologies such as computer-aided design and computer integrated manufacturing. CNC also serves as the building block for flexible manufacturing systems (FMS).

The generation of CNC part programs can be done as a component of the CAD process. The geometric database constructed in the computer by an interactive CAD system can be used to generate tool paths with a few extra commands. These minimize the total design-to-production time, increase engineering efficiency, and improve quality. Checking of a CNC program is aided by animation of the tool path on a CAD system. This enables the part programmer to visualize tool motions.

Thus CAD integrates directly with CAM and can result in increased productivity of both engineering and production personnel by factors of up to an order of magnitude or more, while improving quality control and reducing the design to production time.

The Robotic Institute of America defines the industrial robot as 'A programmable, multi-functional manipulator designed to move materials, parts, tools or specialized devices through various programmed motions for the performance of a variety of tasks'. The basic purpose of the industrial robot is to replace human labour under certain conditions. The programmable nature of the robot provides the flexibility to make a variety of products. The industrial robot was developed to generate higher output at lower cost in situations that require high repetition, high precision, large capacity workload and hazardous environments such as paint, chemical processing and welding. Robots also serve as the building block for flexible manufacturing systems (FMS).

Bibliography

1. Batini, C., Ceri, S. and Navathe, S.B., 1992: *Conceptual Database Design*. Benjamin/Cummings.
2. Delorge, D., 1992: *Product Design and Concurrent Engineering*. SME CASA/SME.
3. Feru, F., Cocquebert, E., Chaouch, H., Deveneux, D. and Soenen, R., 1992: *Feature Based Modeling: State of the Art and Evolution, Manufacturing in the Era of Concurrent Engineering*. North-Holland IFIP.
4. French, M.G., 1988: *Invention and Evolution – Design in Nature and Engineering*. Cambridge University Press.
5. Halevi, G., 1980: *The Role of Computers in Manufacturing Processes*. John Wiley & Sons.
6. Halevi, G. and Weill, R., 1992: *Manufacturing in the Era of Concurrent Engineering*. North-Holland.
7. Gardan, Y. and Minich, C., 1993: Feature-based models for CAD/CAM and their limits, *Computers in Industry*, **23**, 3–13.
8. Lahti, A. and Ranta, M., 1997: Capturing and deploying design decisions. In M. Pratt, R.D. Sriram and M.J. Wozny (eds), *Proceedings of IFIP WG 5.2 Geometric Modelling Workshop*, Airlie, Virginia. IFIP Proceedings, Chapman & Hall, London.
9. Mahoney, D.P. and Driving, V.R., 1995: *Computer Graphics World (CGW)*, **May**.
10. N.N.: ISO 10303-1 Product Data Representation and Exchange – Part1: Overview and Fundamental Principles.
11. N.N.: ISO 10303-11 Industrial automation systems and integration – Product Data Representation and Exchange – Part 11: Description methods: The EXPRESS Language Reference Manual.
12. N.N.: ISO 10303-26 Industrial automation systems and integration – Product Data Representation and Exchange – Part 26: Implementation methods: Standard data access interface – IDL language binding.
13. Ohsuga, S., 1989: Towards intelligent CAD systems, *Computer Aided Design*, **21**(5), 315–337.

14. Tomiyama, T., Montyli, M. and Finger, S. (eds), 1996: Knowledge intensive CAD, Volume 1. *Proceedings of the First IFIP WG 5.2 Workshop on Knowledge-Intensive CAD*. IFIP Proceedings, Chapman & Hall, London.

15. Tomiyama, T. and Yoshikawa, H., 1984: *Requirements and Principles for Intelligent CAD System, Conference on k. E. In CAD*. North-Holland IFIP, 1984.

16. Ullman, G.D., 1992: *The Mechanical Design Process*. McGraw-Hill series in mechanical engineering.

17. Yoshikawa, H., 1981: General design theory and a CAD system, man/machine communication in CAD/CAM, North-Holland IFIP, pp. 1–23.

Cellular manufacturing

M – 2c; 4c; 5d; 6b; 8c; 12c; * 1.1d; 1.3b; 1.4c; 2.4c; 2.5c; 3.2c; 3.5c; 3.6b; 4.5d

Cellular manufacturing is a modern version of the concept of the group technology work cell. The cellular approach objective is that only the amount of product needed by the customer should be produced. It usually requires single-piece flow or, at the least, small batch sizes. The method used to meet this objective is to form families of parts, and to rearrange plant processing resources to form manufacturing cells.

The implementation of cellular manufacturing requires the following steps: analyse the open orders for a specified long period; decide upon a product family of parts; determine the operations required in the cellular environment; design jigs and fixtures that will reduce setup time; balance operations between operators; design the cell layout; move equipment to form the cell. Since most modern processing resources are flexible by nature, and they can perform several jobs, it is easier to practise cellular manufacturing than group technology. The cell might be a virtual cell that will not require the movement of resources every time the product mixes and the orders change.

Introducing manufacturing cells changes the way a company operates. Implementing manufacturing cells affects the production schedule. In many plants today, production schedules depend upon customer forecasts, equipment and material availability, and overdue customer orders. Large batch sizes are run to reduce the number of required equipment changeovers. In cellular manufacturing the batch size can be exactly the quantity required for customer orders. Due to the design of modular fixtures and computerized operated processing resources, set up is not a problem any more.

Production schedules must adapt to the cell's operation. They need to be more flexible in the amount of product produced, and more precise in the amounts of product output.

Traditional standard cost systems that rely upon high equipment utilization and overhead absorption are ineffective in a cellular environment.

New methods of measuring performance (completed orders or jobs performed, for example) must be introduced so management doesn't force practices upon operators that negatively affect the cell's goals. Equipment utilization in a cellular environment can be lower than a machine's capacity would indicate.

Other functions affected by manufacturing cells include the accounting and reporting systems. Today, most companies continue to require timely reports on equipment utilization. These reports are supposedly used to evaluate the effectiveness of each piece of equipment in the facility. In addition, the financial department often uses such reports to justify equipment purchases and paybacks. Under such guidelines, to keep equipment utilization high operators may be asked to produce material on a resource even when it is not needed.

Inventories such as work-in-process (WIP), raw material, and finished goods are listed as assets on a company's balance sheet. But high inventories are really liabilities that tie up company resources. An operation must introduce methods of reducing raw material, WIP, finished goods inventories, and setup times for a cell manufacturing system to work.

It is advisable that the cellular approach be applied to the entire production line. Picking isolated areas in which to implement manufacturing cells results in islands of success, but may not allow a product line to become efficient. The company may still depend upon operations that run in the traditional manufacturing environment. If the cell or group of cells doesn't include all operations in a product line/family, a cellular system will have minimal impact on the overall production process. The cell contains processing resources of several capabilities. Operators have to be flexible as well as the resources in the cell, therefore they have to be able to operate all the resources in the cell, and know how to set up each resource.

Many of the support functions normally handled by different individuals or departments become the responsibility of operators in a cellular system. Cellular manufacturing calls for teamwork. The responsibility for quality and meeting due dates as well as internal scheduling lies with the group as a unit. Operators need training in teamwork as well as manufacturing techniques. They need cross-training to run each piece of equipment in the cell, and this can be a time-consuming issue to resolve. Each station or piece of equipment requires varying degrees of skill to operate it.

This training must be done before the cell layout is designed, because it is very important that the operators are involved in the cell's layout and planned operation. They are the people who know how the equipment operates and understand how to do their assigned jobs. Operators need to understand what cells are, how they work, how they differ from traditional 'batch and queue' operations, and the objectives of the cellular environment. In addition to equipment and team training, operators need training on how to perform setups, setup reduction, inspections, preventive maintenance, proper equipment cleaning procedures, and other such activities.

A training schedule must be developed for every operator before cell implementation. Trainers must be engaged to provide the different types of training required, and to ensure that training does not interfere with normal day-to-day operations. Training will require several weeks or even months to complete.

Bibliography

1. Byrne, G., Dornfeld, D., Inasaki, I., Ketteler, G., Konig, W. and Teti, R., 1995: Tool condition monitoring (TCM) – the status of research and industrial application, *Annals of the CIRP*, **44**(2), S. 541–567.
2. Chan, H.M. and Milnrer, D.A., 1982: Direct clustering algorithm for group formation in cellular manufacturing, *Journal of Manufacturing Systems*, **1**, 65–75.
3. Chandrasekharan, M.P. and Rajagopalan, R., 1986: An ideal seed non-hierarchical clustering algorithm for cellular manufacturing, *International Journal of Production Research*, **24**, 451–464.
4. Choobineh, F., 1988: Framework for design of cellular manufacturing systems, *International Journal of Production Research*, **26**, 1511–1522.
5. Co, H.C. and Arrar, A., 1988: Configuration cellular manufacturing systems, *International Journal of Production Research*, **26**, 1511–1522.
6. Deitz, D. and Drucker, F.P., 1991: The new productivity challenge, *Harvard Business Review*, **Nov.–Dec.**, 69–79.
7. Drucker, F.P., 1990: The emerging theory of manufacturing, *Harvard Business Review*, **May–June**, 94–102.
8. Merchant, M.E., 1984: *Computer Integration of Engineering Design and Production*, Manufacturing Studies Board, National Research Council, Washington DC, National Academy Press.
9. Pritschow, G. *et al.*, 1993: Open system controllers – a challenge for the future of the machine tool industry, *Annals of the CIRP*, **41**(1), pp. 449–453.
10. Rajamani, D., Singh, N. and Aneja, Y.P., 1990: Integrated design of cellular manufacturing system in the presence of alternative process plans, *International Journal of Production Research*, **28**, 1541–1554.
11. Vakharia, A.J. and Wemmerlov, U., 1990: Designing a cellular manufacturing systems: a material flow approach based on operation sequences, *IIE Transactions*, **22**, 84–97.
12. Weck, M., Kaever, M., Brouer, N. and Rehse, M., 1997: NC Integrated process monitoring and control for intelligent, autonomous manufacturing systems, *Proceedings of the 29th CIRP International Seminar on Manufacturing Systems, New Manufacturing Era – Adaption to Environment, Culture, Intelligence and Complexity*, Osaka University, Japan, May 11–13, pp. S. 69–74.
13. Yoshida, H. and Hitomi, 1985: *Group Technology – Applications to Production Management*, Kluwer-Nijhoff, Boston.

Client/server architecture

X – 1b; 2b; 3c; 4c; 5d; 6b; 7b; 13c; * 1.3b; 2.3c; 2.4b; 2.5c; 3.2c; 3.5c; 4.3c
See Manufacturing execution system (MES).

Collaborative manufacturing in virtual enterprises

T – 3d; 7b; 11c; 13b; * 1.1c; 1.2b; 3.3c; 4.3b

The main task of collaborative manufacturing in virtual enterprises is to support communication both within a production plant and among the partners of the virtual enterprise.

The objective of virtual, network-shaped and temporal cooperation of decentralized competencies is to increase flexibility and satisfy customer demands. From the point of view of information processing, the shift of coordination tasks from internal coordination within a company to external coordination of several companies working on a common project is critical. In the borderline case of a virtual enterprise the problems arising can serve as an example.

There are many challenges to the information systems architecture when setting up a virtual enterprise. Potential barriers to cooperation spanning different enterprises are:

1. High degree of distribution. Applications and relevant data are highly distributed.
2. Highly heterogeneous environment. The environment consists of heterogeneous applications, information systems, communication systems, operating systems, hard- and software, which all have to integrate and operate seamlessly.
3. Coordination and cooperation mechanisms. In order to achieve controlled and coordinated cooperation of different applications, a controlling mechanism spanning the partners of a virtual enterprise is needed.
4. Dynamic reorganization. Virtual enterprises must be able to form and dissolve quickly. Therefore, communication links have to be set up and dissolved quickly.
5. Insufficient security. Companies participating in a virtual enterprise necessarily offer insights of their own company to the others. A high level of security concerning access to company-specific data has to be guaranteed.

Collaborative manufacturing in virtual enterprises leads in some ways to specific requirements concerning the information management and the respective information systems architecture. On the one hand, integrated data and process management within the whole production network is a prerequisite to coordinate and supervise the process of fabrication along the whole process chain. Therefore, the access of external cooperation partners has to be restricted to a subset of the process data by means of security mechanisms. On the other hand, monitoring, diagnostics and simulation are important applications used at planning level as well as at supervisory level. In order to enable the user at planning level to adapt the processes immediately to changes of production conditions, seamless integration of planning and process level is required. However, real enterprises do not match this scenario, because the data itself is highly distributed and there is no global database. Therefore, it has to be the task of the information system and the applications to provide the model of a global database and to support interoperability for the applications. Across enterprise boundaries, in particular, this turns out to be extremely difficult because of different hardware platforms and operating systems. Moreover, today's information systems lack support for coordinated production within a production network, e.g. the link-up of simulation models of distributed manufacturing systems and the synchronization of production plans. Considering the task of process management, available tools do not offer the possibility to integrate external partners in the enterprises' workflow. In order to run linked simulation models, transparent access to parts of the operating data at shop-floor level is necessary. However, the shop-floor level lacks support for an open, connective information system. Vendor-specific hardware and software solutions are dominant, comprising non-standardized interfaces. Thus, isolated applications are the consequence. Exchange of process data between these applications and the planning level therefore results in implementing vendor-specific interfaces, which is time and money consuming. As a consequence, when setting up virtual enterprises, access to process data is one of the major problems.

Bibliography

1. Feldmann, K., Rauh, E., Collisi, T. and Steinwasser, P., 1997: Modular tool for simulation parallel to production planning. In *Proceedings of the 16th IASTED International Conference*, Insbruck, Austria.
2. Feldmann, K. and Rottbauer, H., 1997: Achieving and maintaining competitiveness by electronically networked and globally distributed assembly systems. In *29th CIRP International Seminar on Manufacturing Systems*, Osaka.
3. Feldmann, K. and Stackel, T., 1997: Utilization of Java-applets for building device specific man–machine interfaces. In *Conference Proceedings Field Comms UK*.
4. Hinckley, Hardwick, M., Spooner, D.L., Rando, T. and Morris, K.C., 1996: Sharing manufacturing information in virtual enterprises, *Communications of the ACM, Object Management Group*, **39**(2), pp. 46–54.
5. Shen, C.-C., 1998: Discrete-event simulation on the Internet and the Web. In *Proceedings of the 1998 International Conference on Web-Based Modeling & Simulation*, San Diego.
6. Warneke, G., 1996: *Marktstudie PPS/CAQ. VDI-Verlag, Dusseldorf. N.N.*: ISO 10303–1 Product Data Representation and Exchange – Part 1: Overview and Fundamental Principles.
7. N.N.: *ISO 10303–11 Industrial Automation Systems and Integration* – Product Data Representation and Exchange – Part 11: Description methods: The EXPRESS Language Reference Manual.
8. N.N.: *ISO 10303–26 Industrial Automation Systems and Integration* – Product Data Representation and Exchange – Part 26: Implementation methods: Standard data access interface – IDL language binding.

Common-sense manufacturing – CSM

P – 1c; 2c; 4b; 6b; 8c; * 1.3b; 2.3d; 2.4b; 3.5c; 3.6b; 4.2c

The objective of common-sense manufacturing (CSM) is to regulate work-in-process, and enable the manufacturing line to meet the production goal. It allows operations teams on the shop floor to regulate and adjust the work plan.

Common-sense manufacturing (CSM) results from combining the strengths of materials requirement planning (MRP) and just-in-time (JIT) methods with the concepts of constraints management, strategic buffers, and ongoing yield improvement.

MRP systems approach the production control task from a 'first plan the work and then work the plan' viewpoint. Unfortunately, such systems are often better at planning than they are at working. At the point of production, the execution methodologies of JIT systems, such as pull systems and kanbans, are better utilized.

Common-sense manufacturing is composed of the following components.

Organizational structure: One of the benefits of the CSM system is that it does not dictate the organizational structure of the manufacturing plant. The structure that is in place does not need to change as a result of the implementation of the CSM process.

Control the work-in-process: The CSM system uses trays or work holders (called totes) to gauge lot size and to control the work-in-process. A tote system is a method of handling parts and assemblies during production. It is also a method of tracking lots through the line.

Each area of the production line is analysed to determine the correct tote and the proper lot size. Many factors may influence a decision on lot size. The ideal is usually a lot size of one part. While this would be advantageous for inventory and interval reduction reasons as well as for lot traceability and tracking, it is often not feasible for other practical reasons. The first factor in selecting lot size is often the number of parts that are easily processed together as a batch. Other factors include the production facility size and capacity, the physical size of the parts, and the time required to work on a tote full of parts. Often the lot size is set by the constraint operation after taking into account the run time, setup time, and machine utilization factors.

Constraints management analysis: Constraints management is a term that reflects an understanding of a production line as a chain of processes linked one behind the other. The idea is that the line, like a chain, is only as strong as the weakest link. In this case, the line is only as fast as its slowest process. This process is defined as the bottleneck process or line constraint. The bottleneck receives attention from engineering, production scheduling, line supervisors, and production associates. The entire team tries to find ways to enable this process to run faster and more smoothly. Constraints are identified most easily by determining where the work-in-process inventory is accumulating. Such operations are often crowded with work trays or have a 'storage' problem. By recognizing the constraint, the operations team has the opportunity to regulate the workflow of other processes from this position in the line.

Pull system: Pull systems work on the basis of constraints management and kanban-type work request signals. This is where the JIT execution system comes into operation as part of the CSM process. Once an operation is found to be a line constraint, work is begun to improve its throughput and cycle time. Work that may be offloaded to other operations is taken away from the constraint, and the production effort at the constraint operation is made highly focused. Parts and other inputs to the process are made readily available so that the constraint is able to work in its most efficient manner.

Strategic buffering: Strategic buffering is the simple act of holding a strategic, planned amount of work-in-process inventory in the line. This inventory is there to allow for production problems such as breakdown maintenance. It is there, also, to ensure that the constraint operations always have work available, thus keeping them running. The extra inventory also allows improved responsiveness by the product line to short-internal orders or other unexpected demands. It also affords the opportunity to occasionally perform experiments on the line with the production facilities for such things as process improvement. This enables continuous improvements in yields, interval reduction, and costs of manufacture.

Process yield analysis: Process yields (Y) are simply the number of good parts (n) that are produced at any individual operation, divided by the number (N) that is started at that operation. The values for both n and N are collected at each operation via the shop flow system.

These data are utilized by many different organizations within the plant.

The master production scheduler uses these individual process yields to calculate reverse cumulative yields for each step in a routing. By using these data, expected numbers of good items coming from the work-in-process can be calculated at each step. The number of good items expected from the line can then be matched with the production commitments to customers. When these data are used in conjunction with known intervals, the production scheduler knows the amount of product that is available in the line and when to expect it.

The material ordering organization can also make good use of the yield analysis data. The production scheduler lets the ordering organization know how many finished products are required. By accessing the data generated by the reverse cumulative and knowing where each individual piece part is used in the assembly process, individual part requirements can be generated. The lead times for each piece part can be added to the data to create an integrated ordering system.

The production engineer utilizes the process yield data as well. On a weekly and monthly basis, the yields through both individual operations and specific subassembly routings can be reviewed for problems. Areas that are running below normally planned or expected yields can be identified and investigated. Also, areas with lower yields are often the best places to invest efforts to improve the process. These operations are where ongoing process improvements can result in big savings to the bottom line.

Bibliography

1. Belt, B., 1987: MRP and kanban – a possible synergy? *Production and Inventory Management*, **28**(1).
2. Berry, W.L., 1972: Priority scheduling and inventory control in job lot manufacturing system, *AIIE Transactions*, **4**(4), 267–276.
3. Bose, G.J. and Rao, A., 1988: Implementing JIT with MRP II creates hybrid manufacturing environment, *Industrial Engineering*.
4. Buffa, E.S., 1966: *Models for Production and Operation Management*, John Wiley & Sons.
5. Goldratt, E.M. and Cox, F., 1992: The Goal, revised edition. Croton-on-Hudson, NY: North River Press.
6. Harding, J., Gentry, D. and Parker, J., 1969: Job shop scheduling against due dates, Industrial Engineering, **1**(6), 17–29.
7. Hubner, H. and Paterson, I. (ed.), 1983: *Production Management Systems*, North-Holland.
8. Lambrecht, M.R. and Decaluwe, L., 1988: JIT and constraint theory: the issue of bottleneck management, *Production and Inventory Management Journal*, **29**(3).
9. Lotenschtein, S., 1986: Just-in-time in the MRP II environment, P&IM Review, February.
10. Plenert, G., 1985: Are Japanese production methods applicable in the United States? *Production and Inventory Management*, **26**(2).
11. Best, T.D., 1986: MRP, JIT, and OPT: What's 'Best'? *Production and Inventory Management*, **27**(2), 22–28.
12. Rao, A. and Scheraga, D., 1988: Moving from manufacturing resource planning to just-in-time manufacturing, *Production and Inventory Management Journal*, **29**(1).
13. Schonberger, R.J., 1983: Selecting the right manufacturing inventory system: Western and Japanese approaches, *Production and Inventory Management*, **24**(2).
14. Wilson, G.T., 1985: Kanban scheduling – boon or bane? *Production and Inventory Management*, **26**(3).
15. Wiendahl, H.P., 1995: *Load-oriented Manufacturing Control*, Springer-Verlag.

Competitive edge

P – 9c; 11b; 16c; * 1.1b; 1.2c; 1.5c; 3.4,b; 4.1b; 4.6c

Almost all major corporations today are driven by three priorities: creating shareholder value, a laser-beam focus on their customer, and competing in a global environment. These objectives are interdependent and impossible to achieve in a vacuum.

Distribution is the next competitive battleground and the companies with the best-integrated logistics will have a strong competitive edge. Logistics has become a hot competitive advantage as companies hard-pressed to beat competitors on quality or price try to gain an edge through their ability to deliver the right stuff in the right amount at the right time.

Integrated logistics having the right product in the right place at the right time is the new battleground in economic competitiveness on a global scale. Companies are moving rapidly away from the 'conventional wisdom' to a more aggressive, dynamic, and innovative corporate strategy. They are moving away from the traditions of the past and embarking on new courses of action:

- Away from functional excellence towards the pursuit of total business excellence.
- Away from broad funding of business towards selected capital investment.
- Away from competition based on price and quality to competition based on time.
- Away from top-down management decree to frequent two-way communication with employees.
- Away from a product-driven approach to a market-driven approach.
- Away from technological evolution to technological revolution.
- Away from local-based competition to global competition.
- Away from diversification to a focus on core competencies.
- Away from inventory at rest to inventory in motion.

Today's global economy presents a growing need for sophisticated, information-based logistics and transportation solutions. Logistics has always been important, but top management has not considered it critical to competition until recently. Most companies have explored re-engineering and applied total quality management. They have empowered their employees. They have implemented the latest management tools and product innovations. They have jumped headlong into the information age. And now they are focusing on logistics.

The seven principles of an old (1584) Japanese swordsman may be applied to winning in all phases of business and serve as a tactic in competitive situations. The seven principles represent the core principles of this competitive philosophy.

Ordered flexibility. Ordered flexibility embodies preparation, observation, timing, and readiness to act. Excessive order and structure lead to brittleness and defeat. Balance order with flexibility. Move slowly when conditions are unfavourable; move powerfully when the right course opens up. Think of winning, not of position.

Focus on probable areas of success. No person or company has enough resources to exploit every opportunity. Highly effective executives focus on markets and battles that their companies can win and win big. They direct high-output resources into opportunities that produce the greatest profit for the longest time.

Effective execution. Execution or action produces results. Execution creates profit. Execution wins victories. Effective execution consists of taking an appropriate action at an appropriate time. There is no way to tell, in the heat of battle, whether the actions you are taking are the 'right' actions. A good idea executed promptly today is worth a dozen perfect ideas executed next week; be prepared to act when the opportunity arises. This requires courage and patience, order and flexibility. The ability to perceive and benefit from the moment of advantage is developed through constant study and practice.

Resources. Resources are those assets and skills that each side brings to the conflict. They are the raw material of tactics. In business, resources can include people, plant, equipment, finances, and reputation. In all competitive situations, the most critical resource is timely and accurate information. Information is the fabric of tactics. You can never know too much about your enemy, yourself, or the situation.

Environment. In business, environment includes market trends, economic and political climate, technology, and public opinion. Resources and environment provide the setting in which a competitive situation arises and is resolved. Your initial approach depends on your assessment of environment.

Attitude. The attitude you bring to the conflict will be the attitude you practise in training. You must be confident and competent, aware and ready, neither afraid nor careless. Your choice does not change the facts of the situation. Neither imagined fear nor false optimism can change your real position and circumstances.

Concentration. In every situation, there are tactics that will work and tactics that will not work. Effective tactics are based on the principle of concentrating strength against weakness or resources into opportunity. Every opponent, every challenge you face, whether it is another person, another company, or even change and innovation within your own company, has a weakness or opportunity you can exploit with the proper attention. Concentration utilizes your resources most effectively against the weakness or opportunity, contained in a specific situation of threat.

Timing. The timing of competitive actions is often critical to success. When you engage in competition, you should neither move too quickly nor too slowly. It is not speed in itself, but rhythm and timing that are critical. The appropriate moment is that point in time when the scales are tipped in favour of the tactics you chose. Concentration and timing work together. If you do not concentrate thought and resources at the appropriate moment, your tactics will probably fail.

Bibliography

1. Blackburn, J.D., 1991: *Time-Based Competition: The Next Battleground in American Manufacturing*. Business One-Irwin, Homewood IL.
2. Chrisman, J.J., Hofer, C.W. and Boulton, W.R., 1988: Toward a system for classifying business strategies, *Academy of Management Review*, **13**, 413–28.
3. Gabel, H.L., 1991: *Competitive Strategies for Product Standards*, McGraw Hill, London.
4. Gunn, T.G., 1987: *Manufacturing for Competitive Advantage*. Ballinger, Cambridge, MA.
5. Hayes, R.H. and Wheelwright, S.C., 1984: *Restoring Our Competitive Edge*. John Wiley & Sons, New York.
6. Huber, G.P., 1990: A theory of the effects of advanced information technologies on organizational design, intelligence, and decision making, *Academy of Management Review*, **15**, 47–71.
7. Keen, 1986: *Competing in Time: Using Telecommunications for Competitive Advantage*. Ballinger, Cambridge, MA.
8. Lacity, M. and Hirschheim, R., 1993: *Information Systems Outsourcing*. Wiley,
9. Mannion, D., 1995: Vendor accreditation at ICL: competitive versus collaborative procurement strategies, in R. Lamming and A. Cox (eds), *Strategic Procurement Management in the 1990s*, Earlsgate, Winteringham.
10. Miller, J.G. and Roth, A.V., 1994: A taxonomy of manufacturing strategies, *Management Science*, **40**, 285–304.
11. Peters, T. and Waterman, R., 1982: *In Search of Excellence: Lessons from America's Best-Run Companies*. Harper & Row, New York.
12. Prahalad, C.K. and Hamel, G., 1990: The core competence of the corporation, *Harvard Business Review*, **68**(3), 79–91.
13. Tayeb, M.H., 1996: *The Management of a Multicultural Workforce*. John Wiley & Sons, Chichester
14. Teece, D.J., Pisano, G. and Shuen, A., 1997: Dynamic capabilities and strategic management, *Strategic Management Journal*, **18**, 509–533.

Competitive intelligence – CI

M – 7b; 9d; 11b; 13c; 16c; * 1.1b; 1.2b; 4.1b; 4.3d; 4.4d

The goal of competitive intelligence is to find answers to questions about key competitors, pricing, and the strengths and weaknesses of their product lines.

Five ways in which competitive intelligence can give a company an edge are given below.

1. Identify new and potential competitors.
2. Help determine which industries to enter or exit. If a company is evaluating a new market, an analysis of market forces, coupled with an assessment of the technological and regulatory environment, will give indications of the market potential.
3. Competitive intelligence can ensure that a company's business plans are based on the best and most current information.
4. Identify successful and failed strategies in the market. If a competitor has tried and rejected an option being considered, one can find out why. Also strategies of successful competitors can be examined to see if they can be applied.
5. Learning competitors' strengths, weaknesses, opportunities and threats helps a company understand what motivates them and enables the company to plan strategy in advance. In the case of a merger enquiry, competitive intelligence can help determine which companies have the best strategic fit.

A multitude of tools, techniques, products and services have lowered the costs and vastly improved access to information for competitive intelligence researchers – immensely simplifying data gathering. The World Wide Web changed everything. Among the Internet's greatest contributions to competitive intelligence research is the window it opens onto business relationships. The Internet can expose a variety of relationships that may not be widely publicized. Moreover, either party may not even approve the information uncovered for broadcast. The hyperlinks of the Internet can be used as direct evidence of official and unofficial relationships, with real value in the links pointing to a particular Web site. The Internet also excels at providing swift access to critical news about your rivals. While the Internet offers effortless access to almost limitless information, the information can be suspect.

Some fairly straightforward Internet searches can reveal a multitude of relationships, and hopefully more details about the alliance. One may uncover a rival's client list, a rival's supplier, or details about the competitor revealed in a success story. Such searches don't specify the direction of the relationship: the same search may uncover a rival's clients, or the companies to whom your rival is a client.

Along with opening a window on business relationships, the Internet excels at providing swift access to critical news about your rivals. Certainly, electronic clipping services existed before the Web. However, the electronic highway has expanded the variety, simplified access, and lowered the cost of these services. Beyond just watching for news stories out in the print world, attentive services will monitor changes in Web pages you specify, seek new filings or patents, or continuously monitor the Web through a search engine.

Some free Web sentinels are providing an integrated assortment of useful data for company research. Offering valuable Web-based monitoring of public companies, this will monitor up to ten US public companies. When the selected companies submit or receive patent or trademark approvals, post jobs, release news stories, register internet domains, or are mentioned in several investor-focused discussion groups – you receive an email alert. Web sentinels can silently watch your specified pages, and then notify you via email when changes take place. A setup can monitor a competitor's home page (or any page you specify), signalling when your rival posts news stories, jobs, executive speeches, new products, and more. A setup can monitor the Web site of a rival's hometown newspaper, specifying the rival's name: when the electrons hit the wires with a news story, you receive an email alert.

Free simple searches can be carried out using four well-known search engines: AltaVista, Excite, Info seek and Lycos. Informant will also monitor specified Web pages and notify you when changes take place. The possibilities are limited only by your imagination: patrol for executive speeches, distributors, new locations, trade show exhibits, research papers presented at conferences, whatever strikes your fancy.

Discussion groups on the Internet are serving as Internet-era watering holes offering facts along with gossip, rumour, and innuendo on a wide range of topics including investment-related information. The discussion groups, particularly on Yahoo and AOL, can provide hints and tips from industry and company experts, or they can provide off-the-wall comments from uninformed eccentrics. Some of the experts are a little too expert in fact. A defence industry giant suspects its employees are revealing company secrets. The best bet to pick up gossip is to check out high traffic sites such as Yahoo Finance (http://biz.yahoo.com/news), the Motley Fool's message section (http://www.fool.com), and Silicon Investor (http://www.techstocks.com) for talk about the competition or your own company.

Management profiles are sometimes requested for research projects. What makes management tick makes the company tick as well. The Web now offers effortless access to a useful source of executive profiles: alumni magazines. While a CEO of a mid-sized company may not merit a profile in *Fortune* magazine, they may well be one of Stanford Business School's 'prominent alumnae', meriting a full-length article in *Stanford Business Magazine*, published by Stanford University's Graduate School of Business.

Over the past few years, businesses, investors, and inventors have benefited greatly from free public patents, and trademarks on the Internet. Another large cache of company-specific information is just now finding its way onto the Web public records from state, county, city agencies, and federal courts. For competitive intelligence researchers, the state records are the most appealing, serving up business-related information, such as Uniform Commercial Code (UCC) filings and state incorporation records. However, other records are sometimes available through county and city sites: land records, tax assessor records, court records, and some vital records. State incorporation records, required in all 50 states, can also prove valuable in CI research; especially for private companies. These records often provide the date of incorporation, type of company, officers, and location. Some documents show little more than the owner of the record. Previously, access has been available through commercial online services, dial-up state bulletin boards, and through personal office visits. Now these official records are finally becoming available on the Net, sometimes at no cost.

For the Internet, the data needs to be verified. Verify the data with another resource. Verify the author. Verify the date of the information. Verify the domain's owner. Even if you find data at a company's home site, it could be misinformation, designed to mislead – something for which the company may have to plead forgiveness in front of television cameras at a future press conference.

Search addresses on the Web

http://www.altavista.com
http://www.amnesty.org
http://biz.yahoo.com/news
http://www.brbpub.com/pubrecsites.htmworld, Free Public Record Sites
http://www.companyaddress.com
http://www.companysleuth.com
http://www.corporateinformation.com
http://www. edgar-online.com
http://www.freeedgar.com
http://www.fool.com
http://www.hotbot.com
http://informant.dartmouth.edu
http://www.javelink.com/cat2main. Htm
http://www.netmind.com
http://peacefire. org/tracerlock
http://www.silicon-investor.com
http://www.sosaz.com/UCC. Htm
http://www. techstocks.com
http://w3.uwyo.edu/~prospect/secstate.html

Computer-aided process planning – CAPP

S – 1b; 2c; 4c; * 2.3c; 2.4b; 2.5c; 3.1c; 3.2b

Process planning activities generate the data for all production management activities and are key elements in the manufacturing process. It affects all factory activities, such as company competitiveness, production planning, production efficiency, and product quality. It plays a major part in determining the cost of components and is the crucial link between design and manufacturing.

Process planning is the function that establishes which machining processes and parameters are to be used to convert a product drawing and idea into a product, to convert each item from its raw material form to a final form. Alternatively, process planning could be defined as the act of preparing detailed work instructions to produce a part. The process planning is frequently called an operation sheet, routine sheet, and other similar names. In a conventional production system, an expert human process planner, who examines the item and then determines the appropriate procedures to produce it, creates a process.

Traditional production management regards the process plan as unalterable. Therefore, the method by which the process plan was generated, or the time that it took, was of no importance to the production management activity. The objectives of the computer-aided process planning (CAPP) system were:

1. to optimize the process planning task as a stand alone activity;
2. to reduce the skill required of a process planner;
3. to reduce the process planning time;
4. to reduce both process planning and manufacturing cost;
5. to create more consistent process plans;
6. to produce more accurate process plans;
7. to increase productivity

The development of CAPP systems has undergone several stages of improvement. In the following, the gradual development of computer-aided process planning is reviewed.

CAPP stage 1: The computer is utilized to assist the process planner with clerical work, leaving him free for technical work. The idea is to divide the work between the process planner and the computer, letting each perform the task they know best.

CAPP stage 2: Variant approach. The variant approach to process planning is to examine a part drawing, identify similar parts produced in the past (usually from memory, or from a filing cabinet) examine process plans for these similar parts and adapt or modify them to suit the specific part on hand. The variant approach is derived from group technology (GT) methods where parts are classified and coded into families. The classification task is the most critical part of implementing a variant system.

CAPP stage 3: Decision tree. The idea is to use a decision tree to establish a coding number as a key for retrieving a process, so that the tree leads directly to the process. A simple computer program with many 'IF...THEN' instructions is written. The content and knowledge regarding which node and branches to use, the depth of the branch and the decision attached to the terminal branch are the user's responsibility.

CAPP stage 4: Decision table. A decision table is composed of conditions, data and action, the principle elements of all computer programs. Decision tables and decision trees are reversible.

CAPP stage 5: Expert systems. An expert system is a computer program that exhibits the same level of problem-solving skills as an expert for a narrow problem domain. It embodies knowledge and reasoning capabilities that allow it to draw quality conclusions comparable to those drawn by a human expert. The system is based on technical rules from the expert. The collection of human expert knowledge is the heart of the system, and is not as easy as it may appear.

CAPP stage 6: Generative approach. In the generative process planning approach, the computer programs possess engineering processing knowledge and geometric vision of the product and items. Process plans are generated by means of technical algorithms, decision logic, formulae and geometric base data to perform the many processes decisions to convert a part from raw material to the finished state. The generative approach is complex and difficult to develop, and is not yet in wide use.

CAPP stage 7: Semi-generative approach. The semi-generative approach is an intermediate stage, used until a generative system can be developed. This method may be defined as a combination of the generative and the variant, where a pre-process plan is developed and modified before the plan itself is used in a real production environment.

Today, the market demands for agile manufacturing require new production management objectives. These new objectives call for the integration of CAPP into the production management process, which means that the process plan must now be regarded as a variable. To meet these new objectives, CAPP must generate a process plan within seconds without human intervention. Otherwise, the process planning system is of little value in today's dynamic manufacturing situation. Several CAPP systems have been developed, such as non-linear process planning, Petri net techniques for process planning, neural nets, the matrix method, RCAPP, etc.

Bibliography

1. Aho, A.V., Hocroft, J.E. and Ullman, J.D., 1983: *Data Structures and Algorithms*. Addison-Wesley.
2. Alting, L. and Zhang, H., 1989: Computer aided process planning: the state-of-the-art survey, *International Journal of Production Research*, **27**(4), 553–585.
3. Cecil, J.A., Srihari, K. and Emerson, C.R., 1992: A review of Petri net applications in process planning, *The International Journal of Advanced Manufacturing Technology*, **7**, 168–177.

4. Chang, T.C. and Wyysk, R.A., 1985: *An Introduction to Automated Process Planning Systems*. Prentice-Hall.

5. Davies, B.J., 1986: Application of expert systems in process planning, *Annals of the CIRP*, **35**(2).

6. Desrochers, A. and Al-Jaar, 1995: *Applications of Petri Nets in Manufacturing Systems*. IEEE Press, New York.

7. DiCesare, F., Harhalakis, G., Proth, J.M., Silva, M. and Vernadat, F.B., 1993: *Practice of Petri Nets in Manufacturing*. Chapman & Hall, London.

8. Gupta, S.K., Nau, D.S., Regli, W.C. and Zhang, G., 1994: A methodology for systematic generation and evaluation of alternative operation plans. In J.J. Shah, M. Mantÿla and D.S. Nau (eds), *Advances in Feature Based Manufacturing*. Elsevier Science B.V., pp. 161–184.

9. Gupta, S.K., Regli, W.C., Das, D. and Nau, D.S., 1995: Automated manufacturability analysis: a survey, report ISR-TR-95–14, University of Maryland.

10. Halevi, G., 1980: *The Role of Computers in Manufacturing Processes*. John Wiley & Sons.

11. Halevi, G. and Weill, R.D., 1995: *Principles of Process Planning – A Logical Approach*. Chapman & Hall.

12. Ham, I. and Lu, S.C.-U., 1988: Computer-aided process planning: the present and the future, *Annals of the CIRP*, **37**(2), 591–601.

13. Kiritsis, D. and Porchet, M., 1996: A generic Petri net model for dynamic process planning and sequence optimisation, *Advances in Engineering Software*, **25**(1), 61–71.

14. Kruth, J.P. and Detand, J., 1992: A CAPP system for nonlinear process plans, *Annals of the CIRP*, **41**(1), 489–492.

15. Neuendorf, K.-P., Kiritsis, D., Kis, T. and Xirouchakis, P., 1997: Two-level Petri net modeling for integrated process and job shop production planning, ICAPTN'97, *Proceedings of the Workshop 'Manufacturing and Petri Nets'*, Toulouse, pp. 135–150.

16. Srihari, K. and Emerson, C.R., 1990: Petri nets in dynamic process planning, *Computers Industrial Engineering*, **19**, 447–451.

17. Tönshoff, U., Beckendorff, U. and Anders, N., 1989: FLEXPLAN-A Concept for intelligent process planning and scheduling, *CIRP International Workshop on Computer Aided Process Planning*, Hannover University, pp. 87–106.

Computer integrated manufacturing – CIM

S – 1d; 2c; 3d; 6d; 7b; 10c; 13b; * 1.2b; 1.3c; 2.3c; 3.2c; 3.3b; 3.5c; 3.6c; 4.2b; 4.3c; 4.4c

The objective of computer integrated manufacturing is the complete integration of all functional areas of the company into an interactive computer system, from engineering and manufacturing to marketing and management. Computer integrated manufacturing is a technology that combines all advanced manufacturing technologies into one manufacturing system that is capable of producing and distributing a diversified product through an innovative, flexible process that optimizes resources to achieve the required standards of quality, constancy, cost and delivery.

The three fields of computer applications in industry (computers as data processing, computers as machine members, and computers as engineering aids) were developed as islands of automation. The transfer of data and information between one and the other was by manual means. The computer integrated manufacturing method combines the three separate application fields in one integrated system.

CIM is a technology that combines all advanced manufacturing technologies into one manufacturing system that is capable of:

- rapid response to manufacturing and market demands;
- batch processing with mass-production efficiency;
- mass production with flexibility of batch production;
- reducing manufacturing cost.

CIM keeps a central database, and in addition incorporates design tools such as group technology, simulation models, and a design application. Computer integrated manufacturing encompasses the total manufacturing enterprise. Therefore, it includes marketing, finance, strategic planning and human resource management.

The potential benefits of implementing computer integrated manufacturing began to be demonstrated as a few companies throughout the world began to achieve major improvements in performance. During recent years, many US manufacturers have accepted and successfully implemented CIM into their manufacturing process. Twenty-five companies reported that they boosted productivity by 64.5% in 5 years. They reduced inventory by 46.3% and manufacturing costs by 30.4%.

Despite all the money, energy, and time spent by companies trying to automate their factories, CIM is still an unfulfilled promise for many manufacturers. Managers have continually struggled with the problem of successfully putting the pieces together to get the most out of CIM technology. CIM systems technology is especially sensitive to the neglect of human factors. Successful implementation of computer integrated manufacturing calls for management support and involvement. Occasionally, middle managers actively resist changes. They must become more and more involved in the development of CIM ventures. To make CIM a reality, they must think in terms of optimizing the entire process not just individual processes. Management also needs to think about the overall picture and how CIM and employees will interact to produce low-cost, quality products with a diverse product mix.

Implementation of CIM requires knowledge and technology in the following disciplines:

1. Communication between computers, terminals and machines.
2. Computer science to solve data storage and processing problems.

3. Computer-operated resources such as CNC, robots, automatic guided vehicles, etc.
4. Algorithms and methodology in the field of basic engineering and production management.

The first three requirements have been solved by advances in the information technology field. Communication networks such as manufacturing automation protocol (MAP) that tie systems together, will become more standardized in the future. This standardization will allow users to select equipment without regard to vendor or compatibility. Standardized MAP will also enable users to adopt CIM incrementally since the new equipment can easily be attached to other equipment. MAP also enables factory engineers to use flexible automation systems that can be reprogrammed to adapt to changes in vehicle or component design.

Since the introduction of MAP, networks and networking products and software tools specifically targeted to accomplish CIM integration have become a reality.

Engineering data management (EDM) – This technology provides new efficiencies in the handling of automated system inputs. The main objective is to get data to the right people at the right time. EDM helps to supervise the data that needs to be managed, controlled, and integrated across the organization. It is an information management tool that helps manufacturers convert raw data into finished products on a real-time basis. Without an effective EDM system, successful implementation of CIM is virtually impossible.

Electronic data interchange (EDI) – EDI is the exchange of business documents from computer to computer without human intervention. EDI enables companies to exchange business documents (invoices, purchase orders, payments, or even engineering drawings) electronically via a direct communication link, with no human intervention and in a precise format. The major payback of this technology is realized when EDI information is integrated into the company's CIM system.

Software evolution – Another factor that has boosted market acceptance of CIM technology is the emergence of 'user configurable' application software packages. These packages enable manufacturing engineers to tailor applications to their needs without having to rely on a system integrator. It allows engineers to design much more complex systems.

There was a time that it looked like 'CIM is dead'. However, with the developments in such problematic topics as MAP, EDI, and EDM, CIM is rapidly gaining popularity and new implementations are being actively pursued.

Bibliography

1. Albus, J., Barbera, A. and Nagel, N., 1981: Theory and practice of hierarchical control. In *Proceedings of the 23rd IEEE Computer Society International Conference*, Washington DC, pp. 18–39.
2. Ayres, R.U., 1989: Technology forecast for CIM, *Manufacturing Review*, **2**(1), 43–52.
3. Ayres, R.U. (ed.), 1991: *Computer Integrated Manufacturing*, Volumes I–IV. Chapman & Hall.
4. Beeckman, D., 1989: CIM-OSA: computer integrated manufacturing open systems architecture, *International Journal of Computer Integrated Manufacturing*, **2**(2), 94–105.
5. Caputo, A.C., Cardarelli, G., Palumbo, M. and Pelagagge, P.M., 1998: Computer integrated manufacturing in small companies: a case study, *Industrial Management & Data Systems*, **98**(3), 138–144.
6. Catron, B.A. and Ray, S.R., 1991: ALPS: a language for process specification, *International Journal of Computer Integrated Manufacturing*, **4**(2), 105–113.
7. Chou, Y.-C., 1999: Configuration design of complex integrated manufacturing systems, *International Journal of Advanced Manufacturing Technology*, **15**(12), 907–913.
8. Duffie, N.A. and Piper, R.S., 1987: Non-hierarchical control of a flexible manufacturing cell, *Robotics and Computer Integrated Manufacturing*, **3**(2), 175–179.
9. Gun-Ho-Lee, 1999: Design of components and manufacturing system for material handling in CIM, *International Journal of Computer Integrated Manufacturing*, **12**(1), 39–53.
10. Gyorki, J.R., 1989: How to succeed at CIM, *Machine Design*, October 26.
11. Hatvany, J., 1985: Intelligence and cooperation in heterarchic manufacturing systems, *Robotics and Computer Integrated Manufacturing*, **2**(2), 101–104.
12. Hanna, W.L., 1985: Shop floor communication – MAP. In *22nd Annual Meeting & Technical Conference Proceedings AIM Tech*, May, pp. 294–300.
13. Hashemipour, M. and Kayaligil, S., 1999: Identifying integration types for requirement analysis in CIM development, *Integrated Manufacturing Systems*. **10**(3), 170–178.
14. Idelmerfaa, Z. and Richard, J., 1998: CIM systems modelling for control system re-usability, *International Journal of Computer Integrated Manufacturing*, **11**(3), 195–204.
15. Jones, A.T. and McLean, C.R., 1986: A proposed hierarchical control architecture for automated manufacturing systems, *Journal of Manufacturing Systems*, **5**(1), 15–25.
16. Joshi, S.B., Wysk, R.A. and Jones, A., 1990: A scaleable architecture for CIM shop floor control. In A. Jones (ed.), *Proceedings of Cimcon '90*, National Institute of Standards and Technology, pp. 21–33.
17. Judd, R.P., Vanderbok, R.S., Brown, M.E. and Sauter, J.A., 1990: Manufacturing system design methodology: execute the specification. In A. Jones (ed.), *Proceedings of Cimcon '90*, National Institute of Standards and Technology, pp. 133–152.
18. Lin, G.Y. and Solberg, J.J., 1992: Integrated shop floor control using autonomous agents, *IIE Transactions*, **24**(3), 57–71.
19. Livingston, D., 1990: CIM to the rescue, *Systems Integration*, November, pp. 60–66.

20. Luong, L.H.S., 1998: A decision support system for the selection of computer-integrated manufacturing technologies, *Robotics and Computer Integrated Manufacturing*, **14**(1), 45–53.
21. Mathieson, K. and Wharton, T.J., 1993: Are information systems a barrier to total quality management? *Journal of Systems Management*, September, pp. 34–38.
22. McEwan, A.M. and Sackett, P., 1998: The human factor in CIM systems: worker empowerment and control within a high-volume production environment, *Computers in Industry*, **36**(1–2), 39–47.
23. Nagalingam, S.V. and Lin, G.C.I., 1999: Latest developments in CIM, *Robotics and Computer Integrated Manufacturing*, **15**(6), 423–30.
24. Naylor, A.W. and Volz, R.A. 1987: Design of integrated manufacturing control software, *IEEE Transactions on Systems, Man, and Cybernetics*, **SMC-17**(6), 881–897.
25. Samaddar, S., Rabinowitz, G. and Mehrez, A., 1999: Resource sharing and scheduling for cyclic production in a computer-integrated manufacturing cell, *Computers & Industrial Engineering*, **36**(3), 525–47.
26. Shuguang, L. and Rongqiu, C., 1998: Understanding and implementing CIM through BPR, *International Journal of Operations & Production Management*, **18**(11), 1125–33.
27. Simpson, J.A., Hocken, R.J. and Albus, J.S., 1982: The automated manufacturing research facility of the National Bureau of Standards, *Journal of Manufacturing Systems*, **1**(1), 17–31.
28. Smith, J.S. and Joshi, S.B., 1995: A shop floor controller class for computer integrated manufacturing, *International Journal of Computer Integrated Manufacturing*, **8**(5), 327–339.
29. Tinham, B., 1999: The market for CIM: June 1999 snapshot, *Manufacturing Computer Solutions*, **5**(6), 14–17.
30. Yuejin, Zhou and Chuah, K.B., 1999: The strategic issues in implementation of CIM technology in PRC/HK enterprises, *International Journal of Advanced Manufacturing Technology*, **15**(7), 514–520.
31. Yuliu, C., Tseng, M.M. and Yien, J., 1998: Economic view of CIM system architecture, *Production Planning and Control*, **9**(3), 241–249.

Concurrent engineering (CE)

S – 3b; 4c; 5d; 8c; 13c; * 1.2c; 1.3c; 2.1c; 2.2b; 2.5c; 3.2d; 3.6d

The goal of concurrent engineering is to enable an organization to effectively respond to market demands. More specifically, concurrent engineering should facilitate reduced time to market, reduce cost, improve quality, etc.

Concurrent engineering is directed towards the parallel processing of tasks and provides methods to enable different persons to solve problems by consideration of their specific points of view simultaneously. The term 'engineering' must not limit these tasks to technical areas such as design and manufacturing. Others, like cost accounting, procurement, marketing and distribution, have to be included as well. People of different disciplines must work together in a cooperative manner and understand each other.

The advantages of concurrent engineering are as follows:

1. Reduction in the number of design changes which are necessary because of problems of fabrication or maintenance. In the previous structure if no solution could be found to correct the design, it had to be reworked from the beginning
2. As a consequence of smooth transitions from design to execution to delivery of a product lead times can be reduced. The firm that is able to quickly satisfy the market has a substantial advantage.
3. Reduction in the amount of scrap rework.
4. Use of a common database which enables different departments in an enterprise to work with the same data, e.g. data from customer orders, data from quotations, data from payrolls, data from production planning such as material requirements planning, etc.

Fast communication is established between different modules fulfilling different functions in the manufacturing system.

The way and means to achieve such an integrated approach in manufacturing can be related to two main methodologies.

1. Promoting teamwork among the design, production and inspection departments. This does not necessarily mean working in common groups, but does mean using a common knowledge base to advance simultaneously the different phases of a project.
2. Use of advanced technologies which have been developed during the last decade to computerize design and manufacturing functions, e.g., 3D modelling, computer-aided process planning (CAPP) manufacturing protocols (MAP) knowledge bases, etc.

To work effectively in concurrent engineering teams, employees need team building, as well as training in soft skills like communication, conflict resolution and leadership. A core team of three to six people on the project will work full time and others might work part time.

Concurrent engineering contrasts sharply with the traditional approach to designing new products, in which plans and drawings originate in the engineering department, pass on to production, then to marketing and so on. This is commonly referred to as the 'throwing it over the wall' method of building a new product; meaning little communication goes on between each department as the product travels from function to function. The problem with throwing it over the wall was that designers sometimes created a widget on paper that couldn't actually be built by the production department then they had to go back to the drawing board, as it were, and keep fine-tuning the widget until the production department was happy. This repetitive, or iterative, process was a lot like taking two steps forward and one step back. It was expensive, inefficient, and often did not result in well-made, well-designed products that customers wanted.

In concurrent engineering, on the other hand, all the players from different departments get together to design a product. The design engineers, the production engineers, the quality assurance experts, the reliability specialists, and the marketing professionals decide together what the product will look like. From an engineering perspective, that seems like a logical and simple solution to the problems created by the traditional approach. Of course, when you add humans to the mix, it can get messy. If getting people from different departments to work together sounds an awful lot like the cross-functional teams we've been talking about for years, you're not far off. The differences are probably best explained by the multiple meanings of the word concurrent. It means both 'at the same time' and 'in an integrated way'. In fact integration is more important than timing. A concurrent engineering team must have the ability to see the whole product, even if the team is working on one new component of a bigger machine. Not only must individual team members see each other's perspectives, they also must be able to see the big picture.

Concurrent engineering challenges engineers on at least two levels: power sharing and people skills. The people skills are a delicate issue. It does not mean that engineers are less than socially adept. Most engineers are not good at communication, if they really cared for communication they wouldn't be engineers, they'd be marketing people. That may be one of the reasons the 'throwing it over the wall' approach evolved in the first place. It clearly minimized the amount of time the engineer would have to deal with other people and maximized the time he would spend with the product. It meant engineering's predisposition to say, 'We're going to change this a hundred times before we release it. Why should I show you now?'

There is considerable disagreement about the types of organization best suited to concurrent engineering. Some suggest that a non-hierarchical company with empowered employees provides the most fertile ground. Communication among teams, especially on huge projects, is fundamental to getting the separate projects working concurrently; it is probably better if information doesn't have to travel through too many links in the chain of command. On the other hand, some contend that hierarchies aren't the primary obstacles to concurrent engineering: it's the walls between departments that need to be knocked down, not the organization that needs to be flattened.

Integration is the key to making concurrent engineering successful. Collaboration is vital; integrated product development blurs the lines between what you've contributed and what the next person added. The tasks and functions of departments are integrated. To work effectively in concurrent engineering teams, employees need team-building, as well as training in soft skills like communication, conflict resolution and leadership. The training community has focused efforts on these skills for years, but in some cases, the engineering community is just becoming aware of them. Some engineering types contemplating concurrent engineering don't consider soft skills training much of a factor in their plans. Others directly involve trainers in developing cross-functional teams on a daily basis.

Bibliography

1. Bronsvoort, F.W. and Jansen, W.F., 1993: Feature modeling and conversion – key concepts to concurrent engineering, *Computers in industry*, **2**, 289–328.
2. Breuil, D. and Aldanondo, M., 1995: Global concurrent engineering approach for production systems. In *Proceedings of CAPE'95*. IFIP Chapman & Hall. pp. 587–596.
3. Carter, E.D. and Baker, B.S., 1992: *Concurrent Engineering: the Product Development Environment for the 1990s*. Addison-Wesley.
4. Gu, P. and Kusiak, A., 1993: *Concurrent Engineering*. Elsevier.
5. Halevi, G. and Weill, R. (ed.), 1992: *Manufacturing in the Era of Concurrent Engineering*, IFIP Transactions B-6 North Holland.
6. Hashiba, S. and Kasto, I., 1995: Concurrent engineering with CAM/CAT system to reduce the production preparation lead time of personal computer PCB assembly. In *Proceedings of CAPE'95*. IFIP 1995, Chapman & Hall, pp. 579–586.
7. Jiang, X.S. and Li, B.H., 1994: Integration of product development process – concurrent engineering, In *Proceedings of the 3rd CIMS conference of China, Wuhan*, pp. 1–26.
8. Krause, F.L. and Ochs, B., 1992: Potential and advanced concurrent engineering methods. In G. Halevi and R. Weill (eds), *Manufacturing in the Era of Concurrent Engineering*. North-Holland, IFIP.
9. Molina, A., Mezg, R.I. and Kovacs, G.L., 1992: Concurrent engineering approach to FMS design using a blackboard architecture. In M. Zaremba (ed.), *Pre-prints of IFAC-INCOM '92 SYMPOSIUM*, Toronto, *May 25–28*, Vol. 2, pp. 457–462.
10. Nestler, A. and Schone, Ch., 1995: Methods and tools for technological databases to support concurrent engineering. In *Proceedings of CAPE'95*. IFIP, Chapman & Hall pp. 597–606.
11. Osorio, A.L., Oliveira, N., Camarinha and Matos, L.M., 1998: Concurrent engineering in virtual enterprises: the extended CIM-FACE architecture. In *Intelligent Systems for Manufacturing: Multi-Agent Systems and Virtual Organizations. Proceedings of the BASYS'98–3rd IEEE/IFIP International Conference on Information Technology for Balanced Automation Systems in Manufacturing*. Kluwer Academic Publishers, Norwell, MA, pp. 171–184.
12. Weill, R., 1992: Introduction to the concept of concurrent engineering. In G. Halve and R. Weill (eds), *Manufacturing in the Era of Concurrent Engineering*, North-Holland, IFIP, pp. 1–4.
13. Young, E.R., Greef, A. and O'Grady, P., 1992: An artificial intelligence-based constraint network system for concurrent engineering, *International Journal of Production Research*, **30**(7), 1715–1735.
14. Zheng, F., Shanghui, Y. and Chen, M., 1995: Graphic environment for virtual concurrent engineering. In *Proceedings of CAPE'95*, IFIP Chapman & Hall, pp. 617–623.

Constant work-in-process – CONWIP

P – 1c; 2d; 4b; 6b; 14d; * 1.3b; 2.3d; 2.4b; 3.2d; 3.5c; 3.6c; 4.2c

The objective of constant work-in-process is to reduce inventory level and control production planning and scheduling.

CONWIP is a closed production management system in which a fixed number of containers (or cards) traverse a circuit that includes the entire production line. When a container reaches the end of the line the finished product is removed. The container is then sent back to the beginning of the line where it waits in a queue to receive another batch of items. During each container's cycle all items in the container are of the same type. The amount of material put into the container is set by a predetermined transfer lot size.

Since CONWIP systems are closed manufacturing systems, as is kanban, they have the following advantages over open systems: easier control, smaller variances, and smaller average work-in-process (WIP) levels (and thus also shorter flow times) for the same throughput. They are also self-regulating. In addition, CONWIP systems have the following advantages over kanban.

1. They are very robust regarding changes in the production environment and are easier to forecast.
2. They easily handle the introduction of new products and changes in the product mix.
3. They cope with flow shop operations with large set-up times and permit a large product mix.
4. CONWIP systems also yield larger throughput than kanban systems for the same number of containers.

Work-in-process ensures continuity of production by buffering bottleneck resources. As WIP increases so does throughput, up to the maximum capacity of the manufacturing system. But WIP has a cost and too much is simply wasteful; it increases the mean and variance of flow time resulting in long lead times, poor forecasting, and late feedback. Generally, we want as small a WIP as possible that allows us to approach the maximum throughput of the system.

For a CONWIP production system with infinite demand, the average WIP level is equal to the maximum WIP level. To gain insights into the system and establish a desirable WIP level we first consider the amount of WIP needed in a deterministic system. In such systems we can achieve the ideal situation: the bottleneck machine works continuously, without a queue before it or in any other part of the system. The bottleneck machine is the machine with the largest (deterministic) processing time. Since the bottleneck machine works continuously the WIP level needed to achieve the ideal situation would also give us maximum throughput.

Often a manufacturing line does not sit in isolation, but rather is part of a larger manufacturing environment. Just as machine processing time variance can cause a fast machine to become the bottleneck from time to time, high variance can cause the CONWIP line to become the bottleneck in the overall system.

An analytical model (computed bottleneck, CBN) was developed for predicting the mean and variance flow time. The concept of a virtual bottleneck machine was introduced that allowed the employment of analogies between deterministic and stochastic systems. This concept enables one to handle migrating bottlenecks, an issue that is generally neglected. The results of simulation experiments show that the analytical model very accurately predicts the mean flow time, and is sufficiently accurate at predicting the standard deviations of flow time. Simulation experiments also show that the analytical models are much quicker than simulations. Since simulation does not constrain the type of processing time distribution when developing models, the influence of machine breakdowns can also be considered by including them in the processing time distributions.

Since CONWIP systems can be viewed as closed queuing networks, one may (mistakenly) view the system as a loop (having no beginning nor end). This allows one to 'cut' the line at any point in order to evaluate its performance. This approach, as recognized by the model, is valid for mean performance measures but very inaccurate for variance of performance measures.

Bibliography

1. Burbidge, J., 1990: Production control: a universal conceptual framework, *Production Planning and Control*, **1**, 3–16.
2. Duenyas, I. and Hopp, W.J., 1990: Estimating variance of output from cyclic exponential queuing systems, *Queuing Systems*, **7**, 337–354.
3. Duenyas, I., Hopp, W.J. and Spearman, M.L., 1993: Characterizing the output process of a CONWIP line with deterministic processing and random outages, *Management Science*, **39**, 975–988.
4. Duenyas, I. and Hopp, W.J., 1992: CONWIP assembly with deterministic processing and random outages, *IIE Transactions*, **24**, 97–109.
5. Hendricks, K. and McClain, J., 1993: The output processes of serial production lines of general machines with finite buffers, *Management Science*, **29**, 1194–1201.
6. Hendricks, K., 1991: The output processes of simple serial production lines. Working Paper, Georgia Institute of Technology, Atlanta, GA 30332.
7. Hendricks, K., 1992: The output processes of serial production lines of exponential machines with finite buffers, *Operations Research*, **40**, 1139–1147.
8. Hopp, W.J., Spearman, M.L. and Duenyas, I., 1993: Economic production quotas for pull manufacturing systems, *IIE Transactions*, **25**, 71–79.
9. Hopp, W.J. and Spearman, M.L., 1991: Throughput of a constant work in process manufacturing line subject to failures, *International Journal of Production Research*, **29**, 635–655.
10. Kanet, J., 1988: MRP 96: time to rethink manufacturing logic, *Production and Inventory Management Journal*, **29**, 57–61.

11. Little, J., 1961: A proof of the queuing formula $L = aW$. *Operations Research*, **9**, 383–387.
12. Miltenburg, G.J., 1987: Variance of the number of units produced on a transfer line with buffer inventories during a period of length T. *Naval Research Logistics*, **34**, 811–822.
13. Muckstadt, J. and Tayur, S., 1995: A comparison of alternative kanban control mechanisms, part 1, *IIE Transactions*, **27**, 140–150.
14. Reiser, M. and Lavenberg, S., 1980: Mean-value analysis of closed multichain queuing networks. *Journal of the Association for Computing Machinery*, **27**, 313–322.
15. Spearman, M.L., Woodruff, D.L. and Hopp, W.J., 1990: CONWIP: a pull alternative to kanban, *International Journal of Production Research*, **28**, 879–894
16. Spearman, M.L. and Zazanis, M.A., 1992: Push and pull production systems: issues and comparisons, *Operations Research*, **40**, 521–532.
17. Tayur, S., 1992: Properties of serial kanban systems, *Queuing Systems*, **12**, 297–318.
18. Tayur, S., 1993: Structural properties and a heuristic for kanban controlled serial lines, *Management Science*, **39**, 1347–1368.

Cooperative manufacturing

P – 1b; 3c; 4b; 8c; 12d; 14d; 16d; * 1.3b; 1.4d; 2.4b; 3.3c; 3.5d; 3.6c; 4.2c; 4.5c
Cooperative manufacturing is based on the view that it is difficult and expensive to anticipate disturbances and prepare meaningful programmed responses to a specific situation. The environment is perceived as inherently unstable and difficult to influence. The following are ways to respond to disturbances and variability.

1. Make sure that the organization is closely linked to the environment, so that information about disruptions is acquired quickly. It is not limited to formal information from computer systems, but includes informal information such as gossip and body language.
2. Ensure that people within the organization are inherently flexible and able to respond to new situations through experience, education and training. Further, they should be able to create and work in teams to maximize the effectiveness with which different skills and abilities are directed at developing appropriate responses.
3. Provide flexible manufacturing facilities. This does not usually imply a flexible manufacturing system, but rather machines and people that can be easily adapted to a variety of production tasks either simultaneously or one after another.
4. Link the manufacturing organization with other people and organizations for knowledgeable support and advice. The organization may subcontract support activities that are not central to its mission and use internal and external consultants to address challenging and complex problems.

The cooperative organization relies on speed and variety of response to deal with disruptions. Implementation of cooperative manufacturing usually requires that there be product focus to keep market problems in one product group from affecting other product groups. Production is organized around cells and teams, with the team being largely self-managing. Support is largely directed by the work team to ensure that it is aimed at meeting team goals. Much communication is informal and the role of computers is primarily as a decision aid for specific individuals and team. Team size is limited to a critical size, and manufacturing activities may be organized around a loosely linked network of small units, where different units may be under different ownership.

Cooperative manufacturing is most appreciated when bringing a new product to market and product innovation is the key factor of success. Quality of design is created by the experience and expertise of the team and its ability, because of its close link to the environment, to understand the real needs of customers.

Bibliography

1. Ashby, W.R., 1957: *An Introduction to Cybernetics*. Chapman & Hall.
2. Devenport, T.H., 1993: *Process Innovation: Reengineering Work Through Information Technology*. Harvard Business School Press, Cambridge, MA.
3. Duimering, P.R., Safayeni, F. and Purdy, L., 1993: Integrated manufacturing: redesign the organization before implementing flexible technology, *Sloan Manufacturing Review*, **34**, 47–56.
4. Hammer, M. and Champy, J., 1993: *Reengineering the Corporation: a manifesto for Business Revolution*. Harper Business, New York.
5. Stalk, G. and Hout, T.M., 1990: *Competing Against Time*. Free Press.
6. Salvendy, G. and Seymour, W.D., 1973: *Prediction and Development of Industrial Work Performance*. John Wiley, New-York.
7. Kristensen, P.H., 1990: Technical projects and organizational changes: Flexible specialization in Denmark. In M. Warneer, W. Wobbe and P. Broudner (eds), *New Technology and Manufacturing Management*. John Wiley & Sons, pp. 159–189.

Computer-oriented PICS – COPICS

S – 1b; 2c; 4d; 6d; 7c; 10c; 13c; * 1.2c; 1.3b; 2.3b; 2.4b; 2.5d; 4.2c; 4.3b; 4.4c; 4.5c

Computer-oriented production information and control system (COPICS) is a systematic method of performing the technological disciplines of the enterprise, which consist of the following stages:

- Master production planning
- Material requirement / Resource planning
- Capacity planning

- Shop floor control
- Inventory management and control.

COPICS objectives are exactly as those of PICS, the difference is in the method of collecting feedback information: COPICS uses electronic data collection terminals instead of manual forms. Therefore, it is more accurate and allows work online.

Master production planning transforms the manufacturing objectives of quantity and delivery dates for the final product, which are assigned by marketing or sales, into an engineering production plan. The decisions in this stage depend either on forecast or confirmed orders, and the optimization criteria are meeting delivery dates, minimum level of work-in-process, and plant load balance. These criteria are subject to the constraint of plant capacity and to the constraints set by the routing stage.

The master production schedule is a long-range plan. Decisions concerning lot size, make or buy, addition of resources, overtime work and shifts, and confirm or change promised delivery dates are made until the objectives can be met.

Material requirement planning (MRP – see separate item) – The purpose of MRP is to plan the manufacturing and purchasing activities necessary in order to meet the targets set forth by the master production schedule. The number of production batches, their quantity and delivery date are set for each part of the final product. Decisions at this stage are confined to the demands of the master production schedule, and the optimization criteria are meeting due dates, minimum level of inventory and work-in-process, and department load balance. The parameters are on-hand inventory, in-process orders and on-order quantities.

Capacity planning transforms the manufacturing requirements, as set forth at the MRP stage, into a detailed machine-loading plan for each machine or group of machines in the plant. It is a scheduling and sequencing task. The decisions at this stage are confined to the demands of the MRP stage, and the optimization criteria are capacity balancing, meeting due dates, minimum level of work-in-process and manufacturing lead time. The parameters are plant available capacity, tooling, on-hand material and employees.

Shop floor control occurs where the actual manufacturing takes place. In all previous stages, personnel dealt with documents, information, and paper. At this stage workers deal with material and produce products. Shop floor control is responsible for the quantity and quality of items produced and for keeping the workers busy.

Inventory management and control is responsible for keeping track of the quantity of material and number of items that should be and that are present in inventory at any given moment; it also supplies data required by the other stages of the manufacturing cycle and links manufacturing to costing, bookkeeping, and general management.

The COPICS method must have data from several sources such as customer orders, available inventory, status of purchasing orders, status of items on the shop floor, status of items produced by subcontractors, status of items in the quality assurance department, etc. The data from all sources must be synchronized to the instant that the COPICS programs are updated. For example, because of new jobs and shop floor interruptions, capacity planning must be updated at short intervals. COPICS introduces data collection station terminals for shop floor data collection, and terminals in store rooms and production planning and control departments.

Bibliography

1. Baker, K.R., 1974: *Introduction to Sequencing and Scheduling*, John Wiley & Sons, New York.
2. Barash, M.M. *et al.*, 1975: The optimal planning of computerized manufacturing systems, NSG GRANT No. APR74 15256, Report No. 1, November.
3. Berry, W.L., 1972: Priority scheduling and inventory control in job lot manufacturing system, *AIIE Transactions*, **4**(4), 267–276.
4. Buffa, E.S., 1966: *Models for Production and Operation Management*. John Wiley & Sons.
5. Coffman, E.G., Bruno, J.L., Graham, R.L. *et al.*, 1976: Computer and Job-shop Scheduling Theory. John Wiley & Sons, New York.
6. Hanna, W.L., 1985: Shop floor communication – MAP, *22nd Annual Meeting & Technical Conference Proceedings AIM Tech*, May, pp. 294–300.
7. Harding, J., Gentry, D. and Parker, J., 1969: Job shop scheduling against due dates, *Industrial Engineering*, **1**(6), 17–29.
8. Harrington, J., 1985: Why computer integrated manufacturing, *22nd Annual Meeting & Technical Conference Proceedings AIM Tech*, May, pp. 27–28.
9. Halevi, G., 1980: *The Role of Computers in Manufacturing Processes*. John Wiley & Sons.
10. Halevi, G., 1992: The magic matrix as a smart scheduler, manufacturing in the era of concurrent engineering, North-Holland IFIP.
11. Hubner, H. and Paterson, I. (eds), 1983: *Production Management Systems*, North-Holland.
12. IBM, 1972: COPICS.
13. Rowe, A.G., 1958: Sequential decision rules in production scheduling, Ph.D. dissertation, University of California, Los Angeles.
14. Wiendahl, H.P., 1995: *Load-oriented Manufacturing Control*. Springer-Verlag.

Core competence

P – 3d; 4d; 7c; 9c; 10c; 11c; 13b; 16d; * 1.1c; 1.2c; 1.5c; 1.6b; 3.3c; 4.1b; 4.2c; 4.3c

Many manufacturing executives are facing the dilemma of where do they position their firms in the 'value chain' – the entire series of activities that begins with the processing of raw materials and ends when a finished product in the hands of the end user.

Frequently, facing this challenge starts with an examination of the company's core competencies, the things it does best in creating value for customers. Corporations organize around business units and business units organize around products – not the other way around. Without defined products, it is impossible to rationalize corporate assets efficiently; it is impossible to have a market. It is essential to go through the incremental processes of discovering what their core competencies are and fiercely concentrating on them. Often the result is to become less vertically integrated – to outsource production or logistics or other functions.

Outsourcing can result in loss of control of key capabilities, which, in turn, can affect a company's ability to introduce changes in response to shifts in the market place or simply to improve its efficiency in serving customers. Consequently, there has been a growing impetus to find ways to manage the 'extended enterprise' – to build collaborative relationships and improve both the flow of materials and information throughout the value-creating pipeline. The scope of the challenge extends beyond traditional supply-chain management, although that is a key element.

For manufacturers, one distinction is that the value chain extends in both directions and encompasses trading partners ranging from the supplier's supplier to the customer's customer. Another is the increasing focus on working with trading partners to collectively increase speed, pare costs, and enhance the end customer's perception of value. Shaping a strategy that reflects the reality of the downstream marketplace often leads to new approaches to upstream supplier management.

When a decision to change factory operations is made, one may find that it couldn't be done because it wasn't totally within company control. It might be within the control of the suppliers. To change the business it is necessary that the suppliers change their businesses. The extended-enterprise-management approach called for the supply-chain partners to behave almost as though they are part of a single organization. In deciding where to focus supplier-development initiatives, the emphasis is on manufacturing cycle time. If the cycle time is long, it means that there is a lot of opportunity for cost reduction, and for quality improvement it is important to synchronize the activities between multiple links in the value chain. In some organizations the terms 'supply chain' and 'value chain' are used almost interchangeably. Yet, quite commonly, executives think of supply chains as the flow of incoming materials – not the outbound links to the end customer. And often their attention is limited to a single connection – with either an immediate supplier or a direct customer.

A fundamental question in value-chain management is: How is value created? If improved efficiency lowers the cost to the end customer, does that increase the perception of value? If so, then strategies such as lean manufacturing, which reduces inventory-carrying costs, have a role to play. Lean thinkers would ask: 'How can I add value to the product and at the same time reduce lead time?' In short, how do you eliminate non-value-adding activity?

For a value chain to function well and have little waste, it is important that suppliers deliver in smaller batches and deliver more frequently. The supplier must be able to respond quickly to the needs – but without maintaining a huge inventory upstream of the value chain. In many industries, vendor-managed inventory is becoming a popular value added service – one that not only improves inventory control, but also greatly reduces administrative transactions such as purchase orders.

For many online retailers, keeping fulfilment operations in-house gives them a rare opportunity to link directly with their customers. Such firms believe that in-house fulfilment means better quality control and increased flexibility to master the rapidly changing e-commerce environment. For many of these companies, direct to-consumer selling is synonymous with maintaining core competencies in warehousing and fulfilment, and they are scrambling to expand their own facilities in hopes of avoiding e-commerce backlogs.

Bibliography

1. Blackburn, J.D., 1991: *Time-Based Competition: The Next Battleground in American Manufacturing*. Business One-Irwin, Homewood IL.
2. Chrisman, J.J., Hofer, C.W. and Boulton, W.R., 1988: Toward a system for classifying business strategies, *Academy of Management Review*, **13**, 413–28.
3. Gabel, H.L., 1991: *Competitive Strategies for Product Standards*. McGraw Hill, London.
4. Huber, G.P., 1990: A theory of the effects of advanced information technologies on organizational design, intelligence, and decision making, *Academy of Management Review*, **15**, 47–71.
5. Keen, 1986: *Competing in Time: Using Telecommunications for Competitive Advantage*. Ballinger, Cambridge, MA.
6. Lacity, M. and Hirschheim, R., 1993: *Information Systems Outsourcing*. Wiley.
7. Mannion, D., 1995: Vendor accreditation at ICL: competitive versus collaborative procurement strategies. In R. Lamming and A. Cox (eds), *Strategic Procurement Management in the 1990*s. Earlsgate, Winteringham.
8. Miller, J.G. and Roth, A.V., 1994: A taxonomy of manufacturing strategies, *Management Science*, **40**, 285–304.
9. Peters, T. and Waterman, R., 1982: *In Search of Excellence: Lessons from America's Best-Run Companies*. Harper & Row, New York.
10. Prahalad, C.K. and Hamel, G., 1990: The core competence of the corporation, *Harvard Business Review*, **68**(3), 79–91.
11. Tayeb, M.H., 1996: *The Management of a Multicultural Workforce*. John Wiley & Sons, Chichester.
12. Teece, D.J., Pisano, G. and Shuen, A., 1997: Dynamic capabilities and strategic management, *Strategic Management Journal*, **18**, 509–533.

Cost estimation

M – 2b; 4d; 11d; * 1.2b; 3.2b; 4.2d; 4.4c

Cost estimation is an activity undertaken to calculate and predict the costs of a set of activities before they are actually performed. In the particular domain of manufacturing of mechanical parts, cost estimation can be seen as the prediction of costs of the machining operations and other associated activities necessary for the complete manufacture of a mechanical part.

For process planning purposes, we may distinguish four types of cost:

1. the pure machining cost;
2. the cost of moving a part from one machine to another;
3. the cost of a setup change on a machine; and
4. the cost of a tool change on a machine.

The pure machining cost depends mainly on the time a machine is used for a particular machining operation.

Cost estimating calculations are particularly useful at the early design phase of a product where 70% of its cost is determined. The importance of cost estimation based on process plans is outlined in a manufacturability analysis survey and research in this domain is quite recent and growing together with research in feature-based manufacturing.

Two main types of cost estimation models may be distinguished: the variant model based on machining statistics available in the company; and the generative model, based on analysis of the design of the part. The generative model requires detailed information in order to produce a process plan that determines the costs of the manufacturing of the part. This approach offers the possibility to consider various alternatives in the design and processing and compare the resulting costs.

A new method is proposed for the cost estimation of machining a mechanical part given its feature-based description and the associated alternative manufacturing operations for each manufacturing feature together with the required resources (machines, setups and tools), and is capable of representing:

1. manufacturing knowledge, which has the form of precedence constraints;
2. alternative solutions for the machining of manufacturing features;
3. cost factors influencing the cost of a particular process plan.

Besides normal machine operation costs, costs caused by machine setup and tool changing are taken into account.

Some modelling and cost estimation techniques are based on Petri nets. The potential for extending Petri nets or the matrix method to process planning modelling allows the calculation of costs. The process planning cost system combines net structure with explicit modelling of resources.

Two techniques for the dynamic modelling of process plans for the machining of mechanical parts are proposed.

- The first technique uses specific and independent nets that are then integrated into a common net model for machine, setup and tool changing operations. The various costs (operation cost and machine, setup and tool changing costs) are modelled as cost values of transition in the model and the optimal process plan, i.e. a process plan of minimal cost is given by a minimal weighted path from the initial to final node of the corresponding process planning cost system.
- In the second technique, instead of using separate cost values (depending on process batch size) for machine, setup and tool changing, there costs are an integral part of the process planning task, and affect routing selection. This yields a compact representation of an operation together with the machine, setup and tool associated with this operation. A minimal weighted path algorithm is used to search for a path in the generalized process planning that represents a process plan with minimal cost.

Bibliography

1. Aho, A.V., Hocroft, J.E. and Ullman, J.D., 1983: *Data Structures and Algorithms*. Addison-Wesley.
2. Alting, L. and Zhang, H., 1989: Computer aided process planning: the state-of-the-art survey, *International Journal of Production Research*, **27**(4), 553–585.
3. Anand, S. and Quo, P.C., 1996: CAD directed on line cost estimation using activity based costing, *Proceedings of the 5th Industrial Engineering Research Conference*, Minneapolis, pp. 781–786.
4. Cecil, J.A., Srihari, K. and Emerson, C.R., 1992: A review of Petri net applications in process planning, *The International Journal of Advanced Manufacturing Technology*, **7**, 168–177.
5. Desrochers, A. and Al-Jaar, 1995: *Applications of Petri Nets in Manufacturing Systems*. IEEE Press, New York.
6. DiCesare, F., Harhalakis, G., Proth, J.M., Silva, M. and Vernadat, F.B., 1993: *Practice of Petri Nets in Manufacturing*, Chapman & Hall, London.
7. Eversheim, W., Gupta, C. and Kümper, R., 1994: Methods and tools for cost estimation in mechanical manufacturing (METACOST), *Production Engineering*, **I**(2), 201–204.
8. Feng, C.-X., Kusiak, A. and Huang, C.-C., 1996: Cost evaluation in design with form features, *Computer-Aided Design*, **28**(11), 879–885.
9. Gunther, C., 1998: Batch Delivery Time Calculations Using INA, EPFL report.
10. Gupta, S.K., Nau, D.S., Regli, W.C. and Zhang, G., 1994: A methodology for systematic generation and evaluation of alternative operation plans. In J.J. Shah, M. Mantÿla and D.S. Nau (eds), *Advances in Feature Based Manufacturing*. Elsevier Science B.V., pp. 161–184.
11. Gupta, S.K., Regli, W.C., Das, D. and Nau, D.S., 1995: Automated manufacturability analysis: a survey. Report ISR-TR-95-14, University of Maryland.

12. Ham, I. and Lu, S.C.-U., 1988: Computer-aided process planning: the present and the future, *Annals of the CIRP*, **37**(2), 591–601.
13. Kiritsis, D. and Porchet, M., 1996: A generic Petri net model for dynamic process planning and sequence optimisation, *Advances in Engineering Software*, **25**(1), 61–71.
14. Kiritsis, D. and Xirouchakis, P., 1996: A software prototype for cost estimation of process plans of machined parts, *ISATA '96*, Florence.
15. Kruth, J.P. and Detand, J., 1992: A CAPP system for nonlinear process plans, *Annals of the CIRP*, **41**(1), 489–492.
16. Lee, D.Y. and DiCesare, F., 1992: FMS scheduling using Petri nets and heuristic search, *Proceedings of the 1992 IEEE International Conference on Robotics and Automation*, IEEE, pp. 1057–1062.
17. Liebers, A. and Kals, H.J.J., 1997: Cost decision support in product design, *Annals of the CIRP*, **46**(1), 107–112.
18. Liebers, A., 1996: Integrated cost estimation for assembled products, *CIRP Seminar on Manufacturing Systems*, available at: *http://www.pt.wb.utwente.nl/staff/arthur/papers.html*, Johannesburg.
19. Neuendorf, K.-P., Kiritsis, D., Kis, T. and Xirouchakis, P., 1997: Two-level Petri net modeling for integrated process and job shop production planning, *ICAPTN'97, Proceedings of the workshop Manufacturing and Petri Nets*, Toulouse, pp. 135–150.
20. Ou-Yang, C. and Lin, T.S., 1997: Developing an integrated framework for feature-based early manufacturing cost estimation, *The International Journal of Advanced Manufacturing Technology*, **13**, 618–629.
21. Srihari, K. and Emerson, C.R., 1990: Petri nets in dynamic process planning, *Computers Industrial Engineering*, **19**, 447–451.
22. Starke, P. and Roch, S., 1998: Integrated Net Analyzer: INA, free available from internet, http://*www.informatik.hu-berlin.de/lehrstuehle/automaten/ina/*, 1998.
23. Tönshoff, U., Beckendorff, U. and Anders, N., 1989: FLEXPLAN-A Concept for Intelligent Process Planning and Scheduling, *CIRP International Workshop on Computer Aided Process Planning*, Hannover University, pp. 87–106.
24. Valk R., 1995: Petri nets as dynamical objects. *1st Workshop on Object-Oriented Programming and Models of Concurrency*, 27 June, Turin, Italy.
25. Xirouchakis, P., Kiritsis, D. and Persson, J.G., 1998: A Petri Net Technique for Process Planning

Cross-functional leadership

P – 2c; 3c; 8b; 9c; 12b; 13c; 14c; * 1.1b; 1.2b; 1.3c; 3.1c; 3.2c; 4.2c; 4.5b; 4.6c

Cross-functional work teams came into prominence as a direct result of downsizing, rightsizing, and other staff-reduction efforts. Cross-functional teams have enormous capacity for introducing substantive process improvements.

Cross-functional special interest teams have many names and can occur in a variety of forms. In some firms, they are well organized and widely publicized. In other places, they're informal and not well understood. They typically focus on broad subjects of interest to the enterprise as a whole, such as quality, cost control, waste reduction, contingency planning, strategic sourcing, and so forth. The characteristics of cross-functional leadership are:

1. Create commitment outside of authority.
2. Use the customer as the authority.
3. Ask questions as a means of focusing on problems.
4. Allow anyone to offer an answer.
5. Continually raise the bar to improve performance.
6. Create and maintain continual membership.
7. Set time limits to solve a given problem.

In other words, regard anyone as a partner in company problems and their solution. Construct a business culture that fosters open communication and mutually beneficial relationships in a supportive environment built on trust. A partnering relationship stimulates continuous quality improvement. This might mean moving from numerous suppliers for goods or services to few or one, or increasing information exchange from as little as possible to as much as possible. Some of the principles of this methodology are:

1. Develop relationships before you need the cooperation.
2. When encountering differences, seek a win/win breakthrough rather than lose/lose conflict.
3. Most of us enter into agreements to exchange money, services or goods – and then try to get the best of the exchange. Partners also commit to treating the relationship as more important than any single exchange.
4. To envy another's prosperity is to wish for limited prosperity. Partners celebrate other's prosperity thus promoting opportunity for all.

Flexible technology has begun to change the ground on which the assumptions underlying the emerging organizational paradigm have been built. Application areas have moved beyond the linear flows of factory floor and clerical office to the nonlinear, interactive, mutually interdependent domains of managers and engineers and other professionals, e.g. design to manufacture. As a consequence, the complexity of the design task for both technical and organization designers has increased significantly, and the challenge for designing sociotechnical systems that incorporate these two changing domains has increased even more. In particular, it has outstripped most of the methodology that arose under conditions of linear technical systems and sequential work flows. The rules and procedures that guided decisions have had to be augmented with processes that are open to the flexible possibilities of new technologies.

Team-based organizational arrangements have arisen not only where teams cross organizational and physical locations, but also straddle global, cultural, and ethnic differences.

The need for contemporary organizations to use teams to perform all levels of work and management tasks is well documented Management educators acknowledge the challenge to create exercises and simulations to provide laboratory opportunities to experience these new forms of organization Fortunately, the experiential learning literature offers many exercises that allow a wide range of organizational and interpersonal dynamics to surface for debriefing and classroom study. However, many of these classic exercises were designed with an understanding of yesterday's hierarchical organizational configurations.

Attention to single-person leadership often excludes lessons about the differences made by all other participants in team effectiveness. In addition, exercises with only one leadership role encourage the perpetuation of gender and ethnic role stereotypes and discourage the active participation of all team members as leaders.

In the 1970s, group exercises focused on contingent styles of the single formal leader in influencing functional groups. The 1980s saw the addition of leadership exercises focused on teams operating across functions to solve problems in quality and productivity. However, teamwork was still performed within pyramidal lines of authority, often ad hoc and in parallel to the so-called regular ways of doing business. In contrast, many businesses today are trying fundamentally different organizational designs that allow greater flexibility, rapid redeployment of resources, closer interaction with customers and suppliers, and unremitting innovation. The focus is on accelerating learning to make the timely, continuous improvements demanded by customers who can now shop worldwide. Teams are often the fundamental building blocks in these designs, but understanding team leadership opens uncharted ground.

Many large project design activities now incorporate customers as well as suppliers within the project team and/or via focus groups. Strategic alliances and network organizations explicitly cross traditional organizational frontiers. Concurrent or simultaneous engineering teams cross functional boundaries within companies to include members who can reduce the time needed to design and produce products. Unlike project management arrangements that traditionally incorporated these functions in sequence, these arrangements emphasize the simultaneity of the activity. More often than not, it is the existence of shared manufacturing and product design databases, accessed through information technology, that is facilitating and fostering the redesign of these conceptually new integrative approaches.

Bibliography

1. Beckhard, R. and Prichard, W., 1992: *Changing the Essence: The Art of Creating and Leading Fundamental Change in Organizations.* Jossey-Bass, San Francisco.
2. Blake, R. and Mouton, J., 1974: *The Managerial Grid.* Prentice Hall, Englewood Cliffs, NJ.

3. Burack, E., 1993. *Corporate Resurgence and the New Employee Relationships: After the Reckoning*. Quorum Books, New York.
4. Byrne, J.A., 1993: The horizontal corporation. *Business Week*, **3351**(6), 76–81.
5. Cohen, A. and Bradford, D., 1991: *Influence Without Authority*. John Wiley, New York.
6. Fiedler, E., 1972: *A Contingency Theory of Leadership Effectiveness*. Prentice Hall, Englewood Cliffs, NJ.
7. Hoberman, S. and Mailick, S., 1995: *Experiential Management Development*. Quorum Books, New York.
8. Juran, J., 1989: *Juran on Leadership for Quality*. Free Press, New York.
9. Kolb, D., Rubin, I. and McIntyre, J., 1971: *Organizational Psychology*. Prentice Hall, Englewood Cliffs, NJ.
10. Kouzes, J. and Posner, B., 1995: *Challenge: How to Get Extraordinary Things Done in Business*. Jossey-Bass, San Francisco.
11. Manz, C. and Sims, H., 1990: *Self-leadership*. Berkeley Books, Berkeley, CA.
12. Vaill, P., 1988: *Managing as a Performing Art: New Ideas for a World of Chaotic Change*. Jossey-Bass, San Francisco.
13. Vance, C.M., 1993: *Mastering Management Education*. Sage, Newbury Park, CA.
14. Vroom, V. and Yago, A., 1988: *The New Leadership*. Prentice Hall, Englewood Cliffs, NJ.
15. Whetten, D. and Cameron, K., 1995: *Developing Management Skills*. Harper-Collins, New York.

Customer relationship management – CRM

S – 7c; 9b; 10b; 11c; 13c; 16b; * 1.1b; 1.2c; 1.3b; 1.5b; 1.6b; 3.3c; 3.4c; 4.1c; 4.2c; 4.3c; 4.4c

Customer relationship management is defined as any strategy for managing customers and customer relationships, by developing a network of 'touch points' with customers that establish, cultivate and maintain long-lasting relationships. This goes beyond implementing technologies such as a customer information database and data analysis tools. CRM extends into areas such as strategic decisions regarding delivery channels, customer service approach and even organizational structure.

Customer relationship management means the responsible acquisition and deployment of knowledge about customers to sell more of a company's products and services more efficiently. CRM will advance notions about integrated marketing, so agencies will be better able to boost their clients' bottom lines through technologically advanced, but personal, methods of cross-selling and up-selling to existing customers.

While traditional advertising and sales channels could make prospective buyers aware of the offerings, CRM would allow the marketer to target the prospects most likely to buy, and with offers relevant to their situations.

CRM relies on a robust database. Data comes in from numerous paths or, as CRM practitioners call them, touch points. These touch points include the obvious channels in the integrated marketing mixture – advertising, direct marketing, public relations, interactive – but also include additional touch points, including sales calls, billing records, service orders, customer inquiries, satisfaction surveys to provide a complete picture of how customers interact with a brand.

The fundamental assumption of CRM is that a company that can integrate front-office applications with back-office applications would have a higher value for customers by being able to view both customer and supplier needs. One more benefit to integrating CRM with other applications is the ability to more easily conduct data mining and draw business intelligence from the data within applications.

The convergence of e-commerce with existing supply-chain channels is forcing companies to find better ways to serve customers. The need to improve those interfaces while integrating information technology into readily available access points is driving the market for customer relationship management solutions.

Companies are using CRM applications to enhance their competitive position and boost revenue by identifying and maintaining customers, integrating with back-end enterprise resource planning (ERP) systems to create a single customer contact point, and more efficiently managing business coming in via the Web.

Customers and suppliers could use this information to show a prospective client how its usage costs compare with others in its industry, or to prepare a personalized savings forecast for the upcoming year based on the efficiency of new equipment, including how quickly the equipment will pay for itself. Perhaps this prospect has asked its sales representative to contact a different individual about related services. If this information were stored in the marketing database, CRM would dictate a specific, well-informed strategy for the account. Rather than calling the main contact, the CRM agency could contact an alternative buyer, leverage the success of the original relationship and demonstrate bottom-line savings based on individual-level data.

Companies are now developing business plans with CRM strategies designated as the key to revenue-enhancement opportunities and customer retention. CRM applications, along with e-commerce systems, address these critical issues and are becoming the hub of many companies' marketing strategies.

With so much emphasis being placed on integrating enterprise-wide systems, the trend is to extend the family methods of customer relationship, supply chain management, and enterprise resource planning to overlap each other or to combine them. Suppliers of these packages extend their offering either through new products or by acquiring and integration with others. As customers recognize the power of systems that use information from all parts of the enterprise and automate processes along organizational boundaries, stand-alone CRM applications will find it harder to retain market share.

As information sources proliferate, it becomes harder and harder to get customers to pay attention to your marketing message, especially when they are constantly receiving messages through multiple channels. As customer attention becomes a scarcer resource, cataloguers must attract and maintain customer attention by meeting their needs for information, entertainment and community. Not only is it more difficult to keep customers' attention, but also there are fewer barriers keeping them from buying a competitor's product or service. All a customer has to do to change loyalty is to simply type www. yourcompetitor.com.

To keep your customers' attention, retain and create more interactivity with your customers, implement customer relationship management (CRM) strategies. This may mean doing business in a different way. This may mean that you must offer more convenience by selling via the Web, keep track of the stage of the relationship with your customer to better anticipate behaviour, measure success in terms of lifetime value/profitability and identify customer communication preferences.

CRM strategies need to identify and address value, from both the customer and business perspectives. As a business person analysing your customers, you must put the emphasis on them rather than the product portfolio. So it is essential to understand who your customers are, what and how they buy, why they buy and their value to your organization. Value is typically represented by how much they have spent with your company. Furthermore, the wealth of information gathered from CRM strategies becomes the foundation for prospect modelling – creating what are known as look-alike models – that can be leveraged to maximize the rate of new customer acquisition. The cost of acquiring customers is substantial and will probably increase, so you want to ensure that you are getting the most for your money. Existing customers are responsible for near-term profits, but new customers will contribute in the future.

Customers, on the other hand, must identify what value your company brings to them if you are to keep their attention. Your value could be as simple as offering convenience, or excellent customer service, or a brand that the customer perceives as valuable. In short, any way to meet a customer's need will create value. Creating value for customers yields loyalty, which in turn yields growth, profits and more value. Customer loyalty delivers huge bottom-line business impact because loyal customers spend more money, stay longer, cost less to service and refer more new customers.

Bibliography

1. Blackburn, J.D., 1991: *Time-Based Competition: The Next Battleground in American Manufacturing*, Business One, Irwin, Homewood IL.
2. Chrisman, J.J., Hofer C.W. and Boulton, W.R., 1988: Towards a system for classifying business strategies, *Academy of Management Review*, **13**, 413–428.
3. Gabel, H.L., 1991: *Competitive Strategies for Product Standards*, McGraw Hill, London.
4. Christopher, M., Harrison, A. and Van Hoek, R., 1999: Creating the agile supply chain: issues and challenges. In *Proceedings of the 4th ISL*, Florence, Italy, 1999.

5. Huber, G.P., 1990: A theory of the effects of advanced information technologies on organizational design, intelligence, and decision making, *Academy of Management Review*, **15**, 47–71.
6. Keen, 1986: *Competing in Time: Using Telecommunications for Competitive Advantage*. Ballinger Cambridge MA.
7. Lacity, M. and Hirschheim, R., 1993: *Information Systems Outsourcing*. Wiley.
8. Mannion, D., 1995: Vendor accreditation at ICL: competitive versus collaborative procurement strategies. In R. Lamming and A. Cox (eds), *Strategic Procurement Management in the 1990s*. Earlsgate, Winteringham.
9. Miller, J.G. and Roth, A.V., 1994: A taxonomy of manufacturing strategies, *Management Science*, **40**, 285–304.
10. Peters, T. and Waterman, R., 1982: *In Search of Excellence: Lessons from America's Best-Run Companies*. Harper & Row, New York.
11. Prahalad, C.K. and Hamel, G., 1990: The Core Competence of the Corporation, *Harvard Business Review*, **68**(3), 79–91.
12. Tayeb, M.H., 1996: *The Management of a Multicultural Workforce*. John Wiley & Sons, Chichester.
13. Teece, D.J., Pisano, G. and Shuen, A., 1997: Dynamic capabilities and strategic management, *Strategic Management Journal*, **18**, 509–533.

Customer retention

P – 3d; 7c; 9b; 11c; 12c; * 1.1d; 1.2c; 1.4c; 1.5b; 2.5c; 3.4b; 4.1c; 4.2c; 4.6b
Customers can be retained if their needs are addressed. Most sales and marketing dollars are spent attracting new customers. But getting new customers is about six times more expensive than retaining the ones already in place. This is because of increased advertising and promotional expenses and incremental expenses connected with setting up new accounts. Other expenses include credit searches and operating costs as the firm learns the needs of its new customer, and the customer learns how the firm works.

The key to retaining customers is more than providing 'satisfaction' or competing on price. It means an all-out effort to ensure that your customers have an intimate knowledge of your products and services. This intimacy can be accomplished by implementing targeted, direct marketing campaigns for value-added membership programmes, aimed at precisely defined market segments.

Customer contact is only valuable if it provides customers with value-added products or services. This requires an in-depth understanding of who your customers are and what they want. Big firms like Dell, Mattel, Amazon and Levi Strauss focus on using information technology to understand who their customers are and what products and services they want.

The longer a customer stays with a company, the more the customer is worth to the company. The simple truth about long-term customers is that they buy more, take less of the company's time, are less concerned about price, and bring in new customers. Reducing customer defections by as little as 5% can double profits.

The reasons behind customer defection aren't obvious. An intuitive response to defections might focus on customer satisfaction. Ninety per cent of customers who defect do so not because they are dissatisfied, but because they have found a tempting alternative. The next largest category of defections is due to dissatisfaction related to the way they have been treated. Customers want to feel important. Dissatisfaction is like an infectious plague. About 75% of dissatisfied customers tell at least one other person of their discontent. Only 7% bother to tell their original service provider. Customer dissatisfaction must be eradicated through aggressive and systemic focus on customer service.

When it comes to pleasing customers, operators have to know their markets, identify their customers' needs and desires, and then effectively deliver them. Be thorough and make sure you understand what the customer wants. Research can help identify customer needs, and then management must determine if they can be reasonably fulfilled operationally. The cost–price structure also should be analysed.

The average marketing problem doesn't drive customers away, but the average operations problem probably does. If you advertise a lot, the experience must reflect the advertising. Therefore, you need to solve operations problems, because otherwise a good plan will be turned into a bad one.

You need to get information from the customer, but remember that it is historical; it happened in the past. Also, collecting information is useless unless it is acted upon. For those reasons corporate directors, regional directors and managers all receive reports on the feedback to ensure follow-up.

Maximizing the lifetime value of each customer requires maximizing the rate of new customer acquisition, the conversion rate of enquirers to buyers and the repeat frequency of existing buyers. Properly administered customer relationship management (CRM) strategies will help with the conversion of enquirers to buyers and increase the purchase frequency of your most valued customers. This is done by predicting individual preferences and needs well enough to be anticipatory and proactive in the delivery of the right message to the right person at the right time via the right media.

Companies that don't understand the profit-creating behaviours inherent in their business are at a disadvantage in the marketplace. One of the keys is the recognition that not all customers are created equal because not all customers are equally valuable. Keeping your valuable customers and replicating their behaviour in other lower-value customers will generate a significant economic surplus. Furthermore, the wealth of information gathered from CRM strategies becomes the foundation for prospect modelling – creating what are known as look-alike models – that can be leveraged to maximize the rate of new customer acquisition. The cost of acquiring customers is substantial and will probably increase, so you want to ensure that you are getting the most for your money. Existing customers are responsible for near-term profits, but new customers will contribute in the future.

Customers, on the other hand, must identify what value your company brings to them if you are to keep their attention. Your value could be as simple as offering convenience, or excellent customer service, or a brand that the customer perceives as valuable. In short, any way to meet a customer's need will create value. Creating value for customers yields loyalty that in turn yields growth, profits and more value. Customer loyalty delivers huge bottom-line business impact because loyal customers spend more, stay longer, cost less to service and refer more new customers.

Bibliography

1. Bolton, R.N., Kannan, P.K. and Bramlett, M.D., 2000: Implications of loyalty program membership and service experiences for customer retention and value, *Journal of the Academy of Marketing Science*, **28**(1), 95–108.
2. Gardner, A., Bistritz, S.J. and Klompmaker, J.E., 1998: Selling to senior executives: Part 1, *Marketing Management*, **7**(2), 10–21.
3. McGarity, M., 1998: Keeping your borrowers, *Mortgage Banking Washington*. **58**(9), 12–23.
4. Oppermann, M., 1999: Databased marketing by travel agencies, *Journal of Travel Research*, **37**(3), 231–237.
5. Sirohi, N., McLaughlin, E.W. and Wittink, D.R., 1998: A model of consumer perceptions and store loyalty intentions for a supermarket retailer, *Journal of Retailing*, **74**(2), 223–245.
6. Stanley, E.J, 1999: Famous presidents savings: client acceptance and retention. *Issues in Accounting Education*, **14**(4), 657–674.
7. Zeithaml, Z.A. 2000: Service quality, profitability, and the economic worth of customers: What we know and what we need to learn, *Journal of the Academy of Marketing Science*, **28**(1), 67–85.

Cycle time management (CTM)

P – 2c; 5c; 6b; 8b; 11c; 12b; 15b; * 1.1b; 1.2c; 1.3b; 1.4b; 1.5d; 2.4c; 2.6c; 3.1d; 4.1b; 4.2c; 4.5b

Cycle time management is a manufacturing philosophy dedicated to reducing inventory and waste. Respect for workers is the vehicle that promotes continual improvements. For too long factory workers have been misguided, misused, mismanaged and thought of as drones. Worker involvement in all aspects of CTM leads to manufacturing excellence. Manufacturing excellence is looked upon as a strategic advantage for achieving global competitiveness. Manufacturing excellence is producing a product that meets or exceeds the customer expectations at a competitive price delivered to the customer on time. Manufacturing excellence is much more difficult than buying the latest automated technology. Automated equipment, such as machining centres, is not cheap and has proved to be difficult to debug. CTM may offer the best of automated systems and workers respect.

The main driver of CTM is inventory reduction. In the past, inventory has been thought of as an asset, a security blanket for achieving productivity. CTM contradicts this belief and simply states that inventory is evil. Inventory hides problems such as design problems, machine downtime, long setups, absenteeism, defective parts, poor vendor quality, and past due dates. Reduction of inventory through the utilization of small lots and pull operation exposes problems and gives workers the opportunity to solve control process problems. These improvement opportunities allow shop floor workers, their supervisors, production engineers, and design engineers the opportunity to work together to solve problems and conduct process refinement activities. The potential for breaking down department walls with these process refinement activities is great.

The CTM methodology is structured around short-cycle manufacturing, which is linked to the following subsystems:

1. *People leverage* – Ownership and participation: cross-training workers, small group improvement activities.
2. *Structures flow paths* – Resource dedication: group technology, focused factories.
3. *Dependable supply and demand* – Mutual trust: supplier and customer partnership.
4. *Linear operation* – Plus-minus zero output: 'pull' operation, small lots.
5. *Continuous flow* – Process refinement: total production maintenance, total quality control.

Bibliography

1. Heard, E., Short cycle manufacturing, 'The route to JIT', Ed Heard & Associates, PO Box 2692 Columbia, South Carolina 29202.
2. Massaki, I., 1986: *Kaizen: The Key to Japan's Competitive Success*. Random House, New York, p. 102
3. Stinnett, W., 1986: Total employee involvement: integrating people and technology, *PC Fabrication*, April, 75–77.
4. Susman, G. and Chase, R., 1986: A sociotechnical analysis of the integrated factory, *The Journal of Applied Behavioral Science*, **22**(3), 257–270.
5. Watt, M., 1987: Polishing the image, *Manufacturing Week*, 012, 1.

Demand chain management

S – 3b; 4c; 6c; 7b; 9b; 10c; 11c; 13b; * 1.1d; 1.2b; 1.5c; 1.6c; 3.3c; 3.4c; 4.1d; 4.2b; 4.3c; 4.4d

(See also supply chain management.)

Demand chain management focuses on the continuous flow of demand information from customers and end users through distribution and manufacturing to suppliers. The shared objective of the chain is fulfilling customer demands. The most important controlling inputs are rolling forecasts and plans, point-of-sale data, daily orders, management decisions and performance feedback. The controlling trigger of the chain is the customer order. The order penetration point depends on the optimum way to provide the required level of service in the most efficient way.

The focus in demand chain management is on information management. The information flow can be described as being compact, timely, meaningful and transparent. Material flow from supplier through manufacturing to customer is thin and, as much as possible, controlled by daily consumption in order to guarantee the availability of goods and at the same time minimize inventories.

The difference between supply chain management and demand chain management is the focus and starting point of planning and control. In supply chain management it is the material supply push, in demand chain management it is the end user demand pull. Real pull control can only be achieved by using timely end-user demand information as a pull trigger from end user to suppliers as a primary planning and execution source. This is the way to integrate the supply chain in an effective and efficient manner.

The role of information management is a key enabler for demand chain management. It means capturing the market and end user demand information accurately, timely and in a relevant manner: capturing at all times the point of sales through all channels of inventory information. It also requires the ability to be able to search for alternative supply scenarios, carry out risk and profitability analysis in an almost real time manner and prepare the capability and capacity needed to serve the forecast demand when the triggering order arrives.

The key requirements for a state-of-the-art demand chain management information management solution can be summarized as follows:

1. *Strategic direction and focus*: The strategy needs to be derived from and guided by business strategy and key business process requirements rather than by technology, functional or internal administration and control demands.
2. *Integration*: Integration of information, processes and product management information.
3. *Information coverage and availability*: The foundation for successful demand chain management is access to real-time point-of-sale and channel inventory information and sharing the demand information between all parties in the chain end-to-end including customers and suppliers.
4. *Information quality*: Information quality is described by relevance, timeliness, continuous flow, validity, accuracy, intelligibility, accessibility and visibility.

5. *Decision-making support*: Information systems should be capable of identifying exception situations in order to guide management decision-making in these critical areas. Proper decision-making tools must support handling of these exceptions.
6. *Flexible and adaptability*: Market changes today occur faster than ever, and being able to change and adapt solutions to new requirements rapidly is very important.
7. *Cutting down the cost of flexibility*: The best way to reduce the development and running cost of the information management solution is to narrow down different standards and systems used in the company.

Bibliography

1. Anonymous, 1998: Wilkem Builds Demand Chain, *InternetWeek, Manhasset*, p. 18.
2. Anonymous, 2000: IMA introduces demand chain management, *Call Center Solutions, Norwalk*, **18**(7), 54.
3. Blair, B., 1999: Teenager slain on subway as robbers demand chain, *New York Times*, Oct. 10, Late Edition (East Coast), p. 1.45.
4. Cawthorn, C., 1998: Weather as a strategic element in demand chain planning, *The Journal of Business Forecasting Methods & Systems*, **17**(3), 18.
5. Christopher, M., 1992: *Logistics and Supply Chain Management – Strategies for Reduction Costs and Improved Services*. Pitman Publishing, London.
6. Korhonen, M. and Huttunen, K., 1997: Information management in demand chain management – a global enterprise view. In *Proceedings of IFIP TC5 CAPE'97*, Chapman & Hall, pp. 705–711.
7. Lummus, R.L., 1999: Managing the demand chain through managing the information flow: capturing 'moments of information', *Production and Inventory Management Journal*, **40**(1), 16.
8. Siebel, T., 2000: Demand chain management, *Chief Executive*, 27.
9. Hill, S., 1999: Sell: demand chain tools that watch the store, *Apparel Industry Magazine*, **60**(5), SCM30.
10. Vollmann, T., 1996: Supply chain management, Manufacturing 2000, Business Briefing 8/96. International Institute for Management Developments, Lausanne.
11. Wilson, T., 1999: Service links virtual 'demand chain', *InternetWeek, Manhasset*; Sept. 13, p. 9.

Digital factory

S – 1a; 3a; 4a; 6a; 7b; 13c * 1.1a; 1.5b; 2.xb; 4.xb

The digital factory is a revival of the early 1980s notion of 'Factory of the future' and the 'Unmanned factory' when robots were in their infancy. Today's technology enables achievement of some of those dreams.

The objective of the digital factory is to support the development of a product from its conception throughout its production. It uses computerized manufacturing resources and industrial robots as the tools of production. The digital factory is defined as a computer solution that enables manufacturers to plan, simulate and optimize a complete factory, its production lines and processes, at every level of detail.

Historically, manufacturers were monolithic organizations where the objective was to turn out as many units of a limited number of products as cheaply as possible. In the early 1980s, manufacturers faced fierce competition and recognized that this model no longer worked. New manufacturing methods and tools such as 'lean', 'agile', and 'just-in-time' were proposed and introduced.

The group technology method of cell manufacturing received a second chance with the new method called cellular manufacturing.

Robots were introduced to perform routine tasks that can be detrimental to humans, and to free human labour resources to fill more mentally challenging positions created by automation. As robots continue to become more dexterous, they can handle ever more complex tasks. Robots and automatic guided vehicles (AGV) are performing transport functions on the shop floor.

Computerized production resources with robots and AGVs created autonomous production cells, but these were islands of automation. It has its benefits but it accounted for only part of their manufacturing effort.

In addition the Web is altering sales tactics: it lets buyers personalize almost every feature in a product and deliver it in days. Scheduling will depend more on orders coming in rather than forecasts.

While manufacturing has taken a great leap forward during the past decade, the revolution has only just begun. As product design life cycles continue to shrink and manufacturing operations become more costly and complex, flexibility will be the door to success and the digital factory the key.

A digital factory is software that simulates and controls all aspects of the factory. It recognizes that the real benefits come from using the technology early in the design stage to influence decisions, correct mistakes, and optimize systems. For a digital factory to be effective, the software must be an integral part of the host IT infrastructure and be able to communicate both upstream with the CAD tools and downstream with controllers of the production resources. Advanced technologies and methodologies are enabling seamless integration and communication between CAD, CAPE, and shop floor environments. Process databases and product data management systems are providing central repositories of all the company's information.

Digital factory software is the convergence of two techniques. One simulates queues of products, tools, components and people. Companies use simulation because the efficiency of line layouts makes a difference between winning and losing the competitive fast moving consumer goods battle. The other technique is numerical control (NC) programming. Machine tools have become so complex and expensive that no one can afford to stop them even for programming. Before new vehicles are added to the production mix, their robots are taught new jobs offline. The digital factory consists of a collection of algorithms that precisely describe a particular robot's kinematics, movements and motion planning. It relieves software developers from discovering the kinematics on their own. Users are assured that simulation results reflect what will occur on the factory floor. With Internet connection robot programs can be developed by experts at one site and transfered to other sites for execution.

Software developers accommodate such tactics by writing a single program that runs on whatever computer it must.

The main contributor to line slow-down and the key factor that stops a manufacturer from reaching the goal of a mass customized line is the time and effort it takes for a manufacturer to introduce changes and then adjust the process so that the line's capabilities are fully used.

Within a digital factory, engineers can design products, verify and analyse their assembly, manufacturability and serviceability, and design all the robotic and manual processes that comprise the manufacture of a product, such as welding, painting, press work, and drilling. Because these processes are done digitally, they can be started early in the manufacturing process. Thus processes are verified and optimized and design errors corrected before even the first prototype is built.

The Internet is also changing routines for shop-floor people by letting them learn new tasks online rather than the assembly line. In addition to turning robots into Internet appliances, cameras focused on production cells will also host their own Web pages. These will let manufacturing personnel tune in and see problems first hand. They can then duplicate the problem on their desktop, devise a solution, and see if it works.

Bibliography

1. Choobineh, F., 1988: Framework for design of cellular manufacturing systems, *International Journal of Production Research*, **26**, 1511–1522.
2. Dvorak, P., 2000: Digital factories foster new vision of manufacturing, *Machine Design*, **72**(7), 16–21.
3. Halevi, G. and Weill, R., 1984: On line scheduling for flexible manufacturing systems, *Annals of the CIRP*, **33**(1), 331–334.
4. Harel Beit-On, H., 1999: In the digital factory: The next generation, *Chief Executive*, **144**, 54–57.
5. Lee, Y.H. and Iwwata, K., 1991: Part ordering through simulation optimization in an FMS, *International Journal of Production Research*, **7**, 1309–1323.
6. Liu, J. and MacCarthy, B.L., 1996: The classification of FMS scheduling problems, *International Journal of Production Research*, **34**(3), 647–656.
7. MacCarthy, B.L. and Liu, J., 1993: A new classification scheme for flexible manufacturing systems, *International Journal of Production Research*, **31**, 229–309.
8. Nakamura, N. and Shingu, T., Scheduling of flexible manufacturing systems. In H.J. Bullinger and H.J. Warnecke (eds), *Toward the Factory of the Future*, pp. 147–152.
9. O'Grady, P.J. and Menon, U., 1986: A concise review of flexible manufacturing systems and FMS literature, *Computers in Industry*, **7**, 155–167.

10. Rabelo, L. and Alptekin, S., 1993: A hybrid neural and symbolic processing approach to flexible manufacturing systems scheduling. In A. Kandel (ed.), *Hybrid Architectures for Intelligent Systems*. CRC Press, pp. 379–405.
11. Rajamani, D., Singh, N. and Aneja, Y.P., 1990: Integrated design of cellular manufacturing system in the presence of alternative process plans, *International Journal of Production Research*, **28**, 1541–1554.
12. Roll, Y., Karni, R. and Arzi, Y., 1991: Measurement of processing flexibility in flexible manufacturing cell, *Journal of Manufacturing Systems*, **11**(4), 258–268.
13. Sarin, S. and Dar-El, E., 1984: Approaches to the scheduling problems in FMS, Institute Of Industrial Engineers, *Fall Industrial Engineering Conference*, pp. 225–235.
14. Shanker, K. and Tzen, Y.J., 1985: A loading and dispatching problem in a random flexible manufacturing systems, *International Journal of Production Research*, **23**, 579–595.
15. Shaw, M.J., 1989: A pattern directed approach for FMS: a framework for intelligent scheduling, learning and control, *International Journal of Flexible Manufacturing*, **2**, 121–144.
16. Suri, R. and Hildebrant, R.R., 1984: Modelling flexible manufacturing systems with mean value analysis, *Journal of Manufacturing Systems*, **3**(1), 27–38.
17. Talavage, J.J., Shodham, R. and Harel Beit-On, H., 1999: In the digital factory: The next generation, *Chief Executive*, **144**, 54–57.
18. Harel Beit-On, H., 1992: Automated development of design and control strategy for FMS, *International Journal of Computer Integrated Manufacturing*, **5**(6), 335–348.
19. Tang, L. Yih, Y. and Liu, C., 1993: A study on decision rules of scheduling model in an FMS, *Computers in Industry*, **22**, 1–13.
20. Yoshida, Ham and Hitomi, 1985: *Group Technology – Applications to Production Management*, Kluwer-Nijhoff, Boston.

Drum buffer rope (DBR)

S – 1d; 2d; 4b; 6c; * 1.3c; 1.4c; 2.4c; 3.5c; 4.2c
(See also Theory of constraint – TOC.)

Drum buffer rope (DBR) is a production scheduling technique. The name is based on metaphors that the constraint (drum) determines the pace of production. The rope is the material release mechanism. Material is pulled to the first operation at a pace determined by the constraint. Material release is offset from the constraint schedule by a fixed amount of time (the length of the rope). The fixed amount of time between material release and the constraint schedule coupled with quick flow of material to the constraint ensures that an essentially constant buffer is maintained at the constraint.

There are actually two buffers at a resource constraint. A buffer of material waiting to be processed protects against disruptions upstream from the constraint. Space behind the constraint allows processed material to accumulate and protects the constraint from disruptions downstream. Buffers exist to protect the system from delays in production. Buffer size, however, is a trade-off between protection and lead time. If the buffer size is increased, the protection increases, but so does the manufacturing lead time.

The drum buffer rope (DBR) approach suggests that all efforts should initially be focused on inventory reduction since it has maximum impact on all aspects of running a manufacturing business. Beating the *drum* and building the time *buffer* will ensure high utilization of the capacity constraint and secure throughput and due date performance. When the buffer is full the instruction is simply 'stop working!'. This is a *rope* that connects the buffer behind the operation with material being released from the buffer in front of the operation. The DBR approach demonstrates that putting a rope between every two successive operations is excessive protection that might even reduce throughput. Controlling the first operation in every route is enough. The rope should be between the buffer and the released raw material area.

DBR is a basic element of synchronized manufacturing, since it provides all that is needed to maintain production flow with a given predetermined inventory level. The aim is to operate where the bottleneck (the drum) dictates the overall pace of work, and where inventory is allowed to build up only in finished goods and in front of the bottleneck, to act as a buffer which will enable the crucial function to continue even if there are breakdowns upstream. The rope links all upstream operations to the pace of the bottleneck, to keep those at the front end of the process from churning out more than the bottleneck can handle.

If it all sounds reasonably straightforward, that's because in many ways it is – as ever, it's just the implementation that can prove tricky. And if it all sounds like a history lesson from the dark ages of the 1980s (remember them?), the experts agree that there is still a surprisingly large part for such a basic theory to play in this brave new manufacturing world. The message is not radically new, it just hasn't got through to everyone it should have reached yet. It is a common-sense way of using cellular units where activities are watched carefully to minimize inventory and maximize throughput.

Buffer management is the method developed to control buffer size and, therefore, manufacturing lead time and inventory. Buffer management also warns of potential disruption to the production plan. It is assumed that material-processing time is, on average, only one-third of the time allowed by the buffer. If the materials have not been processed by end of the first third of the buffer, the buffer manager will check to see if the order faces any obstacles to timely completion. If two-thirds of the buffer is consumed and the materials have not yet completed the buffer operations, the buffer manager will expedite the order. Each time an order is checked or expedited, the occurrence is tallied and the cause recorded. The buffer size is determined by the expedite record. If there is frequent expediting, the buffer may be increased. If expediting is rare, the buffer can be reduced, thereby reducing lead time and inventory. The delay tally also provides information used to guide continuous improvement to the production system. The problems causing the most frequent and damaging delays would have a high priority for improvement efforts.

Buffer management is the only shop floor control mechanism needed. Any problem, including quality, manifests itself as material missing from the buffer. Note that focusing the continuous improvement effort on the most frequent and severe disruptions should maximize the rate of improvement in performance. As production performance improves, buffers become smaller, causing inventory and lead time to be further reduced.

Bibliography

1. Cohen, O., 1988: The drum-buffer-rope (DBR) approach to logistics. In IFIP state of the art report edited by A. Rolstadas, *Computer-Aided Production Management*, Springer-Verlag, pp. 51–70.
2. Fogarty, D., Blackstone, J. and Hoffmann, T., 1991: *Production and Inventory Management*, 2nd edn. South-Western, Cincinnati, OH.
3. Fox, R.E., 1982: MRP, Kanaban, or OPT, *Inventory and Production*, July/August.
4. Fox, R.E., 1983: OPT – an answer for America – Part IV, *Inventory and Production*, March/April.
5. Fox, R.E., 1983: OPT vs. MRP – thoughtware vs. software, *Inventory and Production*, November/December.
6. Fuchsberg, G., 1992: Quality programs show shoddy results, *Wall Street Journal*, May 14, B1, B7.
7. Goldratt, E., 1991: Late-night discussions: VI, *Industry Week*, December 2, 51, 52.
8. Goldratt, E., 1989: *The Goal*, 2nd revised edn. North River Press, Croton-on-Hudson, NY.
9. Goldratt, E., 1990: *The Haystack Syndrome*. North River Press, Croton-on-Hudson, NY.
10. Goldratt, E., 1988: The fundamental measurements, *The Theory of Constraints Journal*, **1**(3).
11. Goldratt, E. and Fox, R.E., *The Race*. North River Press, Croton-on-Hudson, NY.
12. Goldratt, E., 1988: Computerized shop floor scheduling, *International Journal of Production Research*, **26**(3), pp. 443–455.
13. Lambrecht, M. and Segaert, A., 1990: Buffer stock allocation in serial and assembly type of production lines, *International Journal of Operations and Production Management*, **10**(2), pp. 47–61.
14. Mathews, J. and Katel, P., 1992: The cost of quality, *Newsweek*, September 7.

E-business

S – 2c; 3c; 4b; 6c; 7c; 9b; 10c; * 1.2b; 1.5b; 1.6b; 3.2d; 3.3d; 3.4c; 4.2c; 4.4.c

(See also e-commerce.)

The objective of E-business is to create or maintain a competitive advantage, followed closely by increased customer feedback and improving customer satisfaction, while keeping pace with the competition.

The growth in the number of transactions carried out between organizations, or organizations and individuals, by means of an electronic network is growing rapidly. For this level of growth it is necessary to develop an effective method to manage and support the authenticity and confidentiality of the messages of the electronic business communications. The electronic business security objectives are to minimize the probability of a successful attack; minimize the damage if an attack occurs; and provide a method to quickly recover in the event of a successful attack.

To understand electronic business through the Internet and its security ramifications, it is necessary to understand the electronic environment. Electronic business is the use of computers, telecommunications and related technologies to conduct business transactions and to communicate between entities for the purpose of conducting business.

For mobile applications e-business proposes the smart card. The smart card is a plastic card with a chip that holds a microprocessor and a data-storage unit. This card is smart in the sense that it is a small computer with its own operating system, programs, and data. Smart cards are small and easy to carry around, and provide a secure data container,

E-business is bigger than Web-enabling systems. It has to allow interaction with company partners, people who aren't part of the enterprise but have to transact business with the enterprise.

E-business may offer a hosted, aggregated procurement service via the Web to its small and midsize business customers.

E-business is for commerce with open markets OM-market on the Internet, buy from catalogue advertisements.

The most common approach could be called immersion – the process of gradually deploying e-business applications and initiatives across most of a company's business units. These initiatives are launched for different reasons in different areas of the company, and some have further-reaching implications than others.

Another most popular approach to e-business involves collaborating with a partner that lives and breathes Internet business every day, a Web-only startup. This practice is especially prevalent among big companies, which perceive that they need such partnerships to successfully tackle the most important challenge of e-business i.e. speed. For many initiatives, the issue is no longer whether it fits in that fiscal year's budget but its time to market. That's a huge change for a major corporation. In building e-business, agility and wisdom is needed at the same time as speed.

There is an ever-increasing complexity in constructing an e-business system. It has to consider strategy, digital marketing and technology. As solutions get larger and more complex, it is not going to be easy for companies to keep pace. Web integrators, will need to partner with other vendors and enterprise partners to keep up with the intensified demands of e-business clients.

The motivation urging large companies to pair with small Web firms isn't just the need to infuse an old-line enterprise with a new, faster culture; it's the simple fact that Web specialists already have a beachhead in online commerce. Such partnerships are a two-way street; the Web startup has to see an adequate level of commitment to e-business and Internet time on the part of the larger partner.

Bibliography

1. Alonso, G., Fiedler, U., Hagen, C., Lazcano, A., Schuldt, H. and Weiler, N., 1999: WISE: business to business e-commerce. In *Proceedings of the IEEE International Workshop on Research Issues in Data Engineering*. 1999, IEEE Computer Society, Los Alamitos, CA, pp. 132–139.
2. Dalton, D., 1999: Is e-business for you? *Strategic Finance*, **80**(9), 74–77.
3. Husemann, D., 1999: Smart card: don't leave home without it, *IEEE Concurrency*. **7**(2), 24–27.
4. Jarvis, N., 1999: E-commerce and encryption: Barriers to growth, *Computers and Security*, **18**(5), 429–431.
5. Johnson, M.-W., 1998: Measuring service levels of Java applets in e-business applications, *CMG Turnersville Proceedings*, Vol. 1, pp. 528–538.
6. Komiya, F., Kusuzaki, T., Soga, S., Ohtani, K., Tsushima, I. and Hiramatsu, A., 1998: Preliminary evaluation of business to business electronic commerce by using qualitative simulation and scenario generation. In *Proceedings of the IEEE International Conference on Systems, Man and Cybernetics 5*. IEEE, Piscataway, NJ, 98CB36218, pp. 4763–4768.
7. Kovacich, G., 1998: Electronic-Internet business and security, *Computers and Security*, **17**(2), 129–135.
8. Lamond, K. and Edelheit, J.A., 1999: Electronic commerce back-office integration, *BT Technology Journal*, **17**(3), 87–96.
9. Mainwaring, J., 1999: E-business: supply chains future? *Manufacturing Computer Solutions*, **5**(7), 44–46.
10. Moreau, T., 1999: Emergence of a legal framework for electronic transactions, *Computers and Security*, **18**(5), 423–428.
11. The complete InformationWeek Research E-Business report is available at informationweek.com/reports.
12. More on E-business transformation: informationweek.com/765/transfor.htm
13. For more information on US Interactive, go to: www.crn.com/thisweek

E-manufacturing – F2B2C

P – 3a; 4a; 7c; 9b; 10c; 11a; * 1.1b; 1.5b; 1.6c; 3.3b; 3.4b; 3.5b; 4.1b
E-manufacturing links the customer (through the marketing person) to the factory (several plants) through engineering on to process planning and cost estimates by internet technology.

Online technology provides a low-cost, extremely efficient way to display merchandise, attract customers and handle purchase orders. Manufacturers and financial services companies are pushing their electronic commerce initiatives especially hard.

The starting application was B2B – business to business. The e-business objective is to create or maintain a competitive advantage, followed closely by increased customer feedback and improving customer satisfaction, while keeping pace with the competition. The customers are other business organizations.

It proliferates to B2C – business to customer where the customer is any individual or organization that wishes to purchase a product. B2C uses the Internet to automate all company business processes. It is suitable for every business, large or small, centralized or distributed, service or manufacturing oriented. Electronic commerce/business opens your company's doors to a world of opportunity and profitability. In fact, the flexibility brought by recent innovations in information technologies (IT) has hastened the creation of a new generation of low-cost IT-based tools.

B2C provides companies with a level of scalability, flexibility and adaptability that enables them to look for new markets and new business suppliers.

B2B uses the Web integrators to search for partnerships with other vendors and enterprise partners to keep up with the intensified demands of e-business clients. As the factory that manufactures the items is not part of the system, the business enterprise must keep a high level of inventory in order to compete on fast delivery of products.

E-manufacturing expands the Web technology to B2F, by connecting manufacturers to the business enterprises over the Internet. B2F provides global businesses with direct, cost-effective, flexible and reliable Internet accesses to modern production facilities and manufacturing resources already existing in factories worldwide to lower production costs and delivery time. The traditional OEM model is changed to a new 'Virtual OEM' business paradigm: virtual factories are created on the WWW.

B2F looks upon all manufacturers of the world as one big factory. As modern machines on the factory floor are mostly computerized, one might look at them as peripheral computers that are directly networked to each other and linked by the Internet. It is now possible to search, identity, simulate, test, schedule, control, monitor, and inspect the machines and their production processes online from thousands of miles away. Business is outsourcing production to OEMs around the world. Some miniature B2F practices already exist in specific businesses. The challenge is how to popularize these practices.

F2B2C technology requires all the technologies that are needed by B2C and B2B. In addition B2F requires having manufacturing flexibility on product, processes and production systems. That means optimization of the total manufacturing system from product and system design through planning for information and materials processing, and includes:

- Design for the market, design for economic manufacture.
- Design of customers, design for customers, design with customers and design by customers.
- From design to functional design.
- Translate design into manufacturing requirements, use dynamic computer aided process planning
  - process plan alternatives,
  - adaptation to new technologies,
  - reaction to quantity variations,
  - adaptation to new industrial organization (from part to function).
- Application of computers to manufacturing systems including system modelling, simulation, monitoring and control and self-organization scheduling.
- Information technology, computer-aided engineering, CAD/CAM, self-optimizing control, expert systems and artificial intelligence applied to manufacturing systems.
- Quality assurance and control for total manufacturing systems, implementing quality improvement programs for total business quality.
- Human factors in manufacturing, education and training.

Bibliography

1. Choobineh, F., 1998: Framework for design of cellular manufacturing systems, *International Journal of Production Research*, **26**, 1511–1522.
2. Dvorak, P., 2000: Digital factories foster new vision of manufacturing, *Machine Design*, **72**(7), 16–21.
3. Giachetti, R.E., 1999: Standard manufacturing information model to support design manufacturing in virtual enterprises, *Journal of Intelligent Manufacturing*, **10**(1), pp. 49–60.
4. Halevi, G. and Weill, R., 1984: On line scheduling for flexible manufacturing systems, *Annals of the CIRP*, **33**(1), 331–334.
5. Harel Beit-On, H., 1999: In the digital factory: The next generation, *Chief Executive*, **144**, 54–57.
6. Lee, Y.H. and Iwwata, K., 1991: Part ordering through simulation optimization in an FMS, *International Journal of Production Research*, **7**, 1309–1323.
7. Liu, J. and MacCarthy, B.L., 1996: The classification of FMS scheduling problems, *International Journal of Production Research*, **34**(3), 647–656.
8. Michel, R., 2000: E-manufacturing essentials, *Manufacturing Systems*, **18**(5), pp. 36–41.
9. Nakamura, N. and Shingu, T., 1985: Scheduling of flexible manufacturing systems. In H.J. Bullinger and H.J. Warnecke (eds), *Toward the Factory of the Future*, pp. 147–152.
10. Pires, J.N. and Sa da Costa, J.M.G., 1999: Object-oriented and distributed approach for programming manufacturing cells, *Robotics and Computer-Integrated Manufacturing*, **16**(1), 20, 29–42.
11. Rahman, M., Sarker, R. and Bignall, 1999: Application of multimedia technology in manufacturing: a review, *Computers in Industry*, **38**(1), 43–52.

12. Rajamani, D., Singh, N. and Aneja, Y.P., 1990: Integrated design of cellular manufacturing system in the presence of alternative process plans, *International Journal of Production Research*, **28**, 1541–1554.
13. Sarin, S. and Dar-El, E., 1984: Approaches to the scheduling problems in FMS, Institute of Industrial Engineers, *Fall Industrial Engineering Conference*, pp. 225–235.
14. Shanker, K. and Tzen, Y.J., 1985: A loading and dispatching problem in a random flexible manufacturing systems, *International Journal of Production Research*, **23**, 579–595.
15. Shaw, M.J., 1989: A pattern directed approach for FMS: a framework for intelligent scheduling, learning and control, *International Journal of Flexible Manufacturing*, **2**, 121–144.
16. Suri, R. and Hildebrant, R.R., 1984: Modelling flexible manufacturing systems with mean value analysis, *Journal of Manufacturing Systems*, **3**(1), 27–38.
17. Talavage, J.J., Shodham, R. and Harel Beit-On, H., 1999: In the digital factory: The next generation, *Chief Executive*, **144**, 54–57.
18. Talavage, J.J., 1992: Automated development of design and control strategy for FMS, *International Journal of Computer Integrated Manufacturing*, **5**(6), 335–348.
19. Tang, L. Yih, Y. and Liu, C., 1993: A study on decision rules of scheduling model in an FMS, *Computers in Industry*, **22**, 1–13.
20. Uu, Fei, Yin, Chao and Uu, Sheng, 2000: Regional networked manufacturing system *Chinese Journal of Mechanical Engineering* (English edition), **13**, Suppl, 97–103.
21. Yoshida, Ham and Hitomi, 1985: *Group Technology – Applications to Production Management*, Kluwer-Nijhoff, Boston.

Electronic commerce

S – 7b; 9b; 11b; * 1.1b; 1.2c; 1.5b; 3.4c; 4.2c
Electronic commerce is doing business on the Internet.
Electronic commerce is a general name for all commerce activities.
B2B links manufacturers and suppliers to buyers.
C2B or B2C links manufacturers to customers.
C2M will link customers with manufacturers.

Online technology provides a low-cost, extremely efficient way to display merchandise, attract customers and handle purchase orders. Manufacturers and financial services companies are pushing their electronic-commerce initiatives especially hard. Media companies, retailers and even utilities all are spending billions of dollars in hopes of mastering the Internet's promise and turning it into a revenue- and profit-generating tool for themselves.

E-commerce uses the Internet to automate all of a company's business processes. It is suitable for every business, large or small, centralized or distributed, service or manufacturing oriented. Electronic commerce/business can open a company's doors to a world of opportunity and profitability. In fact, the flexibility brought by recent innovations in information technologies (IT) has hastened the creation of a new generation of low-cost IT-based tools.

A well designed e-commerce infrastructure provides companies with a level of scalability, flexibility and adaptability that enables them to look for new markets, deliver innovative products and services, achieve a high degree of customer intimacy, and differentiate themselves from their competitors, and at the same time create new barriers to entry.

But getting all the parts of an electronic commerce strategy to work smoothly can be a surprisingly tricky exercise. Even something as basic as choosing an Internet brand name isn't easy. Because customers are less likely to remember long or awkward names, short and snappy Web addresses are at a premium. In many cases, however, the most desirable names already have been claimed. As a result, some businesses are paying more than $1 million just to get the rights to the online names they want.

Designing an attractive, useful home page on the Web is full of challenges, too. The site does not have to be too flashy, or include too many pictures, because it can take a long time to download, especially if customers aren't using high-speed modems to connect to the Internet. Slow response time on a Web site, frequent downtime and difficulty negotiating one's way around the site irritates customers.

The site should include the whole line of products and as much information as possible. Keeping Web-site information up-to-date is a frustrating task. References that seem clever one week become useless and embarrassing when they refer to long-gone events. Outdated content is likely to cause customers to take their business elsewhere.

Increased visitor traffic has its own headaches as well. Many first-generation or second-generation Web sites were patched together with data-management systems meant to handle only light loads. Now, busy Web sites may attract many visitors a day. Customers expect detailed information on thousands or even millions of products. And pretty Web sites that don't connect flawlessly to a company's inventory system and supply chain are considered failures.

If companies themselves aren't sure how to make their Internet operations work well, there's always a consultant available. However, most companies are likely to decide that the Internet is too important to be left to subordinates and the CEOs have been doing double duty as chief e-commerce officers. That high-level involvement is crucial to success on the Internet. If CEOs don't take charge of online initiatives and push for a fundamental rethinking of day-to-day operations companies aren't likely to reap the full promise of the Internet.

Bibliography

1. Cappello, P., 1998: EC strategies for small suppliers [electronic commerce], *Electronic Commerce World*, **8**(6), 44–47.
2. Dalton, D., 1999: Is e-business for you? *Strategic Finance*, **80**(9), 74–77.
3. Migliore, L., 1999: Streamlining the automotive EDI supply chain, *EDI Forum: The Journal of Electronic Commerce*, **12**(1), 26–31.

4. Dewey, A.M. and Bolton, R., 1999: Virtual enterprise and emissary computing technology, *International Journal of Electronic Commerce*, **4**(1), 45–64.
5. Fallows, J., 1999: Net profits [electronic commerce], *Computing & Control Engineering Journal*, **10**(4), 177–180.
6. Gide, E. and Soliman, F., 1999: The economic benefits of Internet-based business operations in manufacturing. In: *Proceedings of the 12th International Conference on Industrial and Engineering Applications of Artificial Intelligence and Expert Systems. Multiple approaches to Intelligent Systems.* Springer-Verlag, Berlin, pp. 830–840.
7. Hoy, P.A., 1998: Cleaning up shop [manufacturing information flow], *Electronic Commerce World*, **8**(12), 26–29.
8. Mainwaring, J., 1999: e-business: supply chains future? *Manufacturing Computer Solutions*, **5**(7), 44–46.
9. Inglesly, T., 1999: Screening the bugs out [ERP/EDI integration], *Electronic Commerce World*, **9**(2), 46–48.
10. McGuffog, T., 1999: E-commerce and the value chain, *Manufacturing Engineer*, **78**(4), 157–160.
11. Osorio, A.L., Gibon, P. and Barata, M.M., 1998: Secure electronic commerce in virtual enterprises of SMEs. In *Proceedings of the BASYS'98–3rd IEEE/IFIP International Conference on Information Technology for Balanced Automation Systems in Manufacturing.*
12. Petrovic, D., Roy, R. and Petrovic, R., 1998: Modelling and simulation of a supply chain in an uncertain environment, *European Journal of Operational Research*, **109**(2), 299–309.
13. Raghavan, V. and Mejia, R., 1999: E-commerce demands a new set of rules for security professionals, *Computer Security Journal*, **15**(3), 29–35.
14. Regina, J., 1999: Netting effective e-commerce, *Communications News*, **36**(4), 48–49.
15. Sherer, S.A., 1999: Information systems in manufacturing networks, *International Journal of Electronic Commerce*, **4**(1), 23–43.
16. Smith, B. and Huff, K., 1998: Building electronic marketplaces to meet the needs of industry, *EDI Forum: The Journal of Electronic Commerce*, **11**(3), 31–37.
17. Stein, T., 1998: ERP's future linked to E-supply chain, *Information WEEK*, **705**, 1.20, 1.22.
18. Tinham, B., 2000: What place MRP II in the new world? *Manufacturing Computer Solutions*, **6**(1), 14–18.
19. Worthington, S.L.S., 1998: How to promote your business online: marketing and the Internet. In *National Manufacturing Week Conference Proceedings '98, 'Preparing Industry for the 21st Century'.* Reed Exhibition, Norwalk, CT, **2**, 201–206.

Electronic data interchange – EDI

X – 2c; 3c; 4b; 6b; 7b; 8b; 9b; 10b; 13b; 16c; * 1.2d; 1.3b; 1.5b; 1.6b; 3.3c; 4.1c; 4.3c

Electronic data interchange is the electronic transfer of data from computer to computer without human intervention.

EDI enables companies to exchange business documents such as invoices, purchase orders, payments, or even engineering drawings, electronically via a direct communication link, with no human intervention and in a precise format. EDI greatly diminishes the number of errors that creep into systems when information is re-keyed. The major payback of this technology is realized when EDI information is integrated into the company's computer integrated manufacturing or enterprise resource planning system.

EDI can benefit many departments within an organization. In manufacturing for instance, EDI will help to reduce excess inventories, to progress JIT management, to promote engineering data interchange, and improve work scheduling. In accounting, it enhances payments, invoicing, electronic fund transfer, and contract progress. Finally, in marketing and sales, it enhances market feedback, customer support, and distribution networks.

Electronic data interchange is based on the straightforward goal of changing processes in order to get the maximum return from resources – interrogating the accepted wisdom of the present in order to progress. The main benefits from using EDI are:

1. reduction in paper handling;
2. elimination of data re-keying;
3. dramatic reduction in data processing errors;
4. savings in communication costs;
5. increase production efficiency;
6. reduction in supply and distribution costs;
7. more flexible and responsive;
8. shorter communication cycle time.

The growing momentum of electronic data interchange goes hand in hand with new thinking about the organization of the value chain and supply chain function. Sales, marketing, production, distribution and purchasing must function as one unit. The company must have some group to look across the whole, to recognize and develop the processes both within and beyond the company. The aims are to improve customer service, reduce working capital and reduce total costs and waste.

The more you go down the supply chain route, the more you realize that the best way is not for the customer to throw the order at the supplier but to understand what each party is doing, what its plans are, how stock could be managed if there was less uncertainty. It all leads to the same conclusion: that buyer and supplier are managing the same process and that the information they need is common.

The key is recognizing that if the parties in a value chain were working more closely and sharing information in advance, much of the complexity of EDI data could be removed from actual transactions and commonly held, in master files or catalogues or perhaps on the Internet. An order message itself could be reduced to just a few data elements: codes for supplier and buyer, an order reference, the item itself, where it is and where you want it to be, quantity and deadline. Combined with common access to data on past and future activity, much of the data uncertainty that leads to inefficiency could be removed.

If people think in terms of value chains and supply chains and the entire virtual enterprise, they start to realize that, just because you can't see it, doesn't mean it's not costing you money. The negative side is that you have to think about all the areas that you don't see and don't control.

The positive side is that with the electronic revolution, providing you think clearly about the information you need to capture, you've got the means of doing that. Just because you don't own it doesn't mean you can't manage it.

It is not really the supply chain function's job to say if we are using the right materials, or are purchasing the right materials from the right suppliers – that is a combined job between technical people, production and professional purchasers. You have to be careful not to pretend that supply chain managers can do everything; but they can look at all processes and ask 'could we do it better?'

Chief among critics' complaints is that EDI makes no allowances for data synchronization. EDI provides only for transmission of data over a value-added network (VAN). This requires that each supply-chain partner keep a copy of the product database on its own system. When changes are made to one partner's copy of the file, EDI automatically notifies the other supply-chain partner. But there is no provision to ensure that the originator of the change knows that the alteration has been mirrored in the trading partner's copy of the database. Often it isn't easy to keep the information consistent between retailer and supplier; the volume of data can be enormous, and with so much data to track in a system without real-time updating, mistakes are inevitable.

Bibliography

1. Sohel, A. and Schroeder, R.G., 1998: Impact of JIT, QM, and EDI on supply chain management: Attaining superior delivery performance. In *Proceedings of the Annual Meeting of the Decision Sciences-Institute*, Atlanta, GA, **3**, 1311–1313.
2. Dosdale, T. and Rasmussen, C.N., 1998: EDI security, *Information Security Technical Report*, **3**(2), 98–110.
3. Barcelo-Rosa, J., 1999: EDI-electronic contracting: Contract formation and evidentiary issues under Spanish Law, *EDI-Law-Review*, **6**(2), 155–172.
4. Kimbrough, S.O. and Tan-Yao-Hua, 1999: On lean messaging with wrapping and unfolding for e-commerce. In *Proceedings of the Hawaii International Conference on System Sciences*, PR00001, p. 227.
5. Kuner, C. and Miedbrodt, A., 1999: Written signature requirements and electronic authentication: A comparative perspective, *EDI Law Review*, **6**(2), 143–154.

6. Inglesly, T., 1999: Screening the bugs out [ERP/EDI integration] *Electronic Commerce World*, **9**(2), 46–48.
7. Mak-Horace-Cheok and Johnston, R.B., 1999: Leveraging traditional EDI investment using the Internet: A case study. In *Proceedings of the Hawaii International Conference on System Sciences*, PR00001, p. 182.
8. McGuffog, T., 1999: E-commerce and the value chain, *Manufacturing Engineer*, **78**(4), 157–160.
9. Migliore, L., 1999: Streamlining the automotive EDI supply chain, *EDI Forum: The Journal of Electronic Commerce*, **12**(1), 26–31.
10. Ratnasingham, P., 1998: EDI security: the influences of trust on EDI risks, *Computers and Security*, **17**(4), 313–324.
11. Ratnasingham, P., 1999: Implicit trust in the risk assessment process of EDI, *Computers and Security*, **18**(4), 317–321.
12. Unitt, M. and Jones, I.C., 1999: EDI – the grand daddy of electronic commerce. *BT Technology Journal*, **17**(3), 17–23.
13. van-Heck-Eric and Ribbers, P.M., 1999: Adoption and impact of EDI in Dutch SMEs. In *Proceedings of the Hawaii International Conference on System Sciences*, PR00001, p. 273.
14. Yao, A.C. and Carlson, J.G., 1999: Impact of real-time data communication on inventory management, *International Journal of Production Economics*, **59**(1), 213–219.

Electronic document management – EDM

X – 2d; 3c; 4c; 6c; 7b; 8c; 13c; * 1.2b; 1.3b; 2.5c; 3.3c; 4.2c; 4.4d

Electronic document management is a technology that captures, stores, retrieves and transmits documents by electronic means. This capability makes it possible to reorganize and streamline workflow into an improved process, often called business process re-engineering (BPR).

Electronic document management technology provides new efficiencies in the handling of automated system output. The main objective is to get data to the right people at the right time. EDM helps to supervise the amount of data that needs to be managed, controlled, and integrated across the organization. It is the information management tool that helps manufacturers convert raw data into finished products on a real-time basis. Without an effective EDM system, successful implementation of computer integrated manufacturing is virtually impossible.

EDM interfaces to standard office applications, like word processing, spreadsheet (excel) power point, graphics and drawing, are needed. To support mobile agent applications, the electronic document management must have tools through which documents can be imported, exported and manipulated.

Effective EDM systems could save companies millions of dollars per year by preventing duplicated effort and engineering corrections. Many companies evaluating EDM systems expect the major benefits of EDM automation to be its project status reporting ability and savings in time to the marketplace.

Recent developments within the realm of typical office applications indicate a paradigm shift from application as a tool for direct manipulation of contents to an approach which centres around the notion of task orientation and assistance. New office systems envision several innovative concepts, including multiple display environments, virtual secretaries and related agent technology. The goal is to enable common tasks which were traditionally fulfilled by human staff to be automatically done by computer applications. Since most of the tasks in an office are related to documents, efficient document management is crucial for such a system.

Traditionally document management in an enterprise has been accomplished through corporate programmes for:

1. Records management: controlling the file folders that contain paper documents.
2. Forms management: controlling the inventory of paper forms used for data collection and reporting.
3. Directives and manuals management: controlling the authoring and distribution of policy and procedure manuals.
4. Archives management: controlling the scheduling, review, disposal, and preservation of records, forms, reports, directives, manuals, and any other official document.

Bibliography

1. Benington, G., 1998: Implementing enterprise document management in power plants. In *International Exhibition and Conference for the Power Generation Industries*, Houston, TX, p. 197.
2. Eastman, C. and Jeng-Tay-Sheng, 1999: Database supporting evolutionary product model development for design, *Automation in Construction*, **8**(3), 305–323.
3. Hameri, A.P. and Nikkola, J., 1999: How engineering data management and system support the main process-oriented functions of a large-scale project, *Production Planning and Control*, **10**(5), 404–413.
4. Peng Ting Kuo and Trappey, A.J.C., 1998: *Robotics and Computer Integrated Manufacturing*, **14**(2), 89–109.
5. Teresko, J., 1990: EDM: The next step towards CIM, *Industry Week*, February, pp. 55–57.
6. Whelan, D.S., 1998: *SIGMOD Record (ACM Special Interest Group on Management of Data)*, **27**(2), 533.

Enterprise resource planning (ERP)

S – 1c; 2b; 3b; 4c; 6b; 7b; 9b; 10c; 13b; * 1.2b; 1.3c; 1.4c; 1.5c; 1.6c; 2.3b; 2.4b; 3.3c; 3.4d; 3.5c; 4.2c; 4.3b

The objective of enterprise resource planning is to improve enterprise communications among all disciplines in the company engaged in the manufacturing process, as well as with customers and suppliers. ERP is a revolution in the 'production engine' of most manufacturers worldwide. By uniting numerous disparate systems under one software umbrella, companies are facilitating best practices and using ERP to drive dramatic cost reductions and increased efficiencies. Additional objectives are:

1. Improve cost/efficient parameters.
2. Overall control and direction of enterprise activities.
3. Customer-oriented information technology (IT).

The method is based on the following concepts:

1. The managing complexity of the enterprise throughout its departments should not be of any interest to the customer.
2. Operating procedures should be aimed at value-added characteristics and not added cost.
3. Construct a single database to serve all enterprise operating disciplines. Use the most advanced IT technology.

The background for developing this method is the inflexibility and conceptual blindness of existing methods. Enterprise resource planning regards the customer as the nucleus of the manufacturing activities. It recognizes that manufacturing is acting in a dynamic environment. It appreciates the available potential and capabilities of computers. Furthermore, it envisions future anticipated developments.

The first manufacturing applications were limited generally to inventory control and purchasing. Essentially, they were a by-product of accounting software and the desire by accountants to know the value of inventory. The need for software specifically designed for manufacturing operations led to the development of material requirements planning (MRP), and subsequently, MRP II packages. Shop floor control modules of MRP II systems have met with only limited success, and only in the simplest manufacturing environments.

With enterprise resource planning solution vendors still use the same basic model as MRPII for the manufacturing planning portions of their systems. Enterprise resource planning represents the application of newer information technology to the MRP II model. These technology changes include the move to relational database management systems, the use of a graphical user interface, open systems and a client/server architecture.

Theoretically, enterprise resource planning applications designed to be real-time, rather than periodic, provides the hour and minute time resolution and plan monitoring needed to deal with changes as they occur.

Enterprise resource planning systems are emerging as the single best way for companies to use their entire data and information resources to better manage their businesses. Enterprise resource planning systems have evolved to help organizations manage their information throughout the company, from the plant to the back office, and now the front office. Initially, enterprise resource planning systems were designed to help get the internal, back-office corporate act together. The availability of the Internet, however, has forced the issue of integrating the front office. The potential for integrating customers and suppliers directly into internal corporate systems is a large step made possible by information technology systems.

In factories, the first enterprise resource planning systems replaced simpler subsystems, dynamically ordering supplies, scheduling labour and production, and arranging shipping–tracking costs all the while. For retailers, the latest enterprise resource planning systems manage inventories that are updated after each sale, and then order replenishment stock. Among the most recent innovations, 'self-service' enterprise resource planning systems are emerging as the single best way for companies to use their entire data and information resources to better manage their businesses.

But, as with all good things, enterprise resource planning systems have a cost. System implementation and maintenance are seldom painless. To get the most value from enterprise resource planning systems some of the basic processes have to be changed. A study should be made to define exactly what the objectives are and understand what the system will deliver. Implemented enterprise resource planning systems will radically change the way companies do business. Once having implemented enterprise resource planning it would be unthinkable to manage finances, customer relationships and supply chains without enterprise resource planning.

Major enterprise resource planning systems providers have developed systems that integrate customer–supplier systems via the Internet, crafting a critical link between front and back offices.

For companies looking to establish a flow manufacturing environment, but who find that a true physical flow layout of the manufacturing process is impractical or impossible, supply chain synchronization enables a virtual flow process. With supply chain synchronization, one can anticipate dramatically improved customer responsiveness. Imagine being able to tell customers the exact status of their orders, initiated either by an alarm signal from the system, a customer-initiated call to customer service, or direct access via the Internet. Manufacturers will know exactly where the order is in the process, which operation or activity is next, whether or not any problems exist, and how much time the remaining order fulfilment steps will take. Customers will know with confidence exactly when their orders will be completed and delivered.

Supply chain synchronization is complementary to ERP and supply chain management. Supply Chain Synchronization solutions should help manufacturers overcome the constraints that they face. To achieve success, such a solution requires that:

1. the entire organization execute a shared plan, optimized to meet a balanced set of business and customer objectives;
2. plan revisions or problems with execution are immediately identified, analysed and communicated throughout the organization;
3. material and other resources are managed by a real-time pull to actual activities rather than the traditional periodic push to infinite capacity-based schedules.

Supply chain synchronization closes the loop between supply and demand. It does so dynamically, in real time, and in a way that matches how a business operates. It is based on reality, not on gross, rough-cut numbers. Now, manufacturers can plan, schedule, and manage the flow of work through the entire order fulfilment process rather than via sequential hand-off between departments. A supply chain synchronization software solution provides a proper balance between optimal planning and synchronized execution. Planning is based on shared objectives that optimally balance demand against available resources.

Synchronized systems represent the next level of performance beyond integrated systems. They share common data, in real time, using exception-driven event triggers to initiate action dynamically. In other words, synchronized systems could be defined as dynamic integration. These systems combine what-if simulation with advanced mathematical methods, such as genetic algorithms, to quickly and effectively assure identification of the best possible course of action.

Bibliography

1. Dash, J., 1998: Enterprise resource planning embraces flow manufacturing, *Managing Automation*, **13**(10), 47–8, 50, 52.
2. Eliot, P., 1999: Volkswagen gets on fast track, *Electronic Commerce World*, **9**(1), 30–33.
3. Fitzgerald, A., 1992: Enterprise resource planning (ERP)-breakthrough or buzzword? In *Third International Conference on Factory 2000. Competitive Performance Through Advanced Technology* (Conference Publication No.359). IEE, London, pp. 291–297.
4. Ford, P., 1999: A market in meltdown? *Business & Technology*, **April**, 53–54.
5. Glass, R.L., 1998: Enterprise resource planning-breakthrough and/or term problem? *Data Base for Advances in Information Systems*, **29**(2), 13–16.
6. Hicks, D.A. and Stecke, K.E., 1995: The ERP maze: enterprise resource planning and other production and inventory control software, *IIE Solutions*, **27**(8), 12–16.
7. Inglesly, T., 1999: Screening the bugs out [ERP/EDI integration], *Electronic Commerce World*, **9**(2), 46–48.
8. Jenson, R.L. and Johnson, I.R., 1999: The enterprise resource planning system as a strategic solution, *Information Strategy: The Executive's Journal*, **15**(4), 28–33.
9. Jetly, N., 1999: ERP's last mile [enterprise resource planning], *Intelligent Enterprise*, **2**(17), 38–40, 42, 44–5.
10. Kempfer, L., 1998: Linking PDM to ERP, *Computer-Aided Engineering*, **17**(2), 58–64.

11. Kim, S.H., 1999: Learning agent architecture for design and manufacturing knowledge on the Web: an extension of enterprise resource planning capabilities, *International Journal of intelligent Systems in Accounting, Finance and Management*, **8**(1), 15–24.
12. Kochan, A., 1999: Getting 'active': a finger on the pulse, *ERP, Manufacturing Computer Solutions*, **5**(5), 26–28.
13. McKie, S., 1998: Packaged solution or Pandora's box? *Intelligent Enterprise*, **1**(2), 38–9, 41, 44, 46.
14. Martin, R., 1999: Dynamic EDP management for introducing enterprise resource planning system, *Industrial Management*, **15**(4), 35–38.
15. Pancucci, D., 1999: ERP for everyone, *Application Development Advisor*, **2**(5), 26–28.
16. Schaeffer, C., 1996: Performance measurement [Control Instruments' use of enterprise resource planning software to manufacture a variety of equipment]. *IIE Solutions*, **28**(3), 20–2, 24–7.
17. Stein, T., 1998: ERP's future linked to E-supply chain, *Information WEEK*, **705**, l.20, 1.22.
18. Tinham, B., 2000: What place MRP II in the new world?, *Manufacturing Computer Solutions*, **6**(1), 14–18.
19. Tinham, B., 1999: Getting the best out of your ERP, *Manufacturing Computer Solutions*, **5**(9), 18–20, 22, 24.
20. White, D., 1998: Soft option [ERP], *Supply Management*, **3**(20), 40–41.

Environment-conscious manufacturing – ECM

P – 11c; 15b; * 1.1b; 1.2c; 2.1b; 2.2b; 2.6b; 3.4c

Environment-conscious manufacturing (ECM) is the deliberate attempt to reduce the ecological impacts of industrial activity without sacrificing quality, cost, reliability, performance, or energy utilization efficiency. The principle of environment-conscious manufacturing is to adopt those processes that reduce the harmful environmental impacts of manufacturing, including minimization of hazardous waste and emissions, reduction of energy consumption, improvement of materials utilization efficiency, and enhancement of operational safety.

'Green manufacturing' is becoming increasingly important. Environmental technology is defined as manufacturing processes, resources, product configuration and design, and material and product handling that preserve energy and natural resources, reduce pollution and protect man and nature.

Competitiveness has introduced this new factor, which is the effect of the company's product and the production process on the environment. Topics such as ecology, energy conservation, natural resources, pollution, and waste are factors in industrial competition.

Both manufacturing and design engineers are confronted with the need to design and manufacture in a more environmentally friendly manner. Hence the field of life-cycle engineering [LCE] is taking on increased importance. The environmental trilogies *reduce*, *reuse* and *recycle* (the three Rs of environmental work), have become familiar and create the challenge of designing and manufacturing in a more environmentally friendly manner.

Environmentally conscious manufacturing and design, has two needs:

1. A philosophy of designing and manufacturing in an environmentally friendly manner.
2. A set of tools based upon solid engineering principles to further enhance the philosophy of environmentally friendly design and manufacture.

It should be noted that manufacturing will always have an environmental impact and the goal should be to optimize manufacturing to have the least environmental impact. Implementation of environment-conscious manufacturing must consider company's internal and external elements. The topics are:

1. *Design for disassembly*. Waste disposal is an important issue. The objective is to reduce waste at the design stage, by using materials that can be recycled and designs that consider ease of disassembly. The use of biodegradable materials are in many cases recommended
2. *Manufacturing for the environment*. The objective is to improve the production processes and product performance by using a 'cleaner' technology that reduces waste and pollution, such as more effective and less-energy-consuming motors.
3. *Total quality environmental management*. The method looks for total harmonic commitment between the organization and nature. Nature is not only a source of resources; the long-range welfare of both nature and organization is interdependent
4. *Industrial ecosystems*. This is a new term in configuring the relationship between organizations. It calls for a relationship between organizations that will supplement each other in terms of ecological conservation. Organizations are linked together so that waste from one can be used as raw material for another.
5. *Technology assessment*. This is a measuring tool to understand and measure the effect of a new technology in one plant on itself, its surroundings, its country and the universe. It researches the cost-effectiveness of the technology in terms of the social, ecological, and political environment. Furthermore, it evaluates the possibility of recycling the tested materials.

It can be seen that design is a prominent feature and that the designer plays an important role in deciding what the environmental impact of a part will be. Life-cycle engineering (LCA) is central to environmental work. LCA is a technique that concentrates not upon one sole environmental facet of a product, but upon all its effects on the environment at all steps in manufacturing, including use, disposal and eventual reuse. Although it is called a technique, one can also consider it as a philosophy. It quantifies inputs and outputs of a product at every stage in terms of energy use, raw materials and polluting emissions. LCA looks at the whole picture instead of focusing upon one negative aspect of a product. Behaviour is assessed in terms of emission outputs in response to varying degrees of input. This can be useful in addressing the issue of governmental environmental regulations aimed at reducing a specific type of emission, be it air pollution, water pollution or some other environmental effect. When designing and producing a part the reduction of one type of emission may lead to a disproportionate increase in another emission; LCA is a technique that strives to correct this. LCA can be used in the following ways:

1. to assess/compare total environmental impacts of product/design alternatives;
2. to improve a product by recording important causes of environmental impact;
3. to develop a new product in an environmentally responsible way.

Some definitions from ISO/TC 207 are included for information.

1. *Life-cycle*: the consecutive and interlinked stages, and all directly associated inputs and outputs, of a system from the extraction or exploitation of natural resources to the final disposal of all materials as irretrievable wastes or dissipated energy.
2. *Environmental burden*: any change to the environment which, permanently or temporarily, results in loss of natural resources or deterioration in the natural quality of air, water or soil.
3. *Environmental impact*: the consequences for human health, for the well-being of flora and fauna or for the future availability of natural resources, attributable to the input and output streams of a system.
4. *Environmental impact assessment (EIA)*: a process to determine the magnitude and significance of environmental impacts within the confines of the goals, scope and objectives defined in the life-cycle assessment.
5. *Recycling*: a set of processes for diverting materials that would otherwise be disposed of as wastes, into an economic system where they contribute to the production of useful material.
6. *Recyclability*: property of a substance or a material and parts made thereof that makes it possible to be recycled.
7. *Sustainability*: development, which meets the needs of the present without compromising the abilities of future generations to meet their own needs.

Bibliography

1. Alting, L., 1995: Life cycle engineering & design, *Annals of CIRP*, **2**, 569.
2. Alting, L., 1978: *Our Common Future*, The Brundtland Report. Oxford University Press.
3. Anderi, R., Daum, B., Weissmantel, H. and Wolf, B., 1999: Design for environment – a computer-based cooperative method to consider the entire life cycle. In *Proceedings*

First International Symposium on Environmentally Conscious Design and Inverse Manufacturing, pp. 380–385.

4. Anonymous, 1993: *Environmental Protection Agency, Life Cycle Assessment, Inventory Guidelines and Principles*. EPA/600/R-92/245, report to EPA by Batelle Memorial Inst. and Franklin Association, Ltd. February.

5. Anonymous, *ISO/TC 207 WG1*. International Standards Organization/Technical Committee 207 Working Group 1, ISO Geneva.

6. Curran, M.A., 1996: *Environmental Life-cycle Assessment*, McGraw Hill, New York.

7. Curlee, T.R. and Das, S., 1991: *Plastic Wastes, Management Control, Recycling and Disposal*. Environmental Protection Agency, Noyes data corporation.

8. Dreer, P. and Koonce, D.A., 1995: Development of an integrated information model for computer integrated manufacturing, *Computers in Industrial Engineering*, **29**(1–4).

9. Erbes, R.E., 1996: *A Practical Guide to Air Quality Compliance*, 2nd edn. John Wiley & Sons.

10. Koonce, D.A. Judd, R.P. and Parks, C.M., 1996: Manufacturing systems engineering and design: an intelligent multi-model, integration architecture, *Computer Integrated Manufacturing*, **9**(6).

11. Lu, C.J.J., Tsai, K.H., Yang, J.C.S. and Yu, Wang, 1998: A virtual testbed for the life-cycle design of automated manufacturing facilities, *International Journal of Advanced Manufacturing Technology*, **14**(8), 608–615.

12. Mills, J.J., 1995: An integrated information infrastructure for agile manufacturing, *Manufacturing Science and Engineering ASME MH*-vol. 3–2.

13. Neton, D.E., 1993: *Global Warming, a Reference Handbook*. ABC-CLIO, Santa Barbara, CA.

14. Orfali, R., Harkey, D. and Edwards, J., 1996: *The Essential Client/Server Survival Guide*. John Wiley&Sons, New York.

15. Smith, M., 1996: *Polymer Products and Waste Management, A Multidisciplinary Approach*. International Books, The Netherlands.

16. Van Beers, M., 1996: *Life cycle analysis*. University of Delft report, January.

Executive Excellence

P – 7b; 8d; 9b; 13c; 16c; * 1.1b; 3.3c; 4.3c; 4.5b

Executive excellence has previously been characterized by leadership in communicating vision, demonstrating integrity, focusing on results, and ensuring customer satisfaction. High-potential future leaders require additional competencies such as:

- Thinking globally
- Appreciating cultural diversity
- Demonstrating technological common sense
- Building partnerships and alliances
- Sharing leadership.

Future leaders may be recruited to help tutor present leaders. If future leaders have the wisdom to learn from the experience of present leaders, and if present leaders have the wisdom to learn new competencies from future leaders, they can share leadership in a way that benefits the organization. Details of these competencies are given below.

1. Sharing leadership. Sharing leadership is a requirement, not an option. In an alliance structure, telling partners what to do and how to do it may quickly lead to having no partners.
2. In dealing with knowledge workers who know more about what they are doing than their managers do, old models of leadership will not work. Future leaders will operate in a mode of asking for input and sharing information. Knowledge workers may well be difficult to keep. They will likely have little organizational loyalty and view themselves as professional free agents who will work for the leader who provides the most developmental challenge and opportunity. Skills in hiring and retaining key talent will be valuable for the leader of the future.
3. Thinking globally. The trend toward globally connected markets will become stronger. Leaders will need to understand the economic, cultural, legal, and political ramifications. Leaders will need to see themselves as citizens of the world with an expanded field of vision and values. Two factors making global thinking a key variable for the future are the dramatic projected increases in global trade and integrated global technology, such as e-commerce. Future leaders will have to learn how to manage global production, marketing, and sales teams to achieve competitive advantage.
4. New technology is another factor that makes global thinking a requirement for future leaders. Technology can help break down barriers to global business. Leaders who can make globalization work in their favour will have a huge competitive advantage.
5. Demonstrating technological common sense. Many future leaders who have been raised with technology view it as an integrated part of their lives. Many present leaders still view technological common sense as important for staff people and operations, but not for them. We need to understand how the intelligent use of new technology can help us recruit, develop, and maintain a network of technically competent people, and know how to make and manage investments in new technology. Without technological common sense, the future of integrated global partnerships and networks would be impossible.
6. Appreciating cultural diversity. Future leaders will also need to appreciate cultural diversity, defined as diversity of leadership style, industry style, individual behaviours and values, race and sex. They will need to understand not only the economic and legal differences, but also the social and motivational differences that are part of working around the world. Understanding other cultures is not just good business practice, it is a key to competing

successfully in the future. Smaller issues, such as the meaning of gifts, personal greetings, or timeliness, will also need to be better understood. The ability to motivate people in different cultures will become increasingly important. Motivational strategies that are effective in one culture may be offensive in another.

7. Building partnerships and alliances. Re-engineering, restructuring, and downsizing are leading to a world where outsourcing of all but core-brand-related activities may become the norm. The ability to negotiate complex alliances and manage complex networks of relationships is becoming increasingly important. Joint leadership of new business models is vital to a successful global venture.

Bibliography

1. Badawy, K.M., 1993: *Management as a New Technology*, McGraw-Hill.
2. Buffa, S., 1984: *Meeting the Competitive Challenge*. Irwin Homewood, IL.
3. Fetcher, W.F., 1987: Achieving manufacturing excellence through the sociotechnical aspects of cycle time management. *Autofact '87 Conference Proceedings*, pp. 8-1–8-11.
4. Flood, R.L. and Romm, N.R.A., 1996: *Diversity Management: Triple Loop Learning*. John Wiley & Sons, Chichester.
5. Gunn, T.G., 1987: *Manufacturing for Competitive Advantage*. Ballinger, Cambridge, MA.
6. Hall, R.W., 1987: *Attaining Manufacturing Excellence*. Business-one, Irwin, Homewood, IL.
7. Hitomi, K., 1991: Strategic integrated manufacturing system: the concept and structures. *International Journal of Production Economics*, **25**(1–3), pp. 5–12.
8. Hitomi, K., Manufacturing excellence for 21st century production, *Technovation*, **16**(1), pp. 33–41.
9. Hitomi, K., 1997: Manufacturing strategy for future production moving toward manufacturing excellence, *International Journal of Technology Management*, **14**(6/7/8), 701–711.
10. Lovereeidge, R. and Pitt, M. (eds), 1990: *The Strategic Management of Technological Innovation*, Wiley, London.
11. Prahalad, C.K. and Hamel, G., 1990: The core competence of the corporation, *Harvard Business Review*, **May/June**.
12. Rumelt, R., 1984: Toward a strategic theory of the firm. In R.B. Lamb (ed.), *Competitive Strategic Management*. Prentice Hall, Engelwood Cliffs, NJ.
13. Stryker, M., 1993: Total leadership key to success in global markets, more one says. *ReviewRensselear Polytechniqe Institute*, **January**, 2.

Expert systems

X – 1c; 3c; 5c; 6c; 7b; 11c; 13c; * 1.3c; 2.2b; 2.3b; 2.4b; 4.1c; 4.2c; 4.4b
See Knowledge management.

Extended enterprise

M – 1c; 2c; 3b; 4b; 6b; 7b; 8b; 9b; 10b; 11b; 13c; * 2.4b; 3.2c; 3.3b; 3.4b; 3.5c; 3.6b; 4.1b; 4.2c; 4.3c; 4.4c
See Supply chain management.

Flat organization

P – 2b; 3b; 4d; 7c; 8c; 9c; 13c; 14c; * 1.1b; 1.2c; 1.3c; 1.5c; 3.2c; 3.3b; 4.2b; 4.3d; 4.4c

Flat organization calls for simplification of the organization procedures by removing any unnecessary level of line management. The number of organizational levels should be kept at a minimum to promote a faster and more cooperative response, where responsibility will be on the workforce.

The objectives of the flat organization are to allow greater flexibility, rapid redeployment of resources, closer interaction with customers and suppliers, and continual innovation. It is linked to a management concept known as the 'horizontal organization'. This refers to a management philosophy that focuses on key organizational processes, a flattened hierarchy, and teams performing to achieve desired outcomes. Technological developments in the computers and communication field make the flat organization a reality. Information sharing, a crucial function as companies grow flatter, is no longer based on mainframes, it has become more networked.

In flat organizations the middle level ranks are being or have been eliminated. The manager's task is to set goals and define strategy. The middle level ranks have their computers and all the information and knowledge required to make a decision at their disposal, and the decisions they make (using built-in algorithms) will be exactly those of the manager. The manager is free to supervise and devote time to finding new business.

A typical organization chart of an industrial enterprise is a vertical organization in which one man is in direct command of a number of subordinates, each of whom carries out the instructions received. The person in command is thus responsible both for giving instructions and seeing that they are carried out effectively. As the business grew the manager found that he/she could not continue to adequately supervise the work of the increasing number of operatives and also carry out the time-consuming tasks of finding new business, corresponding with customers and attending to administrative tasks. Therefore the conventional vertical organizational method came into existence. The general manager of an enterprise controlled all the enterprise information, while each division manager and the operatives controlled and possessed only the relevant information needed to perform their particular task. Information is power, and the manager was controlling the power.

Computers and communication technology brought new manufacturing methods, such as enterprise resource planning and customer relationship management: these methods place enterprise information on the desk of all enterprise operators. With these methods, the manager is not solely in control of information. Therefore, the organization type can be changed. Global competitors are right-sized, flattened, and fully wired with information technology. Their focus is on accelerating learning to make the timely, continuous improvements demanded by customers who can now shop worldwide. Teams are often the fundamental building blocks in these designs, but understanding team leadership treads uncharted ground. Lines between manager and non-manager are blurred to obliqueness. Leadership not only shares a vision but integrates the work of self-directed individuals and self-managed teams to successful completion of the entire effort. This illustrates how integrative leadership really happens when there is no longer the time or the inclination to build permanent management structures.

This changed management concept is known as the horizontal organization. This refers to a management philosophy that focuses on key organizational processes; flattened hierarchy, and teams performing to achieve desired outcomes. In working shorthand, it is referred to as 'managing across, not up and down'.

Organizations have had to confront the unpredictabilities of their environments with workers and work teams, but they have aided them in doing so with conceptually new integrative approaches, e.g. by modelling their production processes and simulating them on computers that can race through alternative scenarios quickly. Simulators, expert systems, and other knowledge-based mechanisms are increasingly being built into the technology that workers themselves operate. There is neither the time nor the omniscience to write rules and procedures for all possible events that unpredictable environments can direct at organizations. With the power of knowledge-based systems and the freedom of open processes, work organizations will increasingly confront and attempt to manage the complexity of their situations rather than reduce the complexity.

Flexible technology has begun to change the ground on which the assumptions underlying the emerging organizational paradigm have been built. Application areas have moved beyond the linear flows of factory floor and clerical office to the nonlinear, interactive, mutually interdependent domains of managers and engineers and other professionals. As a consequence, the complexity of the design task for both technical and organizational designers has increased significantly, and the challenges to designing sociotechnical systems that incorporate these two changing domains have increased even more. In particular, this complexity has outstripped most of the methodology that arose under conditions of linear technical systems and sequential work flows. The rules and procedures that guided decisions have had to be augmented with processes that are open to the flexible possibilities of new technologies.

Team-based organizational arrangements have arisen not only where teams cross organizational and physical locations, but also straddle global, cultural, and ethnic differences.

The characteristic requirements of cross-functional leadership are:

1. Create commitment outside of authority.
2. Use the customer as the authority.
3. Ask questions as a means of focusing on problems.
4. Allow anyone to offer an answer.
5. Continually 'raise the bar' to improve performance.

In other words, regard anyone as a partner in company problems and their solution. Construct a business culture that fosters open communication and mutually beneficial relationships in a supportive environment built on trust. A partnering relationship stimulates continuous quality improvement.

Bibliography

1. Beckhard, R. and Prichard, W., 1992: *Changing the Essence: The Art of Creating and Leading Fundamental Change in Organizations*. Jossey-Bass, San Francisco.
2. Blake, R. and Mouton, J., 1974: *The Managerial Grid*. Prentice-Hall, Englewood Cliffs, NJ.
3. Burack, E., 1993: *Corporate Resurgence and the New Employee Relationships: After the Reckoning*. Quorum Books, New York.
4. Byrne, J.A., 1993: The Horizontal Corporation. *Business Week*, **3351**(6), 76–81.
5. Cohen, A. and Bradford, D., 1991: *Influence Without Authority*. John Wiley, New York.
6. Fiedler, E., 1972: *A Contingency Theory of Leadership Effectiveness*. Prentice Hall, Englewood Cliffs, NJ.
7. Hoberman, S. and Mailick, S., 1995: *Experiential Management Development*. Quorum Books, New York.
8. Juran, J., 1989: *Juran on Leadership for Quality*. Free Press, New York.
9. Kolb, D., Rubin, I. and McIntyre, J., 1971: *Organizational Psychology*. Prentice Hall, Englewood Cliffs, NJ.
10. Kouzes, J. and Posner, B., 1995: *Challenge: How to Get Extraordinary things Done in Business*. Jossey-Bass, San Francisco.
11. Manz, C. and Sims, H., 1990: *Self-leadership*. Berkeley Books, Berkeley, CA.
12. Vaill, P., 1988: *Managing as a Performing Art: New Ideas for a World of Chaotic Change*. Jossey-Bass, San Francisco.
13. Vance, C.M., 1993: Mastering Management Education. Sage, Newbury Park, CA.
14. Vroom, V. and Yago, A., 1988: *The New Leadership*. Prentice Hall, Englewood Cliffs, NJ.
15. Whetten, D. and Cameron, K., 1995: *Developing Management Skills*. Harper-Collins, New York.
16. Steven I. Meisel La Salle University, David S. Fearon Central Connecticut State University.

Flexible manufacturing system – FMS

T – 1a; 3a; 4a; 6a; 7b; 13c; * 1.1b; 2.4b; 2.5c; 3.3b

The objective of flexible manufacturing systems (FMS) is to produce medium to low quantities of products with the efficiency of mass production. A flexible manufacturing system can be defined as a computer-controlled configuration of semi-independent workstations and material handling system designed to efficiently manufacture more than one kind of part at low to medium volumes. The essential physical components of an FMS are:

1. Potentially independent numerical controlled (NC) machines.
2. A conveyance network to move parts and sometimes tools between machines and fixture stations.
3. An overall control network that coordinates machines, the parts-moving elements and workpieces.

In most FMS installations, incoming raw workpieces are fixtured onto pallets at a station or group of stations set apart from the machines. They then move via the material handling system to queues at the production machines where they are processed. In a properly designed system, the holding queues are seldom empty, i.e. there is usually a workpiece waiting to be processed when the machine becomes idle. Pallet exchange times are short and machine idle times are small. The number of machines in a system typically ranges from two to 20. The conveyance system may consist of carousels, conveyors, carts, robots, or a combination of these. The important aspect of these systems is that the machine and conveyance elements combine to achieve enhanced productivity without sacrificing flexibility.

Perhaps the easiest approach to understanding an FMS is to trace the flow of parts through the system. A typical FMS is capable of random piece-part production within a given part mix. In other words, using simulation and other production analysis techniques, a production part is determined which utilizes the system capacity. At any given time, any or all of those parts might be found somewhere in the system.

Part flow begins at the load/unload stations, where the raw material and fixtures are kept. The FMS controll computer keeps track of the status of every part and machine in the system. It continually tries to achieve the production targets for each part type and in doing so tries to keep all the machines busy. In selecting parts to be sent into the system, it chooses part types which are the most behind in their production goals, and for which there are currently empty fixture/pallets or load stations. If an appropriate pallet/fixture combination and a workpiece are available at the load station, the loader will receive a message at the computer terminal to load that part onto the pallet. The loader then enters the part number and pallet code into the terminal, and the computer will send a transporter to move the pallet. The transporter is next sent to the appropriate machine.

Once at the queue in front of the machine, the computer actuates the transfer mechanism in the queue and the pallet is shifted from the transporter onto the shuttle. The transporter is then free and will leave when a new move request is assigned. The part and pallet wait until the part currently being machined is completed, and then the two parts and their pallets exchange position. As the new part is moved onto the machine, the proper NC part program is downloaded to the machine controller from the FMS control computer. After completing the downloading, machining begins.

The finished part now on the shuttle waits for the computer to send a free transporter to collect it and carry it to its next destination. If, for some reason, the part cannot go to that destination, the computer checks its files for an alternative destination. If one exists, the computer decides if conditions in the FMS warrant sending the part to that destination. If it does not, the part either circulates around the system on the transporter until the destination is available, or the transporter unloads it at some intermediate or storage queue, and retrieves it when the destination is available. The last destination is usually the load station, now functioning as an unload station where a part is removed from the pallet and replaced by a new part, or the pallet is stored until needed.

Flexible manufacturing systems (FMS) are designed to combine the efficiency of a mass-production line and the flexibility of a job shop for the batch production of a mid-volume and mid-variety of products. To control FRSs is more complex than transfer lines or job shops because of the flexibility of machines and operations. General FMS operation decisions can be divided into two phases: planning and scheduling. The planning phase considers the pre-arrangement of parts and tools before the FMS begins to process, and the scheduling phase deals with routing parts while the system is in operation. The scheduling phase involves a set of tasks to be performed. There are trade-offs between early and late completion of a task, and between holding inventory and frequent production changeover. Scheduling has been proved to belong to the family of NP-complete problems that are very difficult to solve.

The FMS system must control the CNC equipment, the material handling equipment, the part movement within the system, and the system performance information. The tasks of the software control system are:

1. System data acquisition
2. System data storage and retrieval
3. System data interpretation
4. System status determination and interpretation
5. Decision-making
6. Decision implementation.

There are three levels of control. The first level communicates directly with the process and involves most process control tasks. The second level supervises the first level, makes tactical decisions, communicates with the first level, acquires and manages system data using a local database, determines system decisions status and makes and implements decisions. The third level of control exercises indirect control, makes strategic decisions and maintains a complete database.

FMSs increase the flexibility and productivity of discrete part manufacturing. This technology is not only becoming more complex to control, but also presents a number of decision problems. The environment of a FMS is completely different from that of a conventional job shop. This new environment provides new capabilities but imposes new constraints on the scheduling function, which should be adapted accordingly. In an FMS the hardware and the layout provide flexibility in manufacturing by allowing parts to be transferred automatically, rapidly and without delay, from one machine to another. The machines do not require setup time and thus one can switch from one part to another with minimum loss of time. The utilization of the hardware flexibility, however, depends on the software used and its flexibility. Improper software might cause (and it has happened in some FMS installations) overload on some machines, underemployment of machines not having the proper tooling to carry out the job and high in-process inventory, thus machine utilization is low, the automatic transfer system is overcrowded and overall efficiency is low.

Considering the high investment of FMS, it is certainly worthwhile to select the best dispatching rules of decision-making.

Bibliography

1. Chuah, K.B., Cheung, E.H.M. and Li, X.N., 1994: A study of fast modelling techniques for FMS simulator, *Proceedings of 1994 Pacific Conference on Manufacturing*, The Institute of Engineers, Jakarta, Indonesia, 19–22 December.
2. Halevi, G. and Weill, R., 1984: On line scheduling for flexible manufacturing systems, *Annals of the CIRP*, **33**(1), 331–334.
3. Jin, D. and Kakazu, Y., 1995: The determination of AGV's traffic control model by ID3 through an implicit knowledge learning, *Proceedings of CAPE'95*. IFIP, Chapman & Hall, pp. 679–688.
4. Klahorst, H.T., 1983: How to justify multi-machine systems, *American Machinist*, **September**, pp. 67–70.
5. Kusiak, A. (ed.), 1986: *Flexible Manufacturing Systems: Methods and Studies.* North Holland, Amsterdam.
6. Kusiak, A. (ed.), 1986: *Modelling and Design of Flexible Manufacturing Systems.* Elsevier Science, Amsterdam.
7. Lee, Y.H. and Iwwata, K., 1991: Part ordering through simulation optimization in an FMS, *International Journal of Production Research*, **7**, 1309–1323.
8. Lenz, J.E., 1985: MAST: A simulation tool as advanced as FMS it studies, *Proceedings of 1st Conference on Simulation in Manufacturing*. IFS Publications, Stratford-upon-avon, pp. 313–324.

9. Liu, J. and MacCarthy, B.L., 1996: The classification of FMS scheduling problems, *International Journal of Production Research*, **34**(3), 647–656.
10. MacCarthy, B.L. and Liu, J., 1993: A new classification scheme for flexible manufacturing systems, *International Journal of Production Research*, **31**, 229–309.
11. Mukhopadhyay, S.K., Maiti, B. and Garg, S., 1991: Heuristic solution to the scheduling problems in flexible manufacturing systems, *International Journal of Production Research*, **10**, 2003–2024.
12. Nakamura, N. and Shingu, T., 1985: Scheduling of flexible manufacturing systems. In H.J. Bullinger and H.J. Warnecke (eds), *Toward the Factory of the Future*, pp. 147–152.
13. Newman, S.T. and Bell, R., 1992: The modelling of flexible machining facilities, *Proceedings of 1992 IEE Factory Automation Conference*, York, UK, pp. 285–290.
14. O'Grady, P.J. and Menon, U., 1986: A concise review of flexible manufacturing systems and FMS litrature, *Computer in Industry*, **7**, 155–167.
15. Rabelo, L. and Alptekin, S., 1993: A hybrid neural and symbolic processing approach to flexible manufacturing systems scheduling. In A. Kandel (ed.), *Hybrid Architectures for Intelligent Systems*. CRC Press, pp. 379–405.
16. Roll, Y., Karni, R. and Arzi, Y., 1991: Measurement of processing flexibility in flexible manufacturing cell, *Journal of Manufacturing Systems*, **11**(4), 258–268.
17. Sarin, S. and Dar-El, E., 1984: Approaches to the scheduling problems in FMS, Institute of Industrial Engineers, *Fall Industrial Engineering Conference*, pp. 225–235.
18. Shanker, K. and Tzen, Y.J., 1985: A loading and dispatching problem in a random flexible manufacturing system, *International Journal of Production Research*, **23**, 579–595.
19. Shaw, M.J., 1989: A pattern directed approach for FMS: a framework for intelligent scheduling, learning and control, *International Journal of Flexible Manufacturing*, **2**, 121–144.
20. Sloggy, J.E., 1984: How to justify the cost of an FMS, Tooling & production, dEC, pp. 72–75.
21. Suri, R. and Hildebrant, R.R., 1984: Modelling flexible manufacturing systems with mean value analysis, *Journal of Manufacturing Systems*, **3**(1), 27–38.
22. Talavage, J.J. and Shodham, R., 1992: Automated development of design and control strategy for FMS, *International Journal of Computer Integrated Manufacturing*, **5**(6), 335–348.
23. Tang, L., Yih, Y. and Liu, C., 1993: A study on decision rules of scheduling model in an FMS, *Computers in Industry*, **22**, 1–13.

Fractal manufacturing system

P – 1c; 2c; 3d; 4c; 8d; 9d; 13c; 14c; 16c; * 1.3b; 1.4c; 2.4c; 3.3b; 3.5c; 3.6c; 4.4c; 4.6c

(See also Self-organizing manufacturing method.)

A fractal manufacturing system is designed to solve the shop floor control problem, and is an architecture made up of totally distributed independent autonomous modules that cooperate intelligently to create a future manufacturing system that responds to apparently future manufacturing needs. The needs are specified as:

- to produce by autonomous modules;
- reduction of workforce;
- modular design that ensures integration;
- inexpensive construction of production lines (reduction of 70–80% of investment);
- meeting customers needs;
- fast adjustment to market fluctuations.

The traditional approach to the design of manufacturing systems is the hierarchical approach. The design is based on a top-down approach and strictly defines the system modules and their functionality. Communication between modules is strictly defined and limited in such a way that modules communicate with their parent and child modules only. In a hierarchical architecture, modules cannot take an initiative; therefore, the system is sensitive to perturbations, and its autonomy and reactivity to disturbances are weak. The resulting architecture is very rigid and therefore expensive to develop and difficult to maintain.

Heterarchical control was an approach taken to alleviate the problems of hierarchical systems. The heterarchical approach bans all hierarchy in order to give full power to the basic modules, often called 'agents', in the system. A heterarchical manufacturing system consists of, for instance, workstations and orders only. Each order negotiates with the workstations to get the work done, using all possible alternatives available to face unforeseen situations. This way, it is possible to react adequately to changes in the environment (such as new products that enter the market, new or evolving technologies, unpredictable demands for products) as well as to disturbances in the manufacturing system itself (defects, delays, variable yield of chemical reactors).

The term fractal comes from fractal geometry for describing and analysing objects in multi-dimensional spaces, specially focused on the fractional dimension where Euclidean geometry is not suitable. The main characteristics of fractals are self-similarity, implying recursion, pattern-inside-pattern.

In manufacturing, emphasis is given to factory fractals acting independently. This means the fractals have a current system of goals that they pursue. The goal system works through coordination among fractals, occupying both adjacent hierarchical level and the same levels. The fractals develop their goal independently, while solving conflicts through cooperation and the process is iterative as changes are brought to act in a specified way.

With a fractal manufacturing system the key concepts are self-organization, self-optimization, and dynamics of the people in the manufacturing system.

The fractal factory has a flexible and efficient information and navigation system. Fractals navigate in the sense of constantly checking their target areas, re-assessing their position and progress, and correcting if necessary.

Bibliography

1. Dilts, D.M., Boyd, N.P. and Whorms, H.H., 1991: The evolution of control architectures for automated manufacturing systems, *Journal of Manufacturing Systems*, **10**(1), 79–93.
2. Goldberg, D.E., 1982: SGA: Simple genetic algorithms, University of Michigan, Dept. of Civil Engineering, Ann Arbor, MI.
3. Hayashi, H., 1993: The IMS international collaborative program, *Proceedings of 24th International Symposium on Industrial Robots*, Japan Industrial Robot Association.
4. Iwata, K. and Onosato, M., 1994: Random manufacturing system: a new concept of manufacturing systems for production to order, *Annals of the CIRP*, **43**(1), 379–384.
5. Jones, A.T. and McLean, C.R., 1986: A proposed hierarchical control model for automated manufacturing systems, *Journal of Manufacturing Systems*, **5**(1), 15–26.
6. Kadar, L.M. and Szelke, E., 1997: An object oriented framework for developing distributed manufacturing architectures, *Proceedings of 2nd World Congress on Intelligent Manufacturing Processes and Systems*, June 10–13, Budapest, Hungary, pp. 548–554.
7. Kimura, E., 1993: A product and process model for virtual manufacturing systems, *Annals of the CIRP*, **42**(1), 147–150.
8. Maturana, F., Gu, P., Naumann, A. and Norrie, D.H., 1997: Object-oriented jobshop scheduling using genetic algorithm, *Computers in Industry*, **32**, 281–294.
9. Moriwaki, T., Sugimura, N., Martawirya, Y.Y. and Wirjomartono, S.H., 1992: Production scheduling in autonomous distributed manufacturing system. In *Quality Assurance Through Integration of Manufacturing Processes and Systems*, PED-vol. 56, ASME, New York.
10. Tharumarajah, A., Wells, A.J. and Nemes, L., 1996: Comparison of bionic, fractal and holonic manufacturing system concepts, *International Journal Computer Integrated Manufacturing*, **9**(3), 217–226.
11. Schultz, A.C., Grefenstette, J.J. and De Jong, A.K., 1993: Test and evaluation by genetic algorithms, *IEEE Expert*, **12**, pp. 9–14.
12. Senehi, M.K., Kramer, Th.R., Ray, S.R., Quintero, R. and Albus, J.S., 1994: Hierarchical control architectures from shop level to end effectors. In S.B. Joshi and I.S. Smith (eds), *Computer Control of Flexible Manufacturing Systems, Research and Development*. Chapman & Hall, New York, Chapter 2, pp. 31–62.
13. Simon, H.A., 1990: *The Science of the Artificial*, 2nd edn. MIT Press, Cambridge, MA.
14. Swiercz, 1997: Testing and Evaluation of Manufacturing Systems. Graduation thesis for Warsaw University of Technology, Tempus Bursary at K.U.Leuven. Also available as a K.U.Leuven technical report PMA 97R039.
15. Tharumarajah and Wells, A.J., 1997: A behavior-based approach to scheduling in distributed manufacturing systems, *Integrated Computer Aided Engineering*, **4**(4), 235–249.
16. Ueda, K., 1993: A genetic approach toward future manufacturing systems. In J. Peklenik (ed.), *Flexible Manufacturing Systems, Past, Present, Future*. Ljubljana, Slovenia pp. 221–228.
17. Valckenaers, P., Bongaerts, L. and Wyns, J., 1996: Planning systems in the next century (II). *Proceedings of Advanced Summer Institute (ASI) 96 of the N.O.E. on*

Intelligent Control of Integrated Manufacturing Systems, Toulouse, France, 2–6 June pp. 289–295.

18. Waldrop, M., 1992: *COMPLEXITY, the Emerging Science at the Edge of Order and Chaos*. Viking, Penguin Group.
19. Warnecke, H.J., 1993: *The Fractal Company: A Revolution in Corporate Culture*. Springer-Verlag.

Fuzzy logic

X – 1c; 2c; 3c; 4c; 5d; 11c; 13d; 16c; * 2.2c; 2.3c; 2.4c; 2.5c; 3.1c; 3.2c; 3.5c; 3.6c; 4.3d; 4.4b; 4.6c

Fuzzy logic is a technique that handles problems that cannot be defined in explicit terms. In fuzzy logic, you define the problem in the way humans do things. It involves common-sense reasoning and rules of thumb to process data in cases where a set of conditions is only approximately satisfied. Fuzzy logic allows you to think in qualitative terms, rather than quantitative terms when describing a process.

Traditional logic programs rely on binary logic. Inside the program, the switch is either on or off, yes or no, true or false. With fuzzy logic, on the other hand, inputs are placed into membership sets, in a step called fuzzification. Sets define a realm in which the input can exist and allow for an input to be a member to some degree. Since the set describes a range from completely true to completely false, some developers prefer the expression 'continuous logic' to eliminate perceptions of magic, mystery, or imprecision.

Fuzzy logic is a powerful approach to decision-making built into computer hardware and software. It can be applied in a variety of applications including motion and process control, manufacturing, consumer electronics, modelling and forecasting. The bottom line with fuzzy logic is reduced time to market, lower-cost development, and improved product performance. Fuzzy logic technology is used to advance many industrial topics, such as:

1. Scheduling and production planning
2. Process control
3. Quality control
4. Decision support
5. Sensor design
6. Management
7. Data analysis and data mining
8. Marketing research.

The engineering community can be sceptical about fuzzy logic because they believe that in order to get precision you need precision all the way through the process, but the idea of a trade-off is not really true. Fuzzy logic can be terribly precise.

Fuzzy logic allows engineers to express what they want to accomplish in linguistic terms via a series of if/then 'rules'. For example, if I enter my living room and feel cold, then I turn up the thermostat. Fuzzy logic embraces intuitive terms like hot/cold, high/low, easy/hard, and so on. There's a certain uncertainty about how we decide things, and fuzzy logic allows uncertainty to exist during the process. Then, after considering memberships that are mostly true, almost false, and so forth, the program makes a decision and produces a crisp output.

So real-world inputs go into a fuzzy logic system, and real-world outputs come out, but the black box in between operates in a different way. Compared with traditional logic systems, that way is easier to describe because it is the way a human operator would do it. That way is faster and less costly to design because it is more intuitive and takes fewer, simpler rules. That way is easier to operate, maintain, and modify for the same reasons. That way is more robust and less sensitive to noisy signals and component variation because it doesn't operate in the brittle on/off way. Hardware costs can also be reduced, because the code can be smaller, requires less memory, and runs faster.

Though it can mimic linear control systems, fuzzy logic is best suited to nonlinear control and complex systems. It is excellent where systems are easily described verbally, but difficult to describe mathematically. In fact, mathematical models are not required.

Fuzzy logic is combined with artificial-intelligence-based systems, such as neural networks and genetic algorithms in control and recognition systems. While fuzzy logic provides an element of common sense, neural networks provide intelligent use of data. Unlike fuzzy logic, neural networks identify relationships and learn to recognize patterns on their own based on learning from amounts of data; neural networks have numerous processing elements linked into patterns similar to the human brain. Given an input, these are dynamically interconnected by feedback loops until the network 'learns' an output. Neural networks are currently used for process modelling and character recognition such as confirming signatures on cheques, and they are being evaluated for voice recognition.

Genetic algorithms, on the other hand, cause computer programs to mutate, evolving into a series of new programs. The value of the mutant programs is evaluated externally, and certain mutant programs are selected to mutate anew. This Darwinian process of natural selection generates optimum programs.

Bibliography

1. Atrock, C., 1995: *Fuzzy Logic and Neurofuzzy Applications Explained.* Prentice Hall.
2. Bellmann, R. and Zadeh, L.A., 1970: Decision making in a fuzzy environment, *Management Science*, **17**, B-141–164.

3. Fochem, M., Wischnewski, P. and Hofmeier, R., 1997: Quality control system on the production line of tape deck chasis using self organizing feature maps. *ESIT 97 – First European Symposium on Applications of Intelligent Technologies*, article No. 23954, Aachen, Germany.
4. Jardzioch, A., 1999: Scheduling of production on the base of linguistic decision rules. *Third International Data Analysis Symposium*, 17 September, Aachen Germany.
5. Kandel, A. and Langholz, G. (eds), 1992: *Hybrid Architecture for Intelligent Systems*. CRC Press, Boca Raton.
6. Klein, R.L. and Meethlie, L.B., 1995: *Knowledge Based Decision Support System*, 2nd edn. Wiley, Chichester.
7. Leberling, H., 1981: On finding compromise solutions in multicriteria problems using the fuzzy min-operator, *Fuzzy Sets and Systems*, **6**, 105–118.
8. Maiers, J. and Sherif, Y.S., 1985: Applications of fuzzy sets theory, *IEEE Transactions on Systems, Man and Cybernetics*, **SMC-15**(1), 175–189.
9. Newell, A. and Simon, H.A., 1972: *Human Problem Solving*. Prentice-Hall, Engelwood cliffs, NJ.
10. Saaty, Th.L., 1978: Exploring the interface between hierarchies, multiple objectives and fuzzy logic. *Fuzzy Sets and Systems*, **1**, 57–68.
11. Turban, E., 1988: *Decision Support and Expert Systems*, 2nd edn. Macmillan, New York.
12. Turksen, I.B., 1988: Approximate reasoning for production planning, *Fuzzy Sets and Systems*, **26**, 1–15.
13. Yager, R.R., 1978: Fuzzy decision making including unequal objectives, *Fuzzy Sets and Systems*, **1**, 87–95.
14. Zimmermann, H.J., 1978: Fuzzy programming and linear programming with several objective functions, *Fuzzy Sets and Systems*, **1**, 45–55.
15. Zimmermann, H.J. and Zysno, P., 1980 or 1978: Latent connectives in human decision making, *Fuzzy Sets and Systems*, **4**, 37–51.
16. Zimmermann, H.J. and Zysno, P., 1983: Decisions and evaluations by hierarchical aggregation of information, *Fuzzy Sets and Systems*, **10**, 143–266.
17. Zimmermann, H.J., Zadeh, L.A. and Gaines, B.R. (eds), 1984: *Fuzzy Sets and Decision Analysis*. North Holland, Amsterdam.
18. Zimmermann, H.J., 1987: Fuzzy Sets, Decision Making, and Expert Systems. Boston, Dordrecht, Lancaster.
19. Zimmermann, H.J., 1991: Cognitive science, decision technology and fuzzy sets, *Information Science*, **57/58**, 287–295.
20. Zimmermann, H.J., 1996: *Fuzzy Sets Theory and its Applications*, 3rd edn. Boston.
21. Zimmermann, H.J., 1997: Intelligent decision support system. *European Symposium on Intelligent Techniques*, article No. 23924, Aachen, Germany.

Genetic manufacturing system

P – 1c; 2c; 3d; 4c; 8d; 9d; 13c; 14c; 16c; * 1.3b; 1.4c; 2.4c; 3.3b; 3.5c; 3.6c; 4.4c; 4.6c

(See also self-organizing manufacturing method and Holonic manufacturing system.)

Genetic manufacturing systems are designed to solve the shop floor control problem and have an architecture made up of totally distributed independent autonomous modules that cooperate intelligently to create a future manufacturing system that responds to apparently future manufacturing needs. The needs are specified as:

- to produce by autonomous modules;
- reduction of workforce;
- modular design that assures integration;
- inexpensive construction of production lines (reduction of 70–80% of investment);
- meeting customers needs;
- fast adjustment to market fluctuations.

The traditional approach to the design of manufacturing systems is the hierarchical approach. The design is based on a top-down approach and strictly defines the system modules and their functionality. Communication between modules is strictly defined and limited in such a way that modules communicate with their parent and child modules only. In a hierarchical architecture, modules cannot take an initiative; therefore, the system is sensitive to perturbations, and its autonomy and reactivity to disturbances are weak. The resulting architecture is very rigid and therefore expensive to develop and difficult to maintain.

Heterarchical control was an approach to alleviate the problems of hierarchical systems. The heterarchical approach bans all hierarchy in order to give full power to the basic modules, often called 'agents', in the system. A heterarchical manufacturing system consists of, for instance, workstations and orders only. Each order negotiates with the workstations to get the work done, using all possible alternatives available to face unforeseen situations. This way, it is possible to react adequately to changes in the environment (such as new products that enter the market, new or evolving technologies, unpredictable demands for products) as well as to disturbances in the manufacturing system itself (defects, delays, variable yield of chemical reactors).

The genetic manufacturing system elaborates on the idea and mimics the DNA concept to model production orders.

Bibliography

1. Janson, D.J. and Frenzel, J.F., 1993: Training product unit neural network with genetic algorithms, *IEEE Expert*, 27–28.
2. Maturana, F., Gu, P., Naumann, A. and Norrie, D.H., 1997: Object-oriented job-shop scheduling using genetic algorithm, *Computers in Industry*, **32**, 281–294.
3. Ueda, K., 1993: A genetic approach toward future manufacturing systems. In J. Peklenik (ed.), *Flexible Manufacturing Systems*, Past, Present, Future. Ljubljana, Slovenia, pp. 221–228.

4. Goldberg, D.E., 1982: *Simple Genetic Algorithms*. University of Michigan, Dept. of civil engineering, Ann Arbor, MI.
5. Kimk, J.-U. and Kim, Y.-D., 1996: Simulation annealing and genetic algorithms for scheduling products with multi-level product structure, *Computers Operation Research*, **23**(9), 857–868.
6. Schultz, A.C., Grefenstette, J.J. and De Jong, A.K., 1993: Test and evaluation by genetic algorithms, *IEEE Expert*, pp. 9–14.
7. Uckun, S., Bagchi, S. and Kawamura, K., 1992: Managing genetic search in job-shop scheduling, *IEEE Expert*, 15–24.
8. Ueda, A., 1992: An approach to bionic manufacturing system based on DNA type information. In *Proceedings of ICOOMS 1992*, pp. 303–308.
9. Wiendahl, H.P. and Burkner, S., 1999: Application of genetic algorithm in the scheduling of flexible disassembly cells. In *IFIP WG5.7 SIG on ATPPC'99*, IFA Hanover, pp. 57–72.

Global manufacturing network (GMN)

X – 3b; 5b; 7c; 9c; 10c; * 1.6b; 2.2b

The global manufacturing network uses the Internet as a resource focused solely on manufacturing products and services, providing an unequalled store-house of information to help manufacturing professionals and their companies stay competitive. The Internet has the potential to become a strategic informa-tion management tool for manufacturing companies. Internet users can access four basic functions:

1. e-mail;
2. discussion groups;
3. long-distance computing;
4. file transfer.

When used in the manufacturing arena, these communications tools are powerful concurrent engineering aids allowing the following features.

1. Sending and receiving design and manufacturing information as soon as it's updated.
2. Retrieving or simply running a computer file off a system hundreds of miles away, with the only limitations being that of download time.
3. Researching manufacturing problems to see if some national laboratory has already solved them or is working with a consortium on the problem.
4. Shopping for new capital equipment and comparing specs from several vendors without being inundated with paper.
5. Marketing new products to a global audience.
6. Maintaining a line of communications with technical peers.

Equipment suppliers wanting to boost their marketing efforts may be part of the network. Supplier input to a network may give access to the latest machine tool specs, as well as discussion of the problems a company's specific equipment can solve.

A global manufacturing network (GMN) was launched by the society of manufacturing engineers (SME). GMN users can get practical advice on technical problems, download application software programs, and conduct in-depth manufacturing research on a variety of topics from several sources.

Bibliography

1. Coviello, N.E., 1998: International competitiveness: Empirical findings from SME service firms, *Journal of International Marketing*, **6**(2), 8.
2. Davenport, S., 1999: Rethinking a national innovation system: The small country as 'SME', *Technology Analysis & Strategic Management*, **11**(3), 431.
3. Gilmore, A., 1999: Added value: A qualitative assessment of SME marketing, *Irish Marketing Review*, **12**(1), 27.
4. Hart, S., 1999: The impact of marketing research activity on SME export performance: Evidence from the UK, *Journal of Small Business Management*, **37**(2), 63.
5. Johnson, D., HEI and SME linkages: Recommendations for the future, *International Small Business Journal*, **17**(4), 66.
6. Oztel, H., 1998: Local partnership for economic development: Business links and the restructing of SME support networks in the United Kingdom, *Economic Development Quarterly*, **12**(3), 266.
7. van der Wiele, T., 1998: Venturing down the TQM path for SMEs, *International Small Business Journal*, **16**(2), 50.
8. Yongjiang, Shi, 1998: International manufacturing networks – To develop global competitive capabilities, *Journal of Operations Management*, **16**(2,3), 195.
9. http://www.global mfg.com. SME's Global Manufacturing Network is available to users free of charge 24 hours a day, seven days a week
10. http://www.carrlane.com. The home page of Carr Lane Manufacturing Co. (St. Louis) includes a product listing and company profile.
11. http://www.epoxies.com. The home page of Epoxies Etc.

Global manufacturing system

P – 1b; 2b; 3c; 4b; 5d; 6c; 7c; 11b; 12c; 13b; 14d; * 1.1d; 1.2c; 1.3b; 2.3b; 2.4b; 2.5c; 3.1d; 3.2c; 3.3b; 3.5b; 3.6b; 4.1b

The global manufacturing system is a computer-oriented manufacturing philosophy aimed at global optimization of the manufacturing process. It utilizes the power and capabilities of present day computers to meet the requirements of the manufacturing process. It treats the manufacturing process as one interactive problem starting from product specification to product design to product shipment. It considers the manufacturing process as a nucleus and satellites rather than as a chain of activities. It broadens the scope of alternative solutions and eliminates the artificial constraints.

Global manufacturing systems do not contemplate the relationships between individual stages and activities of the manufacturing process, but rather dissolves them into one single global optimization system.

The manufacturing process requires the knowledge of many disciplines, such as design, process planning, costing, marketing, sales, customer relations, costing, purchasing, bookkeeping, inventory control, material handling, shipping and so on. No one can master and become an expert in all disciplines. Therefore the manufacturing process is divided into several activities, each activity being performed by the appropriate expert. In order to have good performance, the manufacturing process must consider the points of view of many disciplines because each discipline considers the problem at hand from a different angle.

Global manufacturing systems are based on the following axioms:

1. Each stage in the manufacturing process must consider other stages' interests, but make decisions only in its area of expertise. The manufacturing process is a decision-making process, and the decisions are of two kinds: critical decisions, which are mandatory to the function of the task, and fillers, which are not crucial to the function of the task.
2. Optimization of each individual stage of the manufacturing process does not ensure overall optimization.
3. Data transfer between manufacturing stages should include intentions, ideas, alternatives, and reasoning instead of just decisions. A decision-maker who knows the reasons that led to the acceptance of a decision will have an additional degree of freedom in the decisions that must be made.
4. Decisions will be made at the latest moment possible, i.e. at the execution time. An optimum decision that was made at a certain point in time might not be good at another time. The manufacturing process is basically very flexible and this flexibility should be used.
5. Economic decisions should not be restricted by the engineering data used to make it. Engineering, no doubt, is doing the best they can. However, engineering considerations and optimization criteria are not always the same as those of the management. Thus engineering actually carries out the first screening of data that will be considered.
6. Always check the cost and manufacturing implications of the 'best' solution. In many cases, reducing the specified values of the best solution by as little as 5% may result in a cost reduction of more than 60%.

The global manufacturing system makes use of the following notions.

1. There are an infinite number of ways to produce a product.
2. Any available resources can produce any item.

3. The cost and lead time required to produce a component are functions of the process used.
4. There are infinite ways of meeting design objective.
5. In any product and item about 75% of the dimensions and shapes are non-functional (fillers). These shapes can vary considerably without affecting the product performance.
6. The cost and lead time required to produce an item are functions of its design. A minute change in fillers or dimensions to suit a standard tooling or an existing setup on a machine can result in significant cost variation.
7. The process plan has to be altered continuously to comply with these changes with plant resources.
8. With present-day techniques, competition for resources will always occur. The method and logic of resolving this competition, that is, pull forward or backward, defeat the main purpose of production planning.
9. There exists a theoretical manufacturing optimum that is theoretical from a specific shop standpoint, but practical from a technology standpoint.

The basic philosophy of the global manufacturing system is that all parameters in the manufacturing process are flexible, that is, any of them is subject to change if such change contributes to increased productivity in manufacturing the product mix required for the immediate period. In such a flexible and dynamic environment, the only stable parameters are the product to be manufactured and the resources available at the shop. Product objectives are external to the manufacturing cycle and must be preserved.

The global manufacturing system is an overall architecture of the manufacturing process. The architecture is composed of four levels as follows:

Level 1: Company management strategic planning
Level 2: Factory planning
Level 3: Divisional planning
Level 4: Shop floor planning

Management according to its forecasts and financial considerations can reach an intelligent decision as to the desirable objective. Once such a decision is made, the system will accept it as a fixed and frozen constraint and will optimize the manufacturing process accordingly.

The method main concepts are:

1. Engineering stages are incorporated into production and management stages.
2. All stages of the manufacturing process work towards a single objective. Each stage considers the problems and difficulties of the other stages.
3. The objective is to increase productivity, decrease lead times and decrease manufacturing cost of the product mix in any period rather than to optimize any single product, component, or operation.

4. No artificial constraints are created and considered.
5. The manufacturing process is kept dynamic and flexible until the moment processing starts.
6. Each decision is made by the qualified expert.
7. Each decision is based on real facts and not on assumptions.
8. Each decision is made at the time of execution, independent of the other decisions.
9. Each decision may be changed when circumstances change.
10. Keep the system simple.

Bibliography

1. Halevi, G., 1980: *The Role of Computers in Manufacturing Processes*, John-Wiley & Sons, New York.
2. Halevi, G., 1995: *Principles of Process Planning – A Logistic Approach*. Chapman & Hall, London.
3. Halevi, G., 1997: The magic matrix as a smart machine evaluator, *International Journal of Production Planning & Control*, **8**(4), 343–355.
4. Halevi, G., 1997: The magic matrix as a smart resource planning, *International Journal of Production Engineering and Computers*, **1**(1), 21–28.
5. Halevi, G., 1993: The magic matrix as a smart scheduler, *Computer in Industry*, **21**, 245–253.
6. Halevi, G., 1997: Global optimization of the manufacturing process, *CIRP International Symposium on Global Manufacturing*, August 21–22, Hong-Kong, pp. 340–352.
7. Halevi, G., 1999: *Restructuring the Manufacturing Process – Applying the Matrix Method*. St. Lucie Press/APICS Series on Resource Management.
8. Hayes, R.H. and Pisano, G.P., 1994: Beyond world-class: The new manufacturing strategy, *Harvard Business Review*, **72**(1), 77–86.
9. Hayes, R.H. and Wheelwright, S.C., 1984: *Restoring Our Competitive Edge*. John Wiley & Sons, New York.
10. Hyun, J.H. and Ahn, B.H., 1992: A unifying framework for manufacturing flexibility, *Management Review*, **5**(4), 251–260.
11. Sethi, A.K. and Sethi, S.P., 1990: Flexibility in manufacturing: A survey, *International Journal of Flexible Manufacturing Systems*, **2**, 289–328.
12. Suarez, F.F., Cusumano, M.A. and Fine, C.H., 1995: An empirical study of flexibility in manufacturing, *Sloan Management Review*, **37**(1), 25–32.
13. Upton, D.M., 1994: The management of manufacturing flexibility, *California Management Review*, **36**(2), 72–89.
14. Upton, D.M., 1995: What really makes factories flexible? *Harvard Business Review*, **73**(4), 74–84.
15. Vickery, S.K., Droge, C. and Markland, R.R., 1993: Production competence and business strategy: Do they affect business performance? *Decision Sciences*, **24**(2), 435–456.
16. Ward, P.T., Leong, G.K. and Boyer, K.K., 1994: Manufacturing proactiveness and performance, *Decision Sciences*, **25**(3), 337–358.

Group technology

M – 1b; 2b; 3b; 4b; 5d; 6c; 7b; 8c; * 1.3b; 1.4d; 2.2c; 2.3c; 2.4b; 2.5c; 3.2c; 3.3c; 3.5d; 3.6b

Group technology (GT) is a manufacturing philosophy aimed at increasing productivity in manufacturing of the job-shop type. Group technology started in 1950 with the main objective being to gain the advantages of flow line production (mass production) in batch production.

GT is a method of alleviating problems associated with short-run low-batch-size in job shop work. In the job shop, because of the variety of jobs encountered, and the short number of parts in each run, setup time may be the most significant part of the overall production time.

While conventional methods such as computer integrated manufacturing (CIM) or integrated manufacturing systems (IMS) try to increase productivity by using capacity planning to attack the direct machining time, group technology GT is concerned with the lead time. It is claimed that only 5% of the lead time in producing a part is direct working time, whereas for 95% of the lead time the part waits in the shop. Furthermore, the 5% can be divided into 30% actual machining time and 70% for positioning, chucking, gauging, and so on. Hence, only 1.5% of the lead-time is actual machining time, and GT directs its effort towards reducing lead time by attacking the remaining 98.5%. One way to achieve this is by organizing the plant layout into work cells rather than according to functions. A work cell is a unit that includes all the machines required to produce a family of parts. Raw material enters a cell, and a finished part emerges. The reported success in reducing lead time by this method is very impressive.

The shop usually uses a functional layout of equipment with no interrelation between groups of different functions. Each part takes a confused, unpredictable path through the shop in order to reach all the necessary equipment involved in its processing. Every time the job is moved from one (operation) workstation to the next, there is a delay. Production control becomes extremely complicated and it is almost impossible to get realistic up-to-date information on the production status of any particular job.

With GT work cells, savings will be in transfer time between operations and reduced setup times. The work cell method calls for machine layout according to a component flow analysis, in which a component will enter a work cell and be terminated there. Hence, one work cell might include all machines, fixtures and tooling required to produce a family of parts. A family of parts are parts whose routing requires similar machines and tooling. The batch size for a family of parts will be the sum of all parts of the family, thus increasing the number of parts per setup and reducing the setup time considerably. A group of machines in the work cell are placed near each other, thus drastically reducing the scope of production scheduling and control problems and improving material handling and group morale of the workers.

Tooling and fixtures are designed by using group concepts common to the part family. To use tooling and fixtures to the full, operations must be arranged so that the maximum number of parts in the family can be processed in one setup, which means that jigs accepting all members of the family have to be designed. For example, the design of a master jig with additional adapters is one way of dealing with changes in size, number of location points, etc. As a result of these advantages of group technology, cost reductions in tool design, tooling and equipment, production control, etc. become very significant.

There are many definitions of group technology, and they are continuously changing as the scope of GT changes and as it becomes apparent that some planned activities cannot be accomplished by GT. On the other hand, it is realized that this technology can serve as a solution to additional activities.

One of the first definitions of GT was given by E.K. Ivanov, who stated, *the main goal of GT is to produce a single or small quantity items using mass production techniques.* Ivanov claims a 270% rise in labour productivity and 240% rise in shop output by use of GT.

In 1968 we find the definition of GT: *Group Technology is the technique of identifying and bringing together related or similar parts in a production process in order to utilize the inherent economy of flow production method.*

A more general definition proposes to use GT concepts in other fields. The definition is: *Group Technology is the realization that many problems are similar and that by grouping together similar problems, a single solution can be found to a set of problems, thus saving time and effort.*

Thus the goals and applications of GT are expanded beyond the original requirement of the work cell manufacturing technique, and the broad meaning of Group Technology now covers all areas of the manufacturing process.

Design. Creating a new part design involves the design time, detail drafting time, prototyping, testing, and documentation and certainly drawing maintenance. When the new part design hits manufacturing many things happen. There is advance manufacturing engineering from a central location and possibly at remote plant locations. There is tool design. Tools have to be either made or bought. Time study is involved. Production control has to schedule the part; cost accounting is involved; data processing, purchasing, quality control, N/C programming are all affected – we could go on and on. It is expensive to support new parts. With the GT technique some of these expenditures can be avoided.

The GT concept is to carefully examine the active parts of the company, and create families of products and parts and make them company standards. When a new part is required, before rushing to design, comparisons are made with available parts to decide if one can be used. Experiments show that at least 5% of new required parts can be obtained by using standard parts rather than new designs.

Process planning. Savings in process planning result from using the same process for a family of parts. Examining the actual process plans in a shop usually reveals that for similar parts belonging to the same family, many different processes are on company files. This can be explained by the fact that several process planners were involved in this task, it was made at different times, and many other personal reasons. GT proposes to examine the different process plans and evaluate them in order to find the 'best' process. This process will be the master process plan. It is suitable for a 'virtual' family part. The specific part will retrieve the master process plan and update it to suit the specific part. By applying the master process plan to the available part, immediate improvements and benefits will be achieved. When a new processing technique becomes available, the master process plan will be updated.

Material management and purchasing. The use of a group of materials has led to greater purchasing efficiency, lower stock levels, and savings in procurement. GT using a family of parts may reduce the number of orders through blanket orders and through larger lot sizes. Parts are bought on a 'family of parts' basis. Blanks may be purchased to suit a family of parts and not any specific part. It might increase processing time, but reduces purchasing and inventory expenses, and probably lower blank cost.

Production control. Production planning and control becomes simple, the only decisions to make are which work cell to direct the job to and setting a due date. Work cell personnel are responsible for internal scheduling and quality.

Cost estimating. Determine to which family of parts the new parts belong. Retrieve the cost of the master part cost and perhaps add a factor and arrive at estimated cost. Experience shows that a very accurate cost is determined.

For practical applications of GT it is essential to create part families. A part family is defined as a collection of related parts that are nearly identical or similar. They are related by geometric shapes and/or size and require similar machining operations. Alternatively, they may be dissimilar in shape, but related by having all or some common machining operations. Parts are said to be similar in respect to production techniques when the type, sequence and number of operations are similar. This similarity is therefore related to the basic shape of the parts or to a number of shape elements contained within the part shape. The type of operation is determined by the methods of machining, the method of holding the part and the tooling required.

The benefits of a good family-forming method in connection with GT can be summarized as follows:

1. Quick retrieval of designs drawings and production plans.
2. Design rationalization and reduction of design costs.
3. Secure reliable workpiece statistics.
4. Accurate estimation of resource requirements.
5. Reduction of setup time and overall processing time.
6. Improvement of tool design and reduction of tool design time and cost, and processing time.
7. Rationalization of production planning procedures and scheduling.
8. Accurate cost accounting and cost estimating.
9. Better utilization of processing resources.

The general manufacturing philosophy of group technology is accepted, although it was practised under different names, or without any label whatever, even before receiving formal recognition. In order to practise group technology as a systematic scientific technology, tools for the identification of the family groups must be prepared. There are three basic methods to form part families, namely:

  (i) manual – walk around the shop and look;
 (ii) production flow analysis;
(iii) classification and coding systems.

Many of the reports on successful group technology applications have come from studies in which the main work on the manufacturing concept was done with families of parts that had been organized manually. Engineers have tended to view each part produced in the company and make a human decision, relying on their memory and on the flexibility of the human mind. Therefore, this method is excellent for small companies, where the human mind might remember all the parts produced in the company.

Production flow analysis is a technique used to analyse the operating sequence and the routing of components through the machines in the plant. Parts with common operations and routes are grouped and identified as a manufacturing part family. Similarly, the machines used to produce the part family can be grouped to form the machines group cell. It should be assumed that the majority of parts in the company belong to clearly defined families and the machines to clearly defined groups. One of the advantages of this method is that it uses the data from operation sheets or route cards instead of part drawings. That is also the disadvantage. Several mathematical algorithms have been developed to compute the family of parts, usually based on Boolean algebra and quite simple in concept.

Industrial classification is a technique for arranging the individual parts comprising any aspect of a business in a logical and systematical hierarchy whereby like things are brought together by virtue of their similarities, and then separated by their essential differences.

There are a number of approaches to the formation of classification systems. Each approach offers some advantages or disadvantages over the others. The coding is done by collecting together drawings and associated production data on one hand and the classification system on the other.

Forming a good classification system is quite a problem, and there are many companies that specialize in this field. Classification systems can be categorized as design oriented, production oriented or resource oriented. Each one calls for different characteristics. Design oriented schemes require that a retrieval request draw only a limited number of drawings. Otherwise the engineer will prefer to design the required part rather than compare many existing drawings with the hope that one might suit. On the other hand, the production oriented technique requires retrieval of as many parts as possible.

The success of any group technology system depends on the ability to form the family of parts.

Bibliography

1. Askin, R.G. and Chiu, K.S., 1990: A graph partitioning procedure for machine assignment and cell formation in group technology, *International Journal of Production Research*, **28**, 1555–1572.
2. Askin, R.G., Cresswell, J.B., Goldberg, S.H. and Vakharia, A.G., 1991: A Hamiltonian path approach to reordering the part–machine matrix for cellular manufacturing, *International Journal of Production Research*, **29**, 1081–1110.
3. Askin, R.G. and Subramainian, S.P., 1987: A cost-based heuristic for group technology configuration, *International Journal of Production Research*, **25**, 101–113.
4. Burbidge, J., 1971: Production flow analysis, *The Production Engineer*, **50**, 139–152.
5. Burbidge, J., 1975: *Introduction to Group Technology*. Wiley, New York.
6. Burbidge, J., 1975: *Production Flow Analysis for Planning Group Technology*. Oxford University Press, Oxford.
7. Carrie, A.S., 1973: Numerical taxonomy applied to group technology and plant layout, *International Journal of Production Research*, **11**, 399–416.
8. Chan, H.M. and Milnrer, D.A., 1982: Direct clustering algorithm for group formation in cellular manufacturing, *Journal of Manufacturing Systems*, **1**, 65–75.
9. Chandrasekharan, M.P. and Rajagopalan, R., 1986: An ideal seed non-hierarchical clustering algorithm for cellular manufacturing, *International Journal of Production Research*, **24**, 451–464.
10. Chandrasekharan, M.P. and Rajagopalan, R., 1986: MODROC – an extension of rank order clustering for group technology, *International Journal of Production Research*, **24**, 1221–1233.
11. Chandrasekharan, M.P. and Rajagopalan, R., 1987: MODROC – an algorithm for concurrent formulation of part-families and machine-cells, *International Journal of Production Research*, **25**, 835–850.

12. Chandrasekharan, M.P. and Rajagopalan, R., 1989: Groupability: an analysis of properties of binary data matrices for group technology, *International Journal of Production Research*, **27**, 1035–1052.
13. De Witte, J., 1980: The uses of similarity coefficients in production flow analysis, *International Journal of Production Research*, **18**, 503–514.
14. Gallagher, C.C. and Knight, W.A., 1987: *Group Technology Production Methods in Manufacturing*. Ellis Horwood.
15. Harhalakis, G., Nagi, R. and Porth, J.M., 1990: An efficient heuristic in manufacturing cell formation for group technology applications, *International Journal of Production Research*, **28**, 185–198.
16. King, J.R., 1986: Machine components grouping in production flow analysis: an approach using a rank order clustering algorithm, *International Journal of Production Research*, **18**, 213–232.
17. Kusiak, A., 1987: The general group technology concept, *International Journal of Production Research*, **25**, 561–569.
18. Kusiak, A. and Chow, W.S., 1987: Effective solving of group technology problem, *Journal of Manufacturing Systems*, **6**, 117–124.
19. Raja Gunasingh, K. and Lasshkari, R.S., 1989: Machine grouping problem in cellular manufacturing systems – an integer programming approach, *International Journal of Production Research*, **27**, 1465–1473.
20. Rajamani, D., Singh, N. and Aneja, Y.P., 1990: Integrated design of cellular manufacturing system in the presence of alternative process plans, *International Journal of Production Research*, **28**, 1541–1554.
21. Vakharia, A.J. and Wemmerlov, U., 1990: Designing a cellular manufacturing systems: a material flow approach based on operation sequences, *IIE Transactions*, **22**, 84–97.

Holonic manufacturing systems (HMS)

P – 1c; 2c; 3d; 4c; 8d; 9d; 13c; 14c; 16c; * 1.3b; 1.4c; 2.4c; 3.3b; 3.5c; 3.6c; 4.4c; 4.6c

Holonic manufacturing systems are designed to solve the shop floor control problem and have an architecture made up of totally distributed independent autonomous modules that cooperate intelligently to create a future manufacturing system that responds to apparently future manufacturing needs. The needs are specified as:

- produce by autonomous modules (50% of production lines);
- reduction of workforce (by 40%);
- modular design that assures integration;
- inexpensive construction of production lines (reduction of 70–80% of investment);
- meeting customers needs;
- fast adjustment to market fluctuations.

The word 'holon' comes from the Greek word 'holos' – which means perfection – plus the suffix 'on' to represent a particle such as neutron or proton.

Holons are the building blocks of HMS. Each holon may change, transfer, store, or validate information regarding information or physical objects. A holon is part of information processing and part of product processing. Each holon can stand alone or be part of a holonic manufacturing system. The HMS is organized in an oligarchy hierarchy (holarchy) that defines the cooperation rules and the authority of each holon. The definitions are dynamic and may be changed during the manufacturing process. This is the main difference between HMS and the agents driven approach. The autonomy of the holon does not mean that humans cannot be an integral part of the holon. Holons are autonomous but unite in order to adjust themselves to the common objective, which is called 'reconfigurability'. Each holon continuously checks its objective and interaction with other holons, and if required merges temporarily with another holon. This is analogous to traffic control. Each vehicle is autonomous on the road, but must obey traffic regulations.

The traditional approach to the design of manufacturing systems is the hierarchical approach. The design is based on a top-down approach and strictly defines the system modules and their functionality. Communication between modules is strictly defined and limited in such a way that modules communicate with their parent and child modules only. In a hierarchical architecture, modules cannot take an initiative; therefore, the system is sensitive to perturbations, and its autonomy and reactivity to disturbances are weak. The resulting architecture is very rigid and therefore expensive to develop and difficult to maintain.

Heterarchical control was an approach taken to alleviate the problems of hierarchical systems. The heterarchical approach bans all hierarchy in order to give full power to the basic modules, often called 'agents', in the system. A heterarchical manufacturing system consists of, for instance, workstations and orders only. Each order negotiates with the workstations to get the work done, using all possible alternatives available to face unforeseen situations. This way, it is possible to react adequately to changes in the environment (such as new products that enter the market, new or evolving technologies, unpredictable demands for products) as well as to disturbances in the manufacturing system itself (defects, delays, variable yield of chemical reactors).

A heterarchical system is very hard to operate according to a predefined plan, so predictability is very low. Heterarchical control typically works well in simple environments, for instance a shop floor comprised of identical workstations and with spare capacity.

Holonic control tries to combine the advantages of both hierarchical and heterarchical control while avoiding their drawbacks. To avoid the rigid architecture of hierarchical systems, holonic manufacturing systems provide autonomy ('freedom of decision making') to the individual modules (holons). This provides the system with a fast response to disturbances and the ability to reconfigure itself to face new requirements. It also allows integration of the system modules in a wider range of manufacturing systems.

Compared to holonic control, heterarchical control systems lack controllability and may suffer from unpredictable system performance. This is caused by the banning of all hierarchy, while hierarchy is an essential tool to master complexity. Therefore, holonic manufacturing systems do have hierarchy, but this hierarchy is flexible, or 'loose'. This hierarchy differs from the traditional hierarchical control in that holons can belong to multiple hierarchies, and holons can form temporary hierarchies, and holons do not rely on the proper operation of each holon in the hierarchy to get their work done.

Holonic systems originate from a philosophical theory on the creation and evolution of complex adaptive systems (such as, social systems, evolutionary theory). Since philosophers do not only observe phenomena but also try to explain them, holonic manufacturing may have more solid foundations than many of its challengers.

The basic building blocks of a holonic manufacturing system are order holons, product holons, and resource holons. Using object-oriented design principles such as aggregation and specialization, structure is created in this large pool of heterogeneous holons. Typical holons resulting from this structuring activity are the workstation holon and the transport system holon (a fleet manager for transport resources). With basic building blocks, aggregated or not, control of the HMS is still completely heterarchical. Holonic manufacturing, however, stands for more than object-oriented, multi-agent systems. To introduce a flexible control hierarchy in the HMS, staff function holons are introduced, giving advice to the basic building block holons. This results in the definition of more central scheduling holons, online shop floor control holons, process sequencing holons, CAD holons, and so on. The entire holarchy consists of two sub-holarchies: a resource allocation holarchy and a process planning and execution holarchy.

The construction of a working holonic manufacturing system should follow several phases. In the first phase identification of all appropriate holons and the definition of their responsibilities should result. In comparison with traditional design methodologies, each holon is assigned a general responsibility rather than a precise function. This enforces the designer of the individual holon to explicitly design the holon for reusability in a vaguely defined situation. The designer therefore really has to think bottom-up instead of relying on former design decisions, as would be the case in a top-down design methodology. The identification of manufacturing holons should be carried out by suppliers of information technology for the holonic manufacturing system, as well as by the company installing the holonic manufacturing system. The software suppliers should know which holons to develop, while the user of the HMS needs to know which holons to buy or eventually develop.

In the second phase, the holons are designed and implemented in a bottom-up way. Their design should explicitly aim at reusability over several architectures and, if developed by a vendor, even reusability in different manufacturing systems. This design should preserve the flexibility of the architecture, such that architectural changes can be made on a daily basis. Here, the focus is on autonomy and a capability to cooperate.

In the third phase, the complete manufacturing system is built from its components in a stepwise way. Once the necessary holons are identified and developed or acquired, the configuration of the system should be straightforward. To a large extent, the holonic manufacturing system should be self-configuring, as in bionic manufacturing. However, it should remain possible for humans to influence, overrule, and control the automatic self-configuration because the intelligence, intuition, and expertise of the people in the factory can seldom be exceeded by automated procedures.

The fourth phase of the development is a continuous improvement process where holons may be added or replaced, and where the configuration can continuously be changed to accommodate changing requirements, to react to disturbances, and to have the system evolve together with new developments in technology.

Research on holonic manufacturing is quite new, and only a few implementations have been reported in the literature up to now. Even for these few existing implementations, it is not trivial to evaluate their performance. Some implementations can prove how close their performance is to the optimal value. (The same is true for their centralized scheduling algorithms.) It remains difficult, however, to fairly compare the results of different approaches because of the wide range of production layouts and input parameters.

A more fundamental problem with these experiments is that they show the performance of the control algorithms rather than the quality of the architecture. For the evaluation of architecture, other criteria are more relevant, such as completeness, genericity, ease of use, and flexibility. The goal of a holonic manufacturing architecture is to be reconfigurable and adaptable to the changing needs of the manufacturing system. Therefore, the architecture is designed to be flexible and able to accommodate all control algorithms encountered in holonic manufacturing. There is still a lot of work to be done on the evaluation of architectures.

Bibliography

1. Bongaerts, L., Valckenaers, P., Van Brussel, H. and Peeters, P., 1997: Schedule execution in holonic manufacturing systems. In *Proceedings of 29th CIRP International Seminar on Manufacturing Systems*, May 11–13, Osaka University, Japan, pp. 209–215.
2. Bongaerts, L., Van Brussel, H., Valckenaers, P. and Peeters, P., 1997: Reactive scheduling in holonic manufacturing systems: architecture, dynamic model and cooperation strategy. In *Proceedings of ASI 97, Esprit Network of Excellence on Intelligent Control and Integrated Manufacturing Systems*, Budapest, pp. 14–17.

 3. Christensen, J., 1997: Holonic manufacturing systems – initial architecture and standard directions. In *Proceedings of Ist European Conference on Holonic Manufacturing Systems*, I Dec., Hannover, Germany, pp. 235–249.
 4. Detand, J., Valckenaers, P., Van Brussel, H. and Kruth, J.P., 1996: Holonic manufacturing systems research at PMA-K.U.Leuven. In *Proceedings of PCM96, Pacific Conference on Manufacturing* (Vol. II), 29–31 Oct., Seoul, Korea (Korea Association of Machinery Industry), pp 131–140.
 5. Dilts, D.M., Boyd, N.P. and Whorms, H.H., 1991: The evolution of control architectures for automated manufacturing systems, *Journal of Manufacturing Systems*, 10(1), 79–93.
 6. Hasegawa, T., Gou, L., Tamura, S., Luh, P.B. and Oblak, J.M., 1994: Holonic planning and scheduling architecture for manufacturing. *Proceedings of International Conference on Cooperating Knowledge-Based Systems*, June.
 7. Iwata, K. and Onosato, M., 1994: Random manufacturing system: a new concept of manufacturing systems for production to order, *Annals of the CIRP*, 43(1), 379–384.
 8. Jones, A.T. and McLean, C.R., 1986: A proposed hierarchical control model for automated manufacturing systems, *Journal of Manufacturing Systems*, 5(1), 15–26.
 9. Kadar, L., Monostori and Szelke, E., 1997: An object oriented framework for developing distributed manufacturing architectures. In *Proceedings of 2nd World Congress on Intelligent Manufacturing Processes and Systems*, June 10–13, Budapest, Hungary, pp. 548–554.
10. Kruth, J.P., Detand, J., Tanaya, P.I., Van Ginderachter, T. and Wyns, J., 1996: An NC holon architecture. In *CNMU96, Machine Tool National Conference*, 24–25, Bucharest, Romania.
11. McFarlane, D.C., 1995: Holonic manufacturing systems in continuous processing: concepts and control requirements. In *Preprints of the Advanced Summer Institute (ASI) 95 of the N.O.E. on Intelligent Control of Integrated Manufacturing Systems*, Lisboa, Portugal, pp. 25–28.
12. Senehi, M.K., Kramer, Th.R., Ray, S.R., Quintero, R. and Albus, J.S., 1994: Hierarchical control architectures from shop level to end effectors. In S.B. Joshi and I.S. Smith (eds), *Computer Control of Flexible Manufacturing Systems, Research and Development*. Chapman & Hall, New York, Chapter 2, pp. 31–62.
13. Simon, H.A., 1990: *The Science of the Artificial*, 2nd edn. MIT Press, Cambridge, MA.
14. Sousa, P. and Ramos, C., 1997: A dynamic scheduling holon for manufacturing orders. In *Proceedings of 2nd World Congress on Intelligent Manufacturing Processes and Systems*, June 10–13, Budapest, Hungary, pp. 542–547.
15. Sugimura, N., Tanimizu, Y. and Yoshioka, T., 1997: A study on object-oriented modeling of holonic manufacturing system. In *Proceedings of 29th CIRP International Seminar on Manufacturing Systems*, Osaka, Japan, May 11–13, pp. 215–220.
16. Tharumarajah and Wells, A.J., 1997: A behavior-based approach to scheduling in distributed manufacturing systems, *Integrated Computer Aided Engineeing*, 4(4), 235–249.
17. Tharumarajah, A. Wells, A.J. and Nemes, L., 1996: Comparison of bionic, fractal and holonic manufacturing system concepts, *International Journal of Computer Integrated Manufacturing*, 9(3), 217–226.
18. Ueda, K., 1992: An approach to bionic manufacturing systems based on DNA-type information. In *Proceedings of ICOOMS '92*, pp. 303–308.

19. Ueda, K., 1993: A genetic approach toward future manufacturing systems. In J. Peklenik (ed.), *Flexible Manufacturing Systems, Past, Present, Future*, Ljubljana, Slovenia, pp. 221–228.
20. Valckenaers, P., Van Brussel, H., Bongaerts, L. and Wyns, J., 1997: Holonic manufacturing systems, *Journal of Integrated Computer-Aided Engineering*, **4**(3), 191–201.
21. Valckenaers, P., Bonneville, E., Van Brussel, H., Bongaerts, L. and Wyns, J., 1994: Results of the holonic control system benchmark at the K.U.Leuven. In *Proceedings of CIMAT Conference (Computer Integrated Manufacturing and Automation Technology)*, Troy, NY, 10–12 Oct., pp. 128–133.
22. Valckenaers, P., Bongaerts, L. and Wyns, J., 1996: Planning systems in the next century (II). In *Proceedings of Advanced Summer Institute (ASI) 96 of the N.O.E. on Intelligent Control of Integrated Manufacturing Systems*, Toulouse, France, 2–6 June, pp. 289–295.
23. Valckenaers, P., Van Brussel, H., Bongaerts, L. and Bonneville, E., 1995: Programming, scheduling, and control of flexible assembly systems, *Computers in Industry* (special issue on CIMIA), **26**(3), 209–218.
24. Van Brussel, H., 1994: Holonic manufacturing systems, the vision matching the problem. In *Proceedings of Ist European Conference on Holonic Manufacturing Systems*, 1 Dec., Hannover, Germany.
25. Wyns, J., Van Brussel, H., Valckenaers, P. and Bongaerts, L., 1996: Workstation architecture in holonic manufacturing systems. In *Proceedings of 28th CIRP International Seminar on Manufacturing Systems*, May 15–17, Johannesburg, South Africa, pp. 220–231.

Horizontal organization

P – 2b; 3b; 4d; 7c; 8c; 9c; 13c; 14c; * 1.1b; 1.2c; 1.3c; 1.5c; 3.2c; 3.3b; 4.2b; 4.3d; 4.4c
See Flat organization.

House of quality (HOQ)

M – 3b; 5c; 8c; 9b; * 1.3c; 1.5d; 2.2b; 2.5d; 2.6c; 3.1b; 3.2d; 3.4c
See Quality function deployment – QFD

Human resource management – HRM

M – 8d; 12b; * 1.1b; 1.2c; 1.4b; 4.2d; 4.5b
The aim of human resource management is to improve management–employee relationships upon such issues as communications, empowerment, and commitment. The objective of human resource management is to enable

employees to perform their job with a smile, and to maintain their enthusiasm. This is the most important issue, then come communications skills and then technical skills. HRM is a genuine attempt to increase commitment through high involvement. Human resource management provides choices and opportunities for quality and culture change programmes that have a perceived impact on performance and productivity. HRM cannot match up to unrealistic expectations, even with middle and senior managers believing change programmes have a massive effect.

The social and psychological needs of workers – a central part of the human relations tradition – play a secondary role to the indicators that managers feel will improve organizational performance, although there is some necessary overlap.

Management objectives in introducing human resource management policies are diverse and complex and we should be careful not to overestimate the influence of employee control in shaping management strategies. HRM does not really reinvent individuals, the claim that this is the primary aim of HRM policies is pure rhetoric and appears overstated. On balance, employees are critical of the changes that actually occur although they welcome some of the changes in principle.

Managers apply contradictory HRM policies with the result that employee attitudes toward their companies do not fundamentally change. The main contradiction is in the simultaneous application of policies aimed at 'hard' results and 'soft' employee development.

An inconsistent mix of policies that incorporate poor design, employee expectations, workplace climate, and competing management priorities negatively affects employee attitudes toward human resource management. Employees are more likely to feel that the gap between the high and low paid at their workplace is too large, that management and employee relations are poor, that their jobs are insecure, that their workplaces are not being managed as well as they could be, and that they do not have much say over how their work is organized. Given these reports, it is surprising that there are no underlying trends towards voluntarily leaving jobs, no falls in work commitment, and little apparent change in the attitudes of workers towards their unions and organizations. Employees appear to 'love the work but hate the job'.

Human resource management aims to concentrate on the voice of employees as representing reality. Employee views enable discrimination between practices that sustain HRM and those that negate HRM, providing insights into why policies stand or fall. The inside story represents a realist ontological aim of workers' first-hand accounts as the prime arbiters or consumers of HRM. This is an important aim given a remarkable lack of congruence in some studies between employers' and employees' perceptions of basic facts. As employees bear the burden of adjustment under HRM programmes and reinventing individuals is a primary espoused focus of HRM, the inside story provides criteria to assess the impact of HRM where it is targeted. Reinventing individuals involves employees internalizing a new set of values as defined by management.

Several authors when experiencing human resource management point the way by drawing upon theories with differing levels of specificity, including negotiations at the frontier of job controls, expectancy theory, trust, and the reorganization of control. Where the focus is upon psychological issues, research also needs to be grounded in a deeper understanding of the measurement and conceptual issues frequently discussed in HRM.

Experiencing HRM could have an encouraging and moral impact on employees. Without doubt, the notions of 'poor work', and good and bad jobs are key concepts in capturing developments in both new and neglected workplaces and also in traditional industries. Although defining a good job faces conceptual difficulties, such a focus could combine the need to establish moral criteria for assessing changes with allowing employees an input into defining the measures that they value in jobs. Ethical considerations encompassing the areas of justice, morals, and standards have largely been ignored.

Bibliography

1. Allen, S., 1997: What is work for? The right to work and the right to be idle. In R. Brown (ed.), The Changing Shape of Work. Macmillan, London, pp. 54–68.
2. Becker, B. and Gerhart, B., 1996: The impact of human resource management on organizational performance: Progress and prospects, *Academy of Management Journal*, **39**, 770–801.
3. Beynon, H., 1997: The changing practices of work. In R. Brown (ed.), *The Changing Shape of Work*. Macmillan, London, pp. 20–53.
4. Blyton, P. and Turnbull, P., 1992: HRM: Debates, dilemmas and contradictions. In P. Blyton and P. Turnbull (eds), *Reassessing Human Resource Management*. Sage, London, pp. 1–15.
5. Bryson, A. and McKay, S., 1997: What about the workers'? In R. Jowell, J. Curtice, A. Park, L. Brook, K. Thomson, and C. Bryson (eds), *British Social Attitudes, the 14th Report: The End of Conservative Values*? Ashgate, Aldershot, pp. 23–48.
6. Burchell, B., Elliott, J., Rubery, J. and Wilkinson, F., 1994: Management and employee perceptions of skill. In R. Penn, M. Rose, and J. Rubery (eds), *Skill and Occupational Change*, Oxford University Press, Oxford, pp. 159–189.
7. Dickens, L., 1998: What HRM means for gender equality, *Human Resource Management Journal*, **8**, 23–40.
8. Ezzamel, M., Lilley, S., Wilkinson, A. and Willmott H., 1996: Practices and practicalities in HRM, *Human Resource Management Journal*, **6**, 63–80.
9. Fineman, S. and Gabriel, Y., 1996: *Experiencing Organizations*. Sage, London.
10. Guest, D. and Dewe, P., 1991: Company or trade union; which wins workers' allegiance? A study of commitment in the United Kingdom electronics industry, *British Journal of Industrial Relations*, **29**, 75–96.

11. Harper Simpson, I., 1989: The sociology of work: where have the workers gone? *Social Forces*, **67**, 563–581.
12. Harris, L. and Ogbonna, E., 1998: Employee responses to culture change efforts, *Human Resource Management Journal*, **8**, 78–92.
13. Hart, T., 1993: Human resource management: time to exercise the militant tendency, *Employee Relations*, **15**, 29–36.
14. Kamoche, K., 1995: Rhetoric, ritualism, and totemism in human resource management, *Human Relations*, **48**, 367–385.
15. Kelly, J. and Kelly, C., 1991: 'Them and us': social psychology and 'the new industrial relations', *British Journal of Industrial Relations*, **29**, 25–48.
16. Legge, K., 1995: Human Resource Management: *Rhetorics and Realities*. MacMillan, Houndsmill.
17. Miller, P., 1996: Strategy and the ethical management of human resources, *Human Resource Management Journal*, **6**, 5–18.
18. Noon, M. and Blyton, P., 1997: *The Realities of Work*. MacMillan, Houndsmill.
19. Pahl, R., 1995: *After Success*. Polity Press, Cambridge.
20. Patterson, M., West M., Lawthom, R. and Nickell, S., 1997: Impact of people management practices on business performance. In *Issues in People Management, No 22*. Institute of Personnel and Development, London. (Business ethics and HRM, Personnel).
21. Purcell, J., 1995: Corporate strategy and its links with human resource management strategy. In J. Storey (ed.), *Human Resource Management: A Critical Text*. Routledge, London, pp. 63–86.
22. Rosenthal, P., Hill, S. and Peccei, R., 1997: Checking out service: Evaluating excellence, HRM and TQM in retailing, *Work, Employment and Society*, **II**, 481–503.
23. Rubery, J., 1995: Performance-related pay and the prospects for gender pay equality, *Journal of Management Studies*, **32**, 637–654.
24. Sisson, K., 1993: In search of HRM, *British Journal of Industrial Relations*, **31**, 201–210.
25. Tilly, C., 1997: Arresting the decline of good jobs in the USA? *Industrial Relations Journal*, **28**, 269–274.
26. Thompson, P. and Ackroyd, S., 1995: All quiet on the workplace front? A critique of recent trends in British industrial sociology, *Sociology*, **29**, 615–633.
27. Undy, R. and Kessler, I., 1995: The new employment relationship: Examining the psychological contract. In *Issues in People Management No. 12*. Institute of Personnel and Development, London.
28. Waddington, J. and Whitston, D., 1997: Why do people join unions in a period of membership decline? *British Journal of Industrial Relations*, **35**, 515–546.
29. Wood, S. and De Menezes, L., 1998: High commitment management in the U.K.: Evidence from the workplace industrial Relations Survey, and Employers' Manpower and Skills Practices Survey, *Human Relations*, **51**, 485–515.
30. Worrall, L. and Cooper, C., 1997: *The Quality of Working Life: 1997 Survey of Managers Changing Experiences*. London, Institute of Management.
31. Wrench, J. and Verdee, S., 1996: Organising the unorganised: 'Race', poor work and trade unions. In P. Ackers, C. Smith and P. Smith (eds), *The New Workplace and Trade Unionism*. Routledge, London, pp. 240–278.

Integrated manufacturing system – IMS

M – 1b; 2b; 4c; 6c; 7b; 10d; 13c; * 1.2c; 1.3b; 1.4d; 1.6d; 2.3b; 3.3d; 3.5b; 4.2c; 4.3d

The integrated manufacturing system (IMS) is a system that recognizes and supplies computer services to each phase of the manufacturing cycle independently while at the same time maintaining a database that serves as a single source of data for all company activities and applications. Basic data are maintained in current and accurate condition so that information can be provided on demand.

The manufacturing cycle can be divided into several main phases. Each phase consists of a continuous chain of activities. The main phases are: engineering design; process planning; customers and orders; master production scheduling; material requirement planning; capacity planning; shop floor control; and purchasing.

The IMS must encompass almost all of the above activities, but no single profession has been trained to handle them as a system. Data processing personnel are qualified to handle such computer-related technical problems as database organization, but they are not qualified to handle the application aspect, and neither are mechanical, industrial nor production engineers.

It is very difficult to implement a database IMS. It is a system that involves both materials and people. Therefore, the active involvement of management is mandatory for the successful implementation of the IMS. In addition, IMS reliability is a necessary requirement, since errors could result in irreversible damage.

The integrated manufacturing system is a computerized system based on:

1. General data processing concepts.
2. Specific manufacturing concepts.

The following general data processing concepts are self-explanatory:

1.1 The system should be management-oriented, and not data processing oriented.
1.2 The system should be adaptable to changes, responsive and economical.
1.3 The system should be reliable.
1.4 The system should reduce paperwork.
1.5 The system should be realistic and consider the environment in which it operates.

The specific manufacturing concepts are as shown below.

2.1 In manufacturing processing the computer should have the role of performing tasks and not merely constitute an information centre.

2.2   Let humans define the strategy for a solution, and let the computer perform it precisely.

2.3   Whenever possible a computer should be employed in decision-making.

2.4   Tasks and decisions in engineering design, process planning, and methods, time, and motion study phases cannot be performed by a computer alone and unattended.

2.5   A computer should be used to make decisions in the production phases of the manufacturing process.

2.6   An integrated manufacturing control system should be used.

2.7   The outcome of the engineering phases, bill of materials, and routing will be the starting point for the integrated manufacturing control system.

2.8   Problems should be looked at from a system point of view and not in isolation.

2.9   The integrated database system should capture data and information from the lowest source level available.

2.10   Management and finance systems should be extensions of the engineering and production systems.

One of the most important novelties of an integrated manufacturing system is the introduction of material requirements planning (MRP). The master production schedule sets goals for the production phases of the manufacturing cycle. It specifies what products are to be produced, the quantities, and the delivery dates. Production activities are dependent on the master production schedule; hence, they can be planned and are predictable. Production activities includes plant shop manufacturing as well as subcontracting operations to other shops, purchased items, subassemblies, assemblies and raw material from external sources. At any point in time numerous activities are under way in a working plant. There are open shop orders, open purchased and subcontract orders, and items in storage between operations and activities. All of these activities must be considered when converting the master production schedule into production activities.

A working plant is a dynamic environment, subject to many changes and unplanned interruptions, which may lead to the accumulation of unrequired stock; these changes and interruptions might include:

1. customer orders being added or deleted; quantities and delivery dates being altered;
2. purchasing being restricted by package size, economic consideration, lot size, and change in delivery dates;
3. interruptions in the shop causing early or late finish of jobs or reject rate being higher or lower than anticipated. These will cause imbalance in the quantities of different items required for assembly, the controlling item being the one available in the smallest quantity; excess units of the other items are left over after assembly.

All these factors lead to the accumulation of stock. This stock can often be utilized later in manufacturing.

The objective of material requirements planning is to plan the activities to be performed in order to meet the goals of the master production schedule.

MRP is not a new concept, having previously gone under such different names as items balance sheet, activity planning, inventory management, and requirement planning. The logic and mathematics upon which MRP is based are very simple. The gross requirement of the end product for each specific delivery is compared against on-hand and on-order quantities and then offset by the lead time to generate information detailing when assembly should be started. All items or subassemblies required for the assembly should be available on that date, in the required quantity. Thus, the above computation establishes the gross requirement for the lower level items. The same computation is repeated level by level throughout the entire product structure.

Bibliography

1. Aguiar, M., Wilson, C. and Edwards John, M., 1999: Achieving manufacturing business integration through the combined formalisms of CIMOSA and Petri nets, *International Journal of Production Research*, **37**(8), 1767–1786.
2. Chaturvedi, S. and Allada, V., 1999: Integrated manufacturing system for precision press tooling, *International Journal of Advanced Manufacturing Technology*, **15**(5), 356–365.
3. Cichang-Chen, 1998: Computer integrated manufacturing system for pump. In *Proceedings of the International Conference on Pumps and Fans, ICPF*. Tsinghua University Press, Beijing, China, pp. 103–109.
4. De Souza, Ying-Zhao-Zhen and Yang-Liu-Chao, 1998: Modelling business processes and enterprise activities at the knowledge level, *Artificial Intelligence for Engineering Design, Analysis and Manufacturing: AIEDAM*, **12**(1), 29–42.
5. Fischer, K., 1999: Agent-based design of holonic manufacturing systems, *Robotics and Autonomous Systems*, **27**(1), 3–13.
6. Halevi, G., 1980: The Role of Computers in Manufacturing Process. John-Wiley & Sons.
7. Kang Hee Won, Kim Jong Woo and Park Sung Joo, 1998: Integrated modeling framework for manufacturing systems: A unified representation of the physical process and information system. *International Journal of Flexible Manufacturing Systems*, **10**(3), 231–265.
8. Li, G., Yin, C. and Zheng, H., 1998: Information integration technology in CIMS. In *Proceedings of the 1997 IEEE International Conference on Intelligent Processing Systems, ICIPS '97*, Beijing, China, **1**, 833–837.
9. Nagata Yoichi, Lew Boon Kee, Shimizu Hidetaka, Ye Ning, Koshimitsu Hirokazu and Shibuya Yuki, 1998: Client-server based computer integrated manufacturing system for an epoxy molding compound plant. In *Proceedings of the 1998 24th Annual Conference of the IEEE Industrial Electronics Society, IECON. Part 1 (of 4). Aachen, Germany. IECON Proceedings (Industrial Electronics Conference), vol. 1 1998, IEEE Computer Society*, Los Alamitos, CA, pp. 182–186.

10. Sheu Jinn Jong, 1998: Computer integrated manufacturing system for rotational parts, *International Journal of Computer Integrated Manufacturing*, **11**(6), 534–547.
11. Tseng, H.C., Ip, W.H. and Ng, K.C., 1999: Model for an integrated manufacturing system implementation in China: a case study, *Journal of Engineering and Technology Management, JET M*, **16**(1), 83–101.
12. Xie, M., Goh, T.N. and Lu, X.S., 1997: Computer-aided statistical monitoring of automated manufacturing processes, *Computers and Industrial Engineering*, **35**(1–2), 189–192.

Intelligent manufacturing system (IMS)

P – 2c; 3b; 4c; 7b; 8b; 9b; 11c; 13b; 1.1b; 1.5c; 1.6b; * 2.x c; 3.x c; 4.x c

The objective of an intelligent manufacturing system is to develop and integrate the best ideas on advanced manufacturing systems into the next generation manufacturing system.

An intelligent manufacturing system is a system which takes intellectual activities in the manufacturing sector and uses them to better fuse men and intelligent machines, integrating the entire range of corporate activities – from order booking through design, production and marketing – in a flexible manner which leads to improved productivity.

An intelligent manufacturing system has to support the next generation of manufacturing enterprises, so called 'virtual enterprises' which will consist of a global distributed assembly of autonomous work units linked primarily by the goal of profitably serving specific customers and operating in an environment of abrupt, often unpredictable change.

An intelligent manufacturing system programme is an international partnership formed to propose and conduct pre-competitive research and development projects. It must develop a framework for ensuring the integration of results into a cost-effective intelligent manufacturing system, and develop on-line facilities for tracking advanced technologies and advanced materials that will be used in and by the intelligent manufacturing system (in gauging their readiness application) to compare it with their present technologies. After pilot testing by the intelligent manufacturing system programme partners, these facilities will be made more openly available. An integrated set of models is developed and simulations are used to merge a bottom-up view of the factory floor (as it will be observed by the intelligent manufacturing system) with a top-down view of the globally distributed 'virtual enterprises' that will constitute the tested intelligent manufacturing system.

The intelligent manufacturing system arose from recent changes in the social environment which have caused a number of issues to surface which threaten to undermine the very existence of manufacturing industries in advanced manufacturing nations. Intelligent manufacturing system technology needs to be established in order to solve the following problems.

1. *Change in the labour environment.* Moves away from manufacturing as more and more people do not want jobs in tertiary industries has resulted in a shortage of skills and trained labour; also the workforce is older and better educated. Demands for shorter working hours and more enjoyable work are also increasing.
2. *The appearance of isolated islands of automation in the workplace.* Automation is pursued on a process-by-process basis, which results in a lack of standardized interfaces for various machine tools and industrial robots, making it hard to develop networks.
3. *The globalization of manufacturing.* In recent years, there have been numerous cases of manufacturing industries in advanced, industrialized nations, going beyond national boundaries to set up in each other's territory. Unfortunately, the differences between countries in technology, their lack of unified technical standards and their differences in human interfaces all hamper the development of more effective production systems.
4. *Insufficient systematization of existing technology.* The best of production technology held by advanced, industrialized nations has yet to be given sufficient academic systemization or to be sufficiently covered in databases, especially from the point of view of technological transfer.
5. *Diversifying consumer needs.* Changes in consumer lifestyle in Western countries have led to more individualism, and a shift from mass-produced goods to customized products. Manufacturing is currently unable to supply products that fit the wants of individual consumers either quickly enough or cheaply enough.
6. *Hollowing out of industry and declining production technology.* More and more companies are taking their production technology and systems, and moving them wholesale overseas in search of cheaper labour. Rather than being an effective form of technology transfer, it is feared that this merely means a decline in production technology itself, or maybe even the loss of it.

It was decided to make the intelligent manufacturing system a joint international research and development project funded by Japan, Europe and the USA, for the following reasons.

1. *To avoid redundant investment of development resources.* Redundant development expenditures can be avoided and human resources can be used more effectively if areas in which standardization and common technology can be effected are developed jointly.
2. *To develop better technology.* New technology following on from current trends can be developed if each country pools its areas of technical expertise and research specialties.
3. *To develop a common international understanding regarding production technology.* The establishment of basic production technology is a prerequisite

to the independence and development of any country's economy. Intelligent manufacturing systems will make it possible to develop a common international understanding that this technology should be considered an asset shared by all mankind.

The following research and development projects will be undertaken in order to establish intelligent manufacturing system technology.

Existing technology will be integrated and systematized.
Existing and next-generation production technology will be standardized.
New, high-tech production systems will be developed.

Examples of research and developments topics are listed below.

1. Production system development technologies:
   1.1 Production control technology using artificial intelligence
   1.2 Variable and flexible production technology
   1.3 On-line inspection technology.
2. Production-related information and communications technologies:
   2.1 Technology for integrating production databases
   2.2 Production simulation technology
   2.3 Production controlling and managing technology using fuzzy logic.
3. Production/control equipment and processing technology:
   3.1 Three-dimensional recognition technology
   3.2 Autonomous robot technology
   3.3 Energy beam processing technology.
4. Application technologies for new materials
   4.1 New sensor technology
   4.2 Ultra-high strengthened and toughened materials
   4.3 Technology using holograms.
5. Human factors in production:
   5.1 Artificial reality for technology in production
   5.2 Human mimetic technology
   5.3 Measuring technology using human-like sensors.

Bibliography

1. Ann, B.N.K. and Kai, C.C., 1994: Knowledge base systems for strip layout design, *Computers in Industry*, **25**, 31–44.
2. Batty, D. and Makel, M.S., 1995: Automating knowledge acquisition: a propositional approach to representing expertise as an alternative to repertory grid technique, *IEEE Transactions on Knowledge and Data Engineering*, **7**(1), 53–67.
3. Hatvany, J., 1985: Intelligence and cooperation in heterarchic manufacturing systems, *Robotics, Computer – Integrated Manufacturing*, **2**(2), 101–104.

4. Hayashi, H., 1993: The IMS International Collaborative Program. *Proceedings of 24th International Symposium on Industrial Robots*, Japan Industrial Robot Association.
5. Iwata, K. and Onosato, M., 1994: Random manufacturing system: a new concept of manufacturing systems for production to order, *Annals of the CIRP*, **43**(1), 379–384.
6. Kusiak, A., 1990: *Intelligent Manufacturing Systems*. Prentice-Hall, Englewood Cliffs, NJ.
7. Mathews, J., 1995: Organization foundation of intelligent manufacturing systems – the Holonic view point, *Computers in Integrated Manufacturing Systems*, **8**(4), 237–243.
8. Okino, N., 1993: Bionic Manufacturing Systems. In J. Peklenik (ed.), *Flexible Manufacturing Systems, Past, Present, Future*, Ljubljana, Slovenia, pp. 73–95.
9. Patel, S.A. and Kamrani, A.K.K., 1996: Intelligent decision support systems for diagnosis and maintenance of automated systems, *Computers in Industrial Engineering*, **30**(2), 293–319.
10. Petin, J.F., Iung, B. and Morel, G., 1998: Distributed intelligent actuation and measurement (IAM) system within an integrated shop-floor organization, *Computers in Industry*, **37**, 197–211.
11. Ueda, K., 1992: An approach to bionic manufacturing systems based on DNA-type information, *Proceedings of ICOOMS '92*, pp. 303–308.
12. Valckenaers, P. (ed.), 1998: Special issue: intelligent manufacturing systems, Computers in Industry, **37**(3).
13. Valckenaers, P., Bongaerts, L. and Wyns, J., 1996: Planning systems in the next century (II), Proceedings of Advanced Summer Institute (ASI) 96 of the N.O.E. on Intelligent Control of Integrated Manufacturing Systems, Toulouse, France, 2–6 June, pp. 289–295.
14. Warnecke, H.J., 1993: *The Fractal Company: A Revolution in Corporate Culture*, Springer-Verlag.

Just-in-time manufacturing – JIT

M – 2c; 3d; 4b; 5c; 6b; 8c; 9c; 10c; 13d; 14b; * 1.1b; 1.2c; 1.3b; 1.4c; 1.5c; 1.6c; 2.3c; 2.4b; 2.5c; 3.6c; 4.2c

The goal of just-in-time manufacturing is to eliminate any function in the manufacturing system which burdens the company with overhead, impedes productivity, or adds unnecessary expense to the customer's operating system.

The biggest misconception about JIT is that it is an inventory control system. Although structuring a system for JIT will control inventory, that is not the major intention of the developers of the method.

Simply put, just-in-time manufacturing means having just what is needed, just when it is needed. It means inventory and all other job auxiliaries.

Just-in-time is a system approach to developing and operating manufacturing systems. Many companies have the opportunity to significantly improve their overall manufacturing performance by taking a total system viewpoint and integrating and optimizing procedures and processes for the purpose of preventing waste and inefficiency. The positive results of this effort are reduction in overall cost of manufacturing and improved company profits through reduction or elimination of specific types of overhead. The overhead areas will be most affected by following a total system integration approach involving functions and processes that have developed to address system-related manufacturing problems. Many of these functions and processes do not add value to the product; they exist only to compensate for inadequacies in some part of the manufacturing system. Eliminating unproductive overhead by identifying and removing the system inadequacies that necessitate the overhead will improve profitability in a minimum amount of time and with lowest overall expense.

The term JIT is meant to convey the idea that the three major elements of manufacturing – capital, equipment and labour – are made available only in the amount required and at the time required to do the job.

JIT management has the goal of obtaining a competitive edge through the use of three simple management tools:

1. *Integration and optimization.* Reducing the need for unnecessary functions and systems, such as inspection rework loops and inventory.
2. *Continuous improvement.* Developing internal systems that encourage constant improvement in processes and procedures.
3. *Understanding the customer.* Meeting the customer's need and reducing the customer's overall cost of purchasing and using a product.

The philosophy of JIT manufacturing is to operate a simple and efficient manufacturing system capable of optimizing the use of manufacturing resources such as capital, equipment and labour. This results in the development of a production system capable of meeting a customer's quality and delivery demands at the lowest manufacturing price.

The goal of JIT is to eliminate any function in the manufacturing system that burdens the company with overhead, impedes productivity, or adds unnecessary expense to the customer's operating system. The five basic principles in developing JIT system are:

1. each worker or work unit is both a customer and a supplier;
2. customers and suppliers are an extension of the manufacturing process;
3. continually seek the path of simplicity;
4. it is more important to prevent problems than to solve them;
5. obtain or produce something only when it is needed (just in time).

The five basic goals associated with a JIT manufacturing system are:

1. design for optimum quality/cost and ease of manufacturing;
2. minimize the resources expended in designing and manufacturing a product;

3. understand and be responsive to the customer's needs;
4. develop trust and open relationships with suppliers and customers;
5. develop commitment to improve the total manufacturing system.

The biggest misconception about JIT is that it is an inventory control system. Although structuring a system for JIT will control inventory that is not the major function.

The direct cost savings from a JIT materials system are significant in terms of reducing purchasing, receiving, inspection and stockroom costs. The savings from these functions alone could be in the range of 30 to 50% of aggregate operating costs. Material-related costs are reduced in a JIT system by several means.

1. Reducing the number of suppliers that the company deals with
2. Developing long-term contracts
3. Eliminate expediting
4. Reduce order scheduling
5. Obtaining better unit pricing
6. Eliminating the need to count individual parts
7. Simplifying receiving system
8. Eliminating receiving inspection
9. Eliminating most unpacking
10. Eliminating the breaking down of large material lots
11. Eliminating the stocking of inventory
12. Eliminating excess material spoilage.

Bibliography

1. Sohel, A. and Schroeder, R.G., 1998: Impact of JIT, QM, and EDI on supply chain management: Attaining superior delivery performance. In *Proceedings of the Annual Meeting of the Decision Sciences Institute*, vol. 3 Atlanta, GA, pp. 1311–1313.
2. Bose, G.J. and Rao, A., 1988: Implementing JIT with MRP II creates hybrid manufacturing environment, *Industrial Engineering*.
3. Change, T.C.E. and Podolsky, S., 1993: *Just-in-time Manufacturing*, Chapman & Hall.
4. Goldratt, E.M. and Cox, J., 1986: *The Goal*, revised edn. North River Press, Croton-on-Hudson, NY.
5. Lambrecht, M.R. and Decaluwe, L. 1988: JIT and constraint theory: the issue of bottleneck management, *Production and Inventory Management Journal*, **29**(3), pp. 61–66.
6. Lotenschtein, S., 1986: Just-in-time in the MRP II environment, *P&IM Review*.
7. Lubben, R.T., 1988: *Just-in-Time Manufacturing*. McGraw-Hill.
8. Taiichi, O., 1988: *Toyota Production System – Beyond Large Scale Production*. Productivity Press, Cambridge, MA.

9. Rao, A. and Scheraga, D., 1988: Moving from manufacturing resource planning to just-in-time manufacturing, *Production and Inventory Management Journal*, **29**(1), pp. 44–50.
10. Spencer, M.S., Daugherty, P.J. and Rogers, D.S., 1996: Logistics support for JIT implementation, *International Journal of Production Research*, **34**(3), 701–714.
11. Swenseth, S.R. and Buffa, F.P., 1990: Just in time: some effects on the logistics function, *International Journal of Logistics Management*, **1**(2), 25–34.
12. Best, T.D., 1986: MRP, JIT, and OPT: What's 'Best'? *Production and Inventory Management*, **27**(2), 22–28.
13. Wang, W. and Wang, D., 1999: JIT production planning approach with fuzzy due date for OKP manufacturing systems, *International Journal of Production Economics*, **58**(2), 209–215.
14. Westbrook, R., 1988: Time to forget 'just-in-time'? Observations on a visit to Japan, *International Journal of Operation and Production Management*, **8**(4), 5–20.
15. White, R.E., 1993: An empirical assessment of JIT in US manufacturing, *Production and Inventory Management Journal*, **34**(2), 38–42.

Kaizen blitz

M – 4c; 5c; 6c; 8b; 12c; 14b; * 1.3b; 1.4b; 2.4b; 2.5c; 3.1b; 3.3c

Kaizen, is the Japanese word for 'continuous improvement'.

The production system adopts or renews itself in accordance with changes of product. Some module units, which form the manufacturing equipment, are replaced frequently. It is important to keep the same or better performance by continuously monitoring and maintaining the facilities in the normal condition in the operating phase as defined in the design phase even though the system configuration of the manufacturing facilities is changed. In many Japanese companies, the manufacturing system remains constant through continuous kaizen activity. Kaizen activity is based on the local shop floor level, and is carried out in small groups of several operators and maintenance persons. Therefore, kaizen activity cannot always be applied to the global manufacturing environment because it is not fully supported by the information system technology.

Kaizen blitz, combines kaizen, with blitz, the German term meaning 'lightning'. It comes from kaizen activity adapted by Toledo, Ohio-based Dana Corp. and Dana University's technical school. The impetus to start such a programme came from establishing the company's Excellence in Manufacturing Award. The goal behind Kaizen blitz – to continuously improve – is an everyday part of Dana's culture, succinctly stated in the corporate slogan, People Finding a Better Way. The Dana style translates in everyday practice as a way of doing things that creates a sense of common purpose. Behind this philosophy is the belief that business is 90% people and 10% money. As a result, each Dana employee is given responsibility for the 25 square feet in which they operate and is challenged to suggest ways in which the process or their role in the process could be improved.

The philosophy behind the Kaizen blitz process is to eliminate waste in order to make dramatic and tangible improvements in work processes. Kaizen blitz is about creative brainpower, not creative checkbook power.

In a Kaizen blitz workshop, the typical team is made up of 12 to 14 participants, and there are often two or three teams. The teams are cross-functional, and are composed of operators, engineers, supervisors, maintenance personnel, and managers, as well as participants invited from outside the plant. The visitors' point of view provides a fresh outlook, unencumbered by traditional ways of working, which can often cut to the heart of a problem.

Just before the blitz begins, team leaders establish stretch goals to challenge the teams. The overall objectives of each Kaizen blitz encounter are to increase productivity by 30%, reduce workflow distance by 80%, generate from 120 to 175 productivity improvement ideas (with an implementation goal of 80%), decrease defects by 80%, and implement 20 safety improvements.

On the first day, the Kaizen blitz training team takes stock of the plant and familiarizes itself with the operation, as well as what needs to be changed or otherwise improved. The training team measures how long it takes for the plant to accomplish certain tasks, and demonstrates to employees how and why the Kaizen blitz will be helpful.

On the second and third days, the training team and plant employees develop ideas to improve plant operations. This is the heart of the Kaizen blitz process. As the employees participate in the process, they become more enthused. They see that they can make a meaningful contribution to their own future. Once they see results, the enthusiasm becomes contagious, and the process takes on a life of its own.

On the last day, the training team and the plant employees present their accomplishments to management.

Plant managers can see an immediate return on their time and investment. Kaizen blitz improvements usually do not need lots of money to improve productivity. In one case, the only investment made to generate the 400% improvement was $56 for a new piece of equipment that modernized an outdated process.

Another Kaizen blitz victory resulted from simple organization. In one warehouse, random and unplanned storage procedures resulted in more than 4000 areas where employees could not store their parts; these were called over storage areas. During the Kaizen blitz process, it was reorganized around short- and long-term storage needs, parts were placed closer to their process, and the time people wasted looking for parts was drastically cut.

Bibliography

1. Cuscela, K.N., 1998: Kaizen blitz: attacks work processes at Dana Corp. *IIE Solutions*, **30**(4), 29–31.
2. Massaki, I., 1986: *The Key to Japan's Competitive Success*. Random House, New York, p. 102.

3. Minton, E., 1998: Luke Faulstick: 'Baron of Blitz' has boundless vision of continuous improvement, *Industrial Management*, **January–February**, **40**(1), pp. 14–21.
4. Oakeson, M., 1997: Kaizen makes dollars and sense for Mercedes-Benz in Brazil, *IIE Solutions*, **April**, **29**(4), pp. 32–35.

Kanban system

M – 1c; 2d; 4c; 6b; 8c; 14d; * 1.3b; 1.4b; 2.4b; 3.3c; 3.5c; 3.6c

Kanban ('tag') is a production planning and scheduling system based on a pull instead of a push system. The goal of eliminating waste is also highlighted by kanban. Kanban is a powerful force to reduce manpower and inventory, eliminate defective products, and prevent the recurrence of breakdowns.

A kanban is a tool for managing and assuring just-in-time. Kanban is a simple and direct form of communication, always located at the point where it is needed. In most cases, a kanban is a small piece of paper inserted in a rectangular vinyl envelop. On this piece of paper is written how many of what part to pick up or which parts to assemble.

Kanban is a Japanese word that means 'visual record' and refers to a manufacturing control system developed and used in Japan. The kanban, or card, as it is generally referred to, is a mechanism by which a workstation signals the need for more parts from the preceding station. The type of signal used for a kanban is not important. Cards, coloured balls, lights and electronic systems, have all been used as kanban signals. A unique feature that separates a true kanban system from other card systems, such as a 'travel card' used by most companies, is the incorporation of a 'pull' production system. Pull production refers to a demand system whereby products are produced only on demand from the using function.

Kanban always moves with the needed goods and so becomes a work order for each process. In this way, a kanban can prevent overproduction, and prevent large revenue losses in production.

Kanban, in essence, becomes the automatic nerve of the production line. Based on this, production workers start work by themselves, and make their own decisions concerning overtime. The kanbam system also makes it clear what managers and supervisors must do. This unquestionably promotes improvement in both work and equipment.

The main characteristic of a kanban system is its operating simplicity, and its ability to reduce work-in-process. It is based on working to buffers, which exist to protect the system from delays in production. Buffer size, however, is a trade-off between protection and lead time. If buffer size is increased, the protection increases, but so does the manufacturing lead time.

Once a kanban-activated workstation has filled its output buffer it is not authorized to produce output again until the output buffer is depleted to its reorder point. The workstation is said to be 'blocked'.

Kanban, requires a buffer of material for each possible part in front of each resource. Therefore, for multi-product environments kanban requires substantial inventory to achieve the necessary throughput.

Kanban is a tool for realizing just-in-time. For this tool to work well, the production process must be managed to flow as much as possible. Other important conditions are levelling production as much as possible and always working in accordance with standard work methods.

Some kanban rules are as follows:

1. The earlier process produces items in the quantity and sequence indicated by the kanban.
2. The later process picks up the number of items indicated by the kanban at the earlier process.
3. No items are made or transported without a kanban.
4. Always attach a kanban to the goods.
5. Defective products are not sent to the subsequent process. The result is 100% defect-free goods. This method identifies the process making the defectives.
6. Reducing the number of kanban increase their sensitivity. This reveals existing problems and maintains inventory control.

The kanban system is most likely to be associated with just-in-time (JIT) systems and the theory of constraints (TOC).

The success of kanban systems appears to depend heavily on complete implementation. Even in cases where the implementation is complete, kanban systems are unable to cope with product variety and demand fluctuation. It may be that when kanban is used as part of a continuous improvement programme, as with JIT philosophy, it is likely to produce increased benefits to the user.

Bibliography

1. Belt, B., 1987: MRP and kanban – a possible synergy? *Production and Inventory Management*, **28**(1), pp. 71–80.
2. Bose, G.J. and Rao, A., 1988: Implementing JIT with MRP II creates hybrid manufacturing environment, *Industrial Engineering*, **September**, **20**(1), pp. 49–53.
3. Goldratt, E.M. and Cox, J., 1986: *The Goal*, revised edn. North River Press, Croton-on-Hudson, NY.
4. Lambrecht, M.R. and Decaluwe, L., 1988: JIT and constraint theory: the issue of bottleneck management, *Production and Inventory Management Journal*, **29**(3).
5. Lotenschtein, S., 1986: Just-in-time in the MRP II environment, *P&IM Review*, **February**, pp. 61–66.
6. Plenert, G., 1985: Are Japanese production methods applicable in the United States? *Production and Inventory Management*, **26**(2), p. 25.
7. Best, T.D., 1986: MRP, JIT, and OFT: what's 'best'? *Production and Inventory Management*, **27**(2), 22–28.

8. Rao, A. and Scheraga, D., 1988: Moving from manufacturing resource planning to just-in-time manufacturing, *Production and Inventory Management Journal*, **29**(1), pp. 44–50.
9. Schonberger, R.J., 1983: Selecting the right manufacturing inventory system: Western and Japanese approaches, *Production and Inventory Management*, **24**(3), pp. 33–44.
10. Wilson, G.T., 1985: Kanban scheduling – boon or bane? *Production and Inventory Management*, **26**(3), pp. 134–142.

Knowledge management

X – 1c; 3c; 5c; 6c; 7b; 11c; 13c; * 1.3c; 2.2b; 2.3b; 2.4b; 4.1c; 4.2c; 4.4b

Knowledge management consists of the distribution, access and retrieval of human experiences and relevant information between related individuals or workgroups. Moreover, it can be seen as a pragmatic further development of the concept of organizational learning.

Knowledge management is more about changing business processes than about upgrading software. The obstacles to knowledge management are collaboration problems that stem from old habits of hoarding knowledge. Getting people to share their knowledge requires not only new processes but also a new covenant between employer and employees. Some companies have not only changed their cultures, but also have hired chief knowledge officers to act as intermediaries between employees and incoming information.

The key focus is to improve organizational skills at all levels of the organization through better handling of resource knowledge. Following this definition and characterization, knowledge management is of vital interest for innovative enterprise as well as institutes of higher education of the future.

One of the key characteristics of knowledge management is the implementation of a knowledge cycle. Effective knowledge management consists of the generation of knowledge by identification, acquisition and development and the application of knowledge by distribution, usage and preservation. Most important is the evaluation of the knowledge application and the re-adjustment and new definition of goals.

A learning organization is defined as a group of people that continuously extend their capacities to accomplish organizational goals. Learning extends knowledge and enables decision-making; the learning rate determines the competitiveness of an organization (competitive advantage). Altogether, learning organization identify learning as a key topic for strategic decision-making. Following this definition the transformation into learning organization is a key requirement for the survival of the organization.

Based on experience in the area of learning and training the classical chain of courseware production and delivery is extended by developing a new concept of internet-based continuous learning, training and qualification. This concept integrates method-oriented learning, tool-oriented training and practice-oriented qualification. It anticipates tomorrow's knowledge-base working style and provides a solution to the key challenges of knowledge transfer and social transfer. The concept is based on two aspects: knowledge domains and Internet communications. Knowledge domains are multi-dimensional information spaces containing theoretical, practical and application-oriented content. This content is interconnected to form specific contexts and can be enriched by individual or group annotations. The participants are interconnected via the Internet and form lively, self-organizing communities. Herewith, the difficulties of traditional learning and training in isolated, often artificial environments lacking practical relevance, can be overcome. This concept can successfully be applied to scenarios such as the introduction of new products in distributed companies.

Implementation of this concept is based on a network centric approach. One of the base layers, the resource of an organization, is connected to form a virtual global resource network. On top of this, the competencies of the organization are interconnected. These competencies comprise diverse areas such as human expertise, know-how in best practice, technology know-how or information in the form of documents or experience. The top layer is built as a human network, the creators and users of knowledge. They work using the globally available resources, benefit from the available competencies and, most important, create new knowledge by reflection and understanding.

Knowledge management is one of the key technologies and applications. It impacts research and development activities as well as industry projects and general management. Knowledge base systems (KBS) are a popular and active research area in artificial intelligence (AI). Its objective is to develop computer software that can employ human experience and knowledge to deal with problems usually needing thinking and reasoning. Artificial intelligence (AI) has become one of the major topics of discussion in computer science. AI can be defined as the ability of a device to perform functions that are normally associated with human intelligence. These functions include reasoning, planning, and problem solving. Applications of AI have been in natural language processing, intelligent database retrieval, expert consulting systems, theorem proving, robotics, scheduling, intelligent design systems, and computer aided process planning.

The Engineering application is a typical problem area where a lot of poorly structured knowledge is available and not all parameters and their effects can be represented in official scientific methods (equations). Therefore, they turn to expert systems (ES), a simplified area in artificial intelligence. In an expert system, the knowledge of a human expert is represented in an appropriate format. The most common approach is to represent knowledge by using rules. Rule-based deduction is frequently used to derive an action. The main problem is that no two experts agree on the rules. Experience is obtained from early training, from books, from discussions, and from years of working in the field. Experience requires a significant period of accumulation. Experience represents only approximate, not exact knowledge. Experience is not directly applicable to new problems or new systems. These have led to a knowledge research study. The expert is not asked to set the rule; knowledge base experts interrogate professional experts on relatively minor issues to understand and form the rules to be applied in the expert system.

Managers who are ready to take the plunge into knowledge management will find it is more about changing business processes than about upgrading software. The obstacles to knowledge management are collaboration problems that stem from old habits of hoarding knowledge. Getting people to share their knowledge requires not only new processes but also a new covenant between employer and employees.

Bibliography

1. Aho, A.V., Hocroft, J.E. and Ullman, J.D., 1983: *Data Structures and Algorithms.* Addison-Wesley.
2. Austin, T., Brian, D. and Jeff, D., 1996: O-plan: a knowledge-base planner and its application to logistics. In A. Tate (ed.) *Advanced Planning Technology, the Technological Achievements of the ARPA/Rome Laboratory Planning Initiative.* AAAI Press, Menlo Park, CA.
3. Cha, J.H. and Yokoyama, M., 1995: A knowledge-based system for mechanical CAD, *ICED'95*, pp. 1382–1386.
4. Chesbrough, H.W. and Teece, D.J., 1996: When is virtual virtuous? *Harvard Business Review*, **74**(1), 65–71.
5. Chesbrough, H.W. and Teece, D.J., 1996: Making companies efficient, *The Economist*, **December**.
6. Covey, S., 1990: *Habits of Highly Effective People.* Simon & Schuster, New York. General references.
7. Coyne, R.D., Rosenman, M.A., Radford, A.D., Balachandran, M. and Gero, J.S., 1989: *Knowledge-based Design Systems.* Addison-Wesley.
8. Co-Davies, B.J., 1986: Application of expert systems in process planning. *Annals of the CIRP*, **35**(2), pp. 451–452.
9. Fischer, K., 1994: Knowledge-base reactive scheduling in a flexible manufacturing system. In R.M. Kerr and E. Szelke (eds) *Proceedings of the IFIP TC5/WG5.7 Workshop on Knowledge Base Reactive Scheduling, Elsevier, Amsterdam*, pp. 1–18.
10. Genesereth, M.R. and Fike, R.E., 1992: Knowledge interchange format version 3.0, reference manual report logic 92–1. Computer Science Department, Stanford University, Stanford.
11. Lahti, A. and Ranta, M., 1997: Capturing and deploying design decisions. In M. Pratt, R.D. Sriram and M.J. Wozny (eds), *Proceeding of IFIP WG 5.2 Geometric Modelling Workshop*, Airlie, Virginia. IFIP Proceedings, Chapman & Hall, London.
12. Montyli, M., Finger, S. and Tomiyama, T. (eds), 1997: Knowledge intensive CAD, Vol. 2. *Proceedings of the Second IFIP WG 5.2 Workshop on Knowledge-Intensive CAD.* IFIP Proceedings, Chapman & Hall, London.
13. Nonaka, I., 1991: The knowledge-creating company, *Harvard Business Review*, **69**(6), 96–109.

14. Rus, D., Gray, R. and Kotz, D., 1997: Transportable information agent, *Journal of Intelligent Information Systems*, **9**, 215–238.
15. Russel, S. and Norvig, P., 1995: *Artificial Intelligence, A Modern Approach*. Prentice-Hall, Englewood Cliffs, NJ.
16. Schierholt, K., 1998: Knowledge systematization for operations planning. In *Proceedings of Artificial Intelligence and Manufacturing Workshop. State of the Art and State of the Practice*. AAAI Press, Menlo Park, CA, pp. 140–146.
17. Stephenson, K. and Haeckel, S.H., 1997: Making a virtual organization work focus, *The Zurich Customer Magazine*, **21**, 26–30.
18. Tomiyama, T., Montyli, M. and Finger, S. (eds), 1996: Knowledge intensive CAD, Vol. 1. *Proceedings of the First IFIP WG 5.2 Workshop on Knowledge-Intensive CAD*. IFIP Proceedings, Chapman & Hall, London.

Lean manufacturing

M – 1c; 2c; 3b; 4b; 5b; 6c; 8c; 9b; 14b; * 1.1b; 1.2b; 1.3b; 1.4b; 1.5c; 1.6c; 2.2b; 2.3b; 2.4b; 2.5b; 3.1b; 3.2c; 3.3b; 3.4b; 3.6c; 4.2b; 4.3c; 4.5b

The objective of lean manufacturing is to cut waste, to shorten the total manufacturing lead time for a product, and continuous improvement.

In practice, lean manufacturing, TQM and JIT use the same tools, which are:

- Process organization (automation with 'a human mind')
- Customer satisfaction
- Teamwork
- Continuous improvement.

Lean manufacturing encompasses many different strategies and activities that are familiar to most industrial engineers. Lean manufacturing production systems were pioneered in Japan. Lean manufacturing began to be implemented in the West's automotive industry from the mid-1980s onwards. Central to the philosophy of lean – and embraced to the full, it assumes the form of an entirely new cultural approach to manufacturing – is a flow-based production architecture in which simplicity is promoted and waste aborted.

The lean system, however, is based on a strong and inseparable relationship between JIT and TQM leading to a virtual circle in which quality is a prerequisite of JIT, and JIT allows quality to be improved through enhanced control and increase visibility of all productive activities. The lean system is also based on Jidoka, which has the dual meaning of automation and autonomous defect control. The underlying concept is automation with 'a human mind'. Automation goes hand in hand with not only worker ability, but also with product and process design. The lean system process capability is built and evolves with limited resources. Capabilities are built around work organization and employee skills, external relationship with suppliers, etc.

Different philosophies and approaches to automation raise questions such as: What kind of relationship exists between such automation approaches and the lean system? Are the lean system and the automation approaches convergent? There are four approaches to automation.

1. Low cost automation.
2. Human fitting automation.
3. Human motivating automation.
4. High technology automation.

The analysis of different approaches to the lean system must highlight both problems raised by its adoption and the other innovative approaches to using problems as learning tools. In many cases such an analysis of approaches must take into account the embedded organizational knowledge and capabilities that influence the evolutionary pattern.

As an example, FIAT adopted lean manufacturing principles. The process began at the end of the 1980s after a period in which FIAT had followed the strategy of the highly-automated factory with a strong emphasis on the automation of assembly operations. The adoption process highlights some specific features:

1. A conceptual priority of TQM over JIT; TQM is key to the adoption of the new lean system.
2. The slow acquisition of JIT practice, and non-acceptance of the stress imposed by its full scale adoption; JIT is seen as counterproductive in terms of good working conditions.
3. Focus on involvement of the workforce rather than on only performances; focus on performances is seen as creating conflict rather than solving it.
4. Resolving conflict and bargaining requires a continuous search for consensus.
5. Not automating 'for the sake of automation'.
6. Preference for a 'slow Japanization' with technological solutions which positively impact both on production flow and work organization

With another example, at Lockheed Martin Tactical Aircraft Systems in Fort Worth, Texas officials acknowledge that the vast amount of lean manufacturing work currently being injected into the F-16 line is grist to the mill for programmes that are, as yet, still on the horizon. 'We're using current programs to prepare for the future'. A cultural change is rapidly taking place despite some union-related resistance to certain aspects of the 'pull' system – one such being the practice of having suppliers deliver items onto the shop floor instead of to union representatives. 'In one and a half days I do what I did in five days under the old system'. They note that lean manufacturing adds job satisfaction and morale. 'Trust is being built here' between shop floor and executives.

'The system is so simple – eventually others will see what we're doing here and want to adopt it for themselves.' Focus is on a regime known as 'one piece flow': the seamless transition of the product from the supply base all the way to the customer. Because it bought in 70% by value of its product from outside its own resources, the supply chain was a high-risk area with enormous potential for improvement.

If lean manufacturing is to work to the full, it has to be embraced by everyone from the boardroom to the shop floor. If successful, it creates a whole new cultural identity that can be mobilized for even greater wealth creation.

It is important to understand that lean manufacturing is a state of mind rather than a pre-designed solution. Each company needs to apply the principles to create an appropriate solution for its own specific challenges and circumstances.

Some steps to implement lean manufacturing are:

- *Design for manufacture and assembly.* Designers and production workers should collaborate during concept development to influence the design in terms of simplicity, standardization and producibility.
- *Factory layout.* Traditional production systems frequently require parts to travel kilometres within the plant and workers had to walk hundreds of metres to complete their assignments. In a lean manufacturing environment everything that the assembler needs is located close to his or her workstation.
- *Just-in-time (JIT).* Ensuring that the right part or component is delivered in the right quantity at the right time in the right place. This not only results in tremendous reductions in inventory but also allows the company to respond quickly to customer-driven changes on the factory floor.
- *Building defect-free products and services.* As JIT lowers the level of available inventory, it is mandatory that you develop and rely on process control. Through various quality control schemes, dependence on inspection to achieve quality ceases, and it relies instead on consistency and predictability to achieve defect-free parts and assemblies.
- *Continuous improvement.* The sense of urgency that a flow-based system creates stimulates the people most closely associated with the process to think about constraints and improve constantly and forever.

Bibliography

1. Anonymous, 1998: Lean manufacturing saves time, *Manufacturing Engineering*, **121**(3), 98.
2. Anonymous, 1998: The importance of ergonomics in lean manufacturing, *Material Handling Engineering*, **53**(10), 30.
3. Jones, C., Medlen, N., Merlo, C., Robertson, M. and Shepherdson, J., 1999: The lean enterprise, *BT Technology Journal*, **17**(4), 15–22.
4. Karthik, A.R., 1999: Lean manufacturing, *Monthly Labor Review*, **122**(1), 50.

5. Kevin, J. and Duggan, K.J.J., 1998: Facilities design for lean manufacturing, *IIE Solutions*, **30**(12), 30.
6. Knill, B., 1999: How lean manufacturing matches today's business, *Material Handling Engineering*, **54**(11), 87.
7. Labow, J., 1999: The last word: on lean manufacturing, *IIE Solutions*, **31**(9), 42.
8. Lee-Post, A., 1999: Information management and lean manufacturing, *Journal of Database Management*, **10**(1), 43.
9. Liker, J., 1999: Advanced planning systems as an enabler of lean manufacturing, *Automotive Manufacturing & Production*, **111**(2), 29.
10. Monden, Y., 1998: *Toyota Production System*. Engineering & Management Press.
11. Munro, S., 1999: Lean manufacturing starts with lean design, *Automotive Manufacturing & Production*, **111**(8), 27.
12. Muffatto, M., 1995: The lean production system: different implementation approaches and evolution. In *Proceedings of the 13th International Conference on Production Research*, Jerusalem, August 6–10, pp. 172–174.
13. Ohno, T., 1988: *Toyota Production System*. Productivity Press.
14. Womack, J. and Jones, D., 1996: *Lean Thinking*. Simon & Schuster.

Life-cycle assessment – LCA

P – 11c; 15b; * 1.1b; 1.2c; 2.1b; 2.2b; 2.6b; 3.4c
See Environment Conscious Manufacturing – ECM.

Life-cycle management

P – 11c; 15b; * 1.1b; 1.2c; 2.1b; 2.2b; 2.6b; 3.4c
See Environment-conscious manufacturing – ECM.

Life-cycle product design

P – 3c; 11c; 15b; * 1.1b; 1.2c; 2.1b; 2.2b; 2.6b; 3.4c
Life-cycle design and recycling are proposed to avert pollution and danger from a used product and to benefit after its usage. An environment-friendly and effective life-cycle economy aims at economically and responsibly dealing with the earth's limited resources. In order to reach economical and environment-friendly cycles the requirements of recycling have to be taken into consideration during product design. Disassembly and recycling companies have to be efficiently organized and have to possess special technology that fulfils the quality and quantity requirements concerning work material and components during the manufacturing process. There is a requirement for cooperation between the manufacturer, the user and the developer of recycling

techniques. The challenge for the management of cycle economy companies lies in an open and continuous flow of information between firms.

Life-cycle-oriented product design leads to maximum usage while minimizing the economical, ecological and social efforts during the life of the product. Requirements of different stages in the product life-cycle compete when designing a product. Using life-cycle assessments, design alternatives can be compared and selected. The assessment of the recycling and the disposal stage includes some special features. When designing products the designer has to face the problem that he cannot fix the type and dimension of recovery exactly. Designer decisions about which components have to be reused or which materials can be utilized strongly depend on design trends, anticipated state of the art of recycling technologies and future economical, ecological and legal conditions.

A recovery plan includes the necessary disassembly operations, their order and the subsequent utilization or disposal. Therefore the designer needs comparable information on disassembly and recycling procedures. The future development of recycling processes requires updated process information concerning the life-cycle of a product. The producer can adapt his recycling strategies to the new conditions and act in time. Actions could be, for example, the contraction of cooperating dissemblers and recyclers or the introduction of a bonus system for returned products in the case of increasing gains due to recycling.

Besides information on recycling techniques, the designer can also receive references for the improvement of his work through cooperation with recycling companies.

The developer of recycling techniques has to arrange his/her facility according to the input that is defined by the designer and to the output that is expected by the recycler. An automatic assignment of recycling alternatives compares the recycling suitability of a product.

The renewing process includes recovery and treatment on a product basis, whereas the material recovery process treats and recovers products as materials. The different recycling methods are classified through:

1. access restrictions related to material and shape;
2. process features – fixed parameters like depreciation, and variable parameters like flow and selectivity;
3. output parameters as a function of input parameters, e.g. energy requirements.

Recycling is proposed to avert pollution and danger from a used product and to provide benefits after its use. Frequently, simple disposal of the product is cheaper than recycling because disassembly, renewing, material recovery and the related processes are too expensive.

The economical organization of cycles is supported by the kind, amount, structure and the condition of a product as well as by ensured access during its use. Diagnostic systems are continuously supplying information about product conditions. Another operational area of diagnostic systems is the registration of product conditions during service and maintenance. Using information from the recycling technique developer, the recycler is able to choose the most suitable process that changes the existing input into the desired output.

During the product life-cycle review assessments verify the results. The producer can adapt recycling strategies to new influences. Recyclers can use existing facilities more effectively to improve the recycling results. Developers of recycling techniques can test their developments and discover new application areas. The access to design data enables the simulation of new recycling procedures and equipment.

A federated database system is used for data administration. The system includes existing heterogeneous databases owned by the companies. A unified data meta-model is defined. The connection of the local databases is user-friendly and automatically executed by an agent-based transformation system.

The first development stage is the integration of the federation members and the search for information in their databases. The second stage is the acquisition of information using information agents. The search within new information systems (data warehouses) via the Internet is possible. Such data structures can now extend the unified data meta-model.

Bibliography

1. Anderi, R., Daum, B., Weissmantel, H. and Wolf, B., 1999: Design for environment – a computer-based cooperative method to consider the entire life cycle. In *Proceedings of the First International Symposium on Environmentally Conscious Design and Inverse Manufacturing*. IEEE Computer Society, Los Alamitos, CA, pp. 380–385.
2. Curran, M.A., 1996: *Environmental Life-cycle Assessment*. McGraw Hill, New York.
3. Curlee, T.R. and Das, S., 1991: *Plastic Wastes, Management Control, Recycling and Disposal*. Environmental Protection Agency, Noyes Data Corporation.
4. Dreer, P. and Koonce, D.A., 1995: Development of an integrated information model for computer integrated manufacturing, *Computers Industrial Engineering*, **29**.
5. Koonce, D.A., Judd, R.P. and Parks, C.M., 1996: Manufacturing systems engineering and design: an intelligent multi-model, integration architecture, *Computer Integrated Manufacturing*, **9**(6).
6. Lu, C.J.J., Tsai, K.H., Yang, J.C.S. and Yu, Wang, 1998: A virtual testbed for the life-cycle design of automated manufacturing facilities, *International Journal of Advanced Manufacturing Technology*, **14**(8), 608–615.
7. Mills, J.J., 1995: An integrated information infrastructure for agile manufacturing, *Manufacturing Science and Engineering ASME MH*, **3**(2).
8. Orfali, R., Harkey, D. and Edwards, J., 1996: *The Essential Client/Server Survival Guide*. John Wiley & Sons.

9. Song, L. and Nagi, R., 1995: An integrated information framework for agile manufacturing. *5th Industrial Engineering Research Conference Proceedings*, No. 1–4, Elsevier Sience.
10. Zussman, E., Kriwet, A. and Seliger, G., 1994: Disassembly-oriented assessment methodology to support design for recycling, *Annals of the CIRP*, **43**(1).

Manufacturing enterprise wheel

P – 5c; 6c; 7c; 8b; 9b; 13b; 14b; 16b; * 1.5b; 2.2c; 2.3c; 2.4c; 2.5c; 2.6c; 3.1c; 3.3b; 3.4b; 4.2b

The Computer and Automated Systems Association of the Society of Manufacturing Engineering (CASA/SME – 1 SME Drive, Dearborn, MI) recently published its vision of enterprise manufacturing. In the past several 'wheels' were recommended. The new 'wheel' demonstrates that manufacturing has entered a new age, an information age, where computer technology helps to manage the manufacturing enterprise. In the mid-1980s the emphasis was on the need to break down the barriers between design and manufacturing. New insight brings a new manufacturing enterprise wheel. The old wheel looked primarily at automation and integration inside the enterprise. The new wheel looks outside as well. It adds understanding in the following areas.

1. The central role of a customer-oriented mission and vision to strive for continuous improvement. A clear understanding of the marketplace and customer desires is the key to success. Marketing, design, manufacturing and support must be aligned to meet customer needs. This is the bull's-eye, the hub of the wheel, the vision and mission of the enterprise.
2. The importance of team and human networking in the new manufacturing environment. The role of people and teamwork in the organization includes the means of organizing, hiring, training, motivation, measuring and communicating to ensure teamwork and cooperation. This side of the enterprise is captured in ideas such as self-directed teams, teams of teams, the learning organization, leadership, metrics, rewards, quality circles and corporate culture.
3. The continuing importance of computer tools now increasingly distributed and networked. These include tools to support networking and concurrent engineering. The revolutionary impact of shared knowledge and systems to support people and processes. Included here are both manual and computer tools to aid research, analysis, innovation, documentation, decision-making, and control of every process in the enterprise.
4. A focus on key processes and best practices throughout the enterprise, from marketing through design, manufacturing and customer support. Key processes from product definition through manufacturing and customer support. There are three main categories of processes: product/process definition;

manufacturing; and customer support. Within these categories 15 key processes complete the product life-cycle.

5. Recognition of the move away from bureaucratic structure, to leaner and more agile organizations. Enterprise resources (input) include capital, people, material, management, information, technology, and suppliers. Reciprocal responsibility (outputs) includes employee, investor, and community relations, as well as regulatory, ethical, and environmental obligations. Administration functions are a thin layer around the periphery. They bring new resources into the enterprise and sustain key processes.

6. The need to integrate and understand the external environment, including customers, competitors, suppliers and the global manufacturing infrastructure. While a company may see itself as self-contained, its success depends on customers, competitors, suppliers, and other factors in the environment. The manufacturing infrastructure includes customers and their needs, suppliers, competitors, prospective workers, distributors, natural resources, financial markets, communities, governments and educational and research institutions.

The new manufacturing enterprise wheel strives for worldwide economies of scale and scope, by networking business units, partners and suppliers. These trends range from virtual co-location of project teams to virtual enterprise spanning the globe.

Bibliography

1. Jordan, J. and Michel, F. (eds), 1999: *Next Generation Manufacturing (NGM)*. SME blue book series.
2. Marks, P. (ed.), 1994: *Process Reengineering and the New Manufacturing Enterprise Wheel: 15 Processes for Competitive Advantage*. SME blue book series.

Manufacturing excellence

P – 2c; 3c; 4c; 8b; 9c; 12b; 14c; * 1.1b; 1.3c; 1.4b; 1.5c; 2.4c; 3.3c; 3.4c; 4.2c; 4.5b

Manufacturing excellence is producing a product that meets or exceeds customer expectations at a competitive price and delivered on time to the customer. Manufacturing excellence is looked upon as a strategic advantage for achieving global competitiveness.

Cycle-time management is a methodology to achieve manufacturing excellence. Cycle time management involves the entire operation from design to service. If management and workers cooperate, cycle time management holds great promise for achieving manufacturing excellence.

Achieving manufacturing excellence is not an easy task. Some believe that automation is the answer. Automated machines that produce quality products with little human intervention is their ultimate goal, but manufacturing excellence will be much more difficult than buying the latest automated technology. Automated equipment, such as machining centres, is not cheap and has proved to be difficult to debug. Creating islands of automation is expensive. Linking these islands of automation together to form the factory of the future is proving difficult. Prerequisites for automation are:

1. Innovative work culture
2. Customer driven
3. Supportive management
4. Long-terms goal
5. Total quality commitment
6. Process of continual improvement
7. De-departmentalizing.

Manufacturing excellence depends on workers involvement and promoting a programme of continual process improvement, just as it also depends on automation.

In the classical definition, the manager's job is to see that a given job gets done. He is supposed to plan, make decisions, tell the workers what to do, and see that they do it. However as dimensions of business have become more complex, managers have begun to find that they do not always have the facts and figures necessary to do this planning, instruction, and supervision at the operational level. Since it is the workers who actually perform the day-to-day operations, they are much closer to these problems and are often better able to find a solution than is the manager. Worker solutions can also have a side effect of enhancing morale. However, management must be receptive to such worker solutions. Getting productive ideas from employees is not so much a matter of having creative employees, as it is one of having supportive management. If a manager cannot encourage workers to introduce productive ideas, most likely he/she is the problem, not the workers.

Business is in business to make profit, but profit at any price can have disturbing long-term outcomes for business and society. For corporate survival and renewed corporate success in the market, industry must change their results-oriented management strategy and replace it with a process-oriented management approach.

Cycle-time management has, as its main driver, inventory reduction; an unlikely candidate for achieving manufacturing excellence. Inventory has been thought of as an asset, a security blanket for achieving productivity. CTM strategy contradicts this belief of inventory and states simply that inventory is evil.

The socio-technical aspects of CTM are many. Implementing such a strategy in an industrial organization bridges both social and technical change. CTM focuses on one product or family of products, which are processed in cells. Cellular manufacturing divides workers into small groups or teams that operate within a focused factory and gives them the responsibility and resources to produce quality products. Small group improvement activities foster a work environment of continuous improvement and give workers what they have desired for many years, participation and ownership. Worker participation is the most important factor in achieving manufacturing excellence.

CTM methodology states that you produce product only when needed, you do not produce product 'just in case'. Following these methodologies might sometimes cause workers to be idle, but this is better than producing product to stock. Idle inventory is evil, not idle workers. Working with small groups improves quality and increases profit. Pull operation and small lots aid workers in gaining control of their production cell. Inventory hides problems such as design problems, machine downtime, long setups, absenteeism, defective parts, poor vendor quality and past due dates.

Customer – supplier's problems might arise. Most of the time workers know the problems best; as they are closest to problems, they should communicate with suppliers and customers. Such meetings of workers with vendors will create an atmosphere of pride and partnership with owners. Creating a climate of trust and mutual benefit will develop a work culture that promotes worker and team development

Worker involvement in all aspects of CTM leads to the accomplishment of the socio-technical aspects necessary to achieve manufacturing excellence. CTM creates an organizational structure that facilitates worker participation and ownership. To get worker involvement it is necessary to provide workers with the required skills, resources, and authority to make meaningful contributions to process improvement.

Bibliography

1. Heard, (ed.), 1991: *Short Cycle Manufacturing*. In *The Route to JIT*, Ed Heard & Associates, P.O. Box 2692 Columbia, South Carolina 29202.
2. Massaki, I., 1986: *Kaizen: The Key to Japan's Competitive Success*. Random House, New York, p. 102.
3. Peters, T. and Waterman, R., 1982: *In Search of Excellence: Lessons from America's Best-Run Companies*. Harper & Row, New York.
4. Stinnett, W., 1986: Total employee involvement: integrating people and technology, *PC Fabrication*, **April**, 75–77.
5. Susman, G. and Chase, R., 1986: A sociotechnical analysis of the integrated factory, *The Journal of Applied Behavioral Science*, **22**(3), 257–270.
6. Watt, M., 1987: Polishing the image, *Manufacturing Week*, July 20, Issue 012, p. 1.

Manufacturing execution system (MES)

T – 1b; 2b; 3c; 4c; 5d; 6b; 7b; 13c; * 1.3b; 2.3c; 2.4b; 2.5c; 3.2c; 3.5c; 4.3c Manufacturing execution systems (MES) aim to increase the functionality and flexibility of factory automation and control. MES technology features distributed, client/server architecture, object-oriented design and implementation, and an intuitive graphical user interface (GUI). By choosing to migrate to MES, manufacturers will realize improvements in yield, cycle times, work-in-process (WIP), equipment utilization, and operator productivity, thereby enhancing delivery performance and overall competitive edge.

The early MES's objective was to identify and track lots of material as it moved through the production process. To accomplish this, the user had to define a routing through which the lot would be tracked. However, this routing was defined solely for the purpose of material tracking. These early systems did not take into consideration the need for a flexible workflow automation environment in which all manufacturing activities would be defined in a flexible manner, and the definitions would then be used to drive the execution of those activities during the production process.

In the late 1980s, sophisticated MES users began to build additional custom functionality and link it into existing MESs. Custom functionality included features such as real-time statistical process control (SPC), equipment status monitoring, and material handling logistics.

Today, manufacturers are facing a new set of business requirements that place greater demands on shop-floor control technology. The focus of manufacturing execution systems is shifting from 'tracking' to planning and optimizing in order to support shorter product life-cycles, more agile production processes, and increased equipment utilization. In order to retain their competitive advantage, many manufacturers are deciding to move to next generation manufacturing execution systems. Next generation MES solutions are based on current information technologies such as distributed applications, client/server architectures, and object-oriented programming. These systems are built around a configuration environment in which users can lay out their manufacturing workflow. In this workflow, all manufacturing activities can be planned and executed at run-time. Thus, this manufacturing execution system has evolved to support the planning and optimization needs of users; they are no longer simply tracking systems.

Since no manufacturing execution system exists as an island of automation, it is critical that all interfaces to external systems be developed and tested in a wide range of operating scenarios prior to implementation. If any interface fails, there is no fallback position. Therefore, to minimize risk, implement a parallel interface test environment to support these integration activities.

Another challenge presented is training of the entire user community and support staff on the new manufacturing execution system. Users must gain and maintain a high level of system competency prior to implementation in order for this approach to be successful. As a result, it is beneficial to motivate as well as train. If users understand how the new system will enhance their job performance and productivity, they will accept the new technology with greater enthusiasm.

One method to implement a manufacturing execution system is by use of a phased implementation approach. Phased implementation represents a medium-risk/medium-cost approach to migration and involves rolling out the new MES in a step-by-step manner. The implementation may be carried out by product types, process flows, manufacturing areas, or application capabilities. For many operations, this approach represents a logical choice for deploying a next-generation MES in an existing manufacturing facility.

Product-type or process-flow implementations will track only certain product types or products that follow certain process flows. Over time, the complete set of products/processes transitions to the new MES. There are various procedures to put in place to facilitate a phased implementation. For example, in the early phases of implementation, a highly visible marking system helps operators identify which parts are to be tracked with which MES.

The primary advantage of a phased implementation is that benefits provided by the new MES are derived very quickly for a limited set of products or flows – without risk of disrupting the entire manufacturing operation should problems arise. A key disadvantage is the need to train a large group of operators in the use of both the old and new MES to reduce the possibility of misprocessing. Furthermore, this approach presents complexities for equipment-state tracking in that both systems must track the status of equipment where products are processed. Maintaining a single repository for equipment-state information, that can be updated and queried by both systems, eliminates synchronization issues.

Phased implementation by application capabilities involves deploying functional elements of the new MES in an incremental manner. For example, new MES functional modules perform equipment status monitoring, whereas old shop-floor control system modules perform WIP tracking. Over time, all system functions migrate to the new MES.

One recommended approach is to migrate the WIP tracking core to the new MES first, followed by the remaining functional areas. In this way, the benefits of the new MES WIP-tracking features can be realized, while potentially reducing some integration issues. With the phased application migration approach, data conversion activities need to focus only on those products or areas where the new MES is to be implemented, thereby reducing the total volume of data that must be converted at one time. In fact, a phased approach of this type may eliminate the need to develop sophisticated data conversion/loading tools.

Suspending operations and loading current state information into the new MES via automated data conversion/loading tools will synchronize the systems, as will developing a 'data tap' for updating the new MES from the old system while operations are executing. It is important to note, however, that data taps may be difficult to implement due to limitations of first-generation MES enabling technologies.

Bibliography

1. Anonymous, 1995: *BPCS Client/Server Distributed Object Computing Architecture.* White paper. System Software Association Inc.
2. Canfora, G., Cimitile, A., De-Lucia, A. and Di-Lucca, G.A., 1998: Decomposing legacy programs: a first step towards migrating to client-server platforms. In *Program Comprehension, Workshop Proceedings*, pp. 136–144. *Proceedings of the 1998 6th International Workshop on Program Comprehension, IWPC'98*, Ischia, Italy.
3. Guengerich, S. and Green, V.G. (eds), 1996: *Introduction to Client/Server Computing.* SME blue book series, CASA/SME.
4. Kubitz, O., Berger, M.O. and Stenzel, R., 1998: Client-server-based mobile robot control. *IEEE ASME Transactions on Mechatronics*, **3**(2), 82–90.
5. Lavington, S., Dewhurst, N., Wilkins, E. and Freitas, A., 1999: Interfacing knowledge discovery algorithms to large database management systems, *Information and Software Technology*, **41**(9), 605–617.
6. Reich, J.R., 1999: Design and implementation of a client-server architecture for taxonomy manager, *Software Practice and Experience*, **29**(2), 143–166.
7. Vetter, R., 1999: Web-based enterprise computing, *Computer*, **32**(5), 112–113.
8. Walborn, G.D. and Chrysanthis, P.K., 1999: Transaction processing in PROMOTION. In *Proceedings of the ACM Symposium on Applied Computing. 1999, Association for Computing Machinery*, New York, pp. 389–398.

Master product design

M – 2c; 3b; 4d; 7c; * 1.2b; 1.5d; 2.1b; 2.2b; 3.2c; 3.4d; 3.6b

Master product design objectives are to reduce the lead time for the design of new or improved products, while creating quality products, product diversity and options.

A product has to seduce the customer with its options and appearance. To arrive at such specifications, many disciplines should be involved in the manufacturing cycle and the product must compare similar products produced all over the world (benchmarking, one of a kind, world class manufacturing, etc.). To arrive at a product design that will result in low cost, ease of manufacture and ease of assembly, design techniques such as design for assembly (DFA), design for manufacturing (DFM), and concurrent engineering must be considered.

Both product specification and product design are innovative tasks and depend on a designer's creativity. The aim of master product design is to improve the creativity of the product specifier and designer by drawing their attention to the requirements of other disciplines, and to flag any decision that increases the cost or lead time.

The basis of a master product design system is that each manufacturing company deals in a specific line of products or business. A line of products usually has many common features. Even different lines of products have several common sub-assemblies, not to mention different models of the same product. Each has its own characteristics and requirements, yet there are features in common. Master product design studies the products in order to come up with a 'master product'. A 'master product' is presented as a schematic block diagram of the product, where each block of the diagram represents its objective and includes alternatives, availability and cost information together with technical specifications.

Master product design schemes have two modules: product definition, and product design. The objective of the product definition module is to assist and guide the product specifier to define a product that will meet all product objectives, drawing attention to the effect of decisions on product cost and lead time. The philosophy behind this idea is that product definition is a process of innovation and as such, must allow the individual who performs this task freedom and judgement. The backbone of the system is technology, not computers. The system draws the attention of the user to the meaning of his decisions and, in some cases, proposes alternatives. However, the final decision is left to the user.

The types of activities in which a company is engaged are displayed in the product definition field.

1. A company manufactures to order. In such cases the product is defined by the customer. However, it is a good idea to consult with the manufacturer on the design of the product in order to reduce manufacturing costs.
2. A company manufactures a line of existing products. In such cases it is a good idea to keep track of possible design changes that might reduce manufacturing costs, increase product appeal to customers, and introduce options and new models of the same product.
3. A company would like to enter a new field of activities.

The master product methodology supply answers to all types.

The manufacturing process must consider the points of view of many disciplines in order to arrive at good performance. Experts in each discipline (marketing, finance, manpower, purchasing, etc.) consider the problem at hand from a different angle. A good balanced and unbiased decision will be achieved by considering the viewpoints of all disciplines and finding a compromise. The need for such compromise is commonly accepted. The problem is: how to arrive at such a compromise. The easy unimaginative answer is to establish committees and discussion groups. Master product design is a computerized answer as a workstation program representing all disciplines.

The master product design main program controls and navigates the design session.

The first step in specifying a product is to understand and have the relevant data for the task. Only then can the product specifications be formalized. The logic in this stage is that it is a natural tendency for someone who specifies product characteristics to aim for the best. However, the product specifier is not always aware of the costs and manufacturing implications. In many cases, reducing the specified values by as little as 5% can result in a cost reduction of more than 60%. The product specifier might well change the specifications if he is aware of this.

Messages that draw the attention of the user are presented whenever the response to an enquiry is outside of standard or reasonable values. To determine if and when to post a message a technical data file is used.

Auxiliary databases are used to assist the product specifier and product designer in fields that are out of their expertise. These databases represent the interest of all other disciplines in the manufacturing process. Hence the user does not have to call a meeting with experts from different disciplines for consultation; the user can achieve the same results by sitting at a workstation. The results are more efficient, more objective, and give better decisions in less time. The databases and files are listed below.

1. *Master product design file*. The purpose of the master product design file is to provide assistance and guidance on forming the dialogue session and to supply data for messages during the session.
2. *Checklist*. The checklist serves as a reminder to draw the attention of the user to many topics and allows the user either to specify that the topic is of no relevance to the specific product, or to enter additional requirements to the product specifications.
3. *Gate list*. The gate list is a project management tool for the controller and follows-up on the project. It is composed of several gates, each one representing a major milestone in the development project. Each gate is then divided into internal milestones.
4. *Technical data file*. The technical data files include a list of available relevant products and subassemblies as well as engineering handbook data, such as data on materials and their specifications, local and international standards, tolerance tables, useful equations, and relevant data for screws, bolts, rivets, etc.
5. *Group B note files*. This file contains the product requirements set by any interested personnel. Group B includes auxiliary or advisory disciplines such as marketing, sales, purchasing, etc.

The master product method is NOT a computerized system; it is a technological system, assisted by computers. One cannot produce a standard, off-the-shelf product like this. It is unique to each plant. The supporting computer program is very simple to write. The file organization of the auxiliary files may be by keyword as referenced in the checklist and a sequential search.

Bibliography

1. Camp, R., 1989: *Benchmarking: The Search for Industry Best* ... ASQC Quality Press.
2. Crawford, J., 1994: TPC auditing: how to do it better, *Quarterly Report*, 9–11.

3. Gardan, Y. and Minich, C., 1993: Feature-based models for CAD/CAM and their limits, *Computers in Industry*, **23**, 3–13.

4. Halevi, G., 1999: *Restructuring the Manufacturing Process – Applying the Matrix Method*. St. Lucie Press/APICS series on resource management.

5. Halevi, G., 1980: *The Role of Computers in Manufacturing Processes*. John Wiley & Sons, New York.

6. Halevi, G., 1995: *Principles of Process Planning – A Logistic Approach*. Chapman & Hall, London.

7. Halevi, G., 1997: Global optimization of the manufacturing process, *CIRP International Symposium in the Global Manufacturing Era*, August 21–22, Hong-Kong, pp. 340–352.

8. Halevi, G. and Weill, R., 1992: *Manufacturing in the Era of Concurrent Engineering*. North-Holland.

9. Halevi, G., 1994: CAD for manufacturing support. *Proceedings of the IFIP International Conference on Feature Modeling and Recognition in advanced CADD/CAM Systems*, Valenciennes, France, pp. 373–390.

10. Rostadas, A. (ed.), 1995: *Benchmarking – Theory and Practice*. Chapman & Hall, London.

11. Scheer, A.-W., 1992: *Architecture of Integrated Information Systems*. Springer-Verlag, Berlin.

12. Watson, H.G., 1993: *Strategic Benchmarking*. John Wiley and Sons, pp. 3–39.

Master Production Scheduling

M – 1b; 2c; 3b; 4c; 7b; 10d; 11c; 13c; 16d; * 1.1b; 1.2c; 1.3d; 2.1d; 2.3c; 3.2c; 3.3b; 3.5b; 3.6c; 4.3b; 4.4b

The master production schedule is a management tool with a 'look ahead' feature – a tool that is needed in order to plan the future of the company. It provides simulation on capacity requirements for different marketing forecasts, on purchasing of new equipment, and on profit or loss forecast. It indicates the necessary requirement planning with respect to shop-floor space, warehousing space, transport facilities and manpower.

The master production schedule is used to prepare the enterprise budget; to plan cash flow, manpower, and resource requirements; and to forecast company profit. The budget is used as a management tool to control the activities of the company.

However, the present-day method of planning the master production schedule assumes fixed, unaltered routing and thereby robs the manufacturing process of its inherent flexibility. Management decisions are thus biased, and in many cases unrealistic decisions will be made.

The master product design and the matrix method assists in preparing and improving the master production schedule, and thereby all its derivatives. Adjusting product design and treating routing as a variable can avoid many scheduling problems and investment in unnecessary resources.

The master production schedule transforms the manufacturing objectives of quantity and delivery dates for the final product, which are assigned by the non-engineering functions of the organization, into an engineering production plan. The master production schedule is a coordinating function among manufacturing, marketing, finance, and management. It is the basis for future detailed production planning. Its main objective is to plan a realistic production programme that ensures even utilization of plant resources – people and machines. This will be the driving input for detailed planning and will guard, as much as possible, against overload and underload of resources. If formulated properly, the master production schedule can serve as a tool for marketing personnel in promising delivery dates.

Master production scheduling is the phase in which delivery dates are established for the production phases. Thus it controls the relative priorities of all open shop orders. If the master production schedule is unrealistic in terms of capacity, many shop orders will be rush orders with high priority, and the entire capacity planning system will not function correctly. To maintain valid shop priorities, the master production schedule must not exceed the gross productive capacity in any period.

Planning the master production schedule is a difficult task, since it normally covers a wide range of products and represents a variety of conflicting considerations, such as demands, cost, selling price, available capital for investment, and company marketing strategy. It is not purely engineering work. The engineers supply information and can simulate different strategies, but the final decision lies with management. In some companies, the sales department is responsible for preparing the master production schedule. In any case, production engineering must be involved in order to ensure a realistic programme.

It is recognized that it is impractical to try out all the combinations possible. Thus human judgement is necessary to predict the most likely combination, and only that combination will be simulated by the system. Basically, from a capacity point of view, the master production schedule represents long-range capacity planning. Suppose that the company plans to produce certain products in certain quantities with different delivery dates. The company needs to know the impact of the plan in terms of production capacity and to enable this the computation system employs the following files:

- The order file – includes the details of all orders.
- The item master file – lists all available products and items.
- The product structure file – lists all the items in the product, the relationship between them and the quantities for each assembly and subassembly.
- The routine file – indicates how each item, and subassembly is being made. It tells in what work centres processing takes place and the sequence

of operations; it also provides such lead time information as setup time and standard machining time.

- The work centre file – lists the available work centres and their available capacity.

By means of the data stored in these files, it is possible to explode each product in the order file into its components and accumulate the workload at each work centre by time and period.

The master production schedule is the driving force behind further detailed production planning. However, it is also a management tool for controlling and planning the future of the company, covering such activities as:

- resource requirement planning;
- human resource requirement planning;
- cash flow planning;
- profit forecasting;
- budget and management controls.

Traditional master production scheduling methods are based on fixed routing. The use of master product design and the matrix manufacturing method will be used to improve the master production scheduling. The methods are:

- Review the product design, before constructing the load profiles.
- Add a new degree of freedom in dealing with load profile fluctuations.

If product design was done a long time before the current period, it is good practice to review the design and incorporate technological improvements, and new customer wishes and needs.

The load profile might indicate continuous overload periods and underload periods. Continuous overloads usually indicate a need to purchase new equipment. However, before making such a major and costly decision, it might be possible to make some design changes or process changes that will balance the load. The matrix method can supply data to management for use in such a decision.

Bibliography

1. Beckhard, R. and Prichard, W., 1992: *Changing the Essence: The Art of Creating and Leading Fundamental Change in Organizations*. Jossey Bass, San Francisco.
2. Blake, R. and Mouton, J., 1974: *The Managerial Grid*. Prentice-Hall, Englewood Cliffs, NJ.
3. Halevi, G., 1980: *The Role of Computers in Manufacturing Processes*. John Wiley & Sons, New York.
4. Halevi, G., 1995: *Principles of Process Planning – A Logistic Approach*. Chapman & Hall, London.

5. Halevi, G., 1993: The magic matrix as a smart scheduler, *Computers in Industry*, **21**, 245–253.
6. Halevi, G., 1997: Global optimization of the manufacturing process, *CIRP International Symposium Global Manufacturing Era*, August 21–22, Hong-Kong, pp. 340–352.
7. Halevi, G., 1999: *Restructuring the Manufacturing Process – Applying the Matrix Method*. St. Lucie Press/APICS series on resource management.
8. Hubner, H. and Paterson, I. (ed.), *Production Management Systems*. North-Holland.
9. Whetten, D. and Cameron, K., 1995: *Developing Management Skills*. Harper-Collins, New York.

Material requirements planning – MRP

S – 1b; 4c; 6c; 7b; 10c; 13c; * 1.2c; 1.3b; 1.6c; 2.3b; 2.4c; 2.5c; 3.5c; 3.6d

The objective of material requirements planning is to plan the activities to be performed in order to meet the goals of the master production schedule.

The logic and mathematics upon which MRP is based are very simple. The gross requirements of the end product for each specific delivery is compared against on-hand and on-order quantities and then offset by the lead time to generate information as to when assembly should be started. All items or sub-assemblies required for the assembly should be available on that date, in the required quantity. Thus, the above computation establishes the gross requirements for the lower level items. The same computation is repeated level by level throughout the entire product structure.

MRP is not a new concept, having previously gone under such different names as items balance sheet, activity planning, inventory management and requirements planning.

MRP represents an integrated communication and decision support system that supports management of the total manufacturing business. The use of optimizing techniques drawn from operations research and management science was frowned upon by MRP. One significant reason why MRP was the technique that was adapted was that it made use of the computer's ability to centrally store and provide access to the large body of information that seemed necessary to run a company. It helped coordinate the activities of various functions in the manufacturing firm such as engineering, production and materials.

Thus the attraction of MRPII lay not only in its role as decision-making support, but more importantly, in its integrative role within the manufacturing organization.

The starting point for MRP is the recognition that products to be manufactured or assembled can be represented by a bill of materials (BOM) which describes the parent/child relationship between an assembly and its components parts or raw material. The bill of materials may have an arbitrary number of levels and have (typically) purchased items at the lowest level in the hierarchy. The MRP system is based on the fact that the BOM relationship allows one to derive the demand for component material based on the demand for the parent item. MRP proposes a technique for management of dependent items demand, by translating the independent demand for top-level products and spares, through the component hierarchy as represented by the BOM. The MRP calculation procedure is extremely simple. MRP plans by a series of discrete time interval periods (assume one week). The procedure starts at the top-level production plan and works down level-by-level and item-by-item through the BOM until all parts are planned. For each item at each level the lead time is retrieved from the routing files and is multiplied by the quantity, to arrive at the interval period that processing the item should start. Assembly of the order (upper level) is the promised delivery date minus the processing time. At the end of this stage each time interval holds the gross requirements of each product, assembly, subassembly, and item on the order book regardless of its origin. The next step is netting off gross requirements against projected inventory and taking into account any open order scheduled for receipt, thus yielding net requirements. Next conversion of the net requirements to a planned order quantity using lot size, and placing the plan order in the appropriate period for purchasing or shop floor processing.

MRP output includes activity planning in the area of purchasing and in-shop processing, and for each it includes the items needed, the quantity and at which date. A third output is a list of items in inventory that are not needed at all (dead stock).

Scheduling in MRP to determine the required dates is based on unlimited capacity. For purchasing, or subcontracting this may be acceptable, however, for in-shop processing the schedule is unrealistic, and in many cases it cannot be done. The effect might be to increase work-in-process and to fail to meet due dates.

To improve the scheduling aspects, and other functions beyond material planning (inventory control and BOM control of MRP), an extension of this functionality is proposed. The extension adds rough-cut capacity planning, production activity control, and capacity requirements planning. It simulates scheduling with finite capacity, but only by simulation, thus it improves the planning. To distinguish it from material requirements planning it is called material requirements planning II (MRPII).

Several areas of the plant are affected by MRPII: production scheduling, quality control, accounting, first-line supervision, production labour, and the MRP system used to develop plant-wide schedules.

MRP-based systems appear to be used in firms belonging to each of the three different process types (job shops, repetitive, and process) and across all size firms. While MRP was the most widely used system in all categories, it especially dominates in those firms whose products are in the early stages of the product life-cycle. In general, MRP users accommodated a wide variety of environments and were able to achieve a reasonably 'good' performance. For example, among MRP users, firms that experienced a complex environment (unsteady demand, etc.) reported best performance results. On the other hand, when there was very little complexity in the environment faced by the firm, the use of MRP does not appear to produce 'good' performance results. This may quite possibly be due to the inherent complexity of MRP systems in terms of information and processing requirements. MRP systems are most versatile and are able to cope with increased complexity. The increased information-processing requirements entailed by MRP systems, however, may prove to be a hindrance for firms that do not need a complex system (i.e. where product variety is low and demand is steady).

Bibliography

1. Belt, B., 1987: MRP and kanban – a possible synergy? *Production and Inventory Management*, **28**(1), pp. 71–80.
2. Bose, G.J. and Rao, A., 1988: Implementing JIT with MRP II creates hybrid manufacturing environment, *Industrial Engineering*, **September**, **20**(9), pp. 49–53.
3. Goldratt, E.M. and Cox, J., 1986: *The Goal*, revised edn. North River Press, Croton-on-Hudson, NY.
4. Lambrecht, M.R. and Decaluwe, L., 1988: JIT and constraint theory: the issue of bottleneck management, *Production and Inventory Management Journal*, **29**(3), pp. 61–66.
5. Lotenschtein, S., 1986: Just-in-time in the MRP II environment, *P&IM Review*, February.
6. Plenert, G., 1985: Are Japanese production methods applicable in the United States? *Production and Inventory Management*, **26**(2), p. 25.
7. Best, T.D., 1986: MRP, JIT, and OPT: what's 'best'? *Production and Inventory Management*, **27**(2), 22–28.
8. Rao, A. and Scheraga, D., 1988: Moving from manufacturing resource planning to just-in-time manufacturing, *Production and Inventory Management Journal*, **29**(1), pp. 44–50.
9. Schonberger, R.J., 1983: Selecting the right manufacturing inventory system: Western and Japanese approaches, *Production and Inventory Management*, **24**(2), pp. 33–44.
10. Wilson, G.T., 1985: Kanban scheduling – boon or bane? *Production and Inventory Management*, **26**(3), pp. 134–142.

Material resource planning – MRPII

S – 1b; 4c; 6c; 7b; 10c; 13c; * 1.2c; 1.3b; 1.6c; 2.3b; 2.4c; 2.5c; 3.5c; 3.6d

See Material requirement planning – MRP.

Matrix shop floor control

P – 1b; 2c; 3d; 4b; 8d; 9d; 13b; 14c; 16c; * 1.2b ;1.3b; 1.4c; 2.3b; 2.4c; 3.3b; 3.5b; 3.6b; 4.4c; 4.6c

Matrix shop floor control is a multi-agent architecture based on the following concepts: the machines take autonomous decisions; machine grouping is dynamic; orders are communicated via a blackboard; and shop floor control is exerted by rewards and penalties. These concepts create a future manufacturing system that responds to apparently future manufacturing needs.

A matrix shop floor control system is a multi-agent architecture made up of totally distributed independent autonomous modules that cooperate intelligently to create a state of the art manufacturing system. The needs are specified as:

- produced by autonomous modules;
- reduction of workforce;
- modular design that assures integration;
- inexpensive construction of production lines (reduction of 70–80% of investment);
- meeting customers needs;
- fast adjustment to market fluctuations.

The traditional approach to the design of manufacturing systems is the hierarchical approach. The design is based on a top-down approach and strictly defines the system modules and their functionality. Communication between modules is strictly defined and limited in such a way that modules communicate with their parent and child modules only. In a hierarchical architecture, modules cannot take an initiative; therefore, the system is sensitive to perturbations, and its autonomy and reactivity to disturbances are weak. The resulting architecture is very rigid and therefore expensive to develop and difficult to maintain.

Heterarchical control was an approach used to alleviate the problems of hierarchical systems. The heterarchical approach bans all hierarchy in order to give full power to the basic modules, often called 'agents', in the system. A heterarchical manufacturing system consists of, for instance, workstations and orders only. Each order negotiates with the workstations to get the work done, using all possible alternatives available to face unforeseen situations. In this way, it is possible to react adequately to changes in the environment (such as new products that enter the market, new or evolving technologies, unpredictable demands for products) as well as to disturbances in the manufacturing system itself (defects, delays, variable yield of chemical reactors).

The matrix shop floor control system basic philosophy is that all parameters in the manufacturing process are flexible, that is, any of them is subject to change if such change contributes to increased productivity in manufacturing the product mix required for the immediate period. In such a flexible and dynamic environment, the only stable parameters are the product to be manufactured and the resources available at the shop. Product objectives are external to the manufacturing cycle and must be preserved. The routing is not explicitly defined, but rather is presented as a 3D matrix of parts, resources and operations. The decision of which routing to use is made in the capacity planning stage and at shop floor operating time. Working product structure is preserved throughout the planning and execution stages.

Bibliography

1. Bongaerts, H. Van Brussel, and Valckenaers, P., 1998: Schedule execution using perturbation analysis. *Proceedings of IEEE International Conference on Robotics and Automation*, Leuven, Belgium, May 16–21, pp. 2747–2752.
2. Dilts, D.M., Boyd, N.P. and Whorms, H.H., 1991: The evolution of control architectures for automated manufacturing systems, *Journal of Manufacturing Systems*, **10**(1), 79–93.
3. Halevi, G., 1980: *The Role of Computers in Manufacturing Processes*. John-Wiley & Sons, New York.
4. Halevi, G., 1995: *Principles of Process Planning – A Logistic Approach*, Chapman & Hall, London.
5. Halevi, G., 1993: The magic matrix as a smart scheduler, *Computers in Industry*, **21**, 245–253.
6. Halevi, G., 1997: Global optimization of the manufacturing process. *CIRP International Symposium Global Manufacturing Era*, August 21–22, Hong-Kong, pp. 340–352.
7. Halevi, G., 1999: *Restructuring the Manufacturing Process – Applying the Matrix Method*, St. Lucie Press/ APICS series on resource management.
8. Jones, A.T. and McLean, C.R., 1986: A proposed hierarchical control model for automated manufacturing systems, *Journal of Manufacturing Systems*, **5**(1), 15–26.
9. Kadar, L., Monostori, and Szelke, E., 1997: An object oriented framework for developing distributed manufacturing architectures, *Proceedings of 2nd World Congress on Intelligent Manufacturing Processes and Systems*, June 10–13, Budapest, Hungary, pp. 548–554.
10. Kimura, E., 1993: A product and process model for virtual manufacturing systems, *Annals of the CIRP*, **42**(1), 147–150.
11. Senehi, M.K., Kramer, Th.R., Ray, S.R., Quintero, R. and Albus, J.S., 1994: Hierarchical control architectures from shop level to end effectors, In S.B. Joshi and I.S. Smith (eds), *Computer Control of Flexible Manufacturing Systems, Research and Development*. Chapman & Hall, New York, pp. 31–62.
12. Swiercz, 1997: Testing and Evaluation of Manufacturing Systems. Graduation thesis for Warsaw University of Technology, Tempus Bursary at K.U.Leuven. Also available as a K.U.Leuven technical report PMA 97R039.

13. Tharumarajah and Wells, A.J., 1997: A behavior-based approach to scheduling in distributed manufacturing systems, *Integrated ComputerAided Engineering*, **4**(4), 235–249.
14. Valckenaers, P., Bonneville, E., Van Brussel, H., Bongaerts, L. and Wyns, J., 1994: Results of the holonic control system benchmark at the K.U.Leuven, *Proceedings of CIMAT Conference (Computer Integrated Manufacturing and Automation Technology)*, 10–12 Oct., Troy, NY, pp. 128–133.

Mission statement

P – 8b; 9c; 12b; 14d; * 1.1b; 1.4b; 3.3c; 4.3c; 4.5b

A mission statement is about how to get an organization fully committed and passionate about its mission; how to get independent people to work and 'buy' the mission. The key to a mission-driven organization is not so much the statement itself, but how it is woven into the daily lives of everyone involved.

Inspiring leadership envisions a clear mission with purpose and passion and calls upon that purpose and that passion to lead to greater heights. A leadership mission describes the values needed to make it reality, and to set a standard of behaviour. Such a mission is not about a code of conduct, rules, systems, and procedures. It is about having a sense of purpose and a set of values that guide everyday actions.

A clear mission statement that includes a clear statement of values is aimed at gaining a high level of commitment from employees and stakeholders.

The quality of the process used to develop and disseminate the mission ultimately determines its effectiveness. Some results show that the process by which the statement is developed might actually be more important than the content of the mission statement. The following steps are recommended for working a mission statement.

1. It is recommended that organizational leaders consider involving as many stakeholder groups as possible in the mission development process, especially those who tend to be under-represented.
2. The mission team should be permitted to follow whatever steps are deemed necessary to converge on a suitable mission. Only when the mission statement is believed to have widespread acceptance and support should the process be considered completed.
3. The process should be straightforward and simple. It should not include many complicated exercises aimed at achieving perfection.
4. A successful mission development process is characterized by creativity. Thus, it would appear to be far better for an organization's mission development team to follow an original process rather than simply take one from a textbook and impose it on the organization.

The two areas on which administrators should consider placing greater emphasis when disseminating their mission are customers and shareholders. These are the stakeholders who do not seem to be getting the attention they require. They are the ones, however, that effective communication offers some substantial returns. Communication is a vital tool in the development and acceptance of a mission statement. Many missions fail because important stakeholder groups either do not know what the statements mean in terms of their own work or, worse, they forget them.

The more difficult part is getting everyone to buy into the mission and values: it takes time and effort, and consistency of action, through bad times as well as good. It only takes one reversal of values at the top when conditions are tough to reverse many years of hard work in setting the standard and the climate. For better or for worse, leaders are better known for deeds than for words. There is thus a substantial payoff for those organizations that put the necessary effort into communicating and disseminating their mission so that it is known, understood, accepted and remembered by all important stake-holders – both internal and external.

Lastly, there are many ways of disseminating the mission statement to stakeholders. The most-frequently-used methods appear to be annual reports, posters, plaques and employee. Less-frequently-used methods include company information kits, word of mouth, newsletters, advertisements and company seminars, workshops and training sessions.

Most employees appear not to be enthusiastic in their overall opinion of the effectiveness of the methods used to communicate their mission Thus, not enough effort appears to be going into the quantity and quality of communication methods.

The key to a mission-driven organization is not so much the statement itself, but how it is woven into the daily lives of everyone involved. Here's how one organization mission 'comes alive' for all employees and everyone who visits or associates with the company:

1. Meet individually with each new employee and describe the company's history and its mission.
2. To make the mission come alive, talk about it all the time.
3. Have a monthly breakfast with employees to get feedback on how well the mission is being fulfilled.
4. Send regular e-mails to employees, describing what is being done to fulfil the mission.
5. Talk about the impact of the mission on customers in a monthly chairman's briefing and annual shareholders meeting.
6. The mission is often referred to in business decisions.
7. The mission is an integral part of quality decisions. No product can be released to the market until the Executive Committee has approved it with a formal vote following a quality presentation.

8. Refer to the mission in making people decisions such as layoffs and early retirements, as well as ensuring that all employees are shareholders so they can have 'a means to share in the company's success'.
9. The mission weighs heavily on our ethical decisions.

Despite the frequency of mission statements, there is little guidance available concerning how they should be managed. Research continues to verify that, as an organizational concept, mission does matter and can make a difference in any organization's performance when used wisely. Managers should, therefore, take care during the process of formulating, disseminating and communicating their mission. If they don't, the final product, no matter how good the words sound (or how much money is spent), may not be worth much.

Bibliography

1. Bart, C.K., 1998: Comparison of mission statements and their rationales in innovative and non-innovative firms, *International Journal of Technology Management*, **16**(1–3), 64–77.
2. Campbel, A., 1992: The power of mission: aligning strategy and culture, Planning Review, **October**, **25**(5), pp. 10–13.
3. Edelheit, L.S., 1998: GE's R&D strategy: be vital, *Research Technology Management*, **41**(2), 21–27.
4. Galleher, J.J. and Stift, M.T., 1998: Pipelines in the constructed environment. In *Proceedings of the Pipeline Division Conference*, ASCE, Reston, VA, pp. 721–730.
5. Jago, C., 1999: Partners promise to deliver on time, *Railway Gazette International*, **155**(5), 3.
6. Lark, J.T., 1998: Linking business processes to the CEO's vision. In *Annual International Conference Proceedings American Production and Inventory Control Society*. APICS, Falls Church, VA, pp. 501–506.

Mobile agent system

X – 3b; 7b; 11c; 13c; * 1.1b; 3.3b; 4.1c; 4.2c;4.3c

A mobile agent is defined as a software agent that is able to autonomously migrate an enterprise's information and programs from one host to another in a computer network.

Globalization and recent advances in information technology has led to the emergence of the virtual enterprise, which is an enterprise made up of number of cooperating companies who are generally physically distributed in different parts of the world, but work together to meet some common goal. As the operations of the virtual enterprise are distributed geographically, so must the information systems that support them. Management of the information remains a base requirement of these virtual enterprises, which are therefore charged with the integration of several separate information technology systems to form an operational system in as short a time as possible.

The ability to effectively manage, manipulate, distribute and access an enterprise's information is key to competitiveness within the global marketplace. Developments in information technology (IT) have provided database systems that help support this need. However, companies in the very rapidly changing sectors of the market are demanding increased levels of flexibility.

Mobile agent is described as a computational environment in which running programs are able to transport themselves from host to host over a computer network. By their nature, mobile agents are inherently distributed. As such, they must be executable across a variety of platforms and operating systems to achieve their full potential. In a small, private network there may only be one configuration upon which they must work, but their true advantage comes from being able to migrate to different systems and continue functioning. This need has influenced the way in which mobile agent systems are created, these systems must be written in some type of script or byte code that can be interpreted. Interpretation removes the need to recompile the agent on arrival at a new host, and places the load on ensuring that the host is capable of uniformly executing the agent on arrival.

Mobile agent technology provides a useful software paradigm that enables information technology system designers to model and implement their systems as more natural reflections of the real world they simulate and support. A direct relationship is established between the mobile elements of a distributed information system and the agent-based architecture of the information technology system to evolve in line with the real world they represent. In addition mobile agent technology can help in the rapid formation of these information systems, which can be vital when supporting the creation of virtual enterprises.

Bibliography

1. Anonymous, 1995: *BPCS Client/Server Distributed Object Computing Architecture*. System software Association Inc. White paper.
2. Camarinha-Matos, L.M, Afsarmanesh, and Marik, V., 1998: *Intelligent Systems for Manufacturing, Multi-agent Systems and Virtual Organizations*, Kluwer Academic Publishers, Dordrecht.
3. Chess, D., Harrison, C. and Kershenbaum, A., 1997: Mobile agents: are they a good idea? In J. Vitek and C. Tschudin (eds), *Mobile Object Systems, Toward one Programmable Internet*. Springer Lecture Notes in Computer Science, Vol. 1222. Springer, Berlin.
4. Gray, R., 1997: Agent Tel: A Flexible and Secure Mobile Agent System. Ph.D. Thesis, Department of Computer Science, Dartmouth College, UK, June.
5. Hofmann, M.O., McGovern, A. and Whitebread, K.R., 1998: Mobile agent on digital battlefield. In *Proceedings of the Second International Conference on Autonomous Agents*. ACM, New York, pp. 219–225.

6. Papaioannon, T. and Edwards, J., 1998: Mobile agent technology in support of sales order processing in the virtual enterprise. In L.M. Camarinha-Matos *et al.* (eds), *Intelligent Systems for Manufacturing*. Kluwer Academic Publishers, Dordrecht, pp. 23–32.
7. Papaioannon, T. and Edwards, J., 1999: Using mobile agents to improve the alignment between manufacturing and its IT support systems, *Robotics and Autonomous Systems*, **27**(1–2), 45–57.
8. Rus, D., Gray, R. and Kotz, D., 1997: Transportable information agent, *Journal of Intelligent Information Systems*, **9**, 215–238.

Multi-agent manufacturing system

P – 1c; 2d; 4c; 6d; 8c; 12b; 13c; 14c; * 1.3c; 1.4b; 2.3d; 2.4b; 3.6c; 4.2c; 4.5b

Multi-agent manufacturing systems are designed to solve shop floor control problems. The increased demand for flexibility has led to new manufacturing control paradigms based on the concept of self-organization and on the notion of agents.

Today, computers are used to support various human work activities. They provide the human with powerful tools to perform individual tasks, but usually, teamworking of humans and computers is required. Although teamwork is most popular in human societies, the multi-agent manufacturing system expands the meaning of teamwork to groups of humans and computers collaborating in order to solve a common problem. Human–computer cooperation is used to solve shop floor control problems in manufacturing systems.

The first manufacturing control architectures were usually centralized or hierarchical. The poor performance of these structures in very dynamic environments and their difficulties with unforeseen disruptions and modifications led to new control architectures, based on self-organized systems that change their internal organization on their own account. A multi-agent manufacturing system is composed of self-organizing agents that may be completely informational or represent subsystems of the physical world.

At workshop level, the heterogeneity of the system led to agent identification problems. This system heterogeneity makes agent identification rather unclear, and one agent identification method proposition to overcome this is based on the idea that an agent should be autonomous intelligent. Thus agent basic capabilities should be:

1. To transform its environment in at least one of the dimensions shape, space and time.
2. To verify the search results before presenting them.
3. To roam the network and seek information autonomously.

The control behaviour of each agent is briefly outlined below.

The part agent and the resource agent negotiate with each other to manage the operation of part entities and the functioning of the resources. The intelligence agent provides different bidding algorithms and strategies; the monitor agent is used to supplement system status. The database agent and management agents manipulate inter-agent information. The communication agents carry out all communication between entities.

A multi-agent system can be viewed as a sphere of commitment, which encapsulates the promises and obligations the agents may have towards each other. Spheres of commitment generalize the traditional ideas of information management so as to overcome their historical weaknesses. The multi-agent scenario-based method is composed of three phases: analysis, design, and implementation.

Analysis: representation of the problem domain. The analysis phase is composed of four modelling activities:

1. Scenario modelling: identification of important notions supporting the scenario; human/artificial agents, role of the agents, objects, interaction among agents, object changes, etc.
2. Agent modelling: role description; local data modelling; detailed behaviour description; validation of agent interaction with the scenario.
3. Object modelling: object structure specification, object life-cycle, object behaviour; validation of object/agent interaction in relation to the scenario.
4. Conversation modelling: user/agent interaction; validation of conversation in relation to scenario. The purpose is to verify the search request and results by communication between the user and the agent.

Design: transformation of the agent's transition diagrams and data conceptual structure into specifications.

Implementation: transformation of design into system programs.

For an automated system, implementation is straightforward, however, if there are human operators working at cell level, there is a distinction between workshop levels and cell level. To integrate the operator into the automated system, one solution consists in interfacing an agent with the operator. The artificial agents then take charge of inter-agent organization and the human being is simply considered as a resource. The operators could participate in self-organizing processes at the same level as the artificial agents. This could be realized with reactive agents, which have simple behaviour based on their perceptions. Although individually very simple, a reactive multi-agent system may exhibit very complex group behaviour. Consider, for example, part transport based on use of both human and auto-guided vehicle control using a simple system of sensors. When a workstation needs a transport agent it sends a red light signal. Artificial agents controlling the auto-guided vehicle detect the signal, and if they have no other task to perform, they automatically approach the source. The human transport operator can also see the red light, and may participate in the transport process or not, depending on his/her judgement of the situation.

In the case of a flexible manufacturing system (FMS) there is no basic difference to agent identification in the workshop. There are only two types of agent: the workstation and the transfer system. Parts and storage area are not considered as agents because they have no resources enabling them to be autonomous. Scheduling in FMS is divided into two separate problems.

1. Internal workstation problems: the workstations have several parts to process and must find an optimum schedule.
2. The problem of the allocation of parts to the FMS system. The arrival of a part at the FMS is transmitted to the transfer agent that must find a workstation for it. An offer is broadcast to the workstations with the message 'location' which activates their algorithm. The workstation then sends a message to the transfer agent 'accept part', which contains a proposal for acceptance at a specific date. The transfer agent chooses the workstation and transports the part with minimum processing date.

The multi-agent manufacturing system is one of several methods based on a self-organization concept. Others are agent-based manufacturing, agent-driven manufacturing, holonic, bionic, genetic, fractal, random, matrix scheduling, and virtual manufacturing systems.

Bibliography

1. Agent Builder Environment. http://www.networking.ibm.com/iag/iagsoft.htm.
2. Davies, C.T., 1978: Data processing spheres of control, *IBM Systems Journal*, **17**(2), 179–198.
3. Elmagarmid, A.K. (ed.), 1992: *Database Transaction Models for Advanced Applications*. Morgan Kaufmann, San Mateo,
4. Finin, T., Fritzson, R., McKay, D. and McEntire, R., 1994: Using KQML as an agent communication language. In *Proceedings of the Third International Conference on Information and Knowledge Management (CIKM'94)*. ACM Press.
5. Georgakopoulos, D., Hornick, M. and Sheth, A., 1995: An overview of workflow management: From process modeling to workflow automation infrastructure, *Distributed and Parallel Databases*, **3**(2), 119–152.
6. Gilman, C.R., Aparicio, M., Barry, J., Durniak, T., Lam, H. and Ramnath, R., 1997: Integration of design and manufacturing in a virtual enterprise using enterprise rules, intelligent agents, STEP, and work flow. In *SPIE Proceedings on Architectures, Networks, and Intelligent Systems for Manufacturing Integration*, pp. 160–171.
7. Gray, J. and Reuter, A., 1993: *Transaction Processing: Concepts and Techniques*. Morgan Kaufmann, San Mateo,

8. Huhns, M.N. and Singh, M.P. (eds), 1998: *Readings in Agents*. Morgan Kaufmann, San Francisco.

9. Labrou, Y. and Finin, T., Semantics and conversations for an agent communication language. In M.N. Huhns and M.P. Singh (eds), *Readings in Agents*. Morgan Kaufmann, San Francisco, pp. 235–242.

10. Lefranqois, P., Cloutier, L. and Montreuil, B., 1996: An agent-driven approach to design factory information systems, *Computers in Industry*, **32**, 197–217.

11. Nakamura, J., Takahara, T. and Kamigaki, 1995: Human-computer cooperative work in multi-agent manufacturing system. In E.M. Dar-el (ed.), *Proceedings of the 13th International Conference on Production Research*, Jerusalem, August 6–10, pp. 370–372.

12. Rabelo, R.J. and Spinosa, L.M., 1997: Mobile-agent-based supervision in supply-chain management in the food industry. In *Proceedings of Workshop on Supply-Chain Management in Agribusiness*, Vitoria (ES) Brazil, pp. 451–460.

13. Rabelo, R.J. and Camarinha-Matos, L.M., 1994: Negotiation in multi-agent based dynamic scheduling, *Journal on Robotics and Computer Integrated Manufacturing*, **11**(4), 303–310.

14. Sethi, A.K. and Sethi, S.P., 1990: Flexibility in manufacturing: a survey, *The International Journal of Flexible Manufacturing Systems*, **2**, pp. 289–328.

15. Singh, M.P., 1998: Agent communication languages: rethinking the principles, *IEEE Computer*, **31**(12), 40–47.

16. SMART. http:l/smart.npo.org/

One-of-a-kind manufacturing (OKM)

M – 2c; 3b; 4c; 7c; 14d; * 1.1d; 1.2d; 1.3b; 2.3b; 2.4b; 2.5c; 3.1c; 3.2b; 4.1b; 4.2b

The market of consumer goods shows an increase in variety and a decrease in product life-cycle. This means that producers of these goods are moving more and more towards one-of-a-kind production. In addition, tailoring the product to customer needs is increasingly important in quality improvement. Ultimately, this leads to one-of-a-kind manufacturing (OKM) production.

The theory of production management covers many different issues, including logistics control, quality control, human resources, design, process innovation, etc. These issues are usually treated as if production were a repeat activity, yielding anonymous products. The theory of production management is largely a theory for producing anonymous products. The information systems assume that perfect information is a prerequisite. However, in OKM the situation is often the opposite. Perfect information is only available after the project is finished, and management means motivation of professionals to act as a team.

OKM is usually process oriented, where a considerable investment is made in the development of a production process independent of customer orders. A production process consists of all manufacturing steps required to produce a particular family of products. OKM may be resource oriented – make to order, or product oriented – a defined product with options to suit specific customer needs.

In OKM top management focuses on capacity and capability: capacity creation, capability improvement, capacity maintenance, and selling capacity and capability. There is a strong need for a simple, rough capacity planning and monitoring system. Sophisticated planning and scheduling tools are seldom a success, because there are many uncertainties. Shop floor personnel lack reliable engineering data about the operation of new orders. Therefore, information systems that support manufacturing engineering are most useful. Such systems are completely different from material-oriented information systems.

In a one-of-a-kind business the purpose of an information system is not automatic generation of planned work orders, but rather, user-friendly support of engineering professionals. The traditional distinction between an information system and a logistics system disappears to some extent.

In general practice, most customers use a fuzzy due date rather than exact date when operating their one-of-a-kind product (OKP) manufacturing systems. In order to clearly describe the practical problems, two kinds of model with different types of fuzzy due dates for OKP manufacturing systems are built to control production using the just-in-time (JIT) philosophy. Automated control systems often face a complex problem in situations where the number of resources and tasks to be controlled by the system rises. This complexity gives a reason to subdivide the control system into smaller and thus simpler systems. However, in order to maintain flexibility of the overall system, interoperability of the subdivided systems must exist.

Production planning in the OKM environment is still under research.

Bibliography

1. Fong, S.W., 1998: Value engineering in Hong Kong – a powerful tool for a changing society, *Computers & Industrial Engineering*, **35**(3–4), 627–630.
2. Hameri, A.P., Nihtila, J. and Rehn, J., 1999: Document viewpoint on one-of-a-kind delivery process, *International Journal of Production Research*, **37**(6), 1319–1336.
3. Hameri, A.P. and Nihtila, J., 1998: Product data management – exploratory study on state-of-the-art in one-of-a-kind industry, *Computers in Industry*, **35**(3), 195–206.
4. Horvath, L., Machado, J.A.T., Rudas, I.J. and Hancke, G.P., 1999: Application of part manufacturing process model in virtual manufacturing. In *ISIE '99. Proceedings of the IEEE International Symposium on Industrial Electronics* (Cat. No. 99TH8465). IEEE, Piscataway, NJ, pp. 1367–1372.
5. Jones, C., Medlen, N., Merlo, C., Robertson, M. and Shepherdson, J., 1999: The lean enterprise, *BT Technology Journal*, **17**(4), 15–22.
6. King, A.M. and Sivaloganathan, S., 1998: Development of a methodology for using function analysis in flexible design strategies. In *Proceedings of the Institution of Mechanical Engineers, Part B (Journal of Engineering Manufacture)*, **212**(B3), pp. 215–230.

7. Laursen, R.P., Orum, Hansen, C. and Trostmann, E., 1998: The concept of state within one-of-a-kind real-time production control systems, *Production Planning and Control*, **9**(6), 542–552.

8. Langeland, B., Holm, H. and Schroder, J., 1999: Subdivision of an automated control system in one-of-a-kind production. In *Proceedings of the Eighteenth IASTED International Conference Modelling, Identification and Control*. ACTA Press, Anaheim, CA, pp. 425–427.

9. Marples, A., 1999: Recycling value from electrical and electronic waste. In *Recycling Electrical and Electrical Equipment. Conference Proceedings*. ERA Technology Ltd, Leatherhead, UK, February, pp. 4/1–4/7.

10. Orum, H.C., Laursen, R.P. and Trostmann, E., 1998: Real-time control systems for one-of-a-kind production based on state modelling, *Production Planning and Control*, **9**(5), 435–447.

11. Schierholt, K., 1998: Knowledge systematization for operations planning. In *Proceedings Artificial Intelligence and Manufacturing Workshop. State of the Art and State of the Practice*. AAAI Press, Menlo Park, CA, pp. 140–146.

12. Schneider, J.G., Boyan, J.A. and Moore, A.W., 1998: Value function based production scheduling. In *Machine Learning. Proceedings of the Fifteenth International Conference (ICML '98)*. Morgan Kaufmann Publishers, San Francisco, CA, pp. 522–530.

13. Wei, Wang and Dingwei Wang, 1999: JIT production planning approach with fuzzy due date for OKP manufacturing systems, *International Journal of Production Economics*, **58**(2), 209–215.

14. Yiliu, Tu, Xulin, Chu and Wenyu Yang, 2000: Computer-aided process planning in virtual one-of-a-kind production, *Computers in Industry*, **41**(1), 99–110.

Optimized production technology – OPT

S – 1c; 4c; 6c; * 1.3c; 2.4b; 3.5c
(See also Theory of constraints (TOC).)

Optimized production technology (OPT) was developed as a scheduling system to govern product flow in a production plant. The rules of OPT are derived for capacity constraints and especially bottlenecks. Both capacity and market constraints should be handled by the logistical system. The nine rules of OPT are:

1. Do not balance capacity. The major objective is flow.
2. The level of utilization of a non-bottleneck is not determined by its own potential but by other constraints within the system.
3. Activation and utilization are not synonymous.
4. An hour lost on bottleneck is an hour lost on the system.
5. An hour gained on a non-bottleneck is a mirage.
6. Bottlenecks govern both inventory and throughput.
7. The transfer batch may not be equal to the process batch.

8. The process batch should be variable, not fixed.
9. Schedules should be estimated by looking at all the constraints. Lead times are the results of a schedule and cannot be predetermined.

Unfortunately, OPT does not reveal the theory underlying the software, so that firms that implemented OPT were forced to follow schedules generated by a 'black box'. Supervisors found the schedules counter-intuitive and were reluctant to follow them.

Bibliography

1. Fogarty, D., Blackstone, J. and Hoffmann, T., 1991: *Production and Inventory Management*, 2nd edn. South-Western, Cincinnati, OH.
2. Fox, R.E., 1982: MRP, Kanaban, or OPT, *Inventory and Production*, **July/August**.
3. Fox, R.E., 1983: OPT – an answer for America – Part IV, *Inventory and Production*, **March/ April**.
4. Fox, R.E., 1983: OPT vs. MRP – thoughtware vs. software, *Inventory and Production*, **November/December**.
5. Fuchsberg, G., 1992: Quality programs show shoddy results, *Wall Street Journal*, May 14, B1, B7.
6. Goldratt, E., 1991: Late-night discussions: VI, *Industry Week*, December 2, 51, 52.
7. Goldratt, E., 1989: *The Goal*, 2nd revised edn. North River Press, Croton-on-Hudson, NY.
8. Goldratt, E., 1990: *The Haystack Syndrome*. North River Press, Croton-on-Hudson, NY.
9. Goldratt, E., 1988: The fundamental measurements, *The Theory of Constraints Journal*, **1**(3).
10. Goldratt, E. and Fox, R.E., 19xx: *The Race*. North River Press, Croton-on-Hudson, NY.
11. Goldratt, E., 1988: Computerized shop floor scheduling, *International Journal of Production Research*, **26**(3), pp. 443–455.
12. Lambrecht, M. and Segaert, A., 1990: Buffer stock allocation in serial and assembly type of production lines, *International Journal of Operations and Production Management*, **10**(2), pp. 47–61.
13. Mathews, J. and Katel, P., 1992: The cost of quality, *Newsweek*, September 7, p. 48.

Outsourcing

M – 2c; 3c; 4b; 6c; 9d; 10b; 14c; * 1.1d; 1.2c; 1.3d; 1.6b; 2.4c; 3.2c; 3.3b; 4.1b; 4.2c; 4.5d

Outsourcing is defined as the conscious business decision to move internal work to external suppliers.

Manufacturers purchase subassemblies rather than piece parts. Outsourcing has become prominent in activities ranging from logistics to administrative services, and suppliers are increasingly involved in defining the technical and commercial aspects of the goods and services companies provide. These trends, in effect, have raised the amount a business spends externally. Most importantly, the complexity of purchasing has increased dramatically in terms of the nature of what is purchased, the breadth of categories considered within the realm of procurement, and the expanding geographic scope of supplier options to consider and manage.

What companies buy has changed significantly. This has implications for how companies buy, and translates into highly leverage-able opportunities for significant cost reduction and profit enhancement. Procurement is quickly becoming recognized as a priority function that offers high-impact opportunities for improving the bottom line.

There are several definitions of the term outsourcing, such as:

1. To subcontract any job that is not in the main line of business of the company.
2. Create a long-term strategic partnership with outsiders, which becomes an extension of the company.
3. Purchase products and components, that previously were made in the company.

Outsourcing is management policies that come to establish the following:

1. Align outsourcing with business plans
2. Ensure consistent handling across all business units
3. Identification and definition of core competencies
4. Identification of outsourcing opportunities
5. Consistent procedures and guidelines for evaluation and implementation of outsourcing opportunities
6. Ensure competitive bidding
7. Consistent handling of personnel issues
8. Sales and retention assets
9. Enable technology refresh
10. Consistent contract structure, terms and conditions.

Outsourcing may be done in three ways:

1. Subcontract job to suppliers
2. Employ temporary workers
3. Employ consultants.

The advantages of outsourcing are:

1. Allows the company to concentrate on the main business – what it can do best
2. Using experts in each field, employing advanced technology

3. Reduction of personnel problems
4. Increases production flexibility, because there are many suppliers
5. Seasonal work force flexibility
6. Transfer quality responsibility to the supplier
7. Objective ideas from an external source
8. Reduction in logistic and operation expenses.

The outsourcing policy of what to outsource should include:

1. Anything that is not a core competence is an outsourcing candidate
2. Process of functions where organization adds value
3. Expertise knowledge that enables organizations to maintain competitive advantage.

Outsourcing critical success factors are:

1. Ensuring a clear understanding of objectives
2. Identifying activities suitable for outsourcing
3. Commitment and trust between vendor and company
4. Identifying decision team and allow adequate time
5. Communications
6. Specifying adequate contact terms
7. Seamless transition
8. Establishing the framework and staff to manage the relationship
9. Continuity of executive support.

The disadvantages of implementing outsourcing are:

1. Exposure of company trade secrets to external sources
2. Maintaining industry and company-specific expertise
3. Suppliers do not have the loyalty to the company
4. Suppliers do not care about internal affairs of the company
5. Suppliers are not familiar with the company's labour problems
6. Suppliers are not familiar with company standards and operations procedures
7. Suppliers cannot be regarded as strategic partners and do not share in profits.

Trouble spots in outsourcing:

1. Poor customer management
2. Difficulty in hiring/retaining staff
3. Rapid technology and business changes
4. Unrealized value added
5. Fear of potential change of control
6. Greater customer sophistication

7. Expectations are not realistically set in the beginning
8. Poor contracts.

An outsourcing decision must be based on:

- *Identification of needs*: A need to achieve more effective information systems delivery at an affordable cost.
- *Establishing unique objectives*: An understanding that each business has different requirements and different goals.
- *Gaining consensus*: The degree of support by all functions within the business.
- *Modelling the relationship*: A complete understanding of structure, benefits, and pitfalls.

To identify the needs, the business case should balance both the cost of the outsourcing arrangements – setup fees and ongoing fees – and their internal structure, such as the cost of technology, the cost of recruiting and training people, the cost of space.

Is one strategy more expensive than the other? Whether or not outsourcing makes financial sense depends on a number of differing factors. For example, are there opportunities to create efficiencies through the use of technology? Will moving from a decentralized to a centralized outsourcing approach free up significant internal resources?

It is important to state your objectives up-front. What exactly are you trying to accomplish? As you look at what's important, start collecting data – whether it's performance data or external benchmarking. Many companies conduct an activity-based costing analysis – an analysis that looks at how people are spending their time. Also, you need to capture labour costs, and costs for technology, recruiting, turnover and training. This information can be derived from financial reports.

Bibliography

1. Childe, S.J., 1998: Extended enterprise – a concept of co-operation, *Production Planning and Control*, **9**(4), 320–327.
2. Conn, D., 1999: To outsource or not to outsource? *Medical Device and Diagnostic Industry*, **20**(1), 76, 78, 80.
3. Gregory, A., 1998: Outsourcing – weighing it up, *Manufacturing Computer Solutions*, **4**(3), 39, 41–42.
4. Hare, D., 1999: Succeeding with ERP, *Manufacturing Engineer*, **78**(2), 65–67.
5. Hull, B., Patell, S. and Williams, S., 1999: Taming the supply chain, *Manufacturing Engineer*, **78**(2), 71–72.
6. Jahnukainen, J. and Lahti, M., 1996: Efficient purchasing in make-to-order supply chains, *International Journal of Production Economics*, **59**(1), 103–111.

7. Jones, R. and Kruse, G., 1999: Making a meal of ERP, *Manufacturing Engineer*, **78**(2), 61–64.
8. Lacity, M. and Hirschheim, R., 1993: *Information Systems Outsourcing*, Wiley.
9. Lehtinen, U., 1997: Subcontractors in a partnership environment: a study on changing manufacturing strategy, *International Journal of Production Economics*, **60**, 165–170.
10. Mainwaring, J., 1999: Outsourcing – the way forward! *Manufacturing Computer Solutions*, **5**(3), 44–46.
11. Ng, J.K.C., Ip, W.H. and Lee, T.C., 1998: Development of an enterprise resources planning system using a hierarchical design pyramid, *Journal of Intelligent Manufacturing*, **9**(5), 385–399.
12. Opperthauser, D., 1998: Outsourcing moves to the plant, *Industrial Computing*, **17**(10), 43–45.
13. Padillo, J.M. and Diaby, M., 1999: Multiple-criteria decision methodology for the make-or-buy problem, *International Journal of Production Research*, **37**(14), 3203–3229.
14. Peterson, Y.S., 1998: Outsourcing: opportunity or burden? *Quality Progress*, **31**(6), 63–64.
15. Rothstein, A.J., 1998: Outsourcing: an accelerating global trend in engineering, *EMJ Engineering Management Journal*, **10**(1), 7–14.

Partnerships

P – 3d; 4d; 5c; 6c; 9b; 10b; 11c; * 1.1c; 1.2c; 1.6b; 3.2c; 3.5c

Partnership manufacturing is a business culture that promotes open communication and mutual benefits in a supportive environment built on trust. Partnering relationships stimulate continuous quality improvement and a reduction in the total cost of ownership.

Partnering is usually referred to as a shift from traditional open market bargaining to cooperative buyer and seller relationships. The shift is often referred to in articles and conversation, but is difficult to isolate. It refers to at least five areas.

1. Moving from numerous suppliers for a goods or services to a few or one.
2. Changing the buyer and seller relationship from a credible threat to a credible commitment.
3. Altering conflict management procedures from unyielding negotiations to managing trade-offs.
4. Increasing information exchange from as little as possible to as much as possible.
5. Viewing the marketplace jointly rather than separately.

Depending on the source, partnering is as old as commerce itself, or as new as the new management principles. The explanation for the new interest in partnering is that global competition has spawned the quality movement, which has brought into focus the total-cost-of-ownership. No longer are purchasers of goods and services based solely on price, but on a sophisticated basis that considers all factors such as original cost of equipment, spare parts, service, maintenance, support, throughput, taxes and duties, monetary exchange considerations, up-time available, and cycle time. Total-cost-of-ownership has elevated the purchasing function to a strategic role in many organizations.

The change in nature of purchasing quality can be appreciated by the following comparisons:

Old approach	New approach
Purchasing is a tactical issue	Purchasing is a strategic issue
Deliver can be at any time	Delivery is just-in-time
Quality is conformance to specification	Quality is broadly defined, mainly in terms of the customer
Quality is satisfying customer requirements	Quality is anticipating and exceeding customer expectations
Price is a major factor in buy decision	Quality is equal to price in buy decision
Front-end price is important	Life-cycle costs are critical
Purchasing is cost area	Purchasing is a profit/loss area
Buyer or agent purchases products	Team purchases products
Defects are accepted	Zero defects are expected
Multiple suppliers provide products	Preferably single supplier-partner provides products

Partnering promotes two levels of partnering: basic and expanded. Basic partnering requires the following between customer and supplier:

1. mutual respect
2. honesty
3. trust
4. open and frequent communication
5. understanding each other's needs.

In addition to these requirements, expanded partnering requires:

1. long-term commitment
2. recognition of continuing improvement – objective and factual
3. passion to help each other succeed
4. high priority on relationship
5. shared risk and opportunity
6. shared strategic/technologies road map
7. sharing advanced technology requirements

8. sharing expectations of the future
9. ensuring financial benefit to both parties
10. mutual task forces and cross-organizational teams.

Selecting and assessing the best partners is critical for successful partnership, and the actual assessment process provides significant benefits as well. The process of selecting partners can be programmatic, that is, guidelines, procedures, hierarchy, strategic plans, and technical requirements can govern it. One method is to attempt to do basic partnering with everyone, and then expand to higher levels of partnering with a long-term and strategic supplier. Winning awards as a world class supplier might make a company eligible for expanded partnering, bringing with it executive-level investment and sponsorship, as well as increased communication through scheduled operational and strategic meetings.

It should be obvious that a quality relationship is critical for a successful partnership. Relationships occur between people, not companies. When partnering practitioners speak of the resource investment required for partnering, they speak of the time and personnel costs of relationship building and maintenance within and across companies.

Partnership activity tends to be initiated by the customer and flow from the customer to the supplier.

Bibliography

1. Axelrod, R., 1984: *The Evolution of Cooperation*. Harper Collins, New York.
2. Fisher, R. and Ury, W., 1991: *Getting to Yes: Negotiating Agreement Without Giving In*. Houghton Miffin, Boston.
3. Hutchins, G., 1992: Partnering: A path to total quality in purchasing, *National Productivity Review*, **Spring**, 215.
4. Lambert, D.M., Emmelhainz, M.A. and Gardner, J.T., 1996: Developing and implementing supply chain partnerships, *The International Journal of Logistics Management*, **7**(2), 1–17.
5. Landeros, R. and Monczka, R.M., 1989: Cooperative buyer/seller relationships and firm's competitive posture, *Journal of Purchasing and Material Management*, Fall.
6. *Partnering for Total Quality: A Partnering Guidebook*, vol. 4, 1990. SEMATECH, pp. 9–18.

Performance measurement system

M – 7a; 8b; 9c; 11b; 13b; * 1.3b; 3.3b; 4.1a; 4.3a; 4.4b

Performance measurement is a management tool used to indicate the efficiency of the organization, and how to improve it. In WEB e-business, performance refers to the response time of the system.

Performance measurement compares intentions and planning to the actual performance. The actual performance data is obtained by data collection. If done properly it reflects the real status of business performance. The planning or target settings are usually accepted without question.

Target setting, in many cases, does not reflect the actual potential of the business and therefore the performance measurement does not highlight the real problems in the organization. For example: Suppose a company finds it difficult to compete in the market as their processing costs are relatively high compared to those of the competitors. This does not mean that their process engineers are not capable ones. It might mean that competitors' processing resources are more suited to producing the required product mix. This is managements' responsibility, as they made the wrong decisions concerning resources and planning.

Another example: The performance measurement indicates that delivery dates are not met. This is a fact. But why? What are the conclusions to be drawn from this information? In many cases the production system has performed efficiently, but management (marketing or sales) are to blame as they have promised an unrealistic delivery date.

Thus performance measurement results give an overall efficiency value for a specific enterprise, but do not allow management to point to specific sources of low overall efficiency.

Performance management systems propose individual measurements for each discipline that may affect the level of performance, such as:

1. management performance level
2. sales performance level
3. marketing performance level
4. production planning performance level
5. shop-floor performance level
6. engineering design performance level.

In addition performance management systems make an additional measurement, called 'predicted performance measurement' which may be used to pinpoint the source of low efficiency and also to compare the efficiency of a specific enterprise to other enterprises.

E-business has intensified the need for better ways to manage system performance. The reality that response times of eight seconds or better are critical to ensure a customer does not go to a competitor's site, is putting real pressure on IT organizations to offer optimal performance.

The problem is that most of them continue to struggle with performance management as e-business gains momentum and customers grow more demanding. This is especially problematical given the lack of complete performance management systems available: there are only 'point solutions' available today. While there are innovative products that attack a particular facet of performance management, customers have been left with the chore of trying to integrate a set of disparate elements into something much more useful to them.

Performance management should be a systematic process, with integrated tools to be used as needed. More attention has been focused on real-time performance management products that adjust traffic flows in real time, based upon service level management policies. These products use sophisticated technology to balance loads on servers and networks, redirect new connections to lightly loaded sites, cache information locally for faster access and shape traffic. A performance management system that integrates both real-time and long-term aspects would offer substantial customer value. Real-time information is critical for tuning and optimizing all performance management elements. Data integration is essential; administrators cannot move files between tools.

Bibliography

1. Bititci, U.S., Carrie, A.S. and McDevitt, L.G., 1997: Integrated performance measurement systems: a development guide, *International Journal of Operations Management*, **17**(6), 522–535.
2. Bititci, U.S., Carrie, A.S. and Turner, T.J., 1998: diagnosing the Integrity of your performance measurement system, *Control Institute of Operations Management*, **24**(3), 9–13.
3. Camp, R., 1989: *Benchmarking: The Search for Industry Best…* ASQC Quality Press.
4. Crawford, J., 1994: TPC Auditing: how to do it better, Quarterly Report, 9–11.
5. Daneva, M., 1995: Software benchmarking design and use. In J. Brown (ed.), *Reengineering the Enterprise*. Chapman & Hall, London.
6. Davenport, T.H., 1993: *Process Innovation*. Harvard Business School Press, Boston.
7. Gomolski, B., 2000: Top 10 recommendations on building scalable, high-performance Web sites, *InfoWorld*, **23**(3), 70.
8. Halevi, G., 1980: *The Role of Computers in Manufacturing Process*. John-Wiley & Sons.
9. Hammer, M. and Champy, J., 1993: *Re-engineering the Corporation: A Manifesto for Business Revolution*. Nicholas Brealey, London.
10. Hana, V., Burns, N.D. and Backhouse, C.J., 1996: How we are measured is how we behave. *Proceedings of 2nd International Conference on Managing Integrated Manufacturing (MIM '96)*, Leicester University 26–28 June, pp. 303–308.
11. Chesbrough, H.W. and Teece, D.J., 1996: Making companies efficient, *The Economist*, December.
12. Covey, S., 1990: *Habits of Highly Effective People*. Simon & Schuster, New York. General references.
13. Kueng, P. and Krahn, A.J.W., 1999: Building a process performance measurement system: some early experiences, *Journal of Scientific and Industrial Research*, **58**, March–April, 145–159.
14. McCarthy, J., 2000: Performance evaluations, *Journal of Property Management*, **65**(5), 22–25.
15. McConnell, J., 2000: Better monitoring tools good for e-biz, *Internetweek*, **807**, 35.

16. Mettins, K., Kempf, S. and Siebert, G., 1995: How benchmarking supports re-engineering. In J. Brown (ed.), *Reengineering the Enterprise*. Chapman & Hall.
17. Neely, A., Gregory, M. and Platts, K., 1995: Performance measurement system design: a literature review and research agenda, *International Journal of Operations Management*, **15**(4).
18. Scheer, A.-W., 1992: *Architecture of Integrated Information Systems*. Springer-Verlag, Berlin.

Product data management – PDM & PDMII

S – 2d; 3b; 4c; 6d; 7b; 8d; 14c; 15d; * 1.2c; 1.3d; 2.1c; 2.2b; 2.3c; 2.5c; 2.6c; 3.1d; 3.2c; 4.3c

Product data management (PDM) is a tool for collecting, storing, organizing, managing and making accessible product and process knowledge. It is a set of software tools designed to control and electronically simulate a product throughout its life-cycle.

PDM II is a new vision to achieve quality, time and cost benefits through product development. PDMII integrates three distinct elements, virtual product development management (VPDM), and traditional PDM and ERP systems. VPDM provides product knowledge much earlier in the design cycle, when the cost of change and design experimentation is minimal and enhances innovation of the design.

PDM started as an intelligent file manager add-on for computer-aided design and computer-aided manufacturing (CAD/CAM) systems. CAD systems originally provided electronic drawings, but then evolved to creating designs in 3D. Today, we can build a 3D virtual prototype and, with digital mockup, interactively simulate product performance and check for system interference. But the focus is still very much on creating part geometry. Even when assembly modelling is done, there is very little to manage elements like versions and configurations, maturity and affectivities, or the relationships and links to other information that is being generated during the innovation phase of the design process.

PDM began with manual control of paper, and has evolved to the control of electronic files. PDM systems today provide secure locations for universally accessing product designs. They provide structured workflow with which to evolve a product design through its life-cycle, and share it with downstream manufacturing and other legacy applications. PDM systems can interface with CAD systems to control design files, but are too structured to function well in a conceptual design environment.

Today, the focus is much more on information systems and bill-of-materials applications. An enterprise PDM system is the main central repository for all that there is to know about the product definition and all the many iterations of that definition. PDM is growing increasingly sophisticated. Take product configuration, for example: if the PDM system knew the features and options that a product could have, manufacturers could generate bills of material for product instances that have not yet been created. There is an average of 15 documents per product – and only one of those documents is the product drawing or model. The broad view of PDM now is that while geometry continues to be important, there are 14 other definitions that are important, too. Such additional documents might include purchase orders, fabrication plans, or, perhaps, safety analyses. Engineers design the product. Manufacturing people fabricate it. Service people are out in the field performing maintenance and repair. There are many people who need to tap into a repository of product information above and beyond the engineer who created a geometrical representation of the part in a CAD file. So it's all about leveraging information as opposed to simply managing it.

PDM helps companies automate the arduous task of design reviews and approvals, streamlining how companies take design concepts and translate them into released products for manufacturing. The result is reduced time to market and lower development costs. Innovation requires change. To facilitate innovation, companies must re-examine the way in which they store and share information, and the development processes that use this information.

Early in a product life-cycle, change is good, and, in fact, should be encouraged. The more iteration a product design can experience at this stage when change is inexpensive, the higher quality we can obtain in our final product. As costs are committed against a design, however, change becomes expensive and is discouraged. PDM systems help control engineering changes at this stage, and ensure enterprise acceptance of changes through structured workflow. PDM systems are excellent for managing enterprise information in this portion of the product life-cycle, where information management requires more structure.

Traditional PDM systems allow engineering data to be efficiently shared with downstream systems for enterprise resources planning (ERP), manufacturing process planning, and product obsolescence planning. Also, changes to finalized designs must be completed efficiently with the impact of the change understood by all engineers who rely on the product design.

Modern companies use computers to store all types of information about the products they build. Product data management (PDM) systems provide easy availability of this information, control its access, and manage changes to it. As humans, we have the unique ability to place the information that we obtain from PDM systems within a context that is meaningful to us. Recent software technologies such as CAD, PDM, and ERP have helped reduce development time by automating portions of the development process. But despite their benefits, they do not eliminate the interpretation required by various departments involved in a classical serial development process, nor do they encourage parallel development activities. To maximize compression of the product development life-cycle, companies must not only represent product data in a digital format; they must also ensure that multiple departments can easily and unambiguously interpret the information and access that knowledge at any point in the process.

With the extension of today's enterprises into closely-knit supply chains, all companies in the extended enterprise must effectively collaborate during the entire product-creation process, including conceptual design. They must have efficient access not only to product design data, but also to manufacturing process definitions and other product information that changes as the product design evolves. The vision integrates three distinct elements: virtual product development management (VPDM), traditional PDM, and ERP systems and it is called PDMII.

VPDM provides product knowledge much earlier in the design cycle, when the cost of change and design experimentation is minimal. The overall goal of PDMII is to introduce knowledge, intelligence and innovation at the design stage. The addition of VPDM enables engineering activities to occur in parallel, because it models dependencies among various engineering disciplines, carefully tracking design changes. Their impact can be more easily explored and understood. With VPDM, manufacturing engineers can begin planning for production long before designs are released, and engineers can become more efficient by finding required product data more quickly. VPDM also uses advanced tools for digital mockup, behaviour simulation, and visualization, allowing engineers to spot defects or manufacturing difficulties early. By enabling collaboration in the conceptual design phase, VPDM allows ideas to be shared with people within and outside the design community. VPDM increases a company's ability to innovate and increase revenue from new products.

PDM II attributes, including those for concurrent engineering, can be broken down into two major categories: those that foster an environment of innovation and those that reduce costs and product life-cycles. Another relevant element of PDM II is action flow, which captures actions that need to be done, have been done, and what other parts are affected. Engineers can subscribe to a portion of a design they're working with, and then automatically be notified when changes occur.

Bibliography

1. Choi, Y.K., 1995: The PDM system for CE implementation, *Computer World*, **December**, 162–167.
2. Choi, Y.K. and Huh, K.B., 1995: *Object-oriented Software Engineering*. Korea Silicon.
3. CIMdata, 1994: *Product Data Management: A Technology Guide*.
4. HP, 1993: *Product Data Management: Understanding the Fundamental Technology and Business Concepts*, Hewlett-Packard Co.
5. Kempfer, L., 1998: Linking PDM to ERP, *Computer-Aided Engineering*, **17**(2), 58–64.

6. Kim, K.S. and Kim, C.H., 1992: A modeling methodology for manufacturing information system based on object-orientd approach. *Proceedings of the 1992 Conference KIIE*, pp. 192–201.
7. Kim, S.H. and Yoon, H.C., 1994: The development of drawing information management system for technical document management, *Interfaces: Industrial Engineering*, **7**(3), 213–225.
8. Kim, W., 1990: *Introduction to Object-oriented Databases*. MIT Press.
9. Lee, C.H., 1996: A case study on the development of R&D integrated system using CALS/PDM, *IE Magazine*, **B3**(1), 58–62.
10. McHenry, S., 1993: RDBMS vs. ODBMS for product information management systems. *Proceedings of AUTOFACT '93 Conference* 28/13–30.
11. Taylor, D.A., 1991: *Object-oriented Technology: A Manager's Guide*. Addison-Wesley.
12. Yoo, S.B., Seo, H.Y. and Ko, K.W. 1995: Product data exchange in production systems by using of STEP, *Interfaces: Industrial Engineering*, **8**(3), 75–95.

Product life-cycle management

M – 3c; 4c; 5d; 7b; 9b; 11d; 14c; 15c; 16c; * 1.1d; 1.2b; 1.5b; 2.2c; 2.6b; 3.1d; 3.4c; 4.6c

The objective of product life-cycle management is to reduce overhead and operating expenses, to obtain valuable management information (including causal data).

Product life-cycle management services can provide value information to retailers, manufacturers and the consumer. Product life-cycle management performs both direct logistics, and reverse logistics, simultaneously: direct logistics is getting the product to the consumer, and reverse logistics is getting the product back efficiently.

Product life-cycle management is the seamless integration of distribution and reverse-logistics technologies and operations that provides retailers and manufacturers with the means to capture data throughout the complete life-cycle of a product, category or line of products.

Full product life-cycle management manages products as they progress through the forward- and reverse-logistics pipelines. It enables a company to manage and direct the disposition of its products in a manner that protects its brand and maximizes its recovery. Retailers and manufacturers have identified the need to track the capabilities of a product throughout the supply chain.

Supply chains are optimized, return rates are high and obsolescence rates are short. These market realities and the shifts towards direct-to-consumer marketing and retailing are the driving factors behind product life-cycle management services. Retailers and manufacturers are facing new challenges and opportunities through nontraditional retailing. The immense availability of products through the Internet and catalogues requires that retailers focus on customer service.

Consumers can now view and purchase nearly any product with a point and a click. This dictates that what will differentiate retailers and provide competitive advantage is customer service and the efficiency of their logistics pipeline. Order fill times are constantly being reduced. Overnight delivery, once viewed as nearly impossible, is now the norm. Same-day delivery is already here and will surely grow in popularity. This only reinforces the need for an efficient logistics process, which includes direct logistics, getting the product there, and reverse logistics, getting the product back. These practices together with simultaneously tracking sales demand, billings and credits, and through technology will be a driving factor in determining which retailers and manufacturers develop customer share and market leadership.

Technology is clearly changing the way we shop and transact business. Building the logistical infrastructure to protect today's retailing market share while capturing customer share in the direct-to-consumer market is the main task.

Third-party expertise and technology can help bridge the gap between today's market-share and tomorrow's customer-share requirements. Outsourcing both direct and reverse logistics functions is a viable strategy in this time of changing technology and fundamental market shift.

A number of third parties have developed and are developing superior technology and operating processes adding a dimension of flexibility and responsiveness. The force of change demands dynamic solutions. Solutions that will help manage a product from production to its resting place. Developing a full product life-cycle strategy is a competitive necessity for today and tomorrow. It enables a company to manage and direct the disposition of its products in a manner that protects its brand and maximizes its recovery. Full product life-cycle management is, in essence, cradle-to-grave management of a product as it progresses through forward- and reverse-logistics pipelines.

Bibliography

1. Alting, L., 1995: Life cycle engineering & design, *Annals of CIRP*, **2**, 569.
2. Alting, L., 1998: Our Common Future, The Brundtland Report, © 1978 Oxford University Press. Winter annual meeting, CIRP Life Cycle Group Meeting, 1998, v 47/2/98.
3. Curran, M.A., 1996: *Environmental Life-cycle Assessment*, McGraw Hill, New York.
4. Dreer, P. and Koonce, D.A., 1995: Development of an integrated information model for computer integrated manufacturing, *Computers Industrial Engineering*, **29**(1–4), pp. 109–112.
5. Koonce, D.A., Judd, R.P. and Parks, C.M., 1996: Manufacturing systems engineering and design: an intelligent multi-model, integration architecture, *Computer Integrated Manufacturing*, **9**(6), pp. 443–453.
6. *Limits to Growth*, Club of Rome, © 1972, Universe Books, New York.
7. Mills, J.J., 1995: An integrated information infrastructure for agile manufacturing, *Manufacturing Science and Engineering, ASME MH*, **3**(2).

8. Orfali, R., Harkey, D. and Edwards, J., 1996: *The Essential Client/Server Survival Guide*. John Wiley & Sons.
9. Song, L. and Nagi, R., 1995: An integrated information framework for agile manufacturing. *5th Industrial Engineering Research Conference Proceedings*.
10. Van Beers, M., 1996: Life cycle analysis. TUDElft report, January.

Production information and control system – PICS

S – 1b; 2c; 4d; 6d; 7c; 10c; 13c; * 1.2c; 1.3b; 1.6c; 2.3b; 2.4b; 2.5d; 3.5b

Production information and control system (PICS) is a systematic method of performing the technological disciplines of the enterprise, which consist of the following stages:

- Master production planning
- Material requirement / Resource planning
- Capacity planning
- Shop floor control
- Inventory management and control.

Master production planning transforms the manufacturing objectives of quantity and delivery dates for the final product, which are assigned by marketing or sales, into an engineering production plan. The decisions in this stage depend either on the forecast or confirmed orders, and the optimization criteria are meeting delivery dates, minimum level of work-in-process, and plant load balance. These criteria are subject to the constraint of plant capacity and to the constraints set by the routing stage.

The master production schedule is a long-range plan. Decisions concerning lot size, make or buy, addition of resources, overtime work and shifts, and confirm or change promised delivery dates are made until the objectives can be met.

The purpose of material requirement planning (MRP – see separate item) is to plan the manufacturing and purchasing activities necessary in order to meet the targets set forth by the master production schedule. The number of production batches, their quantity and delivery date are set for each part of the final product.

The decisions at this stage are confined to the demands of the master production schedule, and the optimization criteria are meeting due dates, minimum level of inventory and work-in-process, and department load balance. The parameters are on-hand inventory, in-process orders and on-order quantities.

The capacity planning goal is to transform the manufacturing requirements, as set forth in the MRP stage, into a detailed machine-loading plan for each machine or group of machines in the plant. It is a scheduling and sequencing task. The decisions at this stage are confined to the demands of the MRP stage, and the optimization criteria are capacity balancing, meeting due dates, minimum level of work-in-process and manufacturing lead time. The parameters are plant available capacity, tooling, on-hand material and employees.

The shop floor is where the actual manufacturing takes place. In all previous stages, personnel dealt with documents, information, and paper. In this stage workers deal with material and produce products. Shop floor control is responsible for the quantity and quality of items produced and for keeping the workers busy.

Inventory management and control is responsible for keeping track of the quantity of material and number of items that should be and that are present in inventory at any given moment; it also supplies data required by the other stages of the manufacturing cycle and links manufacturing to costing, bookkeeping, and general management.

The PICS method requires data from a number of sources, including customer orders, available inventory, status of purchasing orders, status of items on shop floor, status of items produced by subcontractors, status of items in quality assurance department. The data from all sources must be synchronized to the instant that the PICS programs are updated. For example: because of new jobs and shop floor interruptions, capacity planning must be updated at short intervals. PICS can do this, however, feedback data must be introduced into the system.

Bibliography

1. Baker, K.R., 1974: *Introduction to Sequencing and Scheduling*, John Wiley & Sons, New-York.
2. Barash, M.M. *et al.*, 1975: The optimal planning of computerized manufacturing systems, NSG GRANT No. APR74 15256, Report No. 1, November 1975.
3. Berry, W.L., 1972: Priority scheduling and inventory control in job lot manufacturing system, *AIIE Transactions*, 4(4), 267–276.
4. Buffa, E.S., 1966: *Models for Production and Operation Management*. John Wiley & Sons.
5. Buffa, E.S., 1966: *Readings in Production and Operation Management*. John Wiley & Sons.
6. Coffman, E.G., Bruno, J.L. and Graham, R.L. *et al.*, 1976: *Computer and Job-shop Scheduling Theory*. John Wiley & Sons, New York.
7. Hanna, W.L., 1985: Shop floor communication – MAP. *22nd Annual Meeting & Technical Conference Proceedings AIM Tech*, May 1985, pp. 294–300.
8. Harding, J., Gentry, D. and Parker, J., 1969: Job shop scheduling against due dates, *Industrial Engineering*, 1(6), 17–29.
9. Harrington, J., 1985: Why computer integrated manufacturing. *22nd Annual Meeting & Technical Conference Proceedings AIM Tech*, May 1985, pp. 27–28.
10. Halevi, G., 1980: *The Role of Computers in Manufacturing Processes*. John Wiley & Sons.
11. Halevi, G., 1992: *The Magic Matrix as a Smart Scheduler, Manufacturing in the Era of Concurrent Engineering*. North-Holland IFIP.

12. Hubner, H. and Paterson, I. (ed.), 1983: *Production Management Systems*. North-Holland.
13. IBM *COPICS* Copyright 1972.
14. Rowe, A.G., 1958: Sequential decision rules in production scheduling. Ph.D. dissertation, University of California, Los Angeles.
15. Wiendahl, H.P., 1995: *Load-oriented Manufacturing Control*, Springer-Verlag.

Quality function deployment – QFD

P – 3b; 5c; 8c; 9b; * 1.3c; 1.5d; 2.2b; 2.5d; 2.6c; 3.1b; 3.2d; 3.4c

Quality function deployment is a product development methodology, the primary aim being to increasing customer focus throughout the product development process. Thus quality function deployment is a market-driven design and development methodology for products and services to meet or exceed a customer's needs and expectations.

Quality function deployment is a system designed to identify customer needs and requirements and introduce them in product design. All company disciplines are involved in a team effort to evaluate competitors' capabilities. Quality function deployment utilizes total quality management (TQM) principles to introduce a high quality product in a short development lead time.

The house of quality (HOQ) is the nerve centre and the engine that drives the entire quality function deployment process. It is a kind of conceptual map that provides the means for inter-functional planning and communication. HOQ is a large matrix that contains seven different elements:

1. *Customer needs*. These are the voice of the customer.
2. *Product features*. Also called design requirements or engineering attributes.
3. *Importance to customer*. Indicates the importance of each attribute to the customer.
4. *Planning matrix*. This portion of the HOQ contains a competitive analysis of the company's products against major competitors' products for each customer need.
5. *Relationship between customer needs and product features*. How much each product feature affects each customer need.
6. *Feature-to-feature correlation*. The extent to which a change in one feature will affect other features.
7. *Prioritized technical description targets*. A summation of the effects of all prior variables on each product feature.

Using these seven elements, the HOQ becomes a repository of information that can be used as a mechanism for applying common-sense engineering.

The benefit of this approach is a more structured and visible decision-making process that spans a number of life-cycle activities. In this way quality function deployment is often regarded as a facilitator of life-cycle engineering techniques such as concurrent engineering. When successful, the benefits obtained from quality function deployment practices have been reported as:

1. Increased level of team working including providing a communication platform for concurrent engineering.
2. Reduced time to market.
3. Reduced amount of re-work.
4. Increased quality of the product.

However, these benefits – or reported successful adoption of quality function deployment – are far from universal. Problems with quality function deployment have arisen due to the subjectivity of decisions that are required in the process. This has been particularly evident at the first stage of the process where it is necessary to translate subjective customer statements into objective engineering measures.

Another problem is the scalability of the methodology; it is often impractical to remain true to principles of methodology when developing anything but the simplest of products.

Customer value deployment – CVD

This is a special blending of VE and QFD into one powerful development and improvement tool.

Bibliography

1. Beskow, C., Johansson, J. and Norell, M., 1998: Implementation of QFD: identifying success factors. In *IEMC '98 Proceedings. International Conference on Engineering and Technology Management. Pioneering New Technologies: Management Issues and Challenges in the Third Millennium* (Cat. No.98CH36266). IEEE, New York, NY, pp. 179–184.
2. Bossert, L.J., 1991: *Quality Function Deployment*, ASQC Quality Press, New York.
3. Chang, H.H., Jae, K.K., Sang, H.C. and Soung, H.K., 1998: Determination of information system development priority using quality function development, *Computers & Industrial Engineering*, **35**(1–2), 241–244.
4. Chan, L.K., Kao, H.P., Ng, A. and Wu, M.L., 1999: Rating the importance of customer needs in quality function deployment by fuzzy and entropy methods, *International Journal of Production Research*, **37**(11), 2499–2518.
5. Dube, L., Johnson, M.D. and Renaghan, L.M., 1999: Adapting the QFD approach to extended service transactions, *Production and Operations Management*, **8**(3), 301–317.
6. Eyob, E., 1998: Quality function deployment in management information systems, *Journal of International Information Management*, **7**(2), 95–100.

7. Ung, R.Y.K., Law, D.S.T. and Ip, W.H., 1999: Design targets determination for inter-dependent product attributes in QFD using fuzzy inference, *Integrated Manufacturing Systems*, **10**(6), 376–383.
8. Hauser, J.R. and Clausing, D., 1988: The house of quality, Harvard Business Review, May-June, 63–73.
9. Jae, K.K., Chang, H.H., Sang, H.C. and Soung, H.K., 1998: A knowledge-based approach to the quality function deployment, *Computers & Industrial Engineering*, **35**(1–2), 233–236.
10. Kwang, J.K., Moskowitz, H., Dhingra, A. and Evans, G., 2000: Fuzzy multicriteria models for quality function deployment, *European Journal of Operational Research*, **121**(3), 504–518.
11. Ming, Z., 1998: Fuzzy logic and optimization models for implementing QFD, *Computers & Industrial Engineering*, **35**(1–2), 237–240.
12. Omar, A.R., Harding, J.A. and Popplewell, K., 1999: Design for customer satisfaction: an information modelling approach, *Integrated Manufacturing Systems*, **10**(4), 199–209.
13. Partovi, F.Y., 1999: A quality function deployment approach to strategic capital budgeting, *Engineering Economist*, **44**(3), 239–260.
14. Ross, P.J., 1988: The role of Taguchi method and design experiments in QFD, *Quality Progress*, **21**(6), 41–47.
15. Temponi, C., Yen, J. and Tiao, W.A., 1999: House of quality: a fuzzy logic-based requirements analysis, *European Journal of Operational Research*, **117**(2), 340–354.
16. Vairaktarakis, G.L., 1999: Optimization tools for design and marketing of new/ improved products using the house of quality, *Journal of Operations Management*, **17**(6), 645–663.
17. Verma, D., Chilakapati, R. and Fabrycky, W.J., 1998: Analyzing a quality function deployment matrix: an expert-system-based approach to identify inconsistencies and opportunities, *Journal of Engineering Design*, **9**(3), 251–261.
18. Xiong, G., Li, B., Chen, J., Li, J., Zhang, Y., Zhu, W. and Bai, S., 1999: Concurrent engineering research and application, *Tsinghua Science and Technology*, **4**(2), 1375–1385.
19. Zhang, Y., Wang, H.P. and Zhang, C., 1999: Green QFD-II: a life cycle approach for environmentally conscious manufacturing by integrating LCA and LCC into QFD matrices, *International Journal of Production Research*, **37**(5), 1075–1091.

Random manufacturing system

P – 1c; 2c; 3d; 4c; 8d; 9d; 13c; 14c; 16c; * 1.3b; 1.4c; 2.4c; 3.3b; 3.5c; 3.6c; 4.4c; 4.6c

(See also Self-organizing manufacturing method.)

Random manufacturing systems are designed to solve the shop floor control problem.

The increased demand for flexibility has led to new manufacturing control paradigms based on the concept of self-organization and on the notion of agents.

The random manufacturing system is a multi-agent architecture based on four concepts: machines take autonomous decisions; machine grouping is dynamic; orders are communicated via a blackboard; and shop floor control is exerted by rewards and penalties. These concepts create a future manufacturing system that responds to apparently future manufacturing needs. The needs are specified as:

- produced by autonomous modules;
- reduction of workforce;
- modular design that assures integration;
- inexpensive construction of production lines (reduction of 70–80% of investment);
- meeting customers needs;
- fast adjustment to market fluctuations.

The traditional approach to the design of manufacturing systems is the hierarchical approach. The design is based on a top-down approach and strictly defines the system modules and their functionality. Communication between modules is strictly defined and limited in such a way that modules communicate with their parent and child modules only. In a hierarchical architecture, modules cannot take an initiative; therefore, the system is sensitive to perturbations, and its autonomy and reactivity to disturbances are weak. The resulting architecture is very rigid and therefore expensive to develop and difficult to maintain.

Heterarchical control was an approach used to alleviate the problems of hierarchical systems. The heterarchical approach bans all hierarchy in order to give full power to the basic modules, often called 'agents', in the system. A heterarchical manufacturing system consists of, for instance, workstations and orders only. Each order negotiates with the workstations to get the work done, using all possible alternatives available to face unforeseen situations. In this way, it is possible to react adequately to changes in the environment (such as new products that enter the market, new or evolving technologies, unpredictable demands for products) as well as to disturbances in the manufacturing system itself (defects, delays, variable yield of chemical reactors).

Bibliography

1. Iwata, K. and Onosato, M., 1994: Random manufacturing system: a new concept of manufacturing systems for production to order, *Annals of the CIRP*, **43**(1), 379–384.
2. Bongaerts, L., Van Brussel, H. and Valckenaers, P., 1998: Schedule execution using perturbation analysis. In *Proceedings of IEEE International Conference on Robotics and Automation*. Leuven, Belgium, May 16–21, pp. 2747–2752.
3. Iwata, K. and Onosato, M., 1994: Random manufacturing system: a new concept of manufacturing systems for production to order. In *Annals of the CIRP*, **43**(1), 379–384.

4. Jones, A.T. and McLean, C.R. 1986: A proposed hierarchical control model for automated manufacturing systems, *Journal of Manufacturing Systems*, **5**(1), 15–26.
5. Kadar, Monostori, L. and Szelke, E., 1997: An object oriented framework for developing distributed manufacturing architectures, In *Proceedings of 2nd World Congress on Intelligent Manufacturing Processes and Systems*, June 10–13, Budapest, Hungary, pp. 548–554.
6. Maturana, F., Gu, P., Naumann, A. and Norrie, D.H., 1997: Object-oriented job-shop scheduling using genetic algorithm, *Computers in Industry*, **32**, 281–294.
7. Schultz, A.C., Grefenstette, J.J. and De Jong, A.K., 1993: Test and evaluation by genetic algorithms, *IEEE Experts*, **12**.
8. Tharumarajah and Wells, A.J., 1997: A behavior-based approach to scheduling in distributed manufacturing systems, *Integrated Computer Aided Engineering*, **4**(4), 235–249.
9. Uckun, S., Bagchi, S. and Kawamura, K., 1993: Managing genetic search in job-shop scheduling, IEEE Expert, 15–24.
10. Ueda, K., 1993: A genetic approach toward future manufacturing systems. In J. Peklenik (ed.), *Flexible Manufacturing Systems, Past, Present, Future*. Ljubljana, Slovenia, 221–228.
11. Valckenaers, P., Bongaerts, L. and Wyns, J., 1996: Planning systems in the next century (II). In *Proceedings of Advanced Summer Institute (ASI) 96 of the N.O.E. on Intelligent Control of Integrated Manufacturing Systems*, Toulouse, France, 2–6 June, pp. 289–295.
12. Valckenaers, P., Van Brussel, H., Bongaerts, L. and Bonneville, E., 1995: Programming, scheduling, and control of flexible assembly systems, *Computers in Industry* (special issue on CIMIA), **26**(3), 209–218.

Reactive scheduling

P – 1b; 2d; 4c; 13d; * 1.3b; 1.4d; 2.4b; 3.3c; 3.5d

Reactive scheduling is the process of revising a given schedule due to unexpected events on the shop floor. Reactive scheduling is concerned with monitoring and controlling the execution of predictive scheduling and making any changes required to bring them in line with unanticipated events or disturbances happening in real time. It can be done by solving the scheduling problem again from scratch or adapting the old schedule to the new situation.

Reactive scheduling is closely allied to predictive scheduling but it has the added dimension of stringent real time execution requirements that constrain the nature and extent of any computations that can occur. More than ever, in reactive scheduling, we are required to pay attention to the computational efficiency of the algorithms or heuristics invoked to choose the best response to a real-time event. Allied to this is the need to develop predictive schedules that are robust against a wide range of contingencies and to investigate trade-offs between robustness and cost.

Usually, reactive scheduling is illustrated by means of deviations of the processing times of operations. A typical scenario goes as follows: because one operation requires a longer processing time than planned, the starting time of the next job is shifted and this causes violation of a due date. Or: one machine is down and the operations allocated to this machine must be performed on another machine, which causes other jobs allocated to the alternative machine to become tardy. Another case altogether is when items are produced on time but are rejected by quality control, or when statistical process control indicates an unfavourable trend.

Several techniques, such as mathematical and statistical models, dispatching rules, knowledge base systems, look head algorithms and heuristics algorithms have been used to solve the scheduling problem. These techniques have proposed increasingly good solutions, but never completely satisfactory because of the complexity of the problem.

Some of the new promising reactive scheduling techniques are:

Artificial neural networks (ANN) – The massively parallel and interconnected structure of neural networks makes them a good candidate for reactive scheduling applications. The two most important characteristics which make ANN a very promising technique to solve reactive scheduling are:

- The approach to the knowledge of the problem is not constructive, but just descriptive.
- Due to the massive parallel interconnections of the system, computing time is very low compared to other scheduling techniques.

Opportunistic scheduler – The opportunist iteration system of reactive scheduling proceeds opportunistically as an iteration of problem state analysis, i.e. the identification and characterization of control events such as bottlenecks, inconsistencies, opportunities, and incompleteness, by analysis knowledge sources and the subsequent formulation and execution of tasks based on a repertoire of scheduling knowledge sources.

Multi-agent – Two agents are considered: machine agent and order agent. Orders should start as late as possible, but they should finish before their due date. Machines require good utilization and to leave small safety gaps before each operation. Each order agent knows on which machines its operations are planned and each machine agent knows its own schedule, and predecessor and successor operations.

Generic algorithm – In this approach a reasoning phase is followed by combinatorial conflict resolution and generic optimization. In the reasoning phase, domain-specific knowledge is used to generate independent pieces of computing advice. The next phase, supervised by interaction, resolves the eventual conflict. The last, most time-consuming phase, uses the generic metaphor, to generate a schedule.

Human learning and machine induction – A simulation model of the plant is used to log the scheduling decisions of an experienced human. Machine-learned decision rules are designed and entirely take over the task of the human scheduler.

Holistic control – The objective is to provide the whole enterprise's production control structure with such a level of flexibility that it can holistically work under a task/customer oriented strategy, toward a virtual company.

Blackboard-based perspective of reactive scheduling – An intelligent interface and expert supervisory unit assist the system to interact in real time with dynamic processes and humans in the shop by using a cognitive operator model and corresponding reactive blackboard architecture with case and rule base knowledge sources as cooperating multi-agent in the reactive scheduling related problem solving.

Bibliography

1. Bezirgan, A., 1993: A case-based approach to scheduling constraints. In Dorn and Foeschl (eds), *Scheduling of Production Processes*. Horwood, Chichester pp. 48–60.
2. Collonpt, A., Le apape, C. and Pinoteam, G., 1988: SONIA: A knowledge based scheduling system, *Artificial Intelligence in Engineering*, **3**(2), 86–94.
3. Dagli, C. and Sittisathanchai, S., 1993: Genetic neuro-scheduler for job-shop scheduling, *Computers & Industrial Engineering*, **25**(1–4), 267–270.
4. Davis, W., Jones, A. and Saleh, A., 1992: Generic architecture for intelligent control systems, *Computer Integrated Manufacturing Systems*, **5**, 105–113.
5. Mitchel, C.M., 1988: Supervisory control: Human information processing in manufacturing systems. In *Concise Encyclopedia Processing in Systems and Organizations*. Pergamon Press, New York.
6. Nii, H. 1986: Blackboard systems, *AI Magazine*.
7. Ow, P.S. and Smith, S.F., 1988: Viewing scheduling as an opportunistic problem solving process. *Proc. AAAI-88*, St. Paul Minn, pp. 77–82.
8. Prosser, P., 1989: A reactive scheduling agent. *Proceedings of the Eleventh IJCAI*, 20–25 August, Detroit, Vol. 2 Morgan Kaufmann.
9. Quinlan, J.R., 1993: *Programs for Machine Learning*. Morgan and Kaufmann.
10. Rolstadas, A., 1994: Beyond year 2000 – production management in virtual company. *Proceedings of IFIP WG5.7 Conference on Evaluation of Production Management Methods*, Gramado, Brazil, pp. 3–9.
11. Smith, F.S., Ow, P.S., Matthys, D.C. and Potvin, J.Y., 1989: *OPIS: an Opportunistic Factory Scheduling System*. Carnegie-Mellon University Pittsburgh, PA.
12. Szelke, E. and Kerr, R.M., 1994: Knowledge-based reactive scheduling, *Production Planning & Control*, **5**, 124–145.

13. Szelke, E. and Markus, G. (eds), 1994: Reactive scheduling – an intelligent supervisor function. In Proceedings of the first IFIP Workshop on Knowledge Based Reactive Scheduling. Elsevier (North-Holland), Amsterdam.
14. Woods, D.D. and Roth, E.M., 1989: Cognitive systems engineering. In Hollander (ed.), Handbook of Human–Computer Interaction. Springer-Verlag, New York.
15. Zhang, C.S., Yan, P.F. and Chang, T., 1991: Solving job-shop scheduling problem with priority using neural network. *Proceedings of the IJCNN*, Singapore, pp. 1361–1366.
16. Zhou, D.N., Cherkassy, V., Baldwin, T.R. and Hong D.W., 1990: Scaling neural networks for job shop scheduling. *Proceedings of the IJCNN*, San Diego, CA, Vol. 3, pp. 898–894.

Self-organizing manufacturing methods

P – 1c; 2c; 3d; 4c; 8d; 9d; 13c; 14c; 16c; * 1.3b; 1.4c; 2.4c; 3.3b; 3.5c; 3.6c; 4.4c; 4.6c

The self-organizing manufacturing method is based on an architecture made up of totally distributed independent autonomous modules that cooperate intelligently to create a future manufacturing system that responds to apparently future manufacturing needs. The needs are specified as:

- produced by autonomous modules;
- reduction of workforce;
- modular design that assures integration;
- inexpensive construction of production lines (reduction of 70–80% of investment);
- meeting customers needs;
- fast adjustment to market fluctuations.

The traditional approach to the design of manufacturing systems is the hierarchical approach. The design is based on a top-down approach and strictly defines the system modules and their functionality. Communication between modules is strictly defined and limited in such a way that modules communicate with their parent and child modules only. In a hierarchical architecture, modules cannot take an initiative; therefore, the system is sensitive to perturbations, and its autonomy and reactivity to disturbances are weak. The resulting architecture is very rigid and therefore expensive to develop and difficult to maintain.

Heterarchical control was an approach used to alleviate the problems of hierarchical systems. The heterarchical approach bans all hierarchy in order to give full power to the basic modules, often called 'agents', in the system. A heterarchical manufacturing system consists of, for instance, workstations and orders only. Each order negotiates with the workstations to get the work done, using all possible alternatives available to face unforeseen situations. This way, it is possible to react adequately to changes in the environment (such as new products that enter the market, new or evolving technologies, unpredictable demand for products) as well as to disturbances in the manufacturing system itself (defects, delays, variable yield of chemical reactors).

Several paradigms have emerged that are based on the above concepts and objectives, and they include:

Agent-based manufacturing
Agent-driven manufacturing
Multi-agent manufacturing system
Holonic manufacturing system
Bionic manufacturing system
Genetic manufacturing system
Fractal manufacturing system
Random manufacturing system
Matrix manufacturing system
Virtual manufacturing system

The concepts of the above paradigms are not necessarily contradictory to each other. Most of them use concepts of multi-agent systems to distribute decision-making. They have many common characteristics and are even complementary (combinations of these approaches are possible and even desirable). However, they can be distinguished by their source of origin – for example, mathematics for the fractal factory, nature for bionic and genetic production systems. In bionic manufacturing, inspired by biological metaphors, the main focus lies on the self-organizing nature of the elements in the manufacturing system. Genetic manufacturing elaborates on these ideas and mimics the DNA concept to model the production orders. In the fractal factory the key concepts are self-organization, self-optimization, and the dynamics of the people in the manufacturing system. Random manufacturing is a multi-agent architecture based on four concepts: the machines take autonomous decisions; machine grouping is dynamic; orders are communicated via a blackboard; and shop floor control is exerted by rewards and penalties. Virtual manufacturing systems have integrated computer models that precisely simulate the manufacturing system to predict and control their operation. 'PEM modelling' structures the modules in a manufacturing system as consisting of planning, execution, and monitoring blocks.

Bibliography

1. Bongaerts, L., Van Brussel, H. and Valckenaers, P., 1998: Schedule execution using perturbation analysis. In *Proceedings of IEEE International Conference on Robotics and Automation*, Leuven, Belgium, May 16–21, pp. 2747–2752.
2. Bongaerts, L., Valckenaers, P., Van Brussel, H. and Peeters, P., 1997: Schedule execution in holonic manufacturing systems. In *Proceedings of 29th CIRP International Seminar on Manufacturing Systems*, May 11–13, Osaka Univ., Japan, pp. 209–215.

3. Bongaerts, L., Van Brussel, H., Valckenaers, P. and Peeters, P., 1997: Reactive scheduling in holonic manufacturing systems: architecture, dynamic model and cooperation strategy. In *Proceedings of ASI 97, Esprit Network of Excellence on Intelligent Control and Integrated Manufacturing Systems*, Budapest, pp. 14–17.

4. Christensen, J., 1997: Holonic manufacturing systems-initial architecture and standard directions. In *Proceedings of Ist European Conference on Holonic Manufacturing Systems*, I Dec., Hannover, Germany, pp. 235–249.

5. Detand, J., Valckenaers, P., Van Brussel, H. and Kruth, J.P., 1996: Holonic manufacturing systems research at PMA-K.U.Leuven. In *Proceedings of PCM96, Pacific Conference on Manufacturing*. (Vol. II), 29–31 Oct. Seoul, Korea (Korea Association of Machinery Industry), pp. 131–140.

6. Dilts, D.M., Boyd, N.P. and Whorms, H.H., 1991: The evolution of control architectures for automated manufacturing systems, *Journal of Manufacturing Systems*, **10**(1), 79–93.

7. Iwata, K. and Onosato, M., 1994: Random manufacturing system: a new concept of manufacturing systems for production to order, *Annals of the CIRP*, **43**(1), 379–384.

8. Janson, D.J. and Frenzel, J.F., 1993: Training product unit neural network with genetic algorithms, *IEEE Experts*, 27–28.

9. Jones, A.T. and McLean, C.R., 1986: A proposed hierarchical control model for automated manufacturing systems, *Journal of Manufacturing Systems*, **5**(1), 15–26.

10. Kadar, Monostori, L. and Szelke, E., 1997: An object oriented framework for developing distributed manufacturing architectures. *Proceedings of 2nd World Congress on Intelligent Manufacturing Processes and Systems*, June 10–13, Budapest, Hungary, pp. 548–554.

11. Kimura, E., 1993: A product and process model for virtual manufacturing systems, *Annals of the CIRP*, **42**(1), 147–150.

12. Koestler, 1989: *The GHOST in the MACHINE*. Arkana Books, London.

13. Maturana, F., Gu, P., Naumann, A. and Norrie, D.H., 1997: Object-oriented job-shop scheduling using genetic algorithm, *Computers in Industry*, **32**, 281–294.

14. Okino, N., 1992: A prototyping of bionic manufacturing system. In *Proceedings of ICOOMS '92*, pp. 297–302.

15. Okino, N., 1993: Bionic manufacturing systems. In J. Peklenik (ed.), *Flexible Manufacturing Systems, Past, Present, Future*, Ljubljana, Slovenia, pp. 73–95.

16. Senehi, M.K., Kramer, Th.R., Ray, S.R., Quintero, R. and Albus, J.S., 1994: Hierarchical control architectures from shop level to end effectors. In S.B. Joshi and I.S. Smith (eds), *Computer Control of Flexible Manufacturing Systems, Research and Development*, Chapman & Hall, Chapter 2, pp. 31–62.

17. Simon, H.A., 1990: *The Science of the Artificial*, 2nd edn. MIT Press, Cambridge, MA.

18. Sousa, P. and Ramos, C., 1997: A dynamic scheduling holon for manufacturing orders. In *Proceedings of 2nd World Congress on Intelligent Manufacturing Processes and Systems*, June 10–13, Budapest, Hungary, pp. 542–547.

19. Sugimura, N., Tanimizu, Y. and Yoshioka, T., 1997: A study on object oriented modeling of holonic manufacturing system. In *Proceedings of 29th CIRP International Seminar on Manufacturing Systems*, Osaka, Japan, May 11–13, pp. 215–220.

20. Tharumarajah and Wells, A.J., 1997: A behavior-based approach to scheduling in distributed manufacturing systems, *Integrated Computer Aided Engineering*, **4**(4), 235–249.

21. Ueda, K., 1992: An approach to bionic manufacturing systems based on DNA-type information. In *Proceedings of ICOOMS '92*, pp. 303–308.
22. Ueda, K., 1993: A genetic approach toward future manufacturing systems. In J. Peklenik, (ed.), *Flexible Manufacturing Systems, Past, Present, Future*. Ljubljana, Slovenia, pp. 221–228.
23. Valckenaers, P., Van Brussel, H., Bongaerts, L. and Wyns, J., 1997: Holonic manufacturing systems, *Journal of Integrated Computer Aided Engineering*, **4**(3), 191–201.
24. Valckenaers, P., Bonneville, E., Van Brussel, H., Bongaerts, L. and Wyns, J., 1994: Results of the holonic control system benchmark at the K.U.Leuven. In *Proceedings of CIMAT Conference (Computer Integrated Manufacturing and Automation Technology)*, 10–12 Oct., Troy, NY, pp. 128–133.
25. Valckenaers, P., Van Brussel, H., Bongaerts, L. and Bonneville, E., 1995: Programming, scheduling, and control of flexible assembly systems, *Computers in Industry (special issue on CIMIA)*, **26**(3), 209–218.
26. Van Brussel, H., 1994: Holonic manufacturing systems, the vision matching the problem. In *Proceedings of Ist European Conference on Holonic Manufacturing Systems*, 1 Dec., Hannover, Germany.
27. Wyns, J., Van Brussel, H., Valckenaers, P. and Bongaerts, L., 1996: Workstation architecture in holonic manufacturing systems. In *Proceedings of 28th CIRP International Seminar on Manufacturing Systems*, May 15–17, Johannesburg, South Africa, pp. 220–231.
28. Zhang, L. and Ren, S., 1999: Self-organization modeling for supply chain based virtual enterprise decision support systems, *Journal of Tsinghua University (Science and Technology)*, **39**(7), 84–88.

Seven paths to growth

M – 11b; 16b; * 1.1b; 1.5b; 2.6c; 4.1b; 4.2c; 4.3c; 4.6c

The seven paths to growth provide management with a guide to preparing a growth strategy. To maintain growth, management must initiate new business opportunities all the time. By employing the seven paths to growth managers may lay the foundation for strong growth in the future.

The seven questions that managers must ask themselves are:

1. How can we increase sales to the present customers with the present product mix?

   Customer relationship management and customer retention methods may propose solutions to this question.
2. How can we extend the business by selling existing products to new customers?
3. How can we grow by introducing new products and services?

   New products must be carefully designed to ensure that they will meet market demand. One method is to define the product mix in broad terms: e.g. instead of defining the line of business as 'insert cutting tools', define it as 'metal cutting'. By this definition a whole new line of products may emerge.

4. How can we expand sales by developing better delivery systems for customers?

The revolution in communications and Internet-based commerce has intensified competition by effectively redesigning the delivery system and allowing innovators to bypass existing sales channels.

5. How and where can we expand into new geographies?

6. How much can we grow by changing the industry structure?

Many of the most successful growth companies pursue opportunities of this kind, usually by means of mergers, acquisitions or alliances.

7. What opportunities are there outside existing industry boundaries?

Expanding out of your industry is one of the most challenging directions for growth, and it requires especially careful consideration.

A determination to grow is a process that calls for a change in company culture and involves all management levels. Managers must not impose constraints on their thinking about corporate growth. They need to open their eyes to hidden opportunities.

A checklist can help to determine whether a business is ready to pursue growth.

1. Do we know who our customers are?
2. What particular aspects or characteristics of our product are especially important in creating value?
3. Are our core businesses generating sufficient earnings to invest in growth?
4. Is our cost structure competitive?
5. Has operating performance been stable?
6. Has market share grown or been stable?
7. How can we best enhance value-creating properties?
8. Are we protected from new competitors, technologies or regulations that could change the rules of the game?
9. Do we have any new businesses capable of creating as much value as the current businesses?
10. Can we improve our products by new releases in order to control quality enhancement?
11. Are these new businesses gaining momentum in the market?
12. Are we prepared to invest heavily to accelerate their growth?
13. Are they attracting entrepreneurial talent to our organization?
14. Does our leadership team set aside time to think about growth opportunities?
15. Do we have a portfolio of options for reinventing existing businesses and creating new ones?
16. Are these ideas very different from those on the list a year or more ago?

17. Are we finding effective ways to turn these ideas into new businesses?
18. Have the ideas been made tangible in concrete, measurable first steps?
19. Are we using the information system in the organization so as to optimize information system benefits?
20. Do we combine information from different separate sources?
21. Do we have the best programme for promoting cooperation and communication within the organization?

Bibliography

1. Anandan, R., Baghai, M., Coley, S. and White, D., 1999: Seven paths to growth, *Management Review*, **88**(10), 39–45.

Simultaneous engineering (SE)

S – 3b; 4c; 5d; 8c; 13c; * 1.2c; 1.3c; 2.1c; 2.2b; 2.5c; 3.2d; 3.6d
See Concurrent engineering.

Single minute exchange of dies (SMED)

X – 2b; 3c; 4c; 14c; * 1.3b; 2.4b; 3.3c
The objective of single minute exchange of dies is to reduce setup times. It is most important for one-of-a-kind manufacturing, or small lot size manufacturing. It aims at reducing the economic lot size to be very close to one. The method proposes a collection of techniques aimed at reducing setup time to a single minute. The method is composed of the following steps:

1. Identify process operations and setup, and analyse them.
2. Separate internal and external setup operations. Internal, means that the machine is idle while performing the setup. External means setup operations that can be done in a tool room and not on the shop floor.
3. Change internal operations to external ones.
4. Re-define the process operations.

This method is appropriate for a company that needs to manufacture a large number of products, in small quantities.

The basic idea of single minute exchange of dies can be appreciated in CNC machines where machine preparation (setup) is done in the office and does not cause idle machine time; in the use of pallets in flexible manufacturing system (FMS); in group technology methodology for modular fixture design; or in designing components with the idea of a single fixture to accommodate a family of parts.

Bibliography

1. Arn, E., 1975: *Group technology*. Springer-Verlag, Berlin.
2. Shigeo, S., 1985: *A Revolution in Manufacturing: the SMED System*. Productivity Press, pp. 1–31.
3. Yoshida, H. and Hitomi, 1985: *Group Technology – Applications to Production Management*. Kluwer-Nijhoff, Boston.

Statistical process control (SPC)

S – 2c; 3d; 5b; 14b; * 1.3d; 1.4b; 2.5b; 3.2d; 4.2c

Statistical process control is the application of statistical techniques to manage the operation of processes. The main goals of SPC are:

1. Improve quality and reliability of products and services without increased cost.
2. Provide practical tools for controlling quality.
3. Establish an ongoing measurement and verification system.
4. Increase productivity and reduce cost.
5. Prioritize problem-solving activities to direct effort in a systematic way.
6. Improve customer satisfaction.

Benefits of SPC include defect or error prevention rather than just detection (as in quality control). This means greater machines up-time, less warranty costs, avoidance of unnecessary capital expenditure on new machines, increased ability to meet production delivery dates, and increased productivity. Additionally, SPC has been used as a basis for product and process design. With detailed knowledge obtained from SPC on product variability with process change, designers have the capability to design and produce items of the required quality from the first piece. Therefore SPC not only helps with design but results in reduced start-up and debugging effort and cost.

The method uses statistical tools to identify problems and technology to solve them. SPC is statistically based and logically built around the phenomenon that variation in a product is ever present. It can be used in making daily decisions about the operation of nearly all processes. SPC identifies changes between items being produced over a given period. Corrective action may therefore be applied before defective material is produced. A properly conducted SPC programme recognizes the importance of quality and need for never-ending search to improve quality by reducing variation in process output. Material will be of the required quality because it is manufactured properly and not because it is inspected. In most cases, quality should not be left to chance. Sorting conforming units from nonconforming units to produce a yield is not usually the most cost-effective method.

Variation will exist within the process. Parts that conform to specifications are acceptable; parts that do not conform are not acceptable. However, to control the process, reduce variation and ensure that the output continues to meet the expressed requirements, the cause of variation must be identified in the data or in the dispersion (spread) of the data. Collections of these data are characterized as mathematical models called 'distributions' that are used to predict overall performance. Certain factors may cause variation that cannot be adequately explained by the process distribution. Unless these factors, also called 'assignable causes', are identified and removed, they will continue to affect the process in an unpredictable manner. A process is said to be in statistical control when the only source of variation is the natural process variation and 'assignable causes' have been eliminated.

Someone directly connected with the process can usually correct a variation that is outside the desired process distribution. For example, a machine set improperly may produce defective parts. The responsibility for corrective/preventive action in this case will belong to the operator, who can readjust the machine to prevent recurring defects. 'Out of control' conditions become evident quickly by using control charts.

A control chart is a graphic representation of process variation plotted against time. The chart compares ongoing performance to control limits calculated from the natural process dispersion. Because of the low probability of data occurring outside the control limits by random chance, such points are considered to arise from an assignable cause that can be identified and corrected. The personnel directly involved in the operation can maintain control charts. Immediate feedback is key to success of any SPC system.

SPC logically identifies responsibilities and accountabilities, and eliminates 'finger pointing' and confusion. There are fewer tendencies to hide or ignore problems when an efficient system is in place to correct problems.

Bibliography

1. Bank, J., 1992: *The Essence of Total Quality Management*. Prentice-Hall.
2. Box, G.E.F. and Biageard, S., 1987: The scientific context of quality improvement, *Quality Progress*, **20**(6), 54–61.
3. Crosby, B.P., 1979: *Quality is Free*. McGraw-Hill, New York.
4. Crosby, B.P., 1989: *Let's Talk Quality*. McGraw-Hill, New York.
5. Daetz, D., 1987: The effect of product design on product quality and product cost, *Quality Progress*, **20**(6), 63–67.
6. DataMyte Corporation, *DataMyte SPC Handbook*.
7. Deming, W.E., 1945: *Statistical Methods from the Viewpoint of Quality*. Lancaster Press, New York.
8. Feigenbaum, A.V., 1951: *Total Quality Control*, McGraw-Hill, New York.
9. Garvin, D.A., 1983: Quality on the line, *Howard Business Review*, **61**(5), 65–75.
10. Gunter, B., 1987: A perspective on the Taguchi methods, *Quality Progress*, **20**(6), 44–52.

11. Isukawa, K., 1976: *Guide to Quality Control*. Asian productivity organization, Tokyo.
12. Juran, J.M., 1945: *Management of Inspection and Quality Control*. Harper and Row, New York.
13. Juran, J.M., 1986: The quality trilogy, *Quality Progress*, August, 19–24.
14. Kackar, R., 1985: Offline quality control, parameter design, and the Taguchi method, *Journal of Quality Technology*, **17**(4), 176–209.
15. Monden, Y., 1998: *Toyota Production System: An Integrated Approach to Just-in-Time*, 3rd edn. Engineering Management Press.
16. Oakland, J.S., 1989: *Total Quality Management*. Heinemann, London.
17. Taguchi, G., 1989: *Quality Engineering in Production Systems*. Mc-Graw-Hill, New York.
18. US Army Material Command, 1987: Statistical Process Control (SPC) requirements, 2 September.

Strategic sourcing

M – 2c; 3d; 4c; 9b; 10b; 11c; 14d; * 1.1c; 1.2b; 1.6b; 3.3c; 4.2c

The objective of strategic sourcing is to gain the full value-added potential of procurement. A key foundation of strategic sourcing is the total cost of ownership concept. The set of interrelated business processes focus on what a company should buy and how to buy it to maximize the value of externally procured goods or services.

Procurement is playing an increasingly important role in helping major corporations achieve their savings and profitability objectives. What companies buy has been increasing in importance, size, and complexity, and thus how companies buy has changed. Leading procurement organizations are exploiting several opportunities to leverage the corporate buy, optimize the supply base, minimize linked costs in the supply chain, and maximize the value of goods and services for users. These opportunities can be described in a systematic framework of strategic sourcing that is applicable to services as well as materials. With the emphasis on shareholder value growth, industry leaders are turning to new business designs to capture and sustain profitable growth. Strategic sourcing can be applied to the business designs that will shape corporate revenue realization as well as competitive cost position. By building sourcing process excellence and aligning capabilities with the requirements of the corporate buy, procurement can have a key role in the corporate quest for value growth.

For many businesses, procurement is becoming an increasingly significant driver of corporate financial performance. Purchases of outside goods and services has always played an important role in the corporate cost structure reaching as high as 80% or more of the total cost of goods sold in some industries.

Over the last decade there has been an increasing reliance on supply chain. Manufacturers are purchasing subassemblies rather than piece parts, outsourcing has become prominent in activities ranging from logistics to administrative services, and suppliers are increasingly involved in defining the technical and commercial aspects of the goods and services companies provide. These trends, in effect, have raised the amount a business spends externally. Most importantly, the complexity of purchasing has increased dramatically in terms of the nature of what is purchased.

In short, what companies buy has changed significantly. This has implications for how companies buy and translates into opportunities for significant cost reduction and profit. Procurement is quickly becoming recognized as a priority function that offers high-impact opportunities for improving the bottom line. Many businesses have begun to realize that cost cutting alone has generally been a disappointing means of improving operating profit and increasing shareholder value. Senior managers are increasingly realizing that profitable growth, rather than cost cutting, is the best way to create sustainable shareholder value. Squeezing supplier margins for significant unit cost reductions has been a popular route to improve short-term profits, although some companies have found the savings to be unsustainable, leading to higher costs and damaged buyer–supplier relationships.

Traditionally, companies have focused on purchase price alone instead of taking a total cost view. Overemphasis on purchase price fails to consider several factors that can be the source of innovative, and more sustainable opportunities for suppliers and buyers alike. These factors include supplier economics and other supply chain costs, such as transportation, quality, inventory, reliability, and other factors of a product or service over its lifecycle. Total cost of ownership considers both supplier and buyer activities, and costs over a product or service's complete life-cycle in the context of the competitive forces at work in the relevant purchase category. This perspective means understanding a wide range of cost and value relationships associated with individual purchases. For instance, from a competitive economics perspective, it may be more effective for a buyer to rationalize its supply base to enable higher supplier capacity utilization and, in turn, lower acquisition prices while preserving acceptable margins for the surviving suppliers. From a life-cycle ownership standpoint, buying a higher quality item with a steeper price tag could be justified because the initial purchase cost would ultimately be offset by fewer manufacturing defects, lower inventory requirements, and lower administrative costs.

Significant savings in total ownership costs can be achieved through a set of specific strategic pathways.

1. Buy for less. Procurement plays a more value-added role by consolidating volume and selecting suppliers that provide the best prices and terms. Savings of 5 to 15% are typical. Some companies are experiencing a 30% or greater cost reduction.
2. Buy better. The objective is to minimize total ownership costs by directly affecting supplier economics – that is, by understanding current market conditions and supplier economics well enough to provide insight into

what prices ought to be. Savings of 10 to 40% are typical with this procurement method.

3. Consume better. Optimizing life-cycle costs and value to consumer. Value engineering, reduced complexity, earlier supplier involvement in product design, and corporate consumption management are examples of ways that buyers and suppliers can work together to make procurement value added.
4. Sell better.

New, innovative strategic variants are being implemented as fast as the supply and individual company situations change. Some variations include:

1. pursuing open competitive bid vs. selective bid invitations;
2. joining a buying consortium;
3. dealing directly with OEMs vs. buying through a distributor;
4. establishing primary and secondary supplier arrangements;
5. buying an equity stake in a supplier;
6. forming long-term, sole-source partnerships;
7. contracting for supplier capacity, rather than specific products;
8. bankrolling the establishment of a new supply option.

Bibliography

1. Carlsson, B., 1989: Flexibility and the theory of the firm, *International Journal of Industrial Organization*, **7**(2), 179–203.
2. Cleveland, G., Schroeder, R.G. and Anderson, J.C., 1989: A theory of production competence, *Decision Sciences*, **20**(4), 655–668.
3. Harrington, L., 1997: Buying better, *Industry Week*, July 21.
4. Hayes, R.H. and Pisano, G.P., 1994: Beyond world-class: The new manufacturing strategy, *Harvard Business Review*, **72**(1), 77–86.
5. Hayes, R.H. and Wheelwright, S.C., 1984: *Restoring Our Competitive Edge*. John Wiley & Sons, New York.
6. Hyun, J.H. and Ahn, B.H., 1992: A unifying framework for manufacturing flexibility, *Management Review*, **5**(4), 251–260.
7. Lau, R.S.M., 1994: Attaining strategic flexibility. Paper presented at the *5th Annual Meeting of the Production and Operations Management Society*, October 8–11, Washington, DC.
8. Lambert, D.M., Emmelhainz M.A. and Gardner, J.T., 1996: Developing and implementing supply chain partnerships, *The International Journal of Logistics Management*, **7**(2), 1–17.
9. Mansfield, E., Schwartz, M. and Wagner, S., 1981: Imitation costs and patents: An empirical study, *The Economic Journal*, **91**, 907–918.
10. Sethi, A.K. and Sethi, S.P., 1990: Flexibility in manufacturing: A survey, *International Journal of Flexible Manufacturing Systems*, **2**, 289–328.
11. Slywotzky, A.J., Morrison, D.J. and Andelman, B., 1997: *The Profit Zone*: How Strategic Business Design will Lead You to Tomorrow's Profits. Random House, New York.

12. Suarez, F.F., Cusumano, M.A. and Fine, C.H., 1995: An empirical study of flexibility in manufacturing, *Sloan Management Review*, **37**(1), 25–32.
13. Swamidass, P.M. and Newell, W.T., 1987: Manufacturing strategy, environmental uncertainty, and performance: A path analytic model, *Management Science*, **33**(4), 509–524.
14. Upton, D.M., 1994: The management of manufacturing flexibility, *California Management Review*, **36**(2), 72–89.
15. Upton, D.M., 1995: What really makes factories flexible? *Harvard Business Review*, **73**(4), 74–84.
16. Vickery, S.K., 1991: A theory of production competence revisited. *Decision Sciences*, **22**(3), 635–643.
17. Vickery, S.K., Droge, C. and Markland, R.R., 1993: Production competence and business strategy: Do they affect business performance? *Decision Sciences*, **24**(2), 435–456.
18. Ward, P.T., Leong, G.K. and Boyer, K.K., 1994: Manufacturing proactiveness and performance, *Decision Sciences*, **25**(3), 337–358.

Supply chain management

M – 1c; 2c; 3b; 4b; 6b; 7b; 8b; 9b; 10b; 11b; 13c; * 2.4b; 3.2c; 3.3b; 3.4b; 3.5c; 3.6b; 4.1b; 4.2c; 4.3c; 4.4c

The goal of supply chain management is to provide suppliers and customers a window into their supply chain so they can reduce inventory, better utilize plant capacity and cut communications costs. The potential cost savings can be tens of millions of dollars to the bottom line.

The successful operation of any enterprise depends in large measure on procurement of the proper equipment, materials, and supplies of the right quantities, with the right qualities, at the right price, and at the right time. Its importance is recognized as a major business function entitled to equality with such functions as sales, production, and engineering.

In most industries, purchased material and services comprise the largest class of expenditures. The investment in raw material, parts and supplies inventory in most companies is substantial, and the efficient management of inventory can contribute significantly to profit.

The stream of salesmen and direct mail advertising entering the purchasing department, day in day out, brings information about how product materials and new improved ways of doing old jobs. Proper communication and relationships with other functions such as engineering, production, and sales provide one means of keeping the entire organization information on new developments. The importance of keeping up-to-date rapid changes and technological developments can hardly be overemphasized.

Manufacturers are purchasing subassemblies rather than piece parts, outsourcing has become prominent in activities ranging from logistics to administrative services, and suppliers are increasingly involved in defining the technical and commercial aspects of the goods and services companies provide. These trends, in effect, have raised the amount a business spends externally. Most importantly, the complexity of purchasing has increased dramatically in terms of the nature of what is purchased. What companies buy has changed significantly. This has implications for how companies buy and translates into highly leverageable opportunities for significant cost reduction and profit enhancement. Procurement is quickly becoming recognized as a priority function that offers high-impact opportunities for improving the bottom line. Manufacturers share production-scheduling and quality-control information daily with the principal supplier of raw materials. Many are using supplier expertise to help reduce the time and money it spends designing and processing.

Improving supply-chain management builds on trends to outsource non-centre activities, reduce the number of suppliers, and build only after orders come in rather than for inventory. But supply-chain integration still can't happen without seamless exchanges of order, marketing, and production information.

Two major roadblocks are precedent and people. The technology is there to tightly couple these supply chains on a daily basis, but the management processes, the way contracts are written for supply and demand between the nodes in the supply chain, just aren't able to support it. Moreover, as information filters through any chain, each participant is sorely tempted to adjust or manipulate it for his own reasons or because of prior experience.

Companies working at integrating frequently start by looking in the direction along the supply chain – upstream or downstream – where initial gains are easiest to obtain. They're in a hurry because they are under stress from new competition or new technology. What follow are closer relationships with suppliers or customers, generally with the help of the Internet. While most of the tales describe new links between independent companies, the last tells of supply-chain improvements that resulted when two companies merged.

By treating the suppliers like partners not only did customers get faster delivery, but in addition they can cut work-in-process inventory.

Many companies are starting to utilize the Internet to help them manage their supply chains and extend their enterprises to include customers, distributors, and suppliers. When combined, the Internet, traditional enterprise resource planning packages (ERP), electronic data interchange, and supply- and demand-forecasting software are redefining supply-chain management.

For companies looking to establish a flow manufacturing environment, but who find that a true physical flow layout of the manufacturing process is impractical or impossible, supply chain synchronization enables a virtual flow process.

With supply chain synchronization, one can anticipate dramatically improved customer responsiveness. Imagine being able to tell customers the exact status of their orders, initiated either by an alarm signal from the system, a customer-initiated call to customer service, or direct access via the Internet. Manufacturers will know exactly where the order is in the process, which operation or activity is next, whether or not any problems exist, and how much time the remaining order fulfilment steps will take. Customers will know with confidence exactly when their orders will be completed and delivered. Supply chain synchronization is complementary to ERP and supply chain management.

Supply chain synchronization closes the loop between supply and demand. It does so dynamically, in real time, and in a way that matches how a business operates. It is based on reality, not on gross, rough-cut numbers. Average companies work with information averages. Winning companies work with information details, finding business value in the margins. Now, manufacturers can plan, schedule, and manage the flow of work through the entire order fulfilment process rather than via sequential between departments. A supply chain synchronization software solution provides a proper balance between optimal planning and synchronized execution. Planning is based on shared objectives that optimally balance demand against available resources.

Synchronized systems represent the next level of performance beyond integrated systems. They share common data, in real time, using exception-driven event triggers to initiate action dynamically. In other words, synchronized systems could be defined as dynamic integration. These systems combine what-if simulation with advanced mathematical methods, such as genetic algorithms, to quickly and effectively assure identification of the best possible course of action. The real-time feedback loop is one of the most important elements of the system design. A so-called optimal plan with infrequent feedback and schedule recalculations cannot meet the challenge of constantly changing conditions.

Sharing common data is not part of the culture and not what they've been taught. They still look at procurement as a semi-adversarial deal where you propose your bids, come up with somebody who has the lowest price, and then try to get that price down. These tough negotiators are now being asked to cooperate and trust. To work effectively you've got to believe that if you make the pie greater, everybody benefits. Accepting that belief will take time. Although people say they like change, they only like it when it doesn't include them.

Of course the Internet brings hazards by making it easier for buyers to obtain bids from anywhere; e-commerce could mean that many are called but few are chosen. Where specs are tight and turnaround is critical, companies will have strong, deep relationships. Companies looking to establish a flow manufacturing environment, may find that a true physical flow layout of the manufacturing process is impractical or impossible with partners. Other suppliers will see their products as commodities as non-strategic items go out for Internet auction among qualified bidders. The low bid today wins this chunk of business. The lowest tomorrow wins the next. To overcome such a situation there will be three levels of security – for managers, sales people and customers. A search engine will enable customers to find new products, but they will also have access to a 'quick' order form for products they already use. In addition, customers will have access to their account history.

Supply chain terminology and details vary in the literature: some call it the 'extended enterprise', while others expound on the 'borderless corporation'. But the gospel is much the same: integrate the supply chain into some sort of virtual keiretsu and, you'll get lightning-speed responsiveness while cutting a layer of inventory.

Bibliography

1. Anupindi, R. and Akella, R., 1993: Diversification under supply uncertainty, *Management Science*, **39**(8), 944–963.
2. Bowersox, D. and Closs, D., 1996: *Logistical Management: The Integrated Supply Chain Process*. McGraw-Hill.
3. Chen, A. and Liu, L. *et al.*, 1999: Modeling and analysis of production and distribution system in supply chain. *Proceedings of the 26th International Conference of Computer and Industrial Engineering*, Vol. 1, Australia.
4. Chen, A., Liu, L. and Li, G., 1999: Agile supply chain management based on agent technology. *Proceedings of the 4th Asia Pacific Decision Sciences Institute Conference*, Shanghai, China, June 9–12, pp. 589–591.
5. Christopher, M., 1992: *Logistics and Supply Chain Management*. London, Pitman Publishing.
6. Douglas, J.T. and Griffin, P.M., 1996: Coordinated supply chain management, *European Journal of Operational Research*, **94**, 1–15.
7. Christopher, M., Harrison, A. and Van Hoek, R., 1999: Creating the agile supply chain: issues and challenges. In *Proceedings of the 4th ISL*, Florence, Italy.
8. Hau, L. Lee, *et al.*, 1997: Information distortion in a supply chain: the bullwhip effect, *Management Science*, **43**(4), 546–558.
9. Lambert, D.M., Emmelhainz, M.A. and Gardner, J.T., 1996: Developing and implementing supply chain partnerships, *The International Journal of Logistics Management*, **7**(2), 1–17.
10. Rabelo, R.J. and Spinosa, L.M., 1997: Mobile-agent-based supervision in supply-chain management in the food industry. In *Proceedings of a Workshop on Supply-Chain Management in Agribusiness*, Vitoria (ES) Brazil, pp. 451–460.
11. Vollmann, T., 1996: Supply chain management, Manufacturing 2000. Business Briefing 8/96. International Institute for Management Developments, Lausanne.
12. Zhang, L. and Ren, S., 1999: Self-organization modeling for supply chain based virtual enterprise decision support systems, *Journal of Tsinghua University (Science and Technology)*, **39**(7), 84–88.

Taguchi method

S – 2c; 3b; 5b; 14b; * 1.3d; 1.4b; 2.5b; 3.2d; 4.2c

The Taguchi method addresses design and engineering (offline) as well as manufacturing (online) quality. This fundamentally differentiates the Taguchi method (TM) from SPC, which is purely an online quality control method.

Taguchi's ideas can be broken down into two fundamental principles. First, quality losses increase as deviation from target occurs. The loss function quantifies these 'losses to society'. The second principle, the achievement of high system quality through design of the manufacturing process, set Taguchi's method apart from SPC. Quality is designed, not manufactured, into a product.

Conventional SPC-based methodologies consider only manufacturing processes that follow predetermined specifications. The engineers use testing for manufacturability as a means of correcting the initial design. The same testing and correcting actions used at the manufacturing processing stage can be used at the design stage.

The heart of the Taguchi philosophy is the quality 'loss function'. Taguchi defines the cost of poor quality as 'the losses a product imparts to the society from the time a product is shipped'. This definition sets the Taguchi method apart from the traditional SPC approach to quality which defines the cost of poor quality chiefly as cost of scrap, rework and warranty repair. Any deviation from target reduces the value of the product to society.

Taguchi calls for a robust design to handle variability in purchasing, manufacturing, production and end use. Instead of tightening SPC control limits (which increase the cost of production) to ensure nominal performance, Taguchi and Deming advocate designing the product so that nominal performance is achieved, even when variability in production and end use conditions exist.

Bibliography

1. Box, G.E.F. and Biageard, S., 1987: The scientific context of quality improvement, *Quality Progress*, **20**(6), 54–61.
2. Crosby, B.P., 1979: *Quality is Free*. McGraw-Hill, New York.
3. Crosby, B.P., 1989: *Let's Talk Quality*, McGraw-Hill, New York.
4. Daetz, D., 1987: The effect of product design on product quality and product cost, *Quality Progress*, **20**(6), 63–67.
5. Deming, W.E., 1945: *Statistical Methods from the Viewpoint of Quality*. Lancaster Press, New York.
6. Garvin, D.A., 1983: Quality on the line, *Harvard Business Review*, **61**(5), 65–75.
7. Gunter, B., 1987: A perspective on the Taguchi methods, *Quality Progress*, **20**(6), 44–52.
8. Isukawa, K., 1976: *Guide to Quality Control*. Asian Productivity Organization, Tokyo.
9. Juran, J.M., 1945: *Management of Inspection and Quality Control*. Harper and Row, New York.
10. Juran, J.M., 1986: The quality trilogy, *Quality Progress*, **August**, 19–24.
11. Kackar, R., 1985: Offline quality control, parameter design, and the Taguchi method, *Journal of quality technology*, **17**(4), 176–209.
12. Monden, Y., 1998: *Toyota Production System: An Integrated Approach to Just-in-Time*, 3rd edn. Engineering Management Press.
13. Taguchi, G., 1989: *Quality Engineering in Production Systems*. McGraw-Hill, New York.

Team performance measuring and managing

M – 8b; 12c; * 1.1c; 1.2b; 1.4d; 4.3b; 4.5b

The objective of team performance measuring and managing is to measure manage and motive the people within working teams in a manner that is consistent with the strategy and objectives of the organization.

In hierarchical organizations people were traditionally organized and managed within functions or departments and their performance (and their career progression) was reviewed by line managers. Performance was measured in many cases against the contribution individuals and teams made to the objectives and performance of their department or function. Today, however, many companies employ people to work within process teams, self-managed work groups and other alternative forms of work organization – yet performance measurement systems have not changed (or else the company is struggling with how to adapt). A real problem arises then, in that employee performance measurement may not be aligned with process performance and organizational objectives.

Companies can now measure the performance of their business, of business units, of divisions and units, and some are even successfully measuring the performance of business processes. But managers are finding it difficult to measure team performance.

Organizations are focusing on business processes and are adopting alternative forms of work organization, appropriate for a process strategy, including process teams and self-managed work groups. However, the majority of organizations are still experiencing problems in introducing performance measurement systems that effectively measure performance in these new work environments and at the same time are aligned to the strategy, actions and performance measures at other levels of the organization. Companies have invested large sums of money on re-engineering activities that have led them to adopt a process view of their organizations, and they have bought into the need for integrated performance measures – but still they feel that they are not successfully deploying performance measures at the team level. They have the knowledge relating to business processes and re-engineering and its effect on the workplace and it should be complemented by performance measurement systems, aligned with consistent motivation and reward systems, at the team level following a business process re-engineering initiative.

Some solutions proposed by the time base competition (TAB) method are:

1. Workers form teams. The team is responsible for making decisions about its part of the manufacturing system. This implies that the team is aware of the goals of the organization and the available resources constraints.
2. Multi-performance criteria. Performance evaluation of manufacturing is determined by criteria of quality in design, manufacture, and service; time to

meet orders; time to bring products to market; and value in terms of the overall costs over the product's life and performance in meeting the required functions. This results in a focus on product quality, speed of response and inventory investment.

Bibliography

1. Bititci, U.S., Carrie, A.S. and McDevitt, L.G., 1997: Integrated performance measurement systems: a development guide, *International Journal of Operations Management*, **17**(6), 522–535.
2. Bititci, U.S., Carrie, A.S. and Turner, T.J., 1998: Diagnosing the integrity of your performance measurement system, *Control Institute of Operations Management*, **24**(3), 9–13.
3. Carrie, A.S. and MacIntosh, R., 1994: A structured approach to process re-design. *Proceedings of the 29th Annual BPICS Conference, Getting Better All the Time*, 5–6 Oct. Birmingham, pp. 153–167.
4. Hana, V, Burns, N.D and Backhouse, C.J., 1996: How we are measured is how we behave. *Proceedings of 2nd International Conference on Managing Integrated Manufacturing (MIM'96)*, Leicester University 26–28 June, pp. 303–308.
5. Kaplan, R.S. and Norton, D.P., 1996: *Translating Strategy into Action: The Balanced Scorecard*. Harvard Business School Press, Boston MA.
6. Kueng, P and Krahn, A.J.W., 1999: Building a process performance measurement system: some early experiences, *Journal of Scientific and Industrial Research*, **58**, 145–159.
7. MacBryde, J.C., 1998: Business Process Re-engineering in UK Universities. Ph.D. thesis, University of Strathclyde.
8. Neely, A., Gregory, M. and Platts, K., 1995: Performance measurement system design: a literature review and research agenda, *International Journal of Operations Management*, **15**(4).
9. Tranfield, D. *et al.*, 1998: Teamworked organisational engineering: getting the most out of teamworking, *Management Decision*, **36**(6), 378–384.
10. Tranfield, D. *et al.*, 1998: Reconfiguring your organisation: a teamwork approach, *Team Performance Management*, **4**(4), 166–176.

Theory of constraint (TOC)

P – 1b; 2d; 4c; 6b; 13d; * 1.2d; 1.3b; 2.3b; 2.5d; 3.5d; 4.3c

The theory of constraints is a general manufacturing philosophy based on understanding the manufacturing processes and identifying its constraints. A constraint is anything that limits a system from achieving higher performance or meeting goals.

Initially the system was developed as a scheduling system called optimized production technology (OPT). OPT governs product flow in the plant. The rules of OPT are derived for the capacity constraints and especially bottlenecks.

Both capacity and market constraints should be handled by the logistical system. The nine rules of OPT are:

1. Do not balance capacity. The major objective is flow.
2. The level of utilization of a non-bottleneck is not determined by its own potential but by other constraints within the system.
3. Activation and utilization are not synonymous.
4. An hour lost on bottleneck is an hour lost on the system.
5. An hour gained on a non-bottleneck is a mirage.
6. Bottlenecks govern both inventory and throughput.
7. The transfer batch may not be equal to the process batch.
8. The process batch should be variable, not fixed.
9. Schedules should be estimated by looking at all the constraints. Lead times are results of a schedule and cannot be predetermined.

OPT did not reveal the theory underlying the software, the firms that implemented OPT were forced to follow schedules generated by a 'black box'. Supervisors found the schedules counter-intuitive and were reluctant to follow them.

Following a fairly disastrous sortie into OPT scheduling software, the ideas on bottleneck management now run under the name of theory of constraints (TOC). TOC has moved on slightly from OPT, however, the basic message is remarkably similar. TOC is claimed to be a useful approach to issues of project management and constraints in company policies. Independent experts say production is where the true value still lies. A lot of work is being done to see how you can apply manufacturing theory outside of manufacturing, but you always come up against the problem of environments that don't even have the stability offered by manufacturing, where at least if something takes an hour to make, it takes an hour to make. Outside of manufacturing, there is so much scope for informal systems.

TOC boils down to the argument that the throughput (that is, output which is sold) of an entire plant is the measure of success for any company; that it is nonsensical for individual departments to work on improving their performance locally since this will only result in stockpiles of inventory or work-in-progress; and that there is always one weakest link in the chain, the point where improvement efforts should be focused first and whose limitations or constraints should inform all other steps. If you optimize already strong links without strengthening the weakest, all you do is heighten the imbalance – which translates into inventory.

There are interdependencies within any organization striving to satisfy customers. Because of the interdependencies organizations are best characterized by a chain rather than a mere pile of links. The theory of constraints (TOC), a systems management philosophy, asserts that constraints determine the performance of a system and that any system contains only a few constraints.

A constraint is anything that limits a system's performance relative to its goal. To improve the strength of the system one would first find the weakest link (constraint) in the chain and strengthen it.

TOC makes it clear that few resources in the manufacturing process need a detailed schedule. TOC assumes that material flows in small transfer batches, the required number of units to process before moving to the next operation. Process batches, the number of units processed with one setup, may be larger than transfer batches, i.e. simultaneous processing by non-constraints is acceptable. The knee-jerk reaction is that this is inefficient, but that is link-based inertia. It is permissible for non-constraints to be inefficient up to a point. Once material is released, it will flow quickly to the constraints. Non-constraint resources will not tend to accumulate inventory. With short or without queues at non-constraints, the decision about which order to work on next becomes trivial. Non-constraint resources work solely to feed the constraint. Thus, traditional capacity management techniques that attempt to optimize the local performance of every resource become obsolete.

The steps of the TOC process are:

1. Identify the system constraints. The two major constraints that the logical system has to accommodate are market demands, and capacity constraint.
2. Decide how to exploit the system constraints. There are very few capacity constraints in any plant. The drum buffer rope approach recognizes that such constraint should dictate the rate of production of the entire plant – the drumbeat.
3. Subordinate everything else to the above decision. Once buffers are built in line with the policy, any additional inventory is a waste of money and may jeopardize the throughput and meeting due dates.
4. Elevate the system constraints. The elevation of the constraints might mean buying more machines, hiring workers for another shift, reducing setups. All such methods may be easily evaluated.
5. If in any previous step a constraint is broken or eliminated, go to step one. Warning: Do not let inertia become the next constraint. The warning on inertia is emphasized because most system problems come from policies that were correct at the time they were created. Companies devote too little time to clearing out dead wood; hence spend far too much time fire fighting. By following these steps a firm improves in the sales and profit. Furthermore, through study of the constraint's interaction with non-constraints, the firm learns where improvement efforts will yield the greatest benefit.

For practical implementation of the TOC theory the drum buffer rope (DBR), a production scheduling technique, was developed. The name of the technique is based on metaphors that the constraint (drum) determines the pace of production. The rope is the material release mechanism. Material is pulled to the first operation at a pace determined by the constraint. Material release is offset from the constraint schedule by a fixed amount of time (the length of the rope). The fixed amount of time between material release and the constraint schedule coupled with quick flow of material to the constraint ensures that an essentially constant buffer is maintained at the constraint.

There are actually two buffers at a resource constraint. A buffer of material awaiting processing protects against disruptions upstream from the constraint. Space behind the constraint allows processed material to accumulate and protects the constraint from disruptions downstream of the constraint. Buffers exist to protect the system from delays in production. Buffer size, however, is a trade-off between protection and lead time. If the buffer size is increased, the protection increases, but so does the manufacturing lead time.

The drum buffer rope (DBR) approach suggests that all efforts should initially be focused on inventory reduction since it has maximum impact on all aspects of running a manufacturing business. Beating the *drum* and building the time *buffer* will ensure high utilization of the capacity constraint and secure throughput and due date performance. When the buffer is full the instruction is simply 'stopworking!'. This is a *rope* that connects the buffer behind the operation with material being released from the buffer in front of the operation. The DBR approach demonstrates that putting a rope between every two successive operations is excessive protection that might even reduce throughput. Controlling the first operation in every route is enough. The rope should be between the buffer and the released raw material area.

DBR is a basic element of synchronized manufacturing, since they provide all that is needed to maintain production flow with a given predetermined inventory level. The aim is to operate where the bottleneck (the drum) dictates the overall pace of work, and where inventory is only allowed to build up in finished goods and in front of the bottleneck, to act as a buffer which will enable the crucial function to continue even if there are breakdowns upstream. The rope links all upstream operations to the pace of the bottleneck, to keep those at the front end of the process from churning out more than the bottleneck can handle.

If it all sounds reasonably straightforward, that's because in many ways it is – as ever, it's just the implementation that can prove tricky. And if it all sounds like a history lesson from the dark ages of the 1980s (remember them?), the experts agree that there is still a surprisingly large part for such a basic theory to play in this brave new manufacturing world. The message is not radically new, it just hasn't got through to everyone it should have reached yet. It is a common-sense way of using cellular units where activities are watched carefully to minimize inventory and maximize throughput.

Buffer management is the method developed for controlling buffer size and, therefore, manufacturing lead time and inventory. Buffer management also warns of potential disruption to the production plan. It is assumed that material-processing time is on average only one-third of the time allowed by the buffer. If the materials have not been processed by end of the first third of the buffer, the buffer manager will check to see if the order faces any obstacles to timely completion. If two-thirds of the buffer is consumed and the materials have not yet completed the buffer operations, the buffer manager will expedite the order. Each time an order is checked or expedited, the occurrence is tallied and the cause recorded. The buffer size is determined by the expedite record. If there is frequent expediting, the buffer may be increased. If expediting is rare, the buffer can be reduced, thereby reducing lead time and inventory. The delay tally also provides information used to guide continuous improvement to the production system. The problems causing the most frequent and damaging delays would have a high priority for improvement efforts.

Buffer management is the only shop floor control mechanism needed. Any problem, including quality, manifests itself as material missing from the buffer. Note that focusing the continuous improvement effort on the most frequent and severe disruptions should maximize the rate of improvement in performance. As production performance improves, buffers become smaller, causing inventory and lead time to be further reduced.

Bibliography

1. Cohen, O., 1988: The drum-buffer-rope (DBR) approach to logistics. In A. Rolstadas (ed.), IFIP state of the art report, *Computer-Aided Production Management*, Springer-Verlag, pp. 51–70.
2. Fogarty, D., Blackstone, J. and Hoffmann, T., 1991: *Production and Inventory Management*, 2nd edn. South-Western, Cincinnati, OH.
3. Fox, R.E., 1982: MRP, Kanban, or OPT, *Inventory and Production*, **July/August**.
4. Fox, R.E., 1983: OPT – an answer for America – Part IV, *Inventory and Production*, **March/April**.
5. Fox, R.E., 1983: OPT vs. MRP – thoughtware vs. software, *Inventory and Production*, **November/December**.
6. Fuchsberg, G., 1992: Quality programs show shoddy results, *Wall Street Journal*, May 14, B1, B7.
7. Goldratt, M.E. 1990: *Theory of Constraints*. North River Press.
8. Goldratt, E., 1991: Late-night discussions: VI, *Industry Week*, December 2, 51, 52.
9. Goldratt, E., 1989: *The Goal*, 2nd revised edn. North River Press, Croton-on-Hudson: NY.
10. Goldratt, E., 1990: *The Haystack Syndrome*, North River Press, Croton-on-Hudson: NY.
11. Goldratt, E., 1988: The fundamental measurements, *The Theory of Constraints Journal*, **1**(3).
12. Goldratt, E. and Fox, R.E., *The Race*. North River Press.
13. Goldratt, E., 1988: Computerized shop floor scheduling, *International Journal of Production Research*, **26**(3), pp. 443–455.
14. Lambrecht, M. and Segaert, A., 1990: Buffer stock allocation in serial and assembly type of production lines, *International Journal of Operations and Production Management*, **10**(2), pp. 47–61.
15. Mathews, J. and Katel, P., 1992: The cost of quality, *Newsweek*, September 7.

Time base competition – TBS

M – 2d; 3b; 4b; 6b; 7c; 8b; 9d; 13c; 14c; * 1.1d; 1.2d; 1.3b; 1.4b; 2.2c; 2.4b; 3.3c; 4.5b; 4.6c

The time base competition manufacturing method emphasizes the topic of time (such as time to market for new products and time to deliver and establish products) as a competitive weapon.

The basic law that time-in-process equals work-in-process multiplied by mean time between successive releases relates time and inventory. The same formula can be applied to the speed of response to orders and delivery speed, so the same approaches of reducing variability and improving response time should be used.

A more significant emphasis of time-base competition is on the time to develop new products. Again the focus is on improving linkages and communication between all activities responsible for a new product. Development of a new product is primarily concerned not with the processing and movement of materials, but with the processing and communication of ideas. In such conceptual tasks, differences in individual capability, expertise, and performance become very significant; apart from developing approaches to minimize variability, it is essential to consider structures that recognize individual differences. In such circumstances, serial structures for processes are not as appropriate as parallel structures or structures that promote collaborative activity and allow offline resolution of infrequent and difficult problems.

Time base competition manufacturing places emphasis on developing structures and approaches that cope with variability, including recognizing that it can and does exist. Next, consideration must be given to how disturbances or variability will be dealt with. The following are possible generic approaches:

1. *Eliminate*. Totally eliminating variability and disturbances is rarely feasible, particularly in manufacturing that involves using sophisticated production technology or new materials. If humans are involved, we know that we cannot eliminate variability; however, through appropriate selection, training, and task design, significant reduction in human variability is possible.
2. *Reduce effect*. The easy way to cope with variability is to use inventory buffers and order backlogs, but this is hardly consistent with the ideas of time competition. An alternative approach is to try to prevent disturbances in one area from affecting others. This suggests breaking down manufacturing into product-focused cells, an idea also advocated by group technology. Cells reduce the impact of variability, particular variability and unpredictability in demand or in the performance of product-specific manufacturing technology.
3. *Develop responses*. In many manufacturing situations, it must be recognized that variability, disturbances, and uncertainty exist. We have to deal

with them, and we should deal with them as soon and as fast as we can. We should ensure that the capability to respond exists by identifying that a particular disturbance has occurred and developing an appropriate response. The best place to provide this capability is as close to the source of the problem as possible. We should respond immediately, not wait until information about the need is transmitted up the organizational hierarchy and down to the staff expert. We should codify and simplify the response, making it automatic if possible. People have to be trained and motivated to deal with problems as they occur, and the closest person who has the capability should deal with the problem. Capability has to be widely diffused, down to the level of the individual worker. Also, different people have different skills and experience, so small groups or teams are more effective than individuals for problem solving.

Time base competition has the following characteristics:

1. *Workers use their intelligence.* Apart from performing basic production tasks, workers are expected to use their intelligence to recognize problems and deal with them rapidly and efficiently. They have to recognize that continual learning about manufacturing goes on, and they have to be able to recognize how to put into action their own capabilities and the capabilities of others. They have to recognize that they are part of a team where each individual brings different skills and abilities.
2. *Staff help workers.* The role of staff is to help workers solve problems. In a certain sense, staff become subservient to the workers, and the organization is turned upside-down, with authority flowing from the workers. Workers ensure that support is available and used, and recognize when to refer infrequent and complex problems to staff so that basic tasks are not disrupted.
3. *Workers form teams.* The team is responsible for making decisions about its part of the manufacturing system. This implies that the team is aware of the goals of the organization and the available resources constraints.
4. *Managers as educators and coaches.* Managers are no longer the symbol of authority and a communication link to the rest of the organization. Their responsibility becomes that of education and training the work group.
5. *Multi-performance criteria.* Performance evaluation of manufacturing is determined by criteria of quality in design, manufacture, and service; time to meet orders; time to bring products to market; and value in terms of the overall costs over the product's life and performance in meeting the required functions. This results in a focus on product quality, speed of response and inventory investment.
6. *Decentralization of control.* To cut down on response delay and improve response to disturbances, the head office is decentralized and middle management functions are eliminated as much as possible. Suppliers and customers interact directly with plants, while the head office focuses on minimizing

disruptions at plant level from outside the organization. Closer links to customers and suppliers reduce planned inventories and provide forward visibility of potential disruptions.

Bibliography

1. Blackburn, J.D., 1991: *Time-Based Competition: The Next Battleground in American Manufacturing*. Business One-Irwin, Homewood IL.
2. Chrisman, J.J., Hofer C.W. and Boulton, W.R., 1988: Toward a system for classifying business strategies, *Academy of Management Review*, **13**, 413–428.
3. Gabel, H.L., 1991: *Competitive Strategies for Product Standards*, McGraw Hill, London.
4. Huber, G.P., 1990: A theory of the effects of advanced information technologies on organizational design, intelligence, and decision making, *Academy of Management Review*, **15**, 47–71.
5. Keen, 1986: *Competing in Time: Using Telecommunications for Competitive Advantage*. Ballinger, Cambridge MA.
6. Lacity, M. and Hirschheim, R., 1993: *Information Systems Outsourcing*, Wiley.
7. Mannion, D., 1995: Vendor accreditation at ICL: competitive versus collaborative procurement strategies. In R. Lamming and A. Cox (eds), *Strategic Procurement Management in the 1990s*. Earlsgate, Winteringham.
8. Miller, J.G. and Roth, A.V., 1994: A taxonomy of manufacturing strategies, *Management Science*, **40**, 285–304.
9. Peters, T. and Waterman, R., 1982: *In Search of Excellence: Lessons from America's Best-Run Companies*. Harper & Row, New York.
10. Prahalad, C.K. and Hamel, G., 1990: The core competence of the corporation, *Harvard Business Review*, **68**(3), 79–91.
11. Tayeb, M.H., 1996: *The Management of a Multicultural Workforce*. John Wiley & Sons, Chichester.
12. Teece, D.J., Pisano, G. and Shuen, A., 1997: Dynamic capabilities and strategic management, *Strategic Management Journal*, **18**, 509–533.

Total quality management (TQM)

M – 2d; 5b; 6d; 8c; 9b; 12c; 14b; * 1.1b; 1.3b; 1.4b; 1.5c; 1.6c; 2.5b; 3.1b; 3.2d; 3.4b

The main goal of total quality management (TQM) is to satisfy the customer. Total quality management is not only concerned with the final customer who wants to buy a product without defect; the product and customer are understood in a wider sense than normally in manufacturing.

1. Products include goods and services.
2. Customers can be internal or external. No part of a company's operation is omitted from this definition.

3. A customer does more than simply take delivery of the goods bought; experience with offers, services, telephone calls, presentations and invoices also influence the customer's satisfaction.

Customer satisfaction leads to sales and cash flow. To turn cash flow into profit, quality cost has to be minimized. Inspection is not the way to improve quality while cutting quality cost. Control and monitoring of the manufacturing process can save the extra cost of inspection, rework and scrap. TQM is the adoption of an approach to the business whereby a company is determined to have better-than-just-acceptable quality and continuous improvement of it, no matter how good it already is.

Sophisticated JIT focuses on the problems that occur within manufacturing and within the scope of the work group or cell; however, variability can also be improved outside the work group and improvements can be exported by the work group. TQM begins with a focus on the customer and meeting the customer's needs. This results in an emphasis on links between work groups, in particular on the impact that variability originating in one group has on other groups. Improved communication and feedback between work groups speeds the path to the immediate customer or supplier of the work group without going through the organizational hierarchy. Within the work group, the major activity associated with TQM is continuous improvement processes. In particular, this means searching for non-value-added activities that can be eliminated. Because the search for improvement opportunities has to involve all members of the work group, it is essential to train them in team skills and problem-solving skills, many of which use similar approaches to improvement as in other manufacturing methods.

One of the outstanding TQM gurus is Deming, and his fourteen points:

1. Constancy of purpose
2. The new philosophy
3. Cease dependence on inspection
4. End 'lowest tender' contracts
5. Improve every process
6. Institute training on the job
7. Institute leadership
8. Drive out fear
9. Break down barriers
10. Eliminate exhortations
11. Eliminate arbitrary numerical targets
12. Permit pride of workmanship
13. Encourage education
14. Top management commitment.

Another guru is Schonberg who lists an 'action agenda for manufacturing excellence' as:

1. Get to know the customer.
2. Cut work-in-process.
3. Cut flow times.
4. Cut setup and changeover times.
5. Cut flow distance and space.
6. Increase make/deliver frequency for each required item.
7. Cut number of suppliers down to a few good ones.
8. Cut number of part numbers.
9. Make it easy to manufacture the part without error.
10. Arrange the workplace to eliminate search time.
11. Cross-train for mastery of more than one job.
12. Record and retain production, quality and problem data at the workplace.
13. Ensure that line people get first crack at problem-solving – before experts.
14. Maintain and improve existing equipment and human work before thinking about new equipment.
15. Look for simple, cheap and movable equipment.
16. Seek to have plural instead of singular workstations, machines, cells and lines for each product.
17. Automate incrementally, when process variability cannot otherwise be reduced.

Juran identified ten steps to quality improvement.

1. Build awareness of the need and opportunity for improvement.
2. Set goals for improvement.
3. Organize to reach the goals by establishing a quality council to identify problems, select projects, appoint teams, and designate facilitators.
4. Provide training.
5. Carry out projects to solve problems.
6. Report progress.
7. Give recognition.
8. Communicate results.
9. Keep score.
10. Maintain momentum by making annual improvement part of the regular systems and processes of the company.

Crosby recommends using the following 14 steps.

1. Management commitment
2. The quality improvement team

3. Quality measurement
4. The cost of quality
5. Quality awareness
6. Corrective action
7. Zero defects planning
8. Supervisor training
9. Zero defects day
10. Goal setting
11. Error-cause removal
12. Recognition
13. Quality councils
14. Do it over again

Many others are practising TQM and have proposed methods for implementation. However, when examining the recommended methods, one can find agreement between all of them on the following points.

• Change must start with top management.
• The change to TQM is cultural.
• Quality is achieved through people.
• Quality involves everyone.
• Quality is not a separate function.
• The change to TQM needs more than motivation.
• Education and training are essential for lasting improvements.
• Continuous improvement requires steadfast management.

The culture of a company is the integrating factor for all the behavioural and attitudinal patterns which prevail in the company. The culture of a company determines the quality of its products and services. Therefore, quality improvements demand cultural changes. Key requirements of the TQM process are as below.

• There must be a common understanding of quality and of the need to change.
• Management must develop operating principles and values which create the environment for continuous improvement.
• Management must create the organization and provide the resources to support the improvement process.
• Everyone must contribute to the end product or service used by the customer.

The problem with TQM seems to be a lack of focus. TQM carries a large bag of powerful techniques. But because the techniques are applied to all of the links, the rate of improvement is slow for the effort expended. When people realize that their efforts are not leading to real improvement in the performance of the company, they start to shy away, giving TQM no more than lip service.

Bibliography

1. Bank, J., 1992: *The Essence of Total Quality Management*. Prentice-Hall.
2. Box, G.E.F. and Biageard, S., 1987: The scientific context of quality improvement, *Quality Progress*, **20**(6), 54–61.
3. Crosby, B.P., 1979: *Quality is Free*. McGraw-Hill, New York.
4. Crosby, B.P., 1989: *Let's Talk Quality*. McGraw-Hill, New York.
5. Daetz, D., 1987: The effect of product design on product quality and product cost, *Quality Progress*, **20**(6), 63–67.
6. Deming, W.E., 1945: Statistical Methods from the Viewpoint of Quality. Lancaster Press, New York.
7. Feigenbaum, A.V., 1951: *Total Quality Control*. McGraw-Hill, New York.
8. Garvin, D.A., 1983: Quality on the line, *Harvard Business Review*, **61**(5), 65–75.
9. Isukawa, K., 1976: *Guide to Quality Control*. Asian Productivity Organization, Tokyo.
10. Juran, J.M., 1945: *Management of Inspection and Quality Control*. Harper and Row, New York.
11. Juran, J.M., 1986: The quality trilogy, *Quality Progress*, **August**, 19–24.
12. Kackar, R., 1985: Offline quality control, parameter design, and the Taguchi method, *Journal of Quality Technology*, **17**(4), 176–209.
13. Monden, Y., 1998: *Toyota Production System: An Integrated Approach to Just-in-Time*, 3rd edn. Engineering Management Press.
14. Oakland, J.S., 1989: *Total Quality Management*. Heinemann, London.
15. Ross, P.J., 1988: The role of Taguchi method and design experiments in QFD, *Quality Progress*, **21**(6), 41–47.
16. Taguchi, G., 1989: *Quality Engineering in Production Systems*, McGraw-Hill.
17. Zhou, Q., Souben, P. and Besant, C.B., 1998: An information management system for production planning in virtual enterprises, *Computers & Industrial Engineering*, **35**(1–2), 153–156.

Value chain analysis

P – 7c; 9c; 11b; 16c; * 1.1b; 3.2b; 4.1b

The objective of value chain analysis is to reduce operating costs. Value chain analysis assumes that companies can be viewed as being composed of two levels. The lower level of the value chain model includes activities ranging from managing raw material to production to sales to after-sales service. The upper level features tasks that span the entire organization.

Businesses all too often concentrate on cutting the direct cost only at the lower level, which typically represents 3–5% of their total operating spend. Value chain analysis proposes to concentrate on the upper level in an attempt to reduce the other 97% of the operating costs.

For value chain analysis it is important to work with a customer across their business to understand business drivers. To identify opportunities it is important to talk to a wide range of decision-makers as well as information technology personnel and managers, It is important to talk to the customer before even selecting the technology or thinking about putting a business proposal on the table.

Quantifying customer needs and buying patterns calls for vast amounts of data to be collected at the point of sale and stored in outsourced data warehouses that are then mined to deduct coherent buying sequences that indicate an underlying need. Such modelling can also help estimate what a customer might need in future, or may even be used to create new needs.

A competitive strategy model is used to define the strategy of the customer's business and the competition it faces. This competitive force analysis identifies the impact of competition on a business and is supposed to determine the profitability. The bargaining power of customers and suppliers determines prices and costs; the threat from substitutes and competitors and the intensity of rivalry influences prices as well as the costs in areas such as plant, product, development, advertising and sales force. These analyses are then used to determine when, where and how a company can cut some processes, while increasing the cost-effectiveness of others.

The technique of marketing services can probably not be replicated by every other agent. Not every agent has the need to do so. Many claim to provide the same levels of service and cost savings without it On the other hand, the strategy would seem to suit only young, growing operators. For larger international consortia that have to contend with the substantial overheads of doing global business, modelling their customer's business would not be a simple and straightforward exercise. And then, there is also the danger that a customer may consider that it is being told how to conduct its business.

Bibliography

1. Billinton, R. and Wang, P., 1998: Distribution system reliability cost/worth analysis using analytical and sequential simulation techniques, *IEEE Transactions on Power Systems*, **13**(4), 1245–1250.
2. Checkland, P. and Holwell, S., 1998: *Information. Systems and Information Systems: Making Sense of the Field*. Wiley, Chichester.
3. Davalos, K.J. and Noble, J.S., 1998: Integrated approach for environmental cost analysis of manufacturing systems, *Engineering Design & Automation*, **4**, (4), 309–323.
4. Drucker, F.P., 1994: The theory of the business, *Harvard Business Review*, 95–102.
5. King, A.M. and Sivaloganathan, S.M., 1998: Development of a methodology for using function analysis in flexible design strategies. *Proceedings of the Institution of Mechanical Engineers, Part B (Journal of Engineering Manufacture)*, **212**(B3), 215–230.
6. Marples, A., 1999: Recycling value from electrical and electronic waste. Recycling electrical and electrical equipment. In *Conference Proceedings*. ERA Technology Ltd, Leatherhead, pp. 4/1–7.
7. Momoh, J.A., Elfayoumy, M. and Mittelstadt, W., 1999: Value-based reliability for short term operational planning. *IEEE Transactions on Power Systems*, **14**(4), 1533–1542.

8. Niessink, F. and Van-Vliet, H., 1999: Measurements should generate value, rather than data [software metrics]. In *Proceedings Sixth International Software Metrics Symposium* (Cat. No.PR00403). IEEE Computer Society, Los Alamitos, CA, pp. 31–38.
9. Rigby, K.D., 1994: How to manage the management tools, *Planning Review*, **21**(6), 8–15.
10. Riggs, L.J. and Felix H. Glenn, 1983: *Productivity by Objectives*, Prentice-Hall.
11. Schneider, J.G., Boyan, J.A. and Moore, A.W., 1998: Value function based production scheduling. In *Machine Learning. Proceedings of the Fifteenth International Conference (ICML'98)*. Morgan Kaufmann, San Francisco, CA, pp. 522–530.

Value engineering

M – 2b; 3b; 5c; 8b; 14b; 16d; * 1.3c; 1.5c; 2.2b; 3.2c

Value engineering is defined as an organized effort directed at analysing the function of system, equipment, facilities, services and suppliers for the purpose of achieving the essential functions at the lowest overall cost. Value engineering is the process of engineering as much value into a part or product as possible. One traditional way to achieve this goal is to monitor the product over the first year of production and make engineering changes as the opportunity arises. Value engineering becomes a planning phase in which engineering takes information from support functions, including those of the supplier and customer, and includes these suggestions and concerns in the design.

One of the most popular tools of value engineering is the 'value engineering workshop'. Such a workshop follows standard activities based on value engineering methodology. The main characteristic of the workshop are as below.

1. *Teamwork*. It has been proved that cost reduction and design improvements are best achieved by teamwork. A value engineering study is conducted by a team of people with skills tailored to the subject or product area. Teams should normally possess engineering, production, logistics and purchasing talents. The team should be of no more than 10 people.
2. *Effort concentration*. Each team meeting should be of several days duration. It is recommended that meetings be held at a remote location in order to have the team participants free from ordinary tasks.
3. *Methodology*. Value engineering sessions are conducted in a manner that forces the team to work in a systematic and organized way. According to value engineering only such a methodology will achieve good results.

The methodology is as follows:

1. *Investigation phase*. In this phase the team study the existing design or method. The team analyses and recognizes the functions of the product and

defines the logistic connections and the importance of the different functions. In the next step the 'worth' of each function is evaluated. It is a subjective evaluation based on team intuition and experience. Comparing the different worths of the functions and the improvement costs indicates the priority of each function.

2. *Speculation phase.* This phase is aimed to generate ideas and alternatives. Techniques such as brainstorming and green light thinking are used. The main procedure is to separate idea generation from the evaluation of ideas. In addition, a checklist might help to steer the thinking flow.

3. *Evaluation phase.* In this phase the alternatives are evaluated, and the real cost of implementing each alternative is established. In order to establish this cost, meetings are held with engineers, suppliers and any one else who can help evaluate the real cost.

4. *Presentation phase.* Even good ideas have to be 'sold'. In this phase the team prepares a presentation for management.

5. *Implementation phase.* Value engineering results are judged by the results and not by the written proposal. Therefore the team must be part of the implementation of the alternative selected.

Bibliography

1. Billinton, R. and Wang, P., 1998: Distribution system reliability cost/worth analysis using analytical and sequential simulation techniques. *IEEE Transactions on Power Systems*, **13**(4), 1245–1250.

2. Farag, A.S., Shwehdi, M.H., Belhadj, C.A., Beshir, M.J. and Cheng, T.C., 1998: Application of new reliability assessment framework and value-based reliability planning. In *Powercon '98. 1998 International Conference on Power System Technology.* Proceedings (Cat. No.98EX151). IEEE, New York, **2**, 961–967.

3. Fong, S.W., 1998: Value engineering in Hong Kong – a powerful tool for a changing society, *Computers & Industrial Engineering*, **35**(3–4), 627–630.

4. Jones, C., Medlen, N., Merlo, C., Robertson, M. and Shepherdson, J., 1999: The lean enterprise, *BT Technology Journal*, **17**(4), 15–22.

5. King, A.M. and Sivaloganathan, S.M., 1998: Development of a methodology for using function analysis in flexible design strategies. *Proceedings of the Institution of Mechanical Engineers, Part B (Journal of Engineering Manufacture)*, **212**(B3), 215–230.

6. Marples, A., 1999: Recycling value from electrical and electronic waste. Recycling Electrical and Electrical Equipment. In *Conference Proceedings.* ERA Technology Ltd, Leatherhead, pp. 4/1–7.

7. Momoh, J.A., Elfayoumy, M. and Mittelstadt, W., 1999: Value-based reliability for short term operational planning, *IEEE Transactions on Power Systems*, **14**(4), 1533–1542.

8. Niessink, F. and Van-Vliet, H., 1999: Measurements should generate value, rather than data [software metrics]. In *Proceedings Sixth International Software Metrics Symposium* (Cat. No.PR00403). IEEE Computer Society Los Alamitos, CA, pp. 31–38.

9. Schneider, J.G., Boyan, J.A. and Moore, A.W., 1998: Value function based production scheduling. In *Machine Learning. Proceedings of the Fifteenth International Conference (ICML'98)*. Morgan Kaufmann, San Francisco, CA, pp. 522–530.
10. Sik-Wah-Fong-P. and Dodo-Ka-Yan-Ip., 1999: Cost engineering: a separate academic discipline? *European Journal of Engineering Education*, **24**(1), 73–82.

Virtual company

S – 3b; 4c; 8c; 11b; 13d; 14c; * 1.1b; 1.2c; 2.2b; 3.3c; 3.6c; 4.2c
See Virtual manufacturing.

Virtual enterprises

M – 2c; 3b; 4c; 7c; 8b; 9c; 10c; 11b; 13b; 16c; * 1.1b; 1.2c; 1.6c; 3.2c; 3.6c; 4.1b; 4.2c; 4.3c
A virtual enterprise is composed of several companies, which are enabled to make joint commitments to their common customers. Although the companies are involved in a tight relationship in order to make joint commitments, they still retain their autonomy.

Virtual enterprise is a technique that enables a large number of interested parties to use and enhance vast quantities of information that involves a number of information sources and component activities. Without principled techniques to coordinate the various activities, any implementation would yield disjointed and error-prone behaviour, while requiring excessive effort to build and maintain.

Sometimes virtual enterprise might take the form of collaborative ventures with other companies, and sometimes it may take the form of a virtual company. The guiding principle of agile enterprise management is not automatic recourse to self-directed workteams, but for full utilization of corporate assets. The key to utilizing assets fully is the workforce. Flexible production technologies and flexible management enable the workforce of the agile manufacturing enterprise to implement the innovations they generate. There can be no algorithm for the conduct of such an enterprise. The only possible long-term agenda is providing physical and organizational resources in support of the creativity and initiative of the workforce.

Manufacturing is a standard application area for any approach that deals with information management in open environments. This is because modern manufacturing is naturally distributed, involves a large number of autonomous commercial entities with a variety of heterogeneous information systems, makes use of human decision making, faces the realities of failure and exception in physical processes and contractual arrangements, and yet requires that the manufactured products meet design specifications and other quality requirements.

Because they were not sensitive to these constraints, previous attempts at applying computing in manufacturing have had only limited success.

With recent advances in the computing and communications infrastructure, there has been a recurrence of interest in manufacturing applications, especially in those dealing with the coordination of processes in different enterprises. Supply chains are the material flows that are arranged among different companies to accomplish a large manufacturing process.

Traditional programming techniques are designed for closed environments, in which the programmer has (at least in principle) complete knowledge of the meaning of the information and full control over the disposition of the participating activities. By contrast, in open environments, a programmer has partial knowledge of and virtually no control over the behaviour of the components created by other designers and being executed by autonomous users. Although preserving the autonomy of participating components is crucial, unrestrained autonomy would be risky, because it may easily lead to undesirable consequences. Nowhere are these concerns more urgent than in manufacturing. As manufacturing becomes increasingly reliant on the dynamic formation and management of extended and overlapping virtual enterprises, agent-based, flexible approaches will play an increasing role.

Virtual enterprise seeks not data consistency directly, but a coherent state in the ongoing interactions of the participating components. This shift in focus from consistency to coherence not only facilitates automation, but is also more intuitive and closer to some aspects of human social behaviour. People cannot make irrevocable promises when they do not fully control their environments, but they can warn each other of potential problems. For example, if an order is not going to come through, a good service would at least notify the others concerned.

Bibliography

1. Davies, C.T., 1978: Data processing spheres of control, *IBM Systems Journal*, **17**(2), 179–198.
2. Dewey, A.M. and Bolton, R., 1999: Virtual enterprise and emissary computing technology, *International Journal of Electronic Commerce*, **4**(1), 45–64.
3. Elmagarmid, A.K. (ed.), 1992: *Database Transaction Models for Advanced Applications*. Morgan Kaufmann, San Mateo.
4. Georgakopoulos, D., Hornick, M. and Sheth, A., 1995: An overview of workflow management. In *Process Modeling to Workflow Automation Infrastructure. Distributed and Parallel Databases* 3, 2 (Apr. 1995), 119–152.
5. Gilman C.R., Aparicio M., Barry J., Durniak T., Lam, H. and Ramnath, R., 1997: Integration of design and manufacturing in a virtual enterprise using enterprise rules, intelligent agents, STEP, and work flow. In *SPIE Proceedings on Architectures, Networks, and Intelligent Systems for Manufacturing Integration*, pp. 160–171.
6. Gray, J. and Reuter, A., 1993: *Transaction Processing: Concepts and Techniques*. Morgan Kaufmann, San Mateo.

7. Huhns, M.N. and Singh, M.P. (eds), 1998: *Readings in Agents*. Morgan Kaufmann, San Francisco.
8. Jain, A.K., Aparicio, M.I.V. and Singh, M.P., 1999: Agents for process coherence in virtual enterprises, *Communications of the ACM*, **42**(3), 62–69.
9. Kimura, F., 1999: Virtual factory, *Systems, Control and Information*, **43**(1), 8–16.
10. Labrou, Y. and Finin, T., 1998: Semantics and conversations for an agent communication language. In M.N. Huhns and M.P. Singh (eds), *Readings in Agents*, Morgan Kaufmann, San Francisco, pp. 235–242.
11. Singh, M.P., 1999: An ontology for commitments in multiagent systems: Toward a unification of normative concepts, *Artificial Intelligence and Law*, to appear.
12. Singh, M.P., 1998: Agent communication languages: Rethinking the principles, *IEEE Computer*, **31**(12), 40–47.
13. Vernadat, F.B., 1996: Enterprise modeling and integration: principles and applications. Chapman & Hall, London.
14. Zhou, Q. and Besant, C.B., 1999: Information management in production planning for a virtual enterprise, *International Journal of Production Research*, **37**(1), 207–218.
15. Zhou, Q., Souben, P. and Besant, C.B., 1998: An information management system for production planning in virtual enterprises, *Computers & Industrial Engineering*, **35**(1), 153–156.
16. SMART. http:l/smart.npo.org/
17. Agent Builder Environment. http:/ /www.networking.ibm.com/iag/ iagsoft.htm.

Virtual manufacturing

S – 3b; 4c; 8c; 11b; 13d; 14c; * 1.1b; 1.2c; 2.2b; 3.3c; 3.6c; 4.2c

Virtual manufacturing is defined as manufacturing whose functionality and performance is independent of the physical distance between system elements. Virtual manufacturing is aimed at reducing product development time. Many companies understand very well that reducing product development time is a highly effective way of improving return on investment.

Often the quickest route to the introduction of a new product is to select organizational resources from different companies and then synthesize them into a single business entity: a virtual company. If the various distributed resources, human and physical, are compatible with one another, that is, if they can perform their respective functions jointly, then the virtual company can behave as if it were a single company dedicated to one particular project. For as long as the market opportunity lasts, the virtual company continues to exist; when the opportunity passes, the virtual company dissolves and its personnel turn to other projects.

The virtual manufacturing system is defined as an optimized manufacturing system synthesized over a universal set of primitive resources with real-time substitutable physical structure where one instantaneous physical structure has a lifetime at most as long as the lifetime of the product. The design (synthesis) and control of the system is performed in an abstract, or virtual, environment.

In virtual manufacturing, a small cross-functional team is formed to stream-line the development process. The team eliminates paper drawings and carries out all design on a single CAD/CAM system, including all required computer-ized tools that may be used to improve the design of a product, production and production management. Such tools includes solid modelling, stress analysis, production line simulation and factory run-time simulation.

Some of the tools are based on the virtual reality principle, which is a means of entering into a three-dimensional environment using computerized control to simulate a real environment.

Some typical applications of virtual manufacturing in industry are:

1. *Production design and factory planning.* Virtual machines and systems model on screen all steps of new plant installation and plant operation. Engineers can plan and change plans and run and debug programs and machines. They can track workflow and create, test, and modify everything from cell models to material handling system, mimicking everything that goes on in the plant.
   Virtual manufacturing supports lean manufacturing; in the case of an inter-ruption, a simulation can be run on the virtual manufacturing system to find the best way to solve the problem.
2. *Virtual prototyping.* Virtual prototyping can significantly reduce the time and cost of building a prototype at the product specification stage. Physical models of the proposed product can be displayed on the computer monitor and examined from different view angles, and in virtual operation, thus reducing development time and improving quality.
   Virtual prototyping can be an integral part of concurrent engineering (CE). Personnel from all disciplines in a company (e.g. customer service, mar-keting, sales, production management, etc.) can participate in the virtual display of the proposed product, and make their comments in a quiet, clean, computerized environment. Viewing a product on screen in picture format makes it more real than detailed drawings.
3. *Training and education.* Training can be done by simulation. The trainee virtually performs the task he or she is being trained to do.

To implement virtual manufacturing, a bridge is needed between the capabil-ities of technology and the user. There is a logical gap between what the soft-ware may offer (which is almost unlimited), and the solution algorithms, i.e. understanding the logic of operation.

One of the main problems in developing virtual manufacturing is the coordination between software engineers and the real process. The software engineers who create and animate machines and systems on screen may not know enough about the limitations and pitfalls and mechanics and physics of the actual process they are planning and optimizing. They certainly do not know the unique approach of a particular plant to a given operation. Programmers downloading programs at the machine may have one idea about a program's readiness, and software engineers delivering those programs for downloading may have another. The plant's manufacturing engineers trying to get production started are, as usual, caught in the middle. They must struggle to understand the logic, assumptions and language of their partners in this virtual effort. Communication breakdowns due to different vocabularies and wrong assumptions, and old-fashioned cultural gaps between specialists add confusion, no matter how technologically advanced a project may be.

Bibliography

1. Anonymous, 1998: Virtual manufacturing software covers NC machining, *Manufacturing Engineering*, **120**(3), 60.
2. Cimento, A.P., 1999: What's behind the move to 'virtual manufacturing', *Machine Design*, **71**(17), 2–4.
3. Dewey, A.M. and Bolton, R., 1999: Virtual enterprise and emissary computing technology. *International Journal of Electronic Commerce*, **4**(1), 45–64.
4. Giachetti, R.E., 1999: A standard manufacturing information model to support design for manufacturing in virtual enterprises, Journal of Intelligent Manufacturing, **10**(1), 49–60.
5. Horvath, L., Machado, J.A.T., Rudas, I.J. and Hancke, G.P., 1999: Application of part manufacturing process model in virtual manufacturing. In *ISIE '99, Proceedings of the IEEE International Symposium on Industrial Electronics* (Cat. No. 99TH8465). IEEE, Piscataway, NJ, **3**, 1367–1372.
6. Jain, A.K., Aparicio, M.I.V. and Singh, M.P., 1999: Agents for process coherence in virtual enterprises, *Communications of the ACM*, **42**(3), 62–69.
7. Kimura, F., 1999: Virtual factory, *Systems Control and Information*, **43**(1), 8–16.
8. Kimura, E., 1993: A product and process model for virtual manufacturing systems, *Annals of the CIRP*, **42**(1), 147–150.
9. Kochan, A., 1999: Virtual manufacturing comes of age, *News, Boston*, **54**(10), 69.
10. Pradhan, S., 1998: Virtual manufacturing information system using Java and JDBC, *Computers & Industrial Engineering*, **35**(1,2), 255.
11. Petrovic, D., Roy, R., Petrovic, R., 1998: Modelling and simulation of a supply chain in an uncertain environment. European Journal of Operational Research, **109**(2), 299–309.
12. Roche, C., Fitouri, S., Glardon, R. and Pouly, M., 1998: The potential of multi-agent systems in virtual manufacturing enterprises. In *Proceedings Ninth International Workshop on Database and Expert Systems Applications* (Cat. No. 98EX130). IEEE Computer Society, Los Alamitos, CA, pp. 913–918.
13. Smith, R.P. and Heim, J.A., 1999: Virtual facility layout design: the value of an interactive three-dimensional representation, *International Journal of Production Research*, **37**(17), 3941–3957.
14. Weyrich, M. and Drews, P., 1999: An interactive environment for virtual manufacturing: the virtual workbench, *Computers in Industry*, **38**(1), 5–15.
15. Zhang, W.J. and Li, Q., 1999: Information modelling for made-to-order virtual enterprise manufacturing systems, *Computer Aided Design*, **31**(10), 611–619.

16. Zhao, Z., 1998: A variant approach to constructing and managing virtual manufacturing environments, *International Journal of Computer Integrated Manufacturing*, **11**(6), 485–499.
17. Zhou, Q., Souben, P. and Besant, C.B., 1998: An information management system for production planning in virtual enterprises, *Computers & Industrial Engineering*, **35**(1–2), 153–156.
18. Zhiyan, Wang, Chengxiang, Gang and Zhichao, Zhang, 1999: Research on holographic virtual manufacturing basis. In *Proceedings 1999 IEEE International Conference on Robotics and Automation* (Cat. No.99CH36288C). IEEE, Piscataway, NJ, **3**, 2406–2409.
19. Zhou, Q. and Besant, C.B., 1999: Information management in production planning for a virtual enterprise, *International Journal of Production Research*, **37**(1), 207–218.
20. Zygmount, J., 1999: Why virtual manufacturing makes sense, *Managing Automation*, **14**(1), 32–3, 36–7, 40–1.

Virtual product development management (VPDM)

P – 2d; 3b; 4c; 6d; 7b; 8d; 14c; 15d; * 1.2c; 1.3d; 2.1c; 2.2b; 2.3c; 2.5c; 2.6c; 3.1d; 3.2c; 4.3c
See Product data management – PDM.

Virtual reality for design and manufacturing

T – 3b; 7c; 8c; * 1.2b; 2.1c; 2.2b; 3.3c; 3.6c; 4.2c
Virtual reality (VR) technologies are used for the rapid creation, editing, analysis and visualizations of products. The application of VR to the human interaction aspect of design is a huge step in many areas of shape design and analysis, including the level of information presented to the designer, the ability of the designer to interact with the design system in a free and creative manner, and the efficiency of the designer.

At Ford Motor Company (Dearborn, MI), for example, the Ford 2000 initiative calls for assigning a team in a design centre anywhere in the world to work on a car platform anywhere in the world. The people who design the car work thousands of miles from the group of manufacturing engineers building it. During build and launch cycles, all parties must see, modify, and interact with the CAD data.

Although the extent of the graphics was way above average it still was not enough; there's a physical world out there that the simulations did not capture.

A virtual reality-based software system developed at the University of Wisconsin-Madison includes a virtual design studio and assembly disassembly in three dimensions for the design and assembly/disassembly of complex artefacts. The principal notion behind these VR-based systems is to provide an intuitive and easy-to-use environment for engineers, designers, and others by facilitating 3D-hand tracking, voice command, and stereoscopic visual display for geometry creation, manipulation and analysis.

Virtual reality technologies play a key role in virtual design and manufacturing of artefacts for analysis or interaction tools, or both, as part of the design. Virtual assembly and disassembly involve evaluating the different aspects of a product assembly during the design phase, including assemblability and disassemblability, part accessibility, path planning, and subassembly analysis.

A virtual reality-based CAD (VR-CAD) system allows concept shape designs to be created and analysed on a computer, using natural interaction mechanisms, such as voice and hand action/motion. As opposed to the Windows–Icons–Menu–Pointer paradigm, common to most CAD systems, the VR-CAD system is based on the Work Space–Instance–Speech–Locator approach.

In a VR-CAD system, the designer creates three-dimensional appliance/product shapes by voice commands, hand motions, and finger motions. The designer grasps objects with his/her hands and moves them around, and detaches parts from assemblies and attaches new parts to assemblies for virtual manufacturing analysis. Virtual reality devices enable such intuitive interactions and thereby allow a designer with a minimum level of experience of using a CAD system to create and analyse concept shapes quickly and efficiently.

Shape creation systems may provide a hierarchical representation that allows high-speed editing of 3D shapes in a virtual environment. To facilitate shape design, this representation allows enforcement of design rules and provides other features, such as intelligent dimensioning to further speed up the task of shape creation. In addition to the parametric component/assembly design, a hierarchical representation for displaying and editing freeform models has been developed.

By combining different input modalities, such as voice and hand inputs, the designer can effectively create the design shape by talking to the system through the voice command and manipulating objects in the design space via hand action and motion.

Virtual assembly – disassembly systems, may perform virtual assembly and disassembly analysis of 3D geometric models. A system may generate, animate, edit, and validate the assembly–disassembly sequences and paths for appliance/product subassemblies. In addition, the user can perform several other virtual manufacturing analyses, such as interception checking, clearance checking, accessibility analysis of components and design rule checking.

Concurrent engineering systems can be used whereby different engineers at the same or different location can share, modify, and discuss the assembly/appliance design. Evaluation of an appliance assembly provides the user with the information regarding the feasibility of assembling the components, the accessibility of the components, and the sequence to assemble the components in an appliance assembly.

Virtual reality allows determination of the sequence and cost of disassembling/assembling components for appliance maintenance. In turn, the designer may perform design changes to facilitate ease of assembly/disassembly for maintenance.

Virtual reality allows determination of the maximal profitable disassembly sequence for separating components of different materials. Maximizing the recycling profit results in greater impetus for companies to recycle an appliance.

Bibliography

1. Bick, B., Kampker, M., Starke, G. and Weyrich, M., 1998: Realistic 3D-visualisation of manufacturing systems based on data of a discrete event simulation. In *IECON '98. Proceedings of the 24th Annual Conference of the IEEE Industrial Electronics Society* (Cat. No.98CH36200). IEEE, New York, **4**, 2543–2548.
2. Giachetti, R.E., 1999: A standard manufacturing information model to support design for manufacturing in virtual enterprises, *Journal of Intelligent Manufacturing*, **10**(1), 49–60.
3. Lu, C.J.J., Tsai, K.H., Yang, J.C.S. and Yu, Wang, 1998: A virtual testbed for the life-cycle design of automated manufacturing facilities, *International Journal of Advanced Manufacturing Technology*, **14**(8), 608–615.
4. Smith, R.P. and Heim, J.A., 1999: Virtual facility layout design: the value of an interactive three-dimensional representation, International Journal of Production Research, **37**(17), 3941–3957.
5. Tseng, M.M., Jianxin, J. and Chuang, J.S., 1998: Virtual prototyping for customized product development, *Integrated Manufacturing Systems*, **9**(6), 334–343.
6. Zamfirescu, C.B., Barbat, B. and Filip, F.G., 1998: The 'coach' metaphor in CSCW decision making system design. In *Intelligent Systems for Manufacturing: Multi-Agent Systems and Virtual Organizations. Proceedings of the BASYS'98– 3rd IEEE/IFIP International Conference on Information Technology for Balanced Automation Systems in Manufacturing*. Kluwer Academic Publishers, Norwell, MA, pp. 241–250.
7. VDS, I-CARVE Lab, http://icarve.me.wisc. edu/groups/virtual
8. A3D, I-CARVE Lab, http:/ icarve. me. wisc. edu/groups/disassembly
9. I-CARVE Lab, UW-Madison, http://icarve. me. wisc. edu
10. CAD-IT Consortium, UW-Madison, http:/ /cad-it.me.wisc. edu

Virtual reality

P – 2c; 3c; 4d; 8d; 9b; 10c; 13c; * 1.1b; 1.2b; 1.3c; 1.6d; 2.2b; 3.2c; 3.3c; 4.1b; 4.2c

Virtual reality provides major opportunities to simplify the way we communicate and run applications, and so improve business processes without costing a large amount of money.

Improved time-to-market and increased information share are just a couple of advantages offered by current simulation and virtual reality packages. Recent advances in simulation software have focused on three main areas – ease of use, enhanced visualization, and ease of interpretation. Consequently, companies are widening the use of simulation within their organization. Virtual reality combined with simulation is one way of achieving better visual representation, but it can add significantly to the time to build models and the cost of the software, and it can be difficult to use.

Today, the virtual process is very strong in the area of product design. Product design begins with the creation of a solid model, which becomes the design reference for the product. Early cost estimation techniques analyse product components, cycle times, and assembly and manufacturing equipment cost. Design-for-assembly techniques directly evaluate the virtual product assemblies for manufacturability, and virtual teams solve problems as they occur.

The technology lets manufacturers transfer training for complex or dangerous jobs to virtual environments. Engineers can find software to analyse machine tool motion, numerical control programs and programmable logic control, and properties of structures and materials, and to check and optimize design and system performance.

A team of designers can work on a design anywhere in the world. The people who design may work thousands of miles from the group of manufacturing engineers who build. During build and launch cycles, all parties must see, modify, and interact with the CAD data.

Another trend of virtual reality is based on electronic data interchange (EDI) and value chain analysis. It is based on the straightforward goal of changing processes in order to get the maximum return from resources – interrogating the accepted wisdom of the present in order to progress.

The growing momentum of electronic data interchange goes hand in hand with new thinking about the organization of the value chain and supply chain function. The existing functions – sales, marketing, production, distribution, purchasing – must operate as one unit. The company must have some group to look across the whole, to recognize and develop the processes both within and beyond the company. The aims are to improve customer service, reduce working capital and reduce total costs and waste.

The more you go down the supply chain route, the more you realize that the best way is not for the customer to throw the order at the supplier but to understand what each party is doing, what its plans are, how stock could be managed if there was less uncertainty. It all leads to the same conclusion: that buyer and supplier are managing the same process and that the information they need is common.

The key is recognizing that if the parties in a value chain were working more closely and sharing information in advance, much of the complexity of EDI data could be removed from actual transactions and commonly held in master files or catalogues or perhaps on the Internet. An order message itself could be reduced to just a few data elements: codes for supplier and buyer, an order reference, the item itself, where it is and where you want it to be, quantity and deadline. Combined with common access to data on past and future activity, much of the data uncertainty that leads to inefficiency could be removed.

If people think in terms of value chains and supply chains and the entire virtual enterprise, they start to realize that, just because you can't see it, doesn't mean it's not costing you money. The negative side is that you have to think about all the areas that you don't see and don't control.

The positive side is that with the electronic revolution, providing you think clearly about the information you need to capture, you've got the means of doing that. Just because you don't own it doesn't mean you can't manage it.

It is not really the supply chain function's job to say if we are using the right materials, or we are sourcing the right materials from the right suppliers – that is a combined job of technical people, production staff and professional purchasers. One has to be careful not to pretend that supply chain managers can do everything; but they can look at all processes and ask 'could we do it better?'

Virtual reality technology has great potential in computerized manufacturing applications. Technical problems, however, have to be resolved before it can be employed in practical manufacturing.

Bibliography

1. Bick, B., Kampker, M., Starke, G. and Weyrich, M., 1998: Realistic 3D-visualisation of manufacturing systems based on data of a discrete event simulation. In *IECON '98. Proceedings of the 24th Annual Conference of the IEEE Industrial Electronics Society* (Cat. No.98CH36200). IEEE, New York, **4**, 2543–2548.
2. Giachetti, R.E., 1999: A standard manufacturing information model to support design for manufacturing in virtual enterprises, *Journal of Intelligent Manufacturing*, **10**(1), 49–60.
3. Holden, E., 1999: Simulation and virtual reality. *Manufacturing-Management*, **8**(10), 31, 33.
4. Kimura, F., 1999: Virtual factory, *Systems, Control and Information*, **43**(1), 8–16.
5. Lu, C.J.J., Tsai, K.H., Yang, J.C.S. and Yu, Wang, 1998: A virtual testbed for the life-cycle design of automated manufacturing facilities, *International Journal of Advanced Manufacturing Technology*, **14**(8), 608–615.
6. Nagalingam, S.V. and Lin, G.C.I., 1999: Latest developments in CIM. *Robotics and Computer Integrated Manufacturing*, **15**(6), 423–430.
7. Osorio, A.L., Oliveira, N. and Camarinha-Matos, L.M., 1998: Concurrent engineering in virtual enterprises: the extended CIM-FACE architecture. In *Intelligent Systems for Manufacturing: Multi-Agent Systems and Virtual Organizations. Proceedings of the BASYS'98–3rd IEEE/IFIP International Conference on Information Technology for Balanced Automation Systems in Manufacturing*. Kluwer Academic Publishers, Norwell, MA, pp. 171–184.

8. McLean, C., 1997: Production system engineering using virtual manufacturing. In *WMC 97. World Manufacturing Congress. International Symposium on Manufacturing Systems – ISMS'97*. ICSC Academic Press, Millet, Alta., Canada, pp. 20–26.

9. Ressler, S., Godil, A., Qiming, W. and Seidmen, G., 1999: A VRML integration methodology for manufacturing applications. In *Proceedings VRML 99. Fourth Symposium on the Virtual Reality Modeling Language*. ACM, New York, pp. 167–172.

10. Smith, R.P. and Heim, J.A., 1999: Virtual facility layout design: the value of an interactive three-dimensional representation. International Journal of Production Research, **37**(17), 3941–3957.

11. Tseng, M.M., Jianxin, J. and Chuang, J.S., 1998: Virtual prototyping for customized product development. *Integrated Manufacturing Systems*, **9**(6), 334–343.

12. Zamfirescu, C.B., Barbat, B. and Filip, F.G., 1998: The 'coach' metaphor in CSCW decision making system design. In *Intelligent Systems for Manufacturing: Multi-Agent Systems and Virtual Organizations. Proceedings of the BASYS'98– 3rd IEEE/IFIP International Conference on Information Technology for Balanced Automation Systems in Manufacturing*. Kluwer Academic Publishers, Norwell, MA, pp. 241–250.

13. Zhang, L. and Ren, S., 1999: Self-organization modeling for supply chain based virtual enterprise decision support systems, *Journal of Tsinghua University (Science and Technology)*, **39**(7), 84–88.

14. Zhao, Z., 1998: A variant approach to constructing and managing virtual manufacturing environments, *International Journal of Computer Integrated Manufacturing*, **11**(6), 485–499.

15. Zygmount, J., 1999: Why virtual manufacturing makes sense, *Managing Automation*, **14**(1), 32–3, 36–7, 40–1.

Waste management and recycling

M – 13d; 15b; * 1.2b; 2.2b; 2.4b; 2.5c; 4.1c; 4.6c

Waste management has many aspects. It may appear as a waste collection problem, or a waste prevention problem. The life-cycle of many products has become short, and therefore the question arises of what to do with the old/used product. The physical presence of large quantities of waste, with high removal expenses, makes the establishment of a waste management system both desirable and necessary.

Waste poses an environmental problem. Environmental policy calls for preventive measures. The waste and environmental impact should be considered during procurement, during the development of new products and services and during selling. Materials used can be selected such that they can be reused, instead of creating waste. It might increase the initial cost, but it will pay at the product end of life. Processes must be selected such that they create the least amount of waste.

Recycling concepts, as they are required in actual waste management legislation, often need the development of disassembly processes to assure efficient separation of hazardous materials, or the accumulation of ingredients worth further recovery. Therefore methods and tools have to be found in order to determinate law-conformal and economic disassembly strategies. Further, efficient disassembly processes and tools have to be developed, considering specific requirements.

Recycling/reuse allows determination of maximal profitable disassembly sequence for separating components of different materials. Maximizing the recycling profit results in greater impetus for companies to recycle an appliance. In addition, a system will allow companies to determine what the cost is to the company, if and when the appliance/product is disassembled for recycling.

Competition is the name of the game in the waste business. Whether it's a municipal system vs. a private hauler or a large international conglomerate vs. a small company, each is looking for ways to sharpen its strategy, satisfy one more customer or improve pricing.

Technology can help a waste collection system. Its primary goal is to make services more time- and cost-efficient by helping collection trucks and equipment to increase the number of customers serviced in a time period, or to reduce the personnel required to do a job. Nevertheless, it doesn't matter whether you're public or private, you also have to be a little entrepreneurial and have a sense of creativity about what feed stocks will be accepted, processing methods and how to add value to the product. The more creative you can be with trucking, processing or marketing, the more profitable you can be. Keep in mind that you want to get as much money as you can on the front end in tip fees as well as on the back end for your product, while spending as little as reasonable in the middle.

To bring in money at the front end of a composting operation, look at what organic businesses in the area need to get rid of, to see if they can be used for other purposes.

In 1996, ISO published an environmental management systems (EMS) standard series 14000 that has been accepted as a reference standard for the certification of environmental management systems. Today, international organizations, states, public corporations and many private companies have implemented such an environmental management system. Most of them acknowledge that their long-term survival depends on their ability to cope with the environmental challenge and make of it a real strategic issue. If we take for granted that external certification is expected to become a criterion in customer/supplier relations, now is the time to promote EMS in a company.

Bibliography

1. Alting, L., 1995: Life cycle engineering & design, *Annals of CIRP*, **2**, 569.
2. Anderi, R., Daum, B., Weissmantel, H. and Wolf, B., 1999: Design for environment – a computer-based cooperative method to consider the entire life cycle. In *Proceedings of First International Symposium on Environmentally Conscious Design and Inverse Manufacturing*. IEEE Computer Society, Los Alamitos, CA, pp. 380–385.

3. Boreux, V., 1999: On the way to ISO 14001 certification. In *21st International Telecommunications Energy Conference. INTELEC '99* (Cat. No.99CH37007). IEEE, Piscataway, NJ.
4. Curran, M.A., 1991: *Environmental Life-cycle Assessment*. McGraw Hill, New York.
5. Curlee, T.R. and Das, S., 1991: *Plastic Wastes, Management Control, Recycling and Disposal*. Environmental Protection Agency, Noyes Data Corporation.
6. Feldmann, K., Trautner, S. and Meedt, O., 1998: Innovative disassembly strategies based on flexible partial destructive tools. In *Intelligent Assembly and Disassembly (IAD'98). Proceedings volume from the IFAC Workshop*. Elsevier Science, Kidlington, pp. 1–6.
7. Goble, TA., 1998: Waste management improvements from decommissioning activities at Big Rock Point, *Transactions of the American Nuclear Society*, **79**, 27.
8. Cheng, E.T., Rocco, P., Zucchetti, M., Seki, Y. and Tabara, T., 1998: Waste management aspects of low activation materials, *Fusion Technology*, **34**(3–2), 721–727.
9. Haigh, A.D., Middleton, R. and Newbert, G., 1999: Waste management aspects of the DTE1 and RTE campaigns, *Fusion Engineering and Design*, **47**(2–3), 285–299.
10. Linninger, A.A. and Chakraborty, A., 1999: Synthesis and optimization of waste treatment flowsheets, *Computers & Chemical Engineering*, **23**(10), 1415–1425.
11. Maniezzo, V., Mendes, I. and Paruccini, M., 1998: Decision support for siting problems, *Decision Support Systems*, **23**(3), 273–284.
12. Neton, D.E., 1993: *Global Warming, A Reference Handbook*. ABC-CLIO, Santa Barbara, CA.
13. Mehlsen, A., 1999: Waste management system at Tele Danmark A/S. In *21st International Telecommunications Energy Conference. INTELEC '99* (Cat. No. 99CH37007). IEEE, Piscataway, NJ.
14. Smith, M., 1996: *Polymer Products and Waste Management, A Multidisciplinary Approach*. International Books, The Netherlands.
15. Stepinski, T. and Wu, P., 1999: Ultrasonic technique for imaging welds in copper. In *IMTC/'99. Proceedings of the 16th IEEE Instrumentation and Measurement Technology Conference* (Cat. No.99CH36309). IEEE, Piscataway, NJ, vol.2, pp. 856–859.
16. Zussman, E., Kriwet, A. and Seliger, G., 1994: Disassembly-oriented assessment methodology to support design for recycling. *Annals of the CIRP*, **43**(1), p. 9.

Workflow management

M – 3c; 6b; 7a; 13a; * 1.1b; 1.6d; 3.2d; 3.3b; 3.5b; 4.1b; 4.2b; 4.3b; 4.4c

Workflow management focuses on improving the effectiveness and efficiency of businesses processes within an organization. Interorganizational workflow offers companies the opportunity to re-shape business processes beyond the boundaries of individual organizations.

Workflow management controls, monitors, optimizes and supports business processes with an explicit representation of the business process logic that allows for computerized support.

Workflow management is becoming a mature technology that can be applied within organizations. However, the number of business processes where multiple organizations are involved is increasing rapidly. Technologies such as Electronic Data Interchange (EDI), the Internet and the World Wide Web (WWW) enable multiple organizations to participate in shared business processes. The rise of electronic commerce (EC), virtual organizations and extended enterprises highlights the fact that more and more business processes are crossing organizational boundaries. This means that workflow management should be able to deal with workflow processes that span multiple organizations. Interorganizational workflows occur where several business partners are involved in shared workflow processes.

Each business partner has private workflow processes connected to the workflow processes of some of the other partners. Loosely coupled workflow processes operate essentially independently, but have to synchronize at certain points to ensure the correct execution of the overall business process. Synchronization of parallel processes is known to be a potential source of errors. Therefore, it is difficult to establish the correctness of complex interorganizational workflows.

Because processes are a dominant factor in workflow management, it is important to use an established framework for modelling and analysing workflow processes.

The various forms of interoperability are as follows.

Capacity sharing – This form of interoperability assumes centralized control, i.e. the routing of the workflow is under the control of one workflow manager. The execution of tasks is distributed, i.e. the resources of several business partners are used to execute the tasks.

Chained execution – The workflow process is split into a number of separate subprocesses that are executed by different business partners in sequential order. This form of interoperability requires that a partner transfers or initiates the flow after completing all the work. In contrast to capacity sharing, control of the workflow is distributed over the business partners.

Subcontracting – There is one business partner that subcontracts subprocesses to other business partners. The control is hierarchical, i.e. although there is a top-level actor, the control is distributed in a tree-like fashion.

Case transfer – Each business partner has a copy of the workflow process description, i.e. the process specification is distributed. However, each case resides at any time at exactly one location. Cases (i.e. process instances) can be transferred from one location to another. A case can be transferred to balance the workload or because tasks are not implemented at all locations.

Extended case transfer – Each of the business partners uses the same process definition. However, it is possible to allow local variations, e.g. at a specific location the process may be extended with additional tasks. It is important that the extensions allow for the proper transfer of cases. This means that the extensions are executed before transferring the case or that there is some notion of inheritance that allows for the mapping of the state of a case during the transfer.

Loosely coupled – With this form of interoperability the process is broken into pieces that may be active in parallel. Moreover, the definition of each of the subprocesses is local, i.e. the environment does not know the process, only the protocol that is used to communicate.

Note that capacity sharing uses centralized control. The other forms of interoperability use a decentralized control. However, note that in the case of subcontracting and (extended) case transfer, part of the control is (can be) centralized. Chained execution, subcontracting, and loosely coupled use a horizontal partitioning of the workflow, i.e. the process is cut into pieces. (Extended) case transfer uses a vertical partitioning of the flow, i.e. the cases are distributed over the business partners.

Each business partner has a private workflow process that is connected to the workflow processes of some of the other partners. The communication mechanism that is used for interaction is asynchronous communication. Loosely coupled workflow processes operate essentially independently, but have to synchronize at certain points to ensure the correct execution of the overall business process.

Interorganizational workflows are described in terms of individual tasks and causal relations. In most cases, the design of an interorganizational workflow starts with the specification of the communication structure, i.e. the protocol.

A technique to specify the communication structure between multiple loosely coupled workflows might be message sequence charts (MSC). Message sequence charts are a widespread graphical language for the visualization of communications between systems/processes. The representation of message sequence charts is intuitive and focuses on the messages between communication entities.

Bibliography

1. van der Aalst, W.M.P., 1998: Modeling and analyzing interorganizational workflows. In L. Lavagno and W. Reisig (eds), *Proceedings of the International Conference on Application of Concurrency to System Design (CSD'98)*. IEEE Computer Society Press, pp. 1–15.
2. Ellis, C.A. and Nutt, G.J., 1993: Modeling and enactment of workflow systems. In M. Ajmone Marsan (ed.), *Application and Theory of Petri Nets*, Volume 691 of Lecture Notes in Computer Science, Springer-Verlag, Berlin, pp. 1–16.

3. Hayes, K. and Lavery, K., 1991: *Workflow Management Software: The Business Opportunity*. Ovum.
4. ITU-TS, 1996: ITU-TS Recommendation Z.120: Message Sequence Chart 1996 (MSC96). Technical report, ITU-TS, Geneva.
5. Kalakota, R. and Whinston, A.B., 1996: *Frontiers of Electronic Commerce*. Addison-Wesley, Reading, MA.
6. Koulopoulos, T.M., 1995: *The Workflow Imperative*. Van Nostrand Reinhold, New York.
7. Lawrence, P. (ed.), 1997: *Workflow Handbook 1997, Workflow Management Coalition*. John Wiley and Sons, New York.
8. Murata, T., 1989: Petri nets: properties, analysis and applications. *Proceedings of the IEEE*, **77**(4), 541–580.
9. WFMC, 1996: Workflow Management Coalition Terminology and Glossary (WFMC-TC-1011). Technical report, Workflow Management Coalition, Brussels.
10. WFMC, 1996: Workflow Management Coalition Standard – Interoperability Abstract Specification (WFMC-TC-1012). Technical report, Workflow Management Coalition, Brussels.

World class manufacturing

P – 5c; 6c; 7c; 8c; 9c; 11d; 14b; 15c; 16d; * 1.1b; 1.2c; 1.3d; 1.4d; 1.5c; 3.1c; 3.2c; 3.3c; 3.4c; 4.1c; 4.3b; 4.4c; 4.5c; 4.6c

Today the world market is regarded as a small village. A company has to compete on a worldwide basis. With manufacturing globalization, new technologies, and new competitive standards, only high-performance companies can compete efficiently. World class manufacturers share four characteristics:

1. they exhibit outstanding leadership;
2. they continually ask why and challenge what they are doing;
3. they meticulously measure results;
4. they place an extremely high priority on education.

The first area is management leadership and respect for workers. Leadership is not management. Leadership creates the vision, sets the pace, takes the risks, and charts the course. Leaders see in their mind what the operation will look like five to ten years ahead. They see the products, people, facility, machines and customers. These are all clear in their mind and they document and communicate this vision to the workforce. The method is divided into three main areas. The first area is management:

1. Leadership with vision
2. Create goals and new ways of thinking
3. Prepare a long-range strategic plan, and work it out
4. Employee participation in company operations and problem solving

5. Clear definition of overall integrated goals
6. Create a performance measurement and incentive system
7. Organizational focus on product and customer
8. Effective communication systems
9. Educate and promote the workforce.

The second area is quality:

1. Develop customer-oriented products
2. Create design and process interdisciplinary teams
3. Personal responsibility for continuous improvement
4. Use SPC – statistical process control
5. Emphasis on novel ideas and experimentation
6. Encourage partnership with suppliers.

The third area is production:

1. Keep production flow
2. Prioritize demands not capacity
3. Use standards. Consider process simplification before automation
4. Make solid maintenance plans.

World class manufacturing focuses on how systems operate. While methodologies exist that focus on a design approach, say business process re-engineering (BPR), the key strength of world class manufacturers is in use of operational processes which maximize efficiency. For example, work-teams are often cited as a useful way of organizing workers. Teamworking is about how a system can operate and so work-teams are an operational issue.

Performance measurement (PM) is complementary to both world class manufacturing and business process re-engineering approaches. By inference it includes the activity of strategic planning. Both WCM and BPR approaches need goals, and these goals are often set through strategic planning. Strategic planning, by its very name, is concerned with 'strategic' issues such as identifying strategic initiatives, defining performance measures and setting performance targets. The project, which ultimately provides mechanisms for improving the performance measures defined in a strategic plan, inevitably begins life through either WCM or BPR. The danger with world class manufacturing is that every possible improvement project will be pursued regardless of its magnitude, ultimately leading to an impairment of the overall achievement of improvement plans.

Another theme that is recurrent in many BPR approaches is the presence of information technology as an enabler of solutions. In sharp contrast, WCM programs are commonly opposed to information solutions.

In manufacturing, two groups usually define projects aimed at meeting performance improvement targets. The information system group within the company is usually set up to design and maintain the company's computer and telecommunication systems. By implication, this includes many processes such as master scheduling, material requirement planning and design. The engineering group, on the other hand is usually responsible for the design and maintenance of shop floor activities such as flexible manufacturing systems, shop floor control, machine layout and system design. The domains for each group are very much defined by their organizational boundaries and, despite the best efforts of some companies, boundaries exist between the two groups which stunt integration and provide gaps where key issues can fall between two stools. WCM often provides the impetus for activities within the engineering group, while BPR provides the impetus for activities within the information system group.

Bibliography

1. Carlsson, B., 1989: Flexibility and the theory of the firm, *International Journal of Industrial Organization*, **7**(2), 179–203.
2. Cleveland, G., Schroeder, R.G. and Anderson, J.C., 1989: A theory of production competence, *Decision Sciences*, **20**(4), 655–668.
3. Hayes, R.H. and Pisano, G.P., 1994: Beyond world-class: The new manufacturing strategy, *Harvard Business Review*, **72**(1), 77–86.
4. Hayes, R.H. and Wheelwright, S.C., 1984: *Restoring Our Competitive Edge*. John Wiley & Sons, New York.
5. Hyun, J.H. and Ahn, B.H., 1992: A unifying framework for manufacturing flexibility, *Management Review*, **5**(4), 251–260.
6. Lau, R.S.M., 1994: Attaining strategic flexibility. Paper presented at *5th Annual Meeting of the Production and Operations Management Society*, Washington, DC, pp. 8–11.
7. Mansfield, E., Schwartz, M. and Wagner, S., 1981: Imitation costs and patents: An empirical study, *The Economic Journal*, **91**, 907–918.
8. Schonberger, R.J., 1986: *World Class Manufacturing*, Free Press, New York.
9. Sethi, A.K. and Sethi, S.P., 1990: Flexibility in manufacturing: A survey. *International Journal of Flexible Manufacturing Systems*, **2**, 289–328.
10. Shecter, E., 1992: *Managing for World-Class Quality*. SME.
11. Suarez, F.F., Cusumano, M.A. and Fine, C.H., 1995: An empirical study of flexibility in manufacturing, *Sloan Management Review*, **37**(1), 25–32.
12. Swamidass, P.M. and Newell, W.T., 1987: Manufacturing strategy, environmental uncertainty, and performance: A path analytic model, *Management Science*, **33**(4), 509–524.
13. Upton, D.M., 1994: The management of manufacturing flexibility, *California Management Review*, **36**(2), 72–89.
14. Upton, D.M., 1995: What really makes factories flexible? *Harvard Business Review*, **73**(4), 74–84.
15. Vickery, S.K., 1991: A theory of production competence revisited, *Decision Sciences*, **22**(3), 635–643.

16. Vickery, S.K., Droge, C. and Markland, R.R., 1993: Production competence and business strategy: Do they affect business performance? *Decision Sciences*, **24**(2), 435–456.
17. Ward, P.T., Leong, G.K. and Boyer, K.K., 1994: Manufacturing proactiveness and performance, *Decision Sciences*, **25**(3), 337–358.

Index _____